Acclaim for

Come Sunday

"Bradford Morrow's long-awaited *Come Sunday* is a sprawling, rich, innovative, panoramic novel whose themes, characters and subplots appear to have been limned by a brush dipped in rainbow." —George Myers Jr., *Columbus Dispatch*

"If only every American first novelist wrote this well and had an imagination so strong. Morrow writes with mellow density and austere finesse. The central situation is both dramatic and exotic, as hard to resist as to exhaust. **I was captivated by the sheer display of mind and nourished by the virtuoso style. Brad Morrow deserves applause for this audacious debut.**"

—Paul West

"**Morrow's first novel...is a** *tour de force* **of narrative inventiveness.**" —*Philadelphia Magazine*

"**A ferociously impressive first novel**, risky and ambitious and conversant with a hundred human dialects. Morrow knows that fiction, like sex, is friction, and he's fearless as to the number and nature of the sticks he rubs together. I'm sure that writing *Come Sunday* was a real adventure of the soul for him, for it is precisely that for the reader." —*Peter Straub*

"*Come Sunday* is a brilliantly written work of political and mythical grandeur, an important first novel." —John Hawkes

by BRADFORD MORROW

COME SUNDAY

Come Sunday

BRADFORD MORROW

COLLIER BOOKS
Macmillan Publishing Company
New York

Copyright © 1988 by Bradford Morrow

Published by arrangement with Weidenfeld & Nicolson, New York, A Division of Wheatland Corporation.

Collier Books
Macmillan Publishing Company
866 Third Avenue, New York, NY 10022
Collier Macmillan Canada, Inc.

Library of Congress Cataloging-in-Publication Data
Morrow, Bradford, 1951–
    Come Sunday / Bradford Morrow. — 1st Collier Books ed.
      p.   cm.
    ISBN 0-02-023001-X
    I. Title
    PS3563.O8754C6   1989
    813'.54—dc19   88-38394   CIP

Cover art © 1988 by George Corsillo

First Collier Books Edition 1989

10 9 8 7 6 5 4 3 2 1

PRINTED IN THE UNITED STATES OF AMERICA

To the seven borrowed houses in which it was written, and Leslie, its home.

Contents

One shall be born from small beginnings which will quickly become vast, and will respect nothing in creation, indeed with its power will transform the essence of almost everything into another.

—Leonardo da Vinci, *Prophecies*

I

The
History of It

1.

THERE was a crackle, like air tearing. It issued from the long, low valley where an orchid-shaped burst rose away into twilight, warm, and the crescent of faint climbing moon tangled with jungle. The flower collapsed into smoke. Afterward it was dissolved by rivers, waterfalls, and breezes.

Undisturbed, the man continued with his dictation. Even as he spoke the fighting could be heard below, for it had crept up here past the border. He paced the dirt yard, tending to his own magnificent slowness, each step creating a diffusion of rumplings and wrinkles across his suit, and read aloud from his notes. Dusky sun through the trees beaded the wide dome of his head, ran across his cheeks, into his eyes. Opposite the moon—itself some mineral flower, a single petal viewed from the side—it played through his thinned bluish hair as a fresh series of fanning blasts broke over the saddle ridge out behind. Quiet. For a moment too long, more quiet. Then a deafening barrage, but farther away, and he finally paused to listen, against his own will really, against some sense of discretion in the face of habit's ruin. He identified weapons and the general movement of the troops (moronic children) and felt assured that again tonight the fire would not find its way up to his poor *bolsón*, his pocket in the midst of the struggle—this group of unguarded adobe houses pitched together at angles that conformed to the rugged terrain covered in brazil wood, wild groves of lemon and orange, cacao festooned with air plants.

When first he had come here the buildings were abandoned by all but a family of monkeys. The clay tile roof of one had fallen in and lay inside a shell of rotting stucco overgrown with vines. With the help of his brother the compound was made habitable. The man lived here in the hope that a turn of fortune would soon take place. He was safe, but he was in exile. Gone was the epoch of comfort when his parents owned plantations spread up and down the resplendent coffee-bearing mountains back in the district of Jinotega. After the government fell the family dispersed in fear to different countries, and the control they'd held over the region for many decades was abrogated by the junta. For four and a half years he had subsisted at the outskirts of El Paraiso north past Nueva Segovia and the homeland, suspended in a limbo from which he tried to solve the problem of how to reclaim his property and assume once more the traditional and, he believed, rightful powers which attend land owned by men. Never would he be at peace with such poverty. Even the kites and hawks that soared in circles on the thermals mocked the one who lived there, so abject, under the crumbling roofs. Still, despite the difficulties of his present state, he managed to remain fat.

All the while the idea had festered. It was all in the letter, all prologue, background for the sales pitch. Would it come through as they had intended?

> *"Where words are gathered together today,*
> *uttered with care, or stuttered in disarray,*
> *a sales pitch is found not far away—"*

Krieger had said that. Krieger, of course. Inevitably Krieger, thought the fat man: white-lipped, disheveled, restless Krieger. He was there, too, and had been watching as the exile's daughter, tongue caught at the corner of her mouth, took down what her father had put together from two sources, history and whimsy. Takes a lot of truth to tell a lie—another Kriegerism.

Meantime rhythmical popping, then nothing. Had someone died? The coming coffee harvest, like religious holidays, could impede the progress of battle. This is why the mountains had been swarming with boys and girls, young warriors running through mined fields, falling down the steep rows of spent cornstalks, dying these recent weeks. Every side was pressing for victory, though none seemed to be at hand for anyone. The fat man, who knew this, leaned against the whitewashed wall and began once more to work on the letter which Krieger would later take to Danlí and mail with other prospectuses and what they referred to as the epistles.

"Let's give it another try, let's ignore them, shall we? so then, Dear Owen Berkeley, your letter to hand, for which very many thanks."

Krieger allowed himself a little disavowing laugh, eyes down, knuckles of one hand pressed to his mouth; he hitched up his pants. Could use a new belt, cheap alligator, the brass plating tarnished and chipping away.

"What," asked the fat man.

Krieger mimicked the other's deeper voice, "Dear Berkeley, your letter to hand?"

"So?"

"So what kind of line is that—*to hand?* Letters don't come to hand anymore, except in expensive finishing schools—you sound like somebody's goddamn polo pony sitting down to tea and tomato sandwiches."

The other daubed the back of his neck with the sheaf of notes, and continued, as if Krieger had not spoken at all, "It was in the mouth of the Black River, whose fresh waters still wash into the salt waves near Trujillo, that the tall-browed, melancholy-eyed, half-blind Columbus, on his fourth and final voyage, El Alto Viaje, as it's known, landed for the first time in Central America, 1502. This was as close as the mighty explorer would ever come to that great country of yours north up the continent."

"Insert," Krieger interrupted. He had come up to the thatched veranda. "That great country of yours where every October the air is filled with apple cider and baseball injuries and the kiddies singing *In fourteen hundred and ninety-two Columbus sailed the ocean blue* and the kiddies stand up and look out the windows with their lazy little beady little eyes into the gold and red trees and begin reciting how the three boats, the *Niña* the *Pinta* the *Santa María*, with those pretty Maltese crosses painted in red on their little Vacuform plastic sails passed proud behind the shadow of the Statue of Liberty straight into the Potomac where Columbus was quickly elected first President. He was a good President, too, made many wondrous discoveries such as *The earth is round not flat*, so your schoolteachers will tell you whereas in fact he calculated that it was shaped like a pear, and attached to the bulge of this pear was a large mountain shaped precisely like a woman's breast—"

"Krieger."

"—on the cosmic nipple of which the Terrestrial Paradise was located, a theory which naturally gave Ferdinand and Isabella reason to pause, wonder what the hell kind of operation the Spanish royalty was subsidizing out there in the land of Oz. I mean, clearly this wasn't Kansas anymore was it, Toto?"

Eyes grown darker, the girl looked away to where an iguana slept, long, black-green, its shabby headcrest blown like a tired pennant in the breeze, lying along the wall where a puff of dust kicked up under the stone Krieger had tossed at it. A sow caked in red mud crossed the clearing unaccosted, stumbled on its skinny, hoary legs down into a thicket canopied by leaves in a dense shade. Several more stones casually were lobbed to tumble innocent into bougainvillea beside the speckled lizard that remained oblivious to the game.

"How did you know that? about the earthly paradise?"

Krieger was gathering rocks along the wall.

"I want you to stay out of my room, Krieger, understood? and watch your language around Perdita."

The iguana had vanished before the girl pared a finer point on her pencil with a shard of glass and licked the lead, and she saw her father again draw the manuscript across the back of his neck. Loose-limbed, Krieger strolled to the smaller house, where he had put up; he had been down here not quite a week and it was time for him to leave. In Danlí, the small town due north which had a road that led to the capital, he would go about getting the supplies needed, and also make the purchase neither his colleague nor anyone else would know about until much later. Afterward, he would undertake the difficult ride back out southeast into the remotest and most pristine range; there he would meet Lupi. Behind him he could hear the fat man clear his throat, moist gurgling, and proceed with his dictation. Krieger smirked and thought, *Chingadero*. Fucker.

"During his earlier voyages Columbus succeeded in discovering most of the major islands that constitute the West Indies Antilles, and had set anchor in the Gulf of Paria to claim Venezuela, but never had he landed on the continent so far north, nor would he walk on mainland so close to what would eventually become the United States. Having pierced the Caribbean archipelago by early summer 1502, his small flotilla of four ships, caravels manned by a hundred forty hands, men and boys, had come upon the Spanish-claimed island of Hispaniola at June's end.

"Seeing that his largest caravel was damaged and in need of refitting and repair, and that his provisions were low, Columbus sent a boat ashore requesting permission to enter the harbor so that he could stock his fleet with fresh supplies, mend the ships, and sit out in port the hurricane that he predicted was coming up from South America. But the governor of Hispaniola, Don Nicolás de Ovando, refused him this request for a number of reasons that for our purposes we need not go into, and so Columbus was forced to anchor on the island's lee side to wait out the storm.

"The hurricane fell with a fury over the island. Everything was chaos.

All the caravels but his own were blown out as helpless tatters into the chocolate sea. Ovando's fleet was also destroyed. But true to the Spaniard in himself (one realizes Columbus was Italian, but it was, I would like to suggest, his Spaniard's heart that saw him through his troubles) he did not give up. A second fleet was recruited at Azua and by mid-July he set once more a westward course, this time for Jamaica.

"Under full sail they threaded the shoals in Jardín de la Reyna, the Queen's Garden, named during an earlier expedition in the honor of Isabella, and were carried over the high, dull bowl of salt water midway between the Cayman Isles and what is known as the Rosilind Bank until the small island of Guanaja (or Bonacca, as it is called) was sighted from the crow's nest. It was here that he learned from an old Indian of a great unbroken stretch of land just a short distance farther west. From the description this Indian gave him, using sign language and tracing maps in the sand, Columbus assumed the grand empire of the Khan, or China itself, was finally at hand. There was great excitement on board the ships— only forty miles of water lay between them and China?

"They set out for the coast. But more disappointment was to come. The waves were too high for the fleet to make an anchorage. After sailing within sight of its shores they were forced to steer as far south as the fifteenth parallel, to where Nicaragua's border now lies, Cabo Gracias a Dios, yet still discovered no safe place to moor. By now the crew was exhausted, even mutinous; the ship's hulls were full of sea worms' holes and taking on water; supplies were running low again. Columbus ordered them to tack back on a north-northeast heading up the coast and, in heavy green breakers churned up by a winter storm, they finally came upon an embouchure, the mouth of a calm river, where they cast anchors, and marveled at the reflected shadows of flocks of birds that raced under the clouds. The foliage was rich and various, the soil was of a black-red. Columbus commanded his men to begin building. And so it came to pass that this, the first Spanish settlement in the American continent, was christened Belém. What a sight it must have been. By spring, their huts dotted the shoreline, and smoke of fried fish went up into the air. Because the windswept coast— which extended up toward Punta Castilla and back to Laguna de Guaymoreto where the Aguán River drains into the Caribbean—because it had been so difficult of access and was bounded by such deep, wild waters, this country which Columbus had claimed for Spain was called Honduras, or The Depths.

"Belém, as we know, was not destined to survive for very long. The settlers argued with the natives. A cacique (local chieftain) was taken prisoner, but he soon escaped, mustered together an army of natives, and returned to destroy the village. Unprepared to defend themselves, Columbus's men fled for the ships. One caravel ran aground a sandbar and had to be abandoned under the shower of spears; the others escaped to Cuba. And so it was that Columbus's dream of leaving his sons an estate in the New World was not to be realized. He made passage back to Spain, where he died three years later, destitute and broken-hearted."

The fat one paused here, glanced around to see if Krieger was anywhere nearby, leaned over and kissed his daughter on the head. She squinted up at him. His face was thick in all its elements, lips, nose, black doughy skin under the eyes. His shirt was missing a button. He returned the squint, teasing, and thought, Her arms are lovely brown like her mother's but thin as bamboo. He searched his pockets for a match, found a half-smoked corn cigarette, lit it, went on with the epistle.

"Two decades passed before the first permanent Spanish settlement appeared on the Honduran coast. That was in 1524. The famous conquistador Hernando Cortés"—the names he spelled out for her from the encyclopedia he had used as a crib—"who'd already defeated Montezuma in the Aztec capital of Tenochtitlán, now the site of Mexico City, heard rumors of empires south of Guatemala whose wealth in gold, silver, and opals was inestimable. According to traveling merchants, gold was so common that Jicaques fishermen used gold weights for their nets. South too they said was where the fabled fountain of youth ran. Endless wealth. Eternal youth. The two deliria of those Europeans who'd come to the New World in the dawn of the sixteenth century. Cortés was not immune to them, these dreams, but who could be? He dispatched his most trusted lieutenant, a man whose name was Olid, to set up a colony in Honduras— an armed outpost where conquistadors loyal to himself might come appropriate these riches.

"Under the command of Olid these settlers set sail. Their flotilla hugged the coast around the Yucatán Peninsula down through the Gulf of Honduras. They enjoyed fair weather during their passage and after some weeks came into the bay, Bahía de Omoa, where they landed and found a sufficiency of fish and game, groves of bananas, and fertile soil for crops, a protected inlet, immediate fresh water feeding down away from a stream. Here Olid halted and ordered his men to cut trees, make a clearing, begin building a settlement they called Naco. What would happen in Naco those first months even the prophetic and wary Cortés could not have predicted.

Who could have guessed that Olid would suddenly decide to make a bid for his own independence, to excuse himself from the universe and against all odds establish himself as the prince of his own distant land?

"As a soldier Olid had been well known to Cortés. Having joined Cortés in the earliest stages of conquest (the same time as Pedro de Alvarado, Alonso de Avila, Juan Velásquez, Alonso Hernández, Gonzalo de Sandoval, and other famous hidalgos), Olid had proved himself to be a courageous and intelligent officer. Spanish insurrectionaries who in 1521 had plotted to murder Cortés and take over rule of Mexico knew that Cristóbal de Olid would also have to be murdered for their scheme to succeed. This is how faithful an officer he was.

"But Olid's temptation was too great to suppress. Cortés seemed so far away, so preoccupied with maintaining rule over the immense empire of Mexico that he would never bother to come to Honduras to reassert his authority. So, as those first huts were erected in Naco, it occurred to Olid he might begin to secure the allegiance of his men by showing himself to be very generous and equitable. Each man was apportioned a tract of land of his own. Gold was discovered in the local rivers and was stockpiled. Crops were planted. Local tribesmen were befriended and native women taken into the compound. Soon enough, even the plans to send forth an expedition to discover the Atlantic-Pacific passage (which if successful would make them all rich) were scuttled. Here was all that was needed. Olid met with little opposition. He was a beneficent dictator. His colony thrived. Like the lotus eaters his men lost interest in any kind of reality beyond the comforts of this land where they'd arrived.

"Now then, news of Olid's seditious behavior reached Cortés through Indian traders. It was inevitable he would find out, inevitable he would take swift action. Under Captain Francisco de Las Casas a caravel of soldiers was sent to Honduras with orders to locate Olid and place him under arrest. Their ship ran into heavy seas in the last leg of its journey and was shipwrecked on the coast near Naco. Las Casas and his crew were easily captured by Olid. When reports of this misfortune reached Cortés it became obvious that he himself would have to right matters. Contrary to what Olid had predicted, Cortés dropped everything he was doing and gathered together an army to reestablish dominion in Honduras. It would turn out to be the hardest march he ever undertook, over the rugged mountains of southern Mexico and Guatemala.

"Late spring, 1525. A wet season. The skies low and heavy. Off the lagoon flats a smothering air. You can just imagine it. In your eyes a sting.

Your mouth dry, lips caked. Thighs weary, hot as molten glass. Over your hands and feet a maze of broken skin, pustules, leathery scars. Your gums white and receding. Your shoulders infolded and trembling. There is a deadness like the shell of a turtle over your flesh.

"Sir, this was the remnant of Cortés's original army reduced to muscles and nerves. And at the outset it had been such a grand gathering! A hundred horsemen, many foot soldiers, three thousand Indian auxiliaries, a butler and steward, musicians and dancers, jugglers, cooks, buffoons for entertainment, concubines to make the night pass. This march required six full months. The land had offered Cortés every possible obstacle. Marshes sucked precious horses down to their girths where, once it was obvious they could not be freed, they were slaughtered for what meat remained accessible above the quicksand and mud. Precipitous sierras strewn with the rubble of surrounding volcanoes. Musty peat bogs, everything the color of whiskey. Strange night sounds. And there was always the threat of ambush. Tangled, interminable forest (—*donde se ponian los pies en el suelo açia arriba la claridad del cielo no se veia*), tall, thick, heavy with hanging vines and foliage that climbed their trunks to get at the sun. River after river that ran across their path, dozens so wide that floating bridges of lashed logs had to be built to cross them. Anopheles mosquitoes that settled silently on your skin to bring their gift of malaria.

"Many men deserted, never to be heard from again. By the time they crossed the Sierras de los Pedernales, at a pace of two miles a day, half their horses had been lost down ravines and over cliffsides. Others were lame, hooves shredded to pieces by sharp flint. The militia that now approached its destination on Golfo Dolce would be forced, as Cortés knew, to depend on an element of surprise in their attack. Cortés could only hope Olid's forces remained smaller than his own and were not augmented by recruits from local tribes.

"Lookouts who were sent ahead to ascertain the rebel's military strength returned to Cortés with unexpected news. Las Casas, who had (as you will remember) been taken prisoner by Olid, had not, as Cortés presumed, been executed. Instead, Olid merely jailed him. Perhaps he had entertained some notion he would be able in time to bring Las Casas around to his own way of thinking. No one knows. But it was a grave tactical error, for Las Casas himself was a crafty and persuasive man who managed from his prison cell to provoke an insurrection within the town of Naco. Escaping his guards with the help of counterrebels, Las Casas succeeded in finding the traitor, and placed him under arrest. Cristóbal de Olid, these scouts reported to their much-pleased commander, was beheaded soon after, out in the village square as all his men looked on.

"The rumors of what took place after his decapitation, though not reported in either Cortés's *Carta Quinta* (Fifth Letter) to the Spanish Emperor Charles V or Bernal Díaz del Castillo's *Historia Verdadera de la Conquista*, would spread through New World colonies and back to Spain. Like Saint Denys, the medieval Bishop of Paris, who was beheaded on Montmartre, like Saint Mitre of Aix-en-Provence, Cristóbal de Olid was said to have knelt down after the ax had severed his neck, knelt down on one knee to lift his head gently off the ground. Scornful of both his executioner and the crowd that looked on, he stood up before them, stood up proud, brushed away the blood and dust that clung to his face, and walked from the center of the clearing into a forest toward the inland mountains, his head held proudly in hands, his eyes unblinking, eyes clear as the stars that are sprayed like bits of ice across the big sky over my poor country this very night—"

II

American
Baedeker
of Matteo Lupi

1.

THE solitude of the room, already breached by a tapestry of sirens and the whispered utterances of the foreigners, was lost when she heard her own voice returning to her after so many years, wayworn, hot, willowy, her own voice which as it returned—in the decrepit light of this place—substantiated just how distant those times were, with their anger and promise. A dry prairie drawl came through the speaker of the machine, bearing against the hiss of static which sounded like so much gravel stirred by a stick in the bed of a creek. Hannah listened, and dark hair trailed forward over the shoulder of the same khaki blouse she had been wearing for days. She pushed her hands into the pockets of her baggy jeans, shifted weight back and forth. To hear herself again was somehow heartening—wasn't it? she had, after all, set matters right, hadn't she? But the voice, her voice, was so grainy and flattened under the raspy old recording; she understood that despite everything there remained a character inside the voice itself which she'd never comprehended. How impressionable she once had been, she thought. How toyed-with.

"Operator . . . I, hello?" and there was a pause before the musical interlude of another answering machine began a kind of waltz whose melody was painfully played out by what could only be an amateur orchestra straining down the tin winkle of a phonograph. Perhaps the words on this other machine were ruined? What came through the line now was a high, hacking, fluttering squeal. As abruptly as the squeal began it stopped and she waited, her eyes (almond, just like mama Opal's in the photograph over the stove) closed.

That voice, and the words, the urgency of what they conveyed, may have slipped away with so many other voices, but there was no question who was responsible for bringing it back. She rewound the tape, heard the tiny reels spin, hoping his envoy was not awake yet or couldn't hear. At least that way she could have time to think through this new facet, this voice business—why he'd felt it necessary to play back a terrible error of youth for her (and he left no other message, just the recording of a recording), as if the past was somehow unsevered, was something he could still work with to her disadvantage. Already, after a night stretched out smoking on the cane settee where she'd made up questions and figured out the possible consequences to the answers, she had come to the conclusion that Lupi and the old man must leave as soon as possible. How to get them to go, and where to send them, was another matter. That Lupi—whose naiveté she believed was genuine—would protest, claiming the old man was his charge and that she couldn't send them out helpless into the streets of the city, she predicted, and it gave her second thoughts which she knew she'd also resent.

"Thank you operator," the message continued, after the music, "yes operator, it's through operator, thank you, yes I know it's the machine again."

The operator—deep Southern even in her *yeah*—got off the line and young-Hannah continued to whisper under the rustle of what she remembered were the heaviest sheets she'd ever slept in, starched and institutional. The stitching, initials of the place, she could picture: a dreary blue.

"Look, I think I'm in trouble. I mean you're, we're in trouble I'm not sure it's seven in the morning so, well, uhm . . . call make sure that—look this makes me very mad I hope you understand—"

But the voice in the recording gained, and as it did the volume gained, too, so that somewhere back farther in the darkness of the present room, a loft, Lupi awakened into the bad music and old words. Behind the Japanese screen, he rustled on the pallet she had made up for him.

Neck ached. Must in the nose. One gets too old for this sort of thing, he thought. He peered around the lacquered screen (this he could smell through the must) into the loft where the television played—its light jumping, jittery—what were those? vegetables? yes, purple squash, coral squash. Hands, numbers flashed over the hands. He had never seen anything like these hands, so quick, so slender, deft, as the squash piled up like coins—

"It slices,
It dices,
It even juliennes!"

The image altered. Children skipped together down a tree-lined block, hips jerkily jabbing sides, and up a lime lawn. The image cut away to the same kids in a kitchen, gathered around a mother. She passed them chocolate bars on sticks as the word *Crunchy* appeared, evanescent, startling in the visual field. The girls giggled, nibbled, licked. One boy ran his eye down his ice cream bar, across the floor, over the mother, who met his smile with her own:

"It's delicious
And nutritious!
Easy to eat
Fun treat!
No muss,
No fuss, and
No mess for Mom!"

Enchanting, like home, thought Lupi, though after a confused lapse filled with more muffled static young-Hannah's voice interrupted again. "Make sure that everything, look, this is me I'm in the hospital down here I've . . . had some kind of—"

She saw the lacquered screen wobble.

"—but we're in trouble or you are, how many times am I going to have to call? no one has phoned me I'm hurt I'm in trouble I'm going to die or something."

Well, she had thought that she was going to die, she was sure of it, and back then, when the voice spoke to Krieger's tape because she had nowhere else to turn, nothing immediately contradicted her fears—just as she could find no reason to feel her apprehension over what might go wrong here was misplaced. Only after she had made the call did she begin to understand why she'd slept with him, why she did any of the things she did. It was not, nor was it ever, a matter of loving or saving him. Krieger wasn't interested in being saved—he wasn't interested in much of anything, was he?—no, that wasn't true, either. The poor girl, me, she said to herself, babbling into the line so angry and moreover hurt that he wasn't there to listen. No one deserved that kind of treatment, let alone someone who had been, and not sweetly, courted.

"I'm hurt I'm going to die or something call me, get me out of this place that's what you promised wasn't it I, sure, so I'm, I'm waiting, here I've got my shoes on in bed I mean there was all that mud it's like clay here I—"and that was it. The squall of a click came before the tone hummed through.

He—Lupi, the envoy—was up (she was right), had pulled his trousers on and buttoned them, fingercombed his dull, black hair, run the back of his hand over a three days' stubble. There was an air of exhaustion in the sequence of movements, yet he felt sharp-headed even though the week—which had begun in Rome, crossed the mountains from Managua to Tegucigalpa and skittered, such was its method, temporarily to rest here—had hardly afforded him the chance to see to daily routines like shaving. Start again, he thought as he stepped forward. This time he did knock the screen over. It teetered in the blackness and toppled with a puff.

Lupi righted it, rearranging its three panels so that it stood free again, and came out away from the wall. "That lady, she's your friend?"

Hannah didn't answer; she rubbed her temples, helping the blood through, chewed on her thumbnail.

"Sorry about the, uhm, what do you call it? but it didn't break," he tried, though it was all happening too quickly to take in. He was convinced he heard a rooster crow far off in another room, below, down under his feet. "What was that?" thinking, That can't be a mistake too, they crow the same everywhere.

But she ignored him. She didn't need to be so suspicious, did she, after all this man was a naïf. He would have to be, to allow himself to have gotten involved with Krieger, wherever he was and whatever it was he was doing, and with her, Hannah herself. Hers was a very finite system, too, and his being here put not just her and her made-up family in jeopardy, but Lupi himself. If he didn't leave, he would find himself absorbed. That's how the place worked. Such a naïf.

"Why're those kids' faces green like that?" standing in front of the television.

No answer. Shrugging, he edged through the shadow-sewn shapes to the kitchen, where he poured coffee into a water glass, after an assertive yawn, chin thrust a little far forward, bit of groan coming out with his breath. He wrapped a dishcloth around the hot glass and sipped, eyes fixed on Hannah—dear sweet Nini she was not, but not unlike Nini in some ways, the proud nose, open nostrils which always made him think of a kind of nobility since open nostrils meant a willingness to take in the world in great sweeps and breaths into one's being, her skin ginger, bangs over her brow, thin-shouldered, lean and—that was it—bowlegged about which there was an honesty, no? honest-legged—American.

What should he say? nothing? something? He was a long way from his tiny flat on the Via Casilina, whose east window looked onto the Piazza di Pigneto with its chestnut trees, whose south allowed an unblocked, imme-diate view of railroad tracks busy with trains from places as far away as Trieste, Hamburg, Paris—and he'd come all this way to end up here with this woman whom he had never met before last night, and still he didn't have the least idea of how to accomplish what was expected of him next. Here he was, he thought, just where the fat one had said he would be, in a room, and although he had not left this room since he'd arrived, he knew that what the man, whom he didn't like, had told him was probably true. New York—an island over which his plane had flown and into which the cab had driven him.

He had slept, not in fact having meant to, for he'd wanted to take in every detail of the trip. Especially he wanted to be able to remember the drive in from the airport, which, as he was led to believe, lay on another island adjacent to this one, one to which he had planned to return in order to catch another plane, fly back to Rome, fabricate some new identity and begin all over again. But he had dozed off as the skyline loomed emerald in the haze at the end of the Long Island Expressway. With the old man's head leaning lightly into his shoulder he slept through the Midtown Tunnel, whose sweating walls opened up and delivered him into Manhattan as the cab crossed town into the part Krieger had told him was Chelsea.

"You sure you got the right address?" the guy asked through the scratched partition.

"I don't, yes I—"

"He okay?" pointing with his pen, having pulled the partition back.

"Sorry?" He looked the driver hard in the eye and the notion that he knew more than he was letting on came and went.

"Old mama there, who else? he okay?"

Lupi read the numbers once more that were written on the piece of paper the fat man had given him, said yes, tugged at the lapel of his companion's jacket. They climbed out into the night street, feet swollen from the flight, to stand together in the silence along the block, before the building whose address matched that written on the paper he clutched as if for equilibrium.

A wet, salt wind gusted and afterward no movement at all. He had never loved his own life so much that the fear of its ending, of its being taken away from him, mattered very much—he had always advocated this to himself, certainly. It was one of his strengths, he knew—still, here on this abandoned street, at the lowest point in the angular canyon, when a sewer-scented whiffet from somewhere down in the bowels of the island had swelled and risen, blown by subterranean bellows through the vents of a manhole cover, he flinched, seeing a scuttle, something driven before it.

Fists raised cheek-high in the dark, Lupi looked closer and saw a bag, a potato chip bag, cocoon of bright cellophane. He glanced at the old Indian standing motionless beside him, and was about to explain, apologize, in the broken Latin they used to communicate, but there was nothing to say, and in any case what was the Latin for potato chip? The Indian's eyes twinkled like the cellophane and he chortled, making a kind of hiss which whistled off his teeth. Lupi knew that if he were more in control of the situation he would tell the old man to shut up.

As it was, he laughed back. Spirit of fraternity.

"Lupi?" washed from the shadow; she had probably been standing there the whole time—she, too, had seen him. He brought the paper up to his face to read her name.

"What are you doing?"

"What," quizzed the recessed door beneath the symmetric web of stone wreaths and fake columns. Squinting, he could make her out in the crepuscular cartoon mass as her head moved to glance up and down the block. She was tall, Lupi could see. Taller than he. Her arms were crossed. Even in the dimness, how girlish her face was, as pale as paraffin wax, but strong in its features, cheek and chin, molasses-colored lips traced out in the flesh.

"Before you say another word I just want you to know that I think you've got to be crazy, I don't know who you are, but you've got to be crazy," which made Lupi feel relieved, for some reason. She unlocked a door.

He took the old man gently by the elbow and said, *"Nunc videbimus quid fiat."* Let's get ourselves clued in—*fiat? fiet?* who knew what anymore—

He couldn't remember whether they had walked up stairs or been carried up in an elevator. The aural details came easier, the chomp of keys, blood that pecked in his wrist, that potato chip bag, its arid rustle. Some welcoming committee.

L'eau qui chante et qui danse. Where had he read that before? There was a poster on the wall. The water that sings and dances. It was an advertisement for seltzer. Pretty old colors, straight out of his childhood, made him feel more at home than he should. *L'eau qui chante et qui danse*—yet now he'd stubbed his toe on the table leg, said, *"Merde."*

She rewound the tape and listened to the first message again before ejecting it from the machine. He had heard. What point was there in hiding it? No one else would ever hear it, though. With the meat hammer on her chopping block she smashed the cassette in one blow. She shucked it, tangled it, stretched the tape into thin strands.

"Would you mind doing something for me?" she said.

He sipped at the muddy coffee, rubbing the toe against the inside of his calf; the toe throbbed.

"I don't want you to mention this tape to anybody, I don't know if you heard it but I just, can I ask you to do this? I'm doing something for you, you can do this for me, right?"

"I didn't hear nothing," Lupi spoke into the hot glass and within a moment he managed to abide by her wish, crumpled up the voice, the rooster's caw also for safe measure, and discarded them both, stowed them under the metal washbasin which stood by the stove, masses of grape ivy growing out of it, spilling to the floor.

"There's a cup there somewhere, might be easier for you to drink your coffee."

In order to create some aura of independence he would refuse the cup. Altogether more awake than he wanted to be, he blinked hard and tried to plumb the darkness of the loft. The yellow face of a small clock glowed on the shelf over an antique six-burner stove. Color of rose gold, size of a rose blossom. This, and the wild little screen with spinning wheels and screaming people, were the only sources of illumination in the room. Clock anemic, television riotous, these lent their light to the objects around them. A pot of coffee looked like a one-horned goat; a rack of miscellaneous dishes on the counter resisted identification. He sipped and let the hot steam penetrate his eyes. He pressed the glass to his forehead and rolled it from temple to temple, the temples themselves fraught with such a train of words worked up into babble over two, three, four tongues, pronouncing evils and absurdities—this taunting, that tracing the profile of the Nicaraguan girl in the filthy chemise (she had been as treacherous as the others). All night trucks had rumbled down in the smoky streets and with them those sirens, endless sirens, he had never heard so many. He imagined they were like the furies of classical drama, spirits of punishment screaming vengeance across the night, stirred up by curses, mysterious powers of blood and earth that crashed through time. That, too, was pure romanticization; would it fit under the washbasin with those other . . . units?

His eyes felt gritty. His belly grumbled. He rubbed it with regret. Back at

Krieger's hut and ignoring his warning he had drunk a quantity of that rusty-red water drawn from the well, water the boy Bautista had drawn not for him but for their pathetic, scrawny horses. Krieger held out his canteen for Lupi to drink from. It reeked of iodine tabs.

"Look. I know it tastes like a can of cat piss but surely you're not going to drink that other stuff?"

"Why not?"

"Catfish piss, man, the water down here's enough to turn any stomach on earth into a science project. Boil it all night, by dawn it's still got creatures from the Pleistocene paddling around just waiting to get their meathooks into your personal link in the food chain."

Even then trying to establish his own sense of identity in a bad situation—no map, no money, no food, no passport, unarmed and lost in the middle of a war zone where all the combatants looked alike to him—where he was wholly dependent on Krieger and his guide Bautista, he had waved Krieger off, pushed the nuzzling horses away and drunk the water from the bucket, cupping his hands to bring it up to his lips. He coughed at its metal taste, which reminded him of butler's breath, and Krieger clapped and threw his head back.

"Well, it's *your* amoeba, Virgil."

When Krieger first called to tell her she could expect these visitors she immediately recognized him by the scalpel-thin intonations, the crafted patrician air. The intervening years had reconciled in him a greater sobriety under the weight of what he seemed to want, Hannah at once discerned, though there was nothing in particular to which she could point as evidence to support the thought. Sobriety in Krieger, it was a daunting notion. To be sure, she did not suppose that it indicated a greater forthrightness in him than what she had seen in the past—if anything, it lent a sharper edge to the insatiability that followed like a vacuum in his wake. Yet the glib side had not left him, as she listened, and it all rushed in upon her as if it had never been further away than some shadow which trailed along behind, acting in its own manner as a confirmation of the body which cast it there.

"These gross attempts at dignity," he had said, "and all in the face of what you have to admit is a pretty simple request, well it's very unbecoming."

That was one to make her wince, she thought; there was nothing to say, in part because she understood the premise to be false. "Gotta run."

"Hannah, Hannah you're acting as if we're strangers."

"What do you mean, dignity?"

"Dignity!—stick a pin in it, all this 'I don't owe you anything Krieger why don't you crawl back under your rock.' "

"I didn't say that."

"It's understood in your tone."

"Why should I be expected to help you with this business when I know that—"

"But it's so simple, you don't have to do anything, you take in two boarders for one day, two days, and you'll be reimbursed for all expenses."

"Who are these people?"

"Hannah, politics was never your forte, was it?"

"What?"

"Political stability of a whole region, prevention of a proxy war blowing back into our faces, fourth estate starting to get down in here like mad, all these reporters starting to think Vietnam, making it so it feels like whenever you think you're thinking aloud, stenographers in the trenches, garbage wagons loaded up with dead villagers, you don't want to know. What you've got is a civilian volunteer who will be accompanying a, he's like this chieftain, and he has to be gotten out of the zone at least temporarily until these troops figure out who it is they're supposed to be blasting away at. As it is now, the word's: unload your munitions into the morning breeze, the whole countryside is shaking. I didn't plan it this way, there was a foul-up and Lupi, that's the civvy, Lupi got caught in a crossfire and there was a mix-up—"

"It sounds like there was more than just a mix-up."

"—and the timing's premature."

"You expect me to believe you are working for the government?"

"I didn't say I was, but it's nothing for you to worry about, finally boils down to a little requital, little amends."

"Just because—"

"There you've got it."

"Got what?"

"Look, Hannah, we're birds of a feather, don't you remember dear sweet Franzy in his petunia-pink stretch jumpsuits, old Miss *I Am Curious (Yellow)*, and how well he took care of both of us, and how I put you up in that great apartment on, what street was that?"

"It doesn't matter."

"I mean I practically saved your life back in the early days you had nothing to eat, fed you delicacies, too, delicacies. Remember the Scotch haggis I made you, sheep's paunch and pluck, suet, served it up all steaming and pretty just like you're supposed to in a bladder tied off with string? haggis, mashed neeps, whiskey neat good whiskey too, Glenfiddich or what, the whole business, great stuff, delicious, you couldn't get enough."

"I hate haggis, it's disgusting."

"You didn't hate me though, did you."

"What are you talking about?"

"And besides preparing your haggis, all that urine stench you think I liked that? your goddamn haggis which you loved so much I tramped all over the whole city, if you'll recall, I even remember walking miles of subway platform because somebody said they thought they had seen Nicholas down there, heard he lived down there, and that was in the middle of August, heat pouring off the girders, even the steam mixing it up with the Mace and the razors and what am I doing? taking off work traipsing around the sewers looking for who? who else? for your father with all his what're they called? fugues—"

"Krieger, stop it."

"—fugues, running off every week with somebody else and with that medical excuse, like he was some Nijinsky so he rated being let off because they found a phrase that would fit him, paranoid schizophrenia, so that they could say"—slowing—"Well yes Vaslav, the simultaneity of your being both a dancer and a horse is readily understood within the psychological context of fused contradictories, horse of a different color type stuff, so whinny away and by the same token, well to make a long windup to a short pitch, Hannah are you listening?"

"Krieger, I can't help you—" Hannah tried to clear away the physical presence of Krieger's words. The question was like the mottled stain of a water burn on glass, at once transparent and opaque. How many times she'd studied that, wondered at it.

"No, see? Of course you didn't. You don't remember, but God knows I remember."

"A good memory is needed after one has lied."

"Wait a minute—Corneille, and where'd you get that? you got it from whom? Nicholas? saint mama Opal? no—from, look, Hannah, that's why you've got to help me I mean I've never asked for anything before, have I? and I don't think even now like I'm asking much."

"What if I just say no?"

"Times like this you know what I feel like doing?"

"Peter, I'm sorry if you're in some kind of trouble, but—"

"No, listen, times like this I feel like it's no longer a question of survival, it's a question of quality in the face of an absolute impossibility of survival, and then I start to thinking, well hell who needs this kind of bullshit, this pasquinade like making me gargle tetanus toxin, no no no, so sometimes I think, Krieger let's give it up man, sell everything go off to Majorca drink myself to death under some pretty olive tree out there, maybe have just enough cash set aside for a proper cremation, let them scatter the ashes or whatever else is left of me out in the tetanus-colored sea."

"So what's stopping you?"

"My sense of responsibility," he said, without hesitation.

Hannah scoffed, "That's the most ridiculous thing I ever heard you say. What kind of trouble are you in, anyway?"

"You ever seen a person's ashes? They look like popcorn rubbed in moon dust."

"Your sense of responsibility."

"Do yourself a favor, Hannah. Give it some thought. Don't be so negative. I'm not asking much. Besides, they're already on their way."

Hannah's mistake was to do what she had always done: hang up on him. This would only strengthen his determination to see that it was accomplished just the way he had originally planned. There may have been a thousand other ways he would have been willing to consider, but as the minutes passed, her fingers drumming the telephone handset in expectation that he would call back—this too had been one of his faults, a lack of subtlety, for it was true he never showed that kind of restraint—it became clear those were no longer negotiable. Her heart was beating hard. She didn't like that. As with most people who lack self-respect, she concluded, Krieger had endless enthusiasm for disciplining others.

"He's all right," she repeated, thinking, Maybe not so naive.

"I'm sure he is, but I need to see him."

Lupi's face was thin and tired against the scrim of plump gold fish and reeds on the lacquered screen. His eyes—so deep-set beneath his brow that he had appeared, from the earliest years of childhood, to be the victim of severe insomnia, regardless of what light he stood in, regardless of how much sleep he had—closed and opened slowly. In his fatigue could she find something to work with? she wondered, as the eyes looked back at her and saw a disarming openness to her whole bearing, her face more expressive than she could imagine or control, although whatever unsubtlety crossed up the need to mask her feelings was offset by what could only be described as goodness of spirit. This was at least how Lupi translated what he saw in her face. It was the moment in which the two of them, locked each into his own course, would come closest to crossing paths—the rest would be only innocent subterfuge and delay. For her part, she considered Lupi not so much obstinate as grouchy, but the shadows which cut those deep half-moons under his eyes made her reconsider.

"He's asleep, that is, I looked in on him before you woke up, he was sleeping."

"He's my burden, not yours," he said, knowing that he himself could use some contact with reality, call it reality, in the face of all this—and, besides, perhaps he felt affection for the old boy, who was, it had to be admitted, more defenseless than he.

A nest of rubble was all that remained of the cassette. Hannah brushed the pieces together, walked past Lupi and led him along a circuitous path to the second room. The sharp odor of age came off the stacks of objects, and Lupi was reminded of the scent of a wax museum he once had visited on a hot day in Naples. Waxy, warm, musty, like the smell of pages in an old prayerbook. His hand encountered a cable or spring as he followed her down a narrow aisle causing the coffee to slosh over the glass rim and burn his hand, and he cursed as they came into a more open area where the darkness paled. Smaller than the other, this room was lit by a soft dirty-ecru beam that entered through a tent-shaped skylight, panes reinforced with wire and streaked with pigeon guano. He looked up. The birds were there and he could hear them moaning. Filthy bird, dove.

The frail Indian lay on the Victorian four-poster bed. His meager frame belied the strength that was obvious in his taut, almost hewn, features. Spanish, Indian, the traits seemed mixed. Beneath the elaborate carved mahogany finials and flames and the host of dwarfish butter-colored angels onlaid on the headboard, he seemed paltry, out of place there, an ancient baby.

"Sardavaal," he murmured.

Hannah asked half to Lupi, half to the old man, "What?"

"Sardavaal," and blinked.

Given what she had deduced about Lupi, the nature of his stewardship, she was surprised to see with what gentleness he placed on the man's lips the capsule which had emerged from the medicine bottle he kept in his shirt pocket. Cradling the adolescent-sized head, tender as a cantaloupe, up in the palm of his hand, Lupi helped him swallow with some of the coffee. The old man raised his hand, waved weakly, thanking him.

"You got any more blankets?" Lupi asked Hannah. "It's damp in here."

"Is there something wrong with him?"

The Indian lay back and burbled Sardavaal's name once more.

"It's damp in here is all, isn't there a heater?"

Hannah pulled a Hudson's Bay blanket down out of a cupboard and handed it to him. She stood away and watched as he spread it over the man. Crossing her arms over the flat front of the blouse she contemplated asking any number of reasonable questions. Whether it was because she sensed she would rather not know their answers, or remembered the labyrinthine ways in which Krieger sometimes went about accomplishing the simplest of tasks—it *had* been he who saw to it the old recording of a voice found its way onto her answering machine—she assumed whatever response Lupi might give would itself be something prepared, prearranged, something opposite of what mama Opal might have blessed as *All wool and a yard wide*.

When they returned to the larger room Hammond was waiting for them. He gnawed at a hard biscuit. Lupi straightened up and stood emphatic to face him, arms wrapped suddenly across his shoulders.

"Who's he?" Hammond asked.

"Don't worry about it."

"Work says him here's up to no good."

"Tell Henry he doesn't know what he's talking about."

"Course he doesn't know what he's talking about I mean I already knew that," through biscuit crumbs.

Lupi cleared his throat with a forced laugh and his eyes riveted upon Hannah for some suggestion. His coal-black brows were frozen in innocent arches and the smile that flustered him made both ears wiggle and caused his hair, black, thick and short, substantial as crockery, to retreat from his forehead. Hammond shook his head and turned. Hidden behind stacks of bookcases—apple crates and peach crates—which stood as sentinels on either side, pine bowed and slats warped where they snaked up the wall, another door came open. Lupi felt it was imperative that he fill this silence—

"Is that today?" he asked. Hannah handed him the newspaper and followed Hammond out what appeared to be the only other entrance to this windowless bunker.

—what had we? a Stradivarius had been sold in London, the President's powerboat-racer son was not invited to Thanksgiving yesterday, Hitler diary forger Konrad Kujan was rearrested in Hamburg, sun would set at four thirty-two. A bulbous vignette, a fat-eyed balloon-cat named Garfield, was reproduced on the front page, he saw, and read beside the image a headline about Contra raids on coffee plantations in the province of Matagalpa in Nicaragua, near where he had just been. We are not killing civilians, a rebel had been quoted. We are fighting armed people and returning fire when fire is directed against us . . . (a new yawn stretched across Lupi's face, war) . . . among the seventeen residents killed during several hours of firing were four women and two small children, aged three months and sixteen months . . . and reading further, the soot-black ink rubbing off on his fingers as he turned the pages, the exceptional story of a man who lost his leg attempting to rescue his dog, Says he has no regrets, dateline San Diego Nov 22, someone named Cole McFarland who leaped in front of an onrushing train having heard the urgent barks—

Dio mio, and shook his head, laid the paper down on a table beside a deep-cushioned chair, looked at the television where this woman dressed up like a tarot card was being interviewed by a man in a tuxedo as she jumped up and down, nearing hysteria when another woman came from behind to drape over the sandwich-board shoulders what seemed to be a full-length sable coat. Settling back into his chair and staring straight at the screen, Lupi held his stomach with his hands, and thought, People willing to lose their legs saving dogs from trains, well, it was a wild kingdom, never different. He wanted more than anything to be asleep. If it were a dream, he decided, he'd prefer to play the role of the train, the locomotive, heavy in its tracks.

2.

UNDER pressure the mind becomes reductive, sometimes metaphoric. As much as he might try to restrain himself, hold back against what his instincts dictated, Lupi wished he could weave into movie. A beam flickered across the room, causing the set to go blank for a moment.

Static.

Bars of electric light.

And bars of music—a way of addressing any given situation as though it were part of a long film projected at wide angle, movie rolled out there before his eyes, echoing in his ears, the blind spots outside his field of vision to right and left outfitted with sprockets and reality suddenly perforated, loaded onto a reel and set running.

What kind of movie could it be?

Hannah might be movie, the old man might—they weren't, at least at the moment they weren't. But he had the power to convert them.

This room could be a set, its as yet undetermined contents switched into props.

Voices could be audio.

Shades and hues in their hands and faces tinted under filter.

Mass and line and enclosure.

Tactile values. Movement. The ground chalked and blocked.

And Lupi himself converted into both a character and a viewer, at whose back stretched many rows of unoccupied seats, while what he faced were skies of cinema impromptu; the world as nickelodeon, it had stood him safe passage through from the simplest discomfiture to moments of pandemonium, like that once in Turin where the riot reached its peak and he discovered himself at the center of the melee helping to turn this van over, to cram a shirt, lit as a torch, into its gas tank.

Movie always had a wit and will to take circumstance and improve its potential for romance, adapt it, make it seem more human (was this a contradiction in terms?)—it helped with the ritual tedium unto death of firing up his stove to get the water boiling for the rice. It helped him through those times when he was all alone in his small flat where the cobbles outside were drowned under rat-brown winter as the whistles of the trains were heard coming in and leaving the station whose acres of tracks spread across the street beneath his window, until steam fogged the window up. It was a spice, an elixir, a principle, a charm, and its style varied with the mood of what it was meant to transform. Hollywood was there, but so was Wim Wenders or Bergman, Fellini if he felt like it, Tati. Chaplin, Brando, Latin lover Rossano Brazzi, but also the simplest hacks from Bud Spencer, the big Neapolitan swimmer, to blue-eyed Terence Hill—the giant heroes of classic spaghettis like *Lo chiamavano Trinità* and *Continuavano a chiamarlo Trinità*—all were models for movies, were movieable. Crises, denouements . . . more crises, more denouements.

Movie itself flowed beyond, deep into a half-world which no screen could ever reflect and whose sounds could never be heard.

Now, denying reality was a periodic necessity. This was a very different act than movie as it provided nothing by way of entertainment, and was far more an exercise of deliberate self-deception. Yet the central thing he had seen, the thing it was incumbent upon him to bear witness to and to validate if necessary, to vouch before Owen Berkeley for its existence with all the authority of firsthand knowledge—this he could not really bring himself to understand. It was a thin line, he thought.

Item, he knew what he had seen in the village.

Item, he knew what he had experienced.

Item, the water was cold and the women's legs were as muscular as the men's. And the men's legs were as naked, smooth, and brown as the women's.

Item, the parrot swore in three languages. He even knew what they were. Latin, Spanish, and Poton. He knew he could only make out the Latin, but what the parrot said was skillfully bawdy. And moreover, he had to admit, none of this was movie, not the parrot, not the villagers whose genitals he could see so clearly from under the baptismal water of the spring, not the shaman, and assuredly not the war, which was a basic problem, since wars are best kept on screens—though battles are staged in theaters and ammunition, like film, is kept in canisters until it, like film, is needed to shoot someone.

Regardless, he found it hard to believe it had all taken place without someone's elaborate preparation. It had gone too well, and too easily. Here he was, being paid to accompany the old man from a point in Honduras to another point on the Hudson River. A stopover in New York. Simple enough, and remunerative. He was asked to carry a parcel, make a presentation of the materials and evidence, to smile (Krieger had demonstrated how to make just the right smile) and let the quality of the product "speak for itself." José Martí, the Cuban revolutionary, had told the story of what it was like to live, as he put it, in the bowels of a monster. Lupi, who lived the better part of his life in rigorous, if foggy, opposition to America and Americans (all an amorphous mass of evil that stirred his heart when he was young and Vietnam was raging), felt he had entered the monster's very blood. Like any good monster's, this blood was green.

The last thing he wanted to know (although, because Krieger already told him, more or less, he did) was the precise nature of the contents of this parcel and why it was Owen Berkeley needed the old man. Bad for personal welfare. Get yourself in trouble. Nor should he have shown any interest in knowing about those who placed these responsibilities in his hands, or those who would take them on at the other end. These were fundamental strictures and yet so far he had not done well abiding by them. Kill the messenger. He knew that one, too—but try as he might he found it almost impossible to recognize those circumstances when it would be better to study his own shoelaces.

He was traveling under psychological inertia, through a plane in space that was more dangerous than he felt equipped to answer to and, he averred, caught upon this bum reel where there seemed no alternative but to conform to the course established—moon orbiting an earth long since burnt out. Item, again. Could he trust that he had even reached New York— was that what this was? Probably yes. No, he could trust that much, yes. Okay, place to start. He was the alien here, not these other people; he liked Hannah, liked the old Indian: he was the one who was out of place, not them. But why had these people, this group, this loose pattern of contacts (that was the phrase used by that guy Bernhardt back in Zurich)— Bernhardt, the fat one, Krieger, all those characters he suspected had to be actors, perhaps even professional pornographers—why had they entrusted him, Lupi, an outsider, to make the crucial connection? And how could he who as a boy had the hobby of indexing reliquaries of all the most famous cathedrals to find out if there was another crusty old metatarsal of St. Catherine there behind the glass, one he could add to his census (seven such holy objects he had tabulated by his fourteenth birthday, several in Tuscany alone)—how could he be expected to believe the old man was really four hundred and eighty years old?

Even a few days ago high in the blue Nicaraguan sierras, packing a trail with his two guides, frail boys in torn cotton pajamas who marched before and after him, taciturn, sullen, escorting him up through the wet red ribbons of foot-wide paths, he had had his doubts and found himself already beginning to wish he'd turned Bernhardt down when the proposition was first made—Bernhardt with his ironed T-shirt; just insane.

"You like cigarettes?" he asked the youth who walked behind the skinny withers and swishing brown-gray tail of the mule. He had dismounted. He was sore from rocking on the thin back of the animal, saddleless, for so long; he fell in step beside the boy, taking in the landscape and waiting for something to happen. "Cigarettes?—these?"

The boy took two of the cigarettes from his pack, and tucked them into his shirt pocket. He kept walking.

"You don't want to smoke it? *Non lo fumi? Fumare?*" he mimed, two fingers pressed V-shaped to his lips, and inhaled exaggeratedly, moving his hand away to the side of his face to exhale. "Smoke? see, like this?"

The boy shook his head from shoulder to shoulder.

"What's your name?" but getting no response he tried in Italian. "*Tuo nome? Ch'é?*"

"*¿Mi nombre? me llamo Bautista.*"

The boy was offered but would accept no more cigarettes, nor the square of half-melted chocolate, pocketknife, nor even the bulky gold ring with the two ruby-eyed intertwined dragons. And they're acting as if it's my trustworthiness that's in question, Lupi thought, almost snapping out at Bautista. He must have been losing his mind to have proffered the ring— which was gaudy, true, but had been a present from Nini, her uncle's, or grandfather's, an heirloom that he declared would never leave his person— with some edgy, unformed thought of coaxing some clues about what he could expect ahead here, as if knowing about anything in advance would make it easier to get through.

Ridiculous idea. Another conceit. He bridled back the horse, got on its back again and rode, reciting multiplication tables to kill time. Bautista had taken the lead, and at the sharp downward bend in the trail, so narrow the party was reduced to single file with Lupi at the middle, they dropped into a green, shaded crevice and picked their way down to the rope-lashed wood bridge which spanned the white water breaking on the rocks. The gorge echoed and reechoed, a continuous needling applause.

When he saw the faces, aloft in the green, spectral, floating in the darkness above the successful artifice of their camouflage uniforms, that roar converted to a wistful pulsing silence. Lupi fell like dead weight down over the horse's head and grabbed with his mud-smeared hands for the rifle the boy toted out before him. Though he caught the cylinder it would not come away from the boy, held by a wide strap over his shoulder. Bautista reeled around suddenly pointing it in Lupi's face. He looked from the cold metal anus of the rifle's bore to Bautista's chipped teeth and back. With his arms outstretched he whispered but to no avail since the boy, who withdrew half a pace, couldn't understand him. The boy tried to make him stand up, jerking his chin, but he refused, pointing out into the foliage where the ash-blackened faces appeared. The faces could be heard crying out, and Bautista ducked down just before the blast of fire cut through overhead. Lupi felt the congealment of fluids spread like hardening fans in his cheeks—carmine fans—as bullets cut branches and distorted air about his head.

He dropped from his knees in a heap to the shallow mud. He lay on his side. His hands touched his cheeks, mouth, neck, forehead, but when he pulled his palms away to see, there was no blood. Bautista left them beside the trail after the fusillade ceased. Birds went silent, but soon sang on as if nothing out of the ordinary had taken place. Perhaps nothing had, Lupi commented to himself as he attended other explosions down the pass, though there too, in the rocky, narrow gorge, sweet sounds reechoed afterward.

Bautista returned half an hour later, and spoke to the other boy rapidly in Spanish. They signaled for Lupi to get back on the horse. He was conducted to an outpost two hours' distance from the site of the skirmish. He asked questions, was disdainfully ignored by both his escorts, and a third boy—a wiry, older figure—who appeared to live in this small house, a farmer. After a supper of orange-yolked eggs mixed with tomatoes, a toasted cob of corn, rice, heavy black coffee, he was left to sleep on a rug-draped board cot. A new guide took him the next morning back to the village where he had begun the day before.

Lupi dismounted, cursing, and was led into the low building with blue graffitied walls.

"What are you doing back here," said the fat man, whose skin, the color of an overripe green olive, bulged into rotundity where it was visible at the extremities of his tired suit. Even the deep, insincere voice conveyed an essential unctuousness as it contended with his lips, continually moistened by his tongue.

"You tell me." A girl came to the table. "*Una cerveza*," he said, and she left.

"*Por favor*," the Nicaraguan added. He drank a clear liquor that smelled of mesquite from the tumbler and his hand, marvelously spherical so bloated it was, replaced the glass on the table. Lupi could hear a game of pool being played in another room. Ivory clicked, the balls caroming over the felt-covered slate.

"So, I quit."

"You quit," returned blankly, in the same tone as the *por favor*, meant as a comment on the lack of manners.

"Look, I've wasted all this time sitting waiting listening to you, day after day you telling me nothing. Telling me all this stuff about how great

Somoza was despite the death squads, the kaibiles, the guardias, the CIA. All your theories on this and that, what do I care? Now I spend the day riding around only to be sent right back? I'm giving back the advance Bernhardt gave me."

Counterpoint of balls and the men's voices mouthing obscenities, advice about strategies to the players, bets, insults, jokes. The girl returned with a bottle and set it on the table. The bottle had no label.

"What did you do that you are back here?" The edges of his smile pressed down.

"Nothing, I rode, I walked. I followed your Bautista."

"What else, señor. You don't go up and come back to me so fast and tell me you did not do anything. What did you do, something you must have done besides enjoy your ride."

"I made sure not to step in the *caca* after the donkey."

"Why did you give a cigarette, such kindness to strangers?" He put his tumbler before him and stared at his fingernails with a grimace, as if he were infuriated by them. "Well, you see, you have your answer already. You wanted to make friends, right. And what are friends for? They are willing to shield us from criticism, to hide our errors, so? and your error, no need to go into it—but you know what would've happened if you fired that rifle, hit somebody, then you would be in the war, we all would be in the war."

"I mean I thought they were going to ambush—"

"Stupid, just stupid. I ask Bernhardt for a man with two qualities, no more, that he be virgin, and that he be smart. No record and intelligent, reliable. But look at this. No good at all. Have you ever heard of a position called the iguana?"

"Position of what?"

"Very popular in Honduras. They tie you up hands and feet together behind your back. They use strips of rubber taken from inner tubes so as to leave no marks. They like to strip you naked and if your, how to put?—credentials—if your credentials are suspicious they hang you all night from the ceiling in the cellar. It can go on for months before you're disappeared."

"So?"

The fat man pushed his chair back from the square-topped table (whose surface was a palimpsest of burn marks, carved initials, crude images) and got to his feet. "You stay here." He pulled a watch out of his pocket, pressed the button that popped the burnished cover away to reveal its face. Nicotine-yellowed fingers snapped it shut and slid it off their tips into the pocket. "You just wait here, have another of those, be polite, huh? say *per favore*."

Lupi stood up. He hadn't intended the chair to tip over behind him. "I already said I quit."

"Right, you wait here," and turned a broad back on Lupi, who helplessly studied the creases of his suit in the dull yellow of the receding afternoon, the sun having dipped low into naked trees, the sky phlegmatic as he retreated under cones thrown from the ceiling lamps.

He moved with an exquisite laboriousness, diligent, attentive to the oddity of his stout branches and weighty drapery. The effect was as if, caught inside these voluminous clothes, he was swimming, belaboredly, across deep water against clashing undertows. Soon at the far end of the bar, the door came open, and beyond Lupi caught sight of a reassuring backdrop of foliage, the red clay street and a wall of volcanic, gray stone on the side overgrown by lush green succulents, a basking place for lizards. He filled the doorway, left the veranda which fronted the building, whose vines toppled and twisted down the length of supporting posts. Lupi picked up the chair and slumped down into it. Enervated, the sheaths along each of his nerve endings had dissolved in acidity, as if from some source in his chest a constant flow of electric charge was pulsing, radiating across these bare nerves. He tried to concentrate on his breath, in out, in out, tried to slow it, allowed it to penetrate only through his nostrils to the shallow ceilings of his lungs. He tried to think of a joke. He finished the rest of his *cerveza*.

The girl appeared at the table to take the empty bottle away. She hesitated at his side, worrying her strings of beads.

"You is American?" the beads delicately clattering, and Lupi glanced up sharply, saw the spheres gathering light in smoke, looked down. "You here with this man?" she persisted and Lupi looked again into her casually lazy eyes, surprised at his own paranoia. He had been thinking, when she began to speak, of how the fat man had confiscated his passport from him before he had been sent out with the two boys into the mountains. "Like a little leash, señor Matteo," and when the girl spoke it was as part of the pyramiding conspiracy—a conspiracy in which he had deemed himself to be partner or at least an employee, until now he began to suspect he might be an object rather than an actor.

"I don't see any man."

"This one, this one is just left," the girl insisted, lifting her hand away from the necklace and pointing in the direction of the door.

"Who cares whether I was or not?" his eyes distracted from the renewed play of fingers and beads to the suggestion of breasts under the fabric. The girl saw this, smoothed her pale brown dress, turned away, not indignantly or coquettishly, but with seeming dissatisfaction. He followed the row of buttons down the length of her back to her hips and watched her as she walked, in the artificial twilight of the bar, back through a doorway hung with hemp strands. In his thighs he experienced a pang, like being burned, at considering the smoothness of those thighs, their musculature. It was easy to imagine his face pressed into the folds of her dress at the base of the row of undone buttons, to imagine how she might move under him.

When he attempted to climb to his feet to seek out the rooms hidden behind the curtain he found he couldn't. His legs were dead on the hard chair. Rapturous, migrant dialogue of the pool players filled the adjoining room. He watched a scrawny dog as it picked its way along the floor, its dry nose spotted black and pink. It sneezed as it wandered forward, tail tightly tucked between bony legs, hipbones alternately rising and falling under the patchy dun coat. It passed into the room where the men were playing. Their dialogue also rose and fell away, unknowingly miming, Lupi saw, the mutt's hips, up and down—and fell to silence as one of the players took aim, shot, sent the cue ball rolling at its target, effecting some reaction based on the luck of the shot.

"*Pobrecito Miguel. Esto es porque su mujer lo pone los cuernos con los soldados,*" came a cry. This is the reason his woman's taken to sleeping with ex-guardias, over at her sister's house, Libyans, Cubans, cattle rustlers, Contras, don't matter who it is so long as they got the third leg, a good long red healthy one and two big balls to keep her busy squealing over.

"*¿Todo está bien en la casa?*" Things all right, honeypie? he asks her after the day picking coffee beans.

"*O yo tengo resfriado, tengo un constipado de cabeza.*" She has a headache, a toothache, no she's caught a cold.

"*Espero que no sea nada.*"

"*Me ha . . . me ha dislocado el pie.*" Dislocated my foot.

These mercenaries get kinky in the sack, the oldest choked. Learn all their funny tricks from the potato-faces.

"*No se puede dejarle embarazada sin aprender que significan el bastón y la bola,*" asserted the man chalking his stick. No no, he'll never get her knocked up until he learns the meaning of a stick and a ball.

At a corner pocket, exploding into laughter, "*Y hoyo, un hoyo.*" A stick, a ball, a hole.

* * *

As the fantasy smile faded Lupi began to feel nauseous. In his mind he began to lose his bearings all over again. When had he ordered the girl to bring him another bottle of beer? Moreover, what were they possibly doing to the stray dog in the next room that would cause it to produce such piteous yelps? The howling cascaded around him but abruptly reached its end. Lupi unclenched his hands. He drank from the bottle, waited for some kind of conclusion to the primitive drama played out before him, around him, but on a stage he could not directly see. In unsettling silence he kept eyes on the archway by which the two rooms communicated, expecting to witness a grotesquerie, one of the men to cross through, dragging the corpse of the dog by its tail, or lank hind leg.

After long minutes, the game resumed. The conversation, with its interjections and laughter, ascended and dropped off as before. The mongrel dog materialized in the breezeway, hobbled back to the porch door (opened again to a solid bar of day), and limped outside. It turned several circles in place before lying down; sniffed its paws in sequence and with a comfortable shudder closed its eyes to nap. Lupi wished he could pat it.

The door remained open. He watched the dog flinch in response to its dreams. Beyond, the resident snake had retreated. Having traveled lower in the sky, the sun left off warming the stones of the wall across the road. Lupi's head was resting on his forearms. His eyelids slackened and there was the withdrawal just as he tumbled down through the precarious crack between planks.

He recalled having been dragged to his feet sometime after he had observed the dog cross the room into where the men were playing pool. He had been escorted through the rear doorway, curtained with hemp string, down a narrow corridor. In this corridor, he could remember, a pervasive smell of overcooked mutton lay in the air, clung to the damp walls. To the right, through a second, low-beamed door, he was directed into a cramped cell with baked tile floor, red as iron ore, and adobe walls of a pure white. On the far wall hung an image of the Virgin in an ornate tin frame; plastic flowers, tied with dried vine around their cock-eyed stems, lay along its top. A small table, cane chair, narrow plank bed. The men who had led him here exchanged a few words. Lupi listened hard but couldn't understand. He was made to sit on the meager bed, whose ungiving surface was draped with horsehair pelts.

When the men left, the girl emerged from where she had been waiting in one corner.

She had removed her dress and Lupi could see it where it hung, limp as a brown flame, from a nail on the back of the door. A chemise clung to the form of her hips. She came to the bed.

"*¿Tu eres bueno con las mujeres?*" You are good with women? You must be very good to me, I don't want you to hurt me, you strong tramontane . . .

No that wasn't right, tramontane? and Lupi tried to speak, but his tongue was crippled, was like tepid tallow just drawn from a wax mold. Her hands were at work in his lap; she half-sat on the bed. She was muttering to him but her words were in the same dialect the men used and he understood nothing. He could feel her fingers on him; trousers unbuttoned, the flaps lay open. Her hands, coarse as heels of calloused feet, roughly stroked him. He winced. Flailing with his arms he caught hold of her neck and tried to draw her head down to his, but he discovered he hadn't the strength to force her to move. Groaned indistinctly, it was like being crushed under a crowd. In a moment she stopped, clasped his hand, pulled it away from her hair, forced it back to the bed at his side.

"*Deja: cállate.*"

She shifted her buttocks on the horsehair pelt so that she sat closer to his face, ferine eyes staring down into his, which were swimming, as were the images they perceived. He watched her helpless as she slid the thin straps of her chemise off her muscular shoulders and leaned over his moving mouth. She gave him her thin blue-veined breast which he aimlessly kissed until by instinct his lips located her nipple and took it, an implacable hard berry, numbly and began to suckle. It seemed as if there were other hands exploring his lap and thighs but he concentrated on sucking at the breast. What the unseen hands tore away from his finger made a gurgling sound; away with the ring came a little of his own skin, a catastrophe.

He bit hard into the girl's flesh and she gave a surprised cry. Somebody else spoke what, he deciphered from rhythm and tone, were words of encouragement, if not instruction. She wedged her thumb and fingers between his teeth which forced his jaw to come unlocked. Her face now smothered his, her mouth clamped down over his nose and she inhaled, withdrawing air from his lungs, forcing him to breathe through his mouth. He could feel the weight of her on his own chest. She had one hand clamped on his erection. She ran her tongue across his eyes, as they both awakened with a start in Lupi's filmy mind.

3.

THE dream that had left him in bed, writhing in the scarifying and oily pelts, had given way to something ominous and solid and crystalline. From across the stained table of the bar the fat man, accompanied by another, regarded him. The fat man's companion was dressed in fatigues, a smart, violet kerchief knotted around his neck. In either side of his face a deep crease ran vertically from cusp of cheekbone, under tiny eyes, to the edge of jaw, a swarthy marionette whose lower lip, teeth and jaw were cut away so that they seemed independent of the rest of the head. His eyes—their blackness lodged in the flat, wide berth of his face—were dead as they stared in at his own nose. Were he a Contra, Lupi wondered, would he be able to move unobstructed in this hamlet? This was not a government soldier. A bottle of the same clear alcohol the fat man had been drinking before rested on a tray with three glasses, each differently shaped.

The fat one said with cheerfulness that renewed memories of the first optimistic day, his face serene as an egg washed in water, "So here we are."

Lupi looked at him, glanced at the door and observed the dog where it slept on the now-lightless porch. There was nothing to be heard from the pool room. "You have been where?" he asked him, head aching with each pinch of his heart, falling back in his chair—he crossed his arm over his chest; forehead wrinkled, pulling brows together. He glanced over at the bar, but the girl who wore the yellow dress was not there. The three of them were alone. This establishment was, after Santa María de la Rosa, the Catholic cathedral that dominated the plaza at the heart of the village (rocky parvis crowned by pigs and children), the most frequented and important in the community. The men who had access to its pool table— table confiscated from the home of a British coffee exporter who had fled in the earliest days of the revolution (having been bought from partisans in Bluefield whose grandparents had appropriated it from yet another Londoner after the first war)—were the hamlet's dominant males: if not guerrillas, at least in possession of matériel. They'd left.

"Drink up, Lupi, and don't worry so much. I can tell you you leave tonight. You're being deported. The government deems your continued presence here dangerous to the security of the state."

"What, that's ridiculous."

"You should be thanking me, that I have been able to make these arrangements on your behalf."

"*Va fa'n culo.*" Lupi rubbed his eyes with the butts of both hands.

"Carlos why don't you kill him?" he said evenly. "This country is, after all, at war. Infiltrators, agitators from outside, common as flies. It's of no consequence to me who misunderstood your aims here and killed you, people are—as an old American friend in the diplomatic corps was fond of saying—so many bubbles on the horse piss, they get popped and what happens—nothing happens . . ." (changing his tone) "a beautiful evening, smells like wattle, smells like cunt."

How many movies had the guy seen? Lupi wondered as the three sat silent for the time it took the fat one to draw a small cigar from his jacket pocket, open a pearl-handled knife which he used to pare one end, twirl it along his teeth, languidly put a match to it and manufacture smoke, rancid willowy cotton, over them. Bad actor, B-grade—he swallowed a cough.

"You were brought here because you're a blank slate."

"I'm not, though."

"Blank enough."

"I thought you said I was done." The inner smile faded.

"Well, you're done, try this, to all purposes you are deceased for two or three days now. Your passport and all those sham papers? We've returned them to the Italian authorities."

He thought, No such thing as Italian authority.

"You were buried in a shallow grave under a little rock salt—Carlos decided he didn't want to eat you for dinner, right?"

Carlos shrugged.

"Right?"

A boy came walking down the road. He was whistling, tunelessly, still too far away to be heard from where Lupi and the others sat. He had a stick in his hand and with it he tapped the dirt ahead of him. Sometimes he slapped a stone away from his path. His clothing flapped in the small breeze that was coming up from the valley below. He walked past an old man whose skin was brown and rilled as bark and who drove two oxen before him. Behind this man trotted a dog. Upon seeing the boy's stick, the dog bared teeth and began to growl. The boy unholstered his revolver and aimed it at the animal's head. The man cried the dog's name and the dog ceased. The boy did not shoot the dog.

* * *

A mocking fly that'd droned in loose spirals over their heads landed on the revolver, walked its length and facets from hammer to cylinder and down the barrel and cast off again. Carlos scratched behind his ear. He had tried to capture the fly in his hand but had missed. Once he had been told that these insects take off just the opposite of a helicopter, that they cast off backwards. To catch them one must bring the palm in swiftly from behind. He discounted this as fallacy, even myth, something a missionary would make up.

The familiar footsteps of his nephew were heard and he looked out on the porch where the mongrel wagged its tail in a patch of sun spiked by shadows tossed across the wooden planks.

"*Con permiso*," Bautista asked, and came in.

"Good, good, fine," then extinguished his cigar on the sole of his shoe. As Bautista's father continued to speak, he pared the ash off the cigar and replaced the unsmoked portion in his pocket. "Now listen to me, señor Matteo. And you must trust what it is I tell you even though I realize your experience here these past few days has not been the most pleasant, has not been what it was you were told last month in Zurich. You must trust me since as a matter of fact I don't see you have other options."

Lupi found it difficult to suppress his disdain for the abundant self-importance the fat man displayed with each fresh statement, the lips puckered as walnut meat within the convoluted shell of this scheme. Here was a man so accustomed to having his way with people the only interest left in it for him was to twist, pervert, entangle.

"You had no future in Italy. If you never go back, no great loss to you, is what I think, a bunch of lazy people stuck eating salami in fancy churches, and your priests over there. I'm a good Catholic myself—but your priests. Thieving embezzling priests and they all like the choirboys, eh, Tista?"

"*¿Sí papa?*"

Lupi interpreted the quick rush of Spanish. The boy swiveled his hips rubbing his groin with his palm, rolled his eyes and moaned "Ohh-ooh." Carlos pounded the table in approval.

"You people don't know the meaning of Mother Mary's scriptures. And Rome. I've visited there. Graveyard, bones, decadence, four hundred fifty years ago you are smart enough to get out, spread the pestilence over here, and look. No. But as far as you are concerned you must admit you worked too many sides of the fence. It was not you were greedy. Just that, well, you were . . . what is the word, disaffiliated maybe, disorganized, short-sighted. But you're already clear on all this. The fact is—and this you may not have figured—fact is, your name was on at least one list, maybe oh, maybe another, not high-priority but eventually you would have been got around to."

"What list?" incredulous.

"You keep asking me questions about things that do not matter. You can guess. But this is why we approached you. Your identity was already shaky, based as it was on poorly printed and worthless documents."

"I . . ."

"You were broke, there was no way you could decline our offer. It was a fair offer it remains fair."

The ring caught Lupi's eye. "Where did you get that?" pointing at the boy's hand. Bautista was wearing Lupi's ring on his thumb. Its ruby eyes winked.

"You gave it to him," the fat man broke in, impatiently. "Boy here admired it lifted it off your body what does it matter, little souvenir. If he hadn't taken it somebody else would."

"I want, give it to me."

"Want this, want to know that, you may get it back or may not. Meantime, the ring is Bautista's. He killed you, one clean shot, just like that, bunng, up on the mountain."

The boy, misjudging the meaning of the dialogue, cocked his hip and moved his palm over his crotch in wide circles. He looked around to Carlos who hadn't noticed.

"Here," as the clean manila envelope was pushed over the table. "Here are your new papers, your tickets. Bautista will take you to the place, this time you ride quietly, you do nothing, you go by a longer but less active route, all right? No one-man wars. From there you will be taken on to Danlí to meet a bus. The papers aren't the highest quality, not even as good as papers you came with which, as I have pointed out, were trash, but they'll work."

"What am I supposed to do in Honduras? *Porca madonna*."

The fat man slapped his hand on the table with such force that two of the empty glasses jumped, toppled; one rolled off the edge of the table to the floor. In a movie it would have broken (Lupi tried to restrain himself)—

"*Oiga—se calle*," with such calm as would completely belie the violence of his prior gesture. "A very fine man my colleague will meet you there. You listen to him. Krieger. He's a good *yanqui* boy. He'll accompany you from Danlí to Tegucigalpa. Then you're on your own. My friend will show you what you need to know. You will go to this address. There's a woman there who will help you. It's all written down. Bautista? Okay, *vaya bien*," and when Lupi agreed, to the surprise of all, the word *si* meaning something to everyone, Carlos upset the fat man though he amused Bautista, by closing his lips around the revolver barrel pumping it subtly in, out, raising his eyebrows. Lupi thought to reach over and punch the gun back into his throat, but he couldn't.

Fireflies were flashing over a calm darkening hillside which rambled up behind the hamlet and its collection of mud-walled huts, their tiny yellow-green points dimpling two dimensions where they ascended in the very heat of the light they made. Lupi blinked and they were gone, replaced by phosphenes, luminescent glowworms that squiggled under his eyes. Smoke from kitchen fires clung in the pure air of the peaceful evening. Women in twos and threes strolled arm in arm down the street. Roosters, as yet unsettled in some faraway rafter, cried against the curtain of night.

It was all so beautiful, Lupi thought. He wished he could tell Bautista that the fireflies flew upward when they flashed because the heat of their tails made them rise in the air but (well) of course, he couldn't. It was something he knew. He was sorry he couldn't say.

Beyond the outskirts of the village, in a clearing beside a river, the party reached a man whose ratchetlike teeth chewed at a length of sugar cane. He was holding their horses. This time Bautista rode, too. Carlos followed them on horseback, trailing at a distance. He deviated into the woods for periods as long as several hours only to reappear behind them without comment or ceremony.

"*El se ama mucho*," Bautista joked. Loves himself better than any girl. Carlos called forward, What's so funny? but neither Lupi nor the boy made any response. The rear guard was eventually spelled by someone else, by several others in turn, as they made their northward journey, through that night and into the next day.

Tight clusters of gunfire were heard early in the morning of the third day. A helicopter's blades battered the jungle air, making its leaves sigh, and seemed to come from across the long ridge. The boy dismounted and signaled Lupi to follow him and they led their horses hurriedly up into pine and brush off the trail, and for an hour scanned the blue rim of sky that topped the ridge out to the east, but they saw no sign of human activity. They were past the border and had crossed over into Honduras and as they did the first movie strains of Dvorak's *From the New World* began to play in his head—

We were at the border. Maybe we had crossed over into Honduras. The fire and the beating of the gunship blades rhapsodic against the humid air.

I can still hear, I'll always hear sounds from before, from back in Parigi, in Milano, and Torino. The canisters of tear gas shot at us. The craziness of the crowds. Chanting and screaming. Running in all directions. Rocks and bottles and bricks and inevitably someone with a gun. People climbing over people running from the Palais de Justice gates toward Notre Dame. The odor of cars burning, overturned in front of the black-and-gold gates. The crackling of the blaze, and battalion of police rushing in across Pont St. Michel. Trying to make the cathedral where the cops wouldn't go inside. Barricades in the side streets and shoulder to shoulder the cops bearing down from this unexpected flank. Stupid cops, with their high-fashion riot gear and fancy shields.

But the gunfire, what a simple, passionate sound it is, a gun or a rifle going off. Who'd ever think that along with that tiny sound no more than the sound of a paper bag blown up with air: you slap it and it busts. With that sound is the possibility, the plausibility. And if the cop can aim it's probable that the sound'll be tied up with another man's being hit. In the head or the shoulder. In the thigh. The groin, the heart.

The air's gathering around my legs. Warm against this animal. Going to have Christ's own case of lice by the time we reach where it is we're going. Back sore. Head pounds, and that son of a bitch not even five meters in front. My ring on his finger.

All these children the same as I was all these children deeply involved committed to some stupid ideal, some idea that can't come to be, the true beauty. But in a local war it must be impossible not to take sides. Your own sister will take you to her bed. Looks like Nini makes you fuck her and fuck her until you say yes god I'll go I'll go die and she'll say you, brother, strong young warrior, now you have had this night of passion and it was good your manhood in me and you are stronger and a man because of this, can go defend our love, this bed, this house, your family. Bautista like he wipes his prick off in her long hair and goes to wage war—

There! there! hear that! there's that sound again for sure mortar or helicopter but farther away this time I wonder if the boy hears it, he must, low little bastard that fucks his own innocent sister.

Nini, but no maybe that's backwards maybe the violence's more mysterious maybe there aren't any ideas behind it at all, maybe just something older, something that has to do with the loss of innocence in isolation, the Indian faces all flat and knowing and noble not with ideas but maybe with just the old blood, Nini.

So here I am, am I not, on this very small horse, this obscenely tiny. Here these shots are ringing around us what is this steep river this river, help me. Carlos, is that you. No no, he left long ago a long time ago. But the beast is working its way through this brown swirl, horse so tiny I should be carrying *it*. Where are those shots coming from. But maybe they are not gunshots at all just in my head.

The eye of this poor beast it is white, must be blind in that eye, poor animal. Bautista seems not to be alarmed by those sounds. If there were ever the chance the right time to move is now in this confusion but I'd never find my way out of here—la diritta via era smarrita, can say that again, old professor Besone at the Liceo that face like something out of one of the frosty dark deep circles, Beson-beson-beson! caion-caion-caion! whee boom! Face like a fish, fingers like old men's pricks. Besone? what are you doing with me here down in this mud-water? you who claw the air with your hands expressive nimble spiders as you?—feverish, explain Alighieri's meaning in this canto in that, inferno purgatorio paradiso and what postlude for a fatalist no no choice at all. It will be up in Mexico City I will get a flight to Rome can go somewhere, Liguria, there Nini I think would take me in. How her beautiful blond hair her roots brown but not dark, and her eyes and her smooth skin, wondrous belly and how I wanted to make a baby. Good young woman so smart her mind her sentences even were alive in the potency of what all she knew and the conviction that was in every word, her tongue, black panties never a brassiere, her black pumps. How her pharmacist father hated me did everything in his power to keep her away from me after she graduated from the Classico. Our fathers such friends, like brothers almost how many hours they must have spent together lamenting my choices my idiotic opinions my hatred for my family my poor father especially, who probably didn't deserve all the fire I leveled at him. Just doing his job and doing it better than most men. How'd mamá stand it? me that is. And Nini she would lie beside me and we would kiss so long in our clothes. After a while off the clothing would come pieces at a time. Sometimes nylon her hose. That sizzle sound as the insides of her thighs. Soft muscles shiny all her panties the same color but how we were incredibly virgin, I more backward maybe than, she was taken in by some pretty remarkable warnings: don't ever let a boy put his finger down here or you will get pregnant. She believed those things her mother told her. The daughter of a pharmacist, too! But we never did it. I never did put my finger down. And how we really did remain virgins because of her mother's miserable dicta—and what did it all mean?

That is, it might never have meant as much to her as it did to me. Means to me still. She was the crossroads. I wonder whether she so much as thinks of me, now, Nini whom I never got to take the pain out and away from. We kept seeing each other that summer after Liceo but she went off to university in Torino study medicine met Claudio. Remember sad breakup saying goodbye and I knew too well the direction I was headed and it wasn't medicine. Because what would perfect health mean to a mind swamped with Plato, More, Saint-Simon, Engels, Marx, Mao, all of them but still slaved by his own puny government? Torino where she met Claudio second-year student in medicine took no time to show my Nini babies are not made with fingers. How she came back at Christmas to visit and Claudio came with her. How she arranged in all innocence for Claudio and me to meet. In of all places Museo del Duomo, in that room where reliefs of the Cantoria, the *Laudate Domini* of beloved Luca della Robbia. She remembered I thought it was one of the greatest pieces of art in all Italy and how I thought about setting a bomb blowing it up would have been the easiest thing in the world. Or did I forget to tell her?

But knew I just knew no one would miss it same way they would piss and moan over losing the *Pietà*. How that (who was that?) Lazlo Toth the mad Hungarian shouting, I am Jesus Christ, *sono Gesú*. He took this hammer to Michelangelo in Rome broke the bitch's nose in seventy-two. How even if it had been a political action not a renegade gotten free of his straitjacket nothing would have been accomplished would it? How despite everything I liked Claudio. He was at least communist, outspoken one too, but Nini's parents found that preferable to me, a radical, an anarchist. And how Claudio gave me a fancy copy of Dante's *Vita nuova* floridly inscribed. I thought florid that is for a communist making a present of this token object this bit of property to make amends for having appropriated as he saw it my Nini. Her love, but he was as much a communist as I was a real anarchist, not really, I was, I was, I had that strength of character in the beginning didn't I? then just lost it? I, just a worm is all I was just a worm and look at this same thing worm in my own wood have made such a mess of things. That night *Vide cor tuum*, behold your heart, study your heart. Claudio. Where is he now? maybe in Sorrento, somewhere south, the ocean green like gray out to the salt the palms in the white breeze and each day a perfection. Me in my white shirt ironed down the sleeves, and cuff and the collar starched stiff like when I was young so that wearing such a shirt was an honor. Was like marble cut by the great della Robbia, young in the school uniform, a new name, young all over again, a fresh life, *una vita nuova* . . .

—then, movie was over abruptly as it had begun. His eyes came back to focus on how the pilgrimage progressed.

The sun was brighter than before. The horse sputtered. A sense of well-being had settled in with Lupi, although he knew there was no sensible place for it. World, beautiful as ever.

Bautista had slowed the pace, increased it, slowed it again. They stopped at the edge of an extensive clearing, hidden within the lower forest. Lupi studied his guide's agitation. Bautista scanned the farthest perimeter of the field. Lupi, used to half-watching Bautista, looked out over the sunlit land, out in the same direction as the boy, and saw the rows of shabby stalks of a harvested crop of corn. A scarecrow presided over the spent puzzle, dead red rag, a tassel really, turning ever so gently in the air just beneath the tarsus of a crow. The crow, like Bautista, studied the field and was dismayed at the prospect of finding nothing in it. With a click-luck of the teeth he spurred on his horse. Three hours later the same scene was played again. This time, no scarecrow, no crow, but a small hut at the upper boundary, thatch-roofed; no smoke, but a man sitting on the cool clay porch.

Krieger is waiting for them when they reach this hut. His khaki pants are fraying at the cuffs and have two rectangular pockets sewn like cloth boxes to the thighs. They puddle over a pair of floppy black tennis shoes and burgundy socks. White shirt, cuffs rolled up, a scuffed-aristocratic quality about him, but ready to get to work. He offers his hand like an old friend. A firm grasp.

His eyes are quick to take in Lupi. Their irises are the color of lettuce, crisp and fresh in a farina-white face. "All right, okay, how come you two are so late? Never mind, I don't want to hear it. You look the worse for wear, not the world's smoothest ride these goddamn puny skeletons. Your ass hurt?"

"Yes," he began to answer, looking to Bautista for some measure of how he ought to behave. The boy had already gone around behind the hut in search of something to feed his horse.

"Well, Lupi, can I call you Lupi? you've come such a long way to see our possession, our product, what it is we have to offer that no one else, absolutely no one has to offer. You must be, what, excited, little puffed-up maybe, to be involved in such a project as this, even though your part may seem to be tangential."

"Project?"

"No need to work yourself into a lather—"

"I'm not in any lather."

"You are. No need to get worked up over it get those glands dumping epinephrine in the blood, but yeah, pride pride, and anyhow it's merely a factor of ignorance on your part at this stage, and we're here to clear that all up for you give you a good understanding of what this is about."

"Ignorance . . ."

"I mean, not ignorance as such, not that, but what I mean is we're about to remedy that and then, as I say, certainly excitement maybe pride, you may feel it. It would be good, these feelings, utterly justified too," and he tossed his head and the shock of hair that had drifted down over his brow found its place along the thin pate of his head.

"The fat one back there, what does he have to do with it?"

"Ah, ah, cautious—well, and why the hell not? I myself've been known to go to extraordinary lengths in order not to have to see my colleague. You can't just pick and choose the people you work with, got to take the bad with the good, etcetera, am I right?" Krieger chuckled, a soft knowing burst of breath. "It's not like I haven't seen all this before. The necessary caution, the cynicism. Old Nicaragua, he's a difficult sort but he's a dependable mind, little sour maybe, little sour, look at his situation here you get shunted out of the good life, kicked from the upper echelons of Somocistas right down into the sump he lives in now, and, well you learn not to trust very many people, right? Taken me years to know him as well as I do and even at that . . . well, but no matter whatever else you want to think about him you got to admire he's a student of history, see, has read all about it. History, that is, and I expect he's come to form an opinion of people based on his readings, his interpretation of history. Madagascar, Micronesia, the Orkneys, Borneo, etcetera" (Krieger snaps his fingers) "—he's got them, their history by heart. Once we were together where was it maybe in Panama City, no it was, it was São Paulo, and we'd drunk too much, but he's a very funny drunk in the sense he's odd, the more loaded he gets the more coherent he gets, must be in the high breeding you catch my drift?"

"Loaded?"

"Drunk, drunk, and anyway here he was very drunk and begins a recital of every major betrayal in all history beginning with Judas Iscariot, Brutus and on down, but to cut a long story his own thesis was at the least pretty compelling, that is at least it was to me on a very warm night some years ago, down in Brazil."

Lupi interrupts. "Mr. Krieger?"

Krieger is a case study in tics. The constant jerk of his head to flip back that unruly length of hair, the quickly batted eyes, the fingers at his shirt buttons. These are heightened to Lupi's scrutiny within the placid green environment, against the sounds of the horses spluttering and of the cicadas and birds. Bautista comes around with a pail of red water (which makes Lupi realize how thirsty he is). Krieger asks does he intend to give the water to the horses before it has settled. The boy either ignores him or has not understood. Americans seldom speak any language but their own, Lupi considers as the diminutive horses press their heads together at the surface of the water and begin to drink. Bautista goes into the hut in search of food for them. Krieger's lettuce eyes casually revert to Lupi, who is speaking, his voice wetted by the water he has just drunk from the pail, against Krieger's advice.

"Your product," he was saying, wiping his lips with his hand, "this possession as you've called it, I need to know, that is I am glad you have told me these things about your, the other man"—Krieger's forehead knits—"that other man, your historian-friend back in Nicaragua, the fat one? but this product, there is no way for you to have heard that I'm no longer in on this project, you see. There were so many—that is I thought that we, that I was not right for your people and I already quit."

"You quit?" says Krieger, who tosses the long hair off his brow again as he steps back.

"Quit yes, it's just it seemed to me I wasn't doing anything right and that this other man, he—"

"You don't quit. You're in. You're in with us."

"It's just he didn't, wasn't very happy with what I did."

"Don't give my friend another thought. My colleague, he likes you, I'm sure he trusts you completely. Listen. Listen to me, I want you to look at it this way, this is an important thing we are trying to do here, a project, something that will come to be seen as a major turning point in the history of science of medicine, the history of, you cannot overestimate it, history of history. What we have here, in time it is going to affect the lives of thousands, maybe even millions of people. It is a matter of, how to express myself? of presentation." His fingers work the top button of his shirt, buttoning, unbuttoning, rebuttoning.

"Presentation," he echoes, and turns a stone over with the tip of his shoe.

"Good boy, of presentation. *Presentazione*. You were approached for a reason. Scrutinized, carefully considered, a candidate among dozens, qualified men believe me. Lupi, this is science and industry, pinch of bad pinch of good. Our part in the larger process is relatively small, ground-breaking yes, but relative, and not so simple as you'd like to think."

He continues to stare at his shoe, guessing it is better not to look the other in the eye. "The possession, the product? show me."

"Well, are you in with us?"

Lupi has not intended to display his exasperation. A smile, one in which his teeth are briefly uncovered, breaks over his face by way of coaxing Krieger to get along with his program. This smile is seen to vanish, but even for the moment it played there on his face it felt foreign. It was almost (Lupi senses) improper. He squints out over at the sun.

Krieger is intransigently silent. Lupi opens his mouth, and is interrupted.

"Come," he says, but Lupi has seen too many motion pictures not to note a quality of fantasy, the theatrical nature in both Krieger's toss of the head—jerked this time not as part of the sequence of unconscious nervous spasms, but to indicate direction—and also a scripted quality (as in, *acted*) of that one word: "Come."

4.

IN the morning Lupi wore Bautista's field glasses. Their sharp strap dug into the skin at the back of his neck. He and Krieger climbed through the foliage. Up ahead of them Bautista carried a machete, which he used to cut through the underbrush, full and heavy. They had spent the night in the hut. From Danlí, Krieger had brought provisions and they had eaten corn tortillas, chicken, and a communally shared Coca-Cola, which Bautista savored. Happy, he smacked his lips, allowing another of the few displays of real youth Lupi would ever see of him: the rest of the time he acted like an old man that had been horsewhipped by years and fate into utter catatonia. Lupi was so struck by this strange, sudden change in his behavior that he let the child drink the rest of the soda when the bottle was passed to him. Bautista was wary. You do not get your ring back, he said in Spanish.

It was an overcast day, but so bright that particles of sky falling through the branches and leaves were silver. Krieger made the ascent with animal ease. He spoke continuously, or so it seemed, throughout the two hours it took to make the crest. Blood sang in Lupi's ears as his heart pulsed under the strain of the climb. He drank in air through his mouth and the air itself weighed down on his shoulders.

"We first heard about him nine or so years ago, that was back in New York."

"New York," breathing through his dry mouth.

"Where else possibly—it was my not-yet-then-colleague's dozenth visit there, diplomatic corps, his family goes back generations as I understand it, part of this very substantial English-speaking community originally lived out there along the eastern coast of Nicaragua"—he gestured vaguely in a direction—"colony there very settled, very rooted, remnants of the British colonialists but some of the Indians too, along the Coco, did you know the word Indians? cowboys and Indians, comes from Columbus's mistake thought he had arrived in India."

"I did."

"You did what."

"Know that, about India and Indians."

Was he done? had he finished? Krieger picked up, "Good for you but anyway pockets of them all up and down the coast and like cancer, coming inland actually all down the Americas, of course mostly confined to seaboards, French, British, Portuguese, not many of you wops represented."

"Well, no, yes. We haven't had that much a role down here I guess, except . . ."

"Pizza hasn't infiltrated the Caribbean in other words, right?"

With difficulty Lupi drew breath.

"Hey Lupi, here's a good one. What kind of sound do flat tires make in Italy?"

"I don't know."

"Dago wop wop wop."

"Huh?"

"—where was I? pizza, Portuguese, anyhow first time we heard about him was in a small coffee shop on MacDougal Street, sitting outside it was in the middle of the day. I'm still not sure in what capacity precisely it was my partner was there, must have been something, oh I know it had something to do with cultural affairs. There was this other kid, you probably won't meet him but his father's very interested in what we're doing down here, anyway, this Jonathan Berkeley kid, straight out of college, spoiled, sort of a richy back-to-the-earth type, grumbling about how his father's blowing all this inherited money into artifacts—the father a gerontologist and some kind of wacky number—"

"What does this have to do with me?"

"Hey Lupi?"

"What."

"Hold your horses—Sardavaal I'm trying to say, he showed up with a gentleman named Miguel Sardavaal. I was supposed to meet Sardavaal, but the Nicaraguan came along too—and everything sort of came together in my head. Sardavaal was an anthropologist, he'd been working for years in this region, here in Honduras, all over from the Sierras de Nombre de Dios to the Montes de Colón."

"These, in other words?"

"Correct, right," like sharp bites: Krieger did not like to be interrupted. "I gather he mostly was focusing on links, evidences of links, between the very earliest colonists, the conquerors, and the indigenous populace, the natives. He was always needing more money to go on with this work and that's where I came in, in the sense that I worked for a petroleum company was into fruit, hardwood export, etcetera, the standard sort of industries you do down here, that is apart from the drug thing which was big from day one, anyway I worked mostly as a consultant, investment adviser that sort of trip more money than they knew what to do with. Those were the days of gas lines, shortages . . . though of course the shortages were as much manufactured by slowdowns as by supply problems, everybody's clear on that and the bastards're going to pay for their prescience. So, well, we were constantly on the lookout for proper places to put funds, that was my job, funding placement, disposition of excess. Consulting, the second-greatest racket on earth—" Lupi wanted to ask the obvious question, but let it go. "Whenever possible the criteria involved were two. A: promote public respect. You know, counter the hostility. Even promote gratitude of a sort by giving the appearance that the money was going into the arts or the social sciences, in any event something that had the aura of social good about it. Second: to make inroads, establish favors owed in areas of the world that might become important to the corporation at some moment in the future, in other words buy friendships in every potentially strategic place right down the line. All pretty obvious stuff. But Sardavaal, his work was the perfect fit."

"Perfect how?"

"He met both criteria as if they were tailored exclusively for him. Or if not, at least vice versa. Honduras was one of the very poorest countries on earth, sixth-poorest I think, in this hemisphere second only to Haiti mortality rate not to be believed, life expectancy straight out of the thirteenth century, seven of ten children dead before they're six, survivors mostly all illiterate of all the Latin American countries Honduras lagged farthest behind in every category you can think of. Constitution after constitution drafted, promulgated and ignored. Oligarchies, inept bastards one after the other, straight through the nineteenth century on into the twentieth. And look at how well United Fruit had done, Standard Fruit, Chase Manhattan, you telling me? whole bunch of them eighty percent of the whole fucking economy was three U.S. corps—three—the military like their own sort of personal gendarmes, whole government bought off for nickels and dimes, and they're still in here to the tune of sixty percent control of the economy. Other twenty percent slack's been picked up by the nips—"

"What's nips?"

"Nips nips. Japs, slants. You know, the squirts, yellow bastards with their eyes like theees? Mitsubishi, on and on, low wages and no division of profits worth spitting at. No, no, we wanted Sardavaal, his reputation so clean you could eat off it. Here was a humanitarian, introduced hygiene to some of these more remote villages, scientific farming ideas, that sort of thing. I remember one thing he wanted was used tires—"

"Tires."

"Tires, yeah, he tried to get these people to make sandals with tire soles, keep them from walking around barefoot in their own shit, and the shit crawling with tapeworm, ringworm, hookworms. No, god, this guy we had to have, an absolute fount of benevolence and carrying the corporation's flag down here. We knew even then, two decades tops before the popular revolt. I mean, you can only feed people a steady diet of malaria pills and jet fighters so long before their digestive systems start to go and the mood turns sour. So this was backup, and the corporations were into the really intelligent strategizing down in here long before the government types even gave it three thoughts. Sardavaal. It was prophetic, really. Let him play till his heart's content with linking images painted on old clay pots and fabrics, whatever, *artículos de piedra y cerámica*, bunch of junk carved in lava etcetera. A small investment and of course the corporation had every logical right to fly somebody in from time to time, visit, see how the old money's being spent, glad-hand around at the Palacio de los Ministerios, the Casa Presidencial, in Teguz. Every strategist worth his salt, every damn one of them knew thirty-forty years ago this was as fine an exhibit of a piece of real estate vulnerable to . . . you know what, as there was on earth. Rich and completely untapped, gold, silver, copper, coffee, cotton, sugar, tobacco, not to mention as I say primo bit of military-industrial strategic acreage, I mean that this would be one of the scenes of the major confrontation in the latter quarter of the century, it was something you could bank on, in fact it's already begun."

"How do you get away with? that is," seemed somewhat sheepish, for Krieger was on a roll, his voice tinged with the kind of hysteria that comes of many years of concentrated thought on a single topic. "How is it, speaking of the fighting and how it's started, I can attest to that, we heard gunfire back there. How is it you people are able to move about so freely?"

"Sardavaal, I'm trying to explain. These investments do pay off. Etcetera, in any case, to continue, the Spaniards had it right in the first place, came here looking for gold, fame, the fountain of youth, honor, the great passage to the Orient, and more or less they found what they were after. All perfectly but perfectly reasonable goals to an expansionist civilization."

"The fountain of youth they never found, of course." Lupi rubbed the back of his neck; his shoulders ached. He glanced up ahead and saw they were nearing the top. The trees thinned out and gave way to green scrub and rough stone.

"The fountain of youth, no. Ponce de León, Cabeza de Vaca?" And with this Krieger gave a clipped laugh. "That, no, and to think of the lives lost, the fortunes squandered trying to find it. But this all pertains, you see."

"How pertains? you mean the Berkeley man—or the—"

"Pertains to the project, fountain of youth, longevity etcetera. You know that Walt Disney—you know Disney, no? Pluto, Minnie Mouse, Mickey, all that crap?—you know that Disney had himself frozen?"

Lupi closed his eyes.

"Cryogenics, sure, sink them in units three hundred and X degrees below zero suspended in canisters until the cure for whatever they've got, cancer, whatever, is found, then you thaw them—but of course the invoice is tendered and check cleared in advance, otherwise? brick ovens or cold ground, take your choice. Clever concept from the marketing angle since they don't slap you on ice until just after you croak, so what value does the money have at that point? High profit yield, theoretically, think of the interest accruals waiting for you when they pop you in the toaster in two thousand eighty-four, however cryogenics' scientific merit about the equal of like treating measles with nannyplum tea, you ever heard of nannyplum tea?"

"No."

"Sure, my grandma loved to steep you up a nice pot of nannyplum for measles, goatshit tea. It had kind of a nice taste to it, mellow, a tad salty's all."

"It worked?" Lupi asked, feeling there wasn't room for the question, but finding that he'd already asked, composed a kind of stern look on his face, one of interest, as if the answer mattered.

"Worked, hell no, obviously not, that's my point. No, Jesus, probably vented a little of her aggressiveness, maybe relieved some perverse psychological need way down deep in the works, but it cleared your sinuses right the hell out, that I can tell you. No, what I'm talking about is money spent on any project you want to name whose point is to keep blessed youth going. We worship youth, have since the sixteenth century, since long before, you sip some secret potion your wrinkles disappear, the glaucoma dries up, the hair on your balls falls off, you're a mewling adolescent again and it's what everybody seems to want. Some more than others. Every culture has its holy grail, or Achilles' heel if you want to look at it from another angle, mix a metaphor, but anyway this grail for the Romans, like it was empire for them, to hold complete dominion. The Greeks were softies for perfection, in art, government, philosophy, boys' rumps, whatever you like. Take us Americans, for us it's the overwhelming desire to be loved, and if you can't see your way clear to loving us, why we'll have to bludgeon a modicum of respect out of you, you got a nation made up of runaways, malcontents, religious nerds, troublemakers who left behind their own cultures to join this single strange hybrid. So here your holy grail is a mix of the others, eternal youth, power, total wealth, but a nation too young to concern itself with perfection anyway, were it even in search of such a thing which, of course, it's not. And that's where Sardavaal and in his own way the noisy Jonathan Berkeley put me onto an idea. I guess some of my annoyance with the guy comes from, well look, I don't know what kind of background you have but you strike me as blue-collarish, and I sat there looking at this kid, really smart, talking telepathy and clairvoyance, growing his hair out so he could go down and live with a tribe of Lacandones, drive around in dugout canoes, blow weed in the milpas or something, and here I was working my ass off, mailed half my pay back to my aunt who lived over the kennel, dogs barking day and night begging to be papped and played with—"

"Mr. Krieger?"

"Huh?"—Krieger seemed distracted for a moment, with the memory.

"You were about to say, what were you going to say about this Sardavaal."

"Come again?"

"Sardavaal, you were saying—"

"Very pleasant individual, honest in the extreme."

"What would a diplomat from Nicaragua want with Sardavaal," asked Lupi, unsuccessfully—in part because of fatigue—trying to conjure an image of that fat man, years younger, dressed conservatively perhaps in the unoffending pinstriped suit of a cultural attaché, one son of a wealthy Third World family.

"Simple, officially, publicly he wanted Sardavaal to extend his research from El Paraiso and Olancho over into the northern provinces of Nicaragua. Of course that was back when you could drive your VW camper down the Pan American highway right down to the tip of South America, ferryboat ride Panama to Colombia, smoking reefer and whoring all the way, and nobody was going to bother shooting your face off just because they felt like appropriating a new set of tires for their jeep, or needed to suck some gasoline off your tank. But anyway, what I was saying about Sardavaal. Prestige, influx of foreign grant money, jobs, the same as what was happening through him in Honduras they wanted to bring over the border into Nica. Granted, on a cultural level quote unquote—not a high priority per se. But as I told you, these things develop. Picture your ordinary provincial deputy, your general, your local governor muckymuck being invited with the wife in tow over to toy at nine holes of peewee golf at the private residence of some U. Fruit exec. Sardavaal was just one of any number of foreigners perceived to be a potential link to one of the bigger concerns coming down, setting up. Corporations don't like revolutions knocking their foreign plants down. Lobby Congress for military aid, stabilize the area, and so forth, all of it elementary. You have to make friends with the potentially powerful, not just those already established. That was what his courting of Sardavaal was about, or so I gathered. Privately, by extension of what I just said, my colleague comes from a landed family, good wealthy old family, and naturally Sardavaal'd be of use to them. Family owned mountain after mountain and the valleys between, all coffee plantations and when you own in Nicaragua mountains of coffee plantations you own, at least in part, in turn, the government, and they did. Very chummy with the American ambassador in Managua before what's his name Pezzullo but I mean back in Somoza's day. Pezzullo, Negroponte, come to think of it you wops *have* been involved in here in your own way haven't you but where was I, so anyway it was the ambassador who was the real head of state there. So these people were doing fine."

"What does all this have to do with—"

"You?"

"Me—the project—"

Krieger brushed his hand at the space between them. "I'm getting there, I'm getting there. So as I'm saying, the whole scene's changed since Somoza was put to pasture. Changed and stayed the same. There's always been the fighting, that's a constant. There've been murders, land reclamations, seizures of property, liberations, all untidy business especially if you happened to be on the wrong side of the fence. But, as I was saying, most of the family, his family, fled the country I believe, up into Honduras, Guatemala, down to Costa Rica, or else went underground. But it's beside the point, you're right. What Sardavaal talked about that day in New York, and I think you have a clear idea about what a trustworthy, even simple almost incredibly simple man we were sitting there with, drinking our iced teas, what Sardavaal talked about was this rumor, apparently persistent rumor that circulated among the Indians up here where he was conducting his studies, excavations, etcetera, that they kept telling him once they had grasped the nature of his project, telling him he must try to visit this man, a Spaniard, one they referred to as El Viejo, as the christ, El Christo, and as Baal or some such. Miracles were attributed to him. He was the object of adulation, worship, and considerable terror. Sardavaal told us how surprised he had been at the consistency of these rumors, also at the—let's face it—undeniably fantastic nature of some of their claims about him. How is a man like Sardavaal supposed to react when he is told, over and over, that this Viejo guy has, that he is generations old, generations surely the oldest living—well one can speculate, clearly one can't afford not to be doubtful, and a scholar like Sardavaal naturally—"

"*Allá está,*" Bautista broke in on Krieger.

Lupi was seized by two strong hands laid on his shoulders and shoved to the ground. Bautista was already in a crouch just above them. Krieger's face was inches from Lupi's and their knees jostled. They had been following Bautista for a hundred yards along the gently snaking mountain ridge just below its jagged summit, paying no attention to anything around them. Now they found themselves in a deep granite blind, a natural formation of boulders whose carbon-blackened walls, protected from the wind and rain and difficult of access, had for centuries been used as a refuge if not a dwelling.

What Bautista'd heard, Krieger and Lupi heard now, too—girls' voices raised in song. The melody carried from some distance, but was distinct. No more than three notes, like a religious litany, rather monotonous in its harmony. Then it ceased, as if on cue, and the echo of the last note held before drifting away.

Viewed in the lenses of binoculars the world is narrowed, sharpened. It is owned by the eye. There is a proprietary quality over what is seen. This arises because in essence it is a solitary act of victimization. The object of study is usually unaware and without recourse. Outside the field of vision lay mere inconsequentials, black walls, a barrenness. Depth is not canceled altogether, but it is metamorphosed and must be imagined through the help of memory. The ocean, for example, the ocean that once splashed over these mountains—the ocean when seen through binoculars seems to stand up, a wall across which the waves melt. The sky seen by them is converted into sleep. The planet, its plants and flowers, is even more abundantly detailed through the glass than when seen by the naked eye. It is all made lavish, particularized, and suspect in its misshapen high-resolve. As a result it can become cinematic, even fictive.

Here is a man whose eyes, cerulean blue faded to the whiteness of coconut, propose something unfeasible, propose to have been witness to more than the experiences of a single lifetime, thousands of nights sunk in sleepless passions, unredeemable ceremony of sunset and moonrise and of seasons turning so often they have become as blurred as two colors—say, blue and red—painted on either half of a top spinning so fast that red and blue relinquish their redness and blueness in order to form a third color, a color like a violet bruise: a color that does not in fact exist.

He is harvesting bananas, this man. Two girls, possibly his daughters, possibly wives—Krieger is unsure—assist him. Their flat adolescent breasts are exposed; each wears a wraparound bark-cloth skirt, but is naked from the waist up. Their strong, wide backs, their torsos the shade of oiled mahogany—a tree which grows in wild abundance around the plantation—shimmer under the high morning light as do the woven bands of glass beads which encircle their necks and wrists. The taller of the girls fetches the bunches of bananas and carries them uphill to a flatbed cart with large wooden wheels; the other keeps a lookout for tarantulas, which enjoy roosting in the bunches hanging in the shady banana grove. She brandishes a bamboo pole which can be used to flick the animal out of its hiding place to the ground, where it is easily crushed under a rock.

The cart is nearly filled with fat green bananas. The ox tethered to the trunk of a tree beside the cart switches its tail and gives its massive head a shake from side to side. It ignores the girl as she swings two weighty loads into the bed. She makes her way barefoot back down the stone-stubbled slope.

The old man has sheathed his machete, and reclines against the bole of the harvested tree. The fruit sways in clusters above, but he has left it to mature and swell more before he will cut it down. His skin is dark, although not quite as dark as the girls'; his eyes are unblinking, seem at once advertent, melancholy. There is a quality—almost voluptuary— about them that is sweeping, unreadable as the quick eye of a bird or a tardy tortoise. At night, when he retires, the girls, who sleep beside him on a bark mattress (Krieger postulates, "Though it would not be typical Carib- bean lowland tribe behavior except the shamans, who get to have their polygyny and eat it too, right?") in the quiet cabana above the rambling houses of the barricade, watch him under the moon that pours through the open window. They are able to discern the moment he has fallen asleep solely by the metamorphosis of his slowing breathing, since he sleeps with eyes unclosed.

A beard of soft gray hair, two fingers wide, follows the concavity of his cheek, along his jaw, and thins around his mouth. His hair is white, but his manner and movement are youthful, quick. The muscles in his arms and legs are supple, but can harden into smooth stones. At his chest, breasts, flat and empty, lean sacs like those of an elderly woman, tipped with black nipples, matte as the powder dust of charcoal. A length of gauzy linen is wrapped around his waist and loins and tied at the side.

The tall girl reaches the man and the other girl, who has lain down beside him and placed her head in his lap. Far away below them, out toward a horizon so unobstructed that the tapered curve of the earth is discernible, banks of clouds, some lithe, some fickle as white yarn drawn off the whorl of a spindle, lie in the mountain valleys. Range after range of mountains rise like blue-brown waves beyond the banana grove. Peaceable kingdom.

The man stares down at the girl's head where it rests against his thigh. He strokes her hair, thick as husk. It is moist at the base of her neck. The tall one sits, leans forward, and kisses his temple. Quiet, he concentrates his attention on the long train of hair that is fanned across his legs. He reaches around the seated one's bare shoulder with his free arm and draws her tight in to his side. Her cheek pressed against the hollow above his collarbone, she joins him in caressing the wave of sparkling black hair in his lap.

Again his face solidifies in blankness, gives up no clue to what thoughts might be forming beneath its surface. However, he has closed his eyes and his heart has begun to pulse; his fingers gently tightening around the tall girl's shoulder, he directs her down, his hand weighing and guiding, so that after a moment the girl's face is adjacent to his breast. She does not speak. With two fingers he pushes past her lips and touches her wet teeth, running the tips back and forth across them several times before they loosen and her mouth comes open; he pinches the tip of his breast and lifts his nipple to her mouth so that she begins to suck.

Behind the lids of the old man's eyes are forms and color like those which can be seen in the homemade kaleidoscope (a photograph of which has been included in the kit Lupi will be entrusted with), the one he fashioned (Krieger advises) for these girls when they were just children. Constructed of bits of quartz and mica dyed in vegetable juices collected at the end of a thick hollow reed and pressed between lenses of wafer-thin marble, its design by Sardavaal's estimation is anthropologically unique. There is also the matter of the armillary sphere, a large device, a celestial globe fashioned of solid gold hoops that represent the equator, tropics, the circles arctic and antarctic, ecliptic, and colures—each a full meter in circumference—set on an axis within a silver horizon; Sardavaal's stumper: to him the most puzzling item seen in the barricade, of Spanish manufacture dating possibly from as early as the fifteenth century and for no earthly reason having any right (Sardavaal's term: "any right") to be here. A rather poor snapshot of this armillary sphere, taken indoors with a flash, is also to be included with the documents in Lupi's envelope.

Through the field glasses, Lupi can see the man whose left hand gathers hair, twists it over and over until it is tight like a tail at the back of a neck. Tacit, slowly, he continues to twist the heavy braid of hair so that the girl who had curled against his leg seemingly comes out of a dream and rolls onto her side facing him. He draws her head up along his thigh until her face is buried at the juncture of his hip. With her tongue she begins to trace the fold of skin. He releases the braid, reaches fluidly in under the coarse dry drapery of loin wrapping and lifts it away so that she can close her mouth around his penis, which he has offered her. His face is as stationary as sculpture. After the sun has climbed down lower into the leaves of the banana tree that canopies the three, he will have first pulled back the knee-length skirt covering one girl's legs and buttocks and have entered her and, after a time, have also taken the other young woman. By dusk they will have followed ox and cart along the high ridge, down the zigzagging narrow road that descends to the river (which cuts through the bottom of the ravine) and back up the side of the far hill to the barricade not visible from here, an ancient village, formed not unlike a medieval town, in circles that radiate from the raised central house. Here—according to Sardavaal, the only "civilized man" ever to have entered its precincts (and by this he wryly'd discounted the season some poor missionary had spent among them, teaching Latin since they steadfastly refused to speak Spanish, trying to sort out whether these were Mosquito, Sumo, Paya, or Jicaque, and reaching no judgment)—the old man lives.

Bautista had fallen asleep, had ignored the entire pantomime which Krieger summed up as "a splendid performance, christ almighty, and to have seen them so close up out away from the barricade and in the very act of . . . well, we've certainly enjoyed a bit of good luck. It's a propitious sign for the success of the entire project."

Binoculars beside him on the lichen-rugged outcropping, Lupi looked at Krieger incredulous, thinking *che cazzo credi che sia*, what kind of a jerk do you think I am, saying, "But what is it you possess?"

"Possess? possess! why him, man, of course. The old one, the one you just saw. Indeed, we own them all." That Krieger even now was whispering, and that his words were shrill and strained, only added to his overall histrionics.

"We do?" resistantly.

"All them, don't you get it? Sardavaal says there are men in there some of them easily a hundred fifty, two hundred years old and, well, they're ours."

". . . they are."

" 'You that are old consider not the capacities of us that are young'—"

"But how is it you own them?"

"Postindustrialism, post-machine age, don't you know diddley-squat? knowledge is property, man, and no one else so much as suspects this remnant-group, as I believe they might be classified, and no one suspects their existence and thus we—*we*, mind you—are the rightful owners and we have buyers, people willing to pay."

"What for?"

"What for? for the good of man's what for."

"The buyers must be idiots."

"Idiots? why not, romantics, moral maniacs, pathomaniacs, small beer, kind of a mix, a brew—the kid's father, don't you see?"

"What?"

"Moral insanity, not a current idea in psychology I guess, but one that ought to be brought back into currency. What I'm saying is progressives, Lupi, men willing to take a plunge, like Faustus, you got to keep thinking what I said before: science and industry . . . and presentation, Faustus don't forget and from what I've seen, some of them are considerably more cunning than all that. We ask a couple hundred thousand *ejemplares* of what *we* need, little purchasing power is all, little power to bust us out of our own various bogs, and in exchange they get full ownership to perform whatever research they wish on them no questions asked, and nothing traceable, and you come through for them at least in most cases at any rate, you come through for them, and are paid, and immediately the crime quote unquote of it goes home to reside just where it belongs—squarely on *their* shoulders. They're the ones that stand to grab all the fame and honor after all, even the real potential financially here. But the responsibility's theirs as it should be and we perform our service, too, and everything's hunky-dory. And there's nothing to come back to roost with us. Here they have custody of an alien, no papers, no past, nameless, who cannot even begin to tell you where he came from, and if you are dissatisfied what are you going to do, go to the police? the Department of Immigration? What have you got."

"Not much."

"Nothing at all. At max a pseudonymous letter or two written out in a child's hand. The thing to keep high in mind, you see, is that, despite some of the details, what we're doing here is good, it's a good thing. As it is now these people don't stand a chance."

"What child's hand?"

Krieger breathed out hard. "You didn't meet her, don't worry about it, etcetera, a letter that makes at best some relatively amicable and businesslike references to a transaction so vague it could involve almost anything from elephants to rivets. Once these people say yes they themselves are the ones who are at risk, not us. But they're willing to gamble, they're adults. They know the difference between yes and no, right and wrong, right?"

"Maybe, maybe not."

"Well, we do don't we. Right and wrong're only words but words are dangerous, words are symbols, and you know how they're shaped? Here I was at college, know-it-all, and I come home for Easter to visit my aunt and she asks me, she said, Peter, how are they shaped? Like hooks, I told her, some people think words are things and that they refer only to themselves and nothing out in the other, I said. And she said, Other what? And I said, Just other. Other. So this is the fancy philosophy you've been in college learning? she said, that's all well and good, these are important things for you to understand but remember when you come back home, you say 'Nice day, huh?' to a kid down from 140th Street and he turns around you're dead. She was absolutely right. Structuralists, commentators on society, on all of us, I've read them, I've seen firsthand this decadence, they think this stuff is pioneering thought, innovation, revolutionary, but you know what it is?"

"I don't, but listen—"

"It's a pack of fags running around, cocks brown with their students' shit, looking to keep themselves in print in order to keep their vermin university jobs. They think they're vanguard whereas they're really rearguard. They don't understand anything but fucking in the ass."

"Mr. Krieger."

"Yeah?"

"You haven't said how we, how it's supposed to go that they're transported, delivered to all these—"

"Not difficult and this is where your talents come in, your Latin, good old dead tongue that that is, leave it to a European to speak Latin, no offense but you people sit around on your thumbs watch everybody else go to the moon, while you sit there hail-Marying and conjugating verbs, read about the glory days, Caesar, Tacitus, Cicero bunch of windbags."

"But getting back, you haven't said how we're, with all these border guards and soldiers, passport control—"

"Lempiras, Lupi. Money. Money into proper hands. We've got official help high up into the military, which is, let's face it, the only branch of government that counts in these countries. You can pay a lot of people to say the word yes, you'd be surprised. Lempiras into the proper mitts. There're echelons of military personnel in every army on earth that are open to bribe, if the plan is feasible, neat, safe. And ours fits all those criteria. After all, this is a sparsely populated region, undeveloped, poor, not much communication with the outside, precisely the region where the Bigger War will come and believe me it's on its way. Of course, we'll be out of here by then, but Montes de Colón, inland, just jungle and mountains.

Were you to take a serious stand against the *norteamericanos* this would be a great place to do it. How is a high-speed jet coming in at two hundred feet supposed to locate targets by turns in rivers, tiny villages at nonexistent bends in nonexistent roads, all based on satellite photographs and old maps. You're past your target before you so much as saw it and you've unloaded your rockets—caahboom—into emptiness. For all the money they spend there's still no way to fight a limited air war over a jungle but as the adage goes some folks never learn, and the handful of politicians who can learn don't want to—"

Lupi looked at his wrist; he had left his watch behind—ring, watch, this was a losing proposition.

"Why do you think they had to strafe with napalm in Vietnam, burn everything out clean? . . . why do you think they had to burn out the foliage in big rectangles, because they were all ace pilots? Hell no, napalm was a retrograde chapter in the history of warfare, like nuclear, since it's not skill or accuracy or even strategy—just burn it *all* out! These mountains are gonna stink of napalm and a zillion other chemicals before the century is out. Napalm's for queers, so's atomic."

Lupi rubbed his wrist. He wished he had remembered to bring his watch. "What's my part in all this, what's Latin got to do with anything?"

"Tomorrow morning you're going in, it's all arranged, you go in, get him, come back here and we'll all go up to Teguz. Then you're on your own."

(Or had Bautista taken it?) "How am I supposed to do, I mean, I'm not going there."

"Sure you are, Cicero, I'll tell you just what to say, give you time to practice, eh?"

"Then what, afterwards."

"Afterwards?"

"Us, us—there are people that are going to disappear, remember?"

"It's nothing. Here's the worst-case scenario: some men show up, some soldiers, they ask questions about the reports of murders, of harboring somebody. They accuse this one that one of being a leftist sympathizer, *guerrilleros* and goddamn trouble, they line the ladies and gentlemen in the village up against a wall, they say rural aid's gonna get cut off, no more bullets no more beans for you folks if you keeping harboring these red *guerrilleros*, and they round up whoever they want and off they go."

"An arrest, like."

"Arrests become disappearances, disappearances become yesterday's news faster than you can say minicam . . . three hundred eighty-something armed rebellions, a hundred-some-odd governments in the past century and a half? Forget it. Everything's yesterday's news. Nobody gives a hoot—so, no prob. Sardavaal's colony managed to stay above it all. Pretty desirable piece of real estate I'd say. Nobody's penetrated it yet, to our knowledge. There're probably more villages like it, like the Tasaday tribe's in the Philippines, Marcos's tourist-trap tribe. The potential's infinite. Think what the vacation industry could do with it. Anyway, northeast of here, up toward Burimac, it's a no-man's-land. For all anybody knows there are scads of pre-Columbian groups up in some of the higher mountain areas. No radios, no Beatles records, no framed photos of Kennedy. Nothing you'd find in any of the one-kilometer grids the good old Army Corps of Engineers made. Even old Sardavaal never got up in there."

"When do I meet this Sardavaal?"

"You heard about the Corps? they're a friendly pack. Here they came in mapped all these countries, helped build bridges, electrical substations, that sort of crap, all an act of neighborly foreign policy, right? and then the maps are given to, say, Nicaragua, and it's all fine except that a second set is popped up to the Pentagon for research into how our own troops—if the need arose—could be moved across the terrain in the most cost-effective way. Nice."

Lupi said again, "What about Sardavaal?"

"Sardavaal . . ." calming suddenly. "I'm afraid he vanished on us, Sardavaal did, at least he's not to be found, just gone . . . not that it's the first time. It's habit with him. He loops in and loops out. It's too bad, too. You're right. I reason he'd have been useful in age verification, help stabilize any negotiation with Mr. Berkeley, that is, could he have been persuaded to come in with us, maybe we could have convinced him it is only a matter of time, that if we didn't extract them, the community, they'd be massacred fairly soon anyway, *accidentes personales*, might have brought him around by pointing up the research value at the other end of the project, all the good that might come of it but on that score just conjecture, etcetera. Moot, etcetera."

The descent down the mountainside was accomplished in silence. Lupi was careful of his footing. He stepped softly in the respite from Krieger's words, the new quiet now, into which the birds did not break, and the soft-turfed path trod by animals, too narrow to be traveled comfortably by men.

He restrained his breathing where it flowed across his tongue, the air itself of such a purity, like an endowment to his spirit. Krieger's ribbons of language splintered up in particles and were left back at a turn in the path; Bautista, his smile was consigned to a bit of vine hung over the lower branches of a tree where it wound round on its natural chase sunward; the fat man shrank to a midnight-blue ant. Alone for the first time in days, and under the spell of . . . perhaps not freedom but independence, as Lupi knew the binoculars up there behind held him in view, by this time the size of a small figure on a beach maybe, and the beach itself reproduced on a postcard, like the one his mother had sent him from a strange island called Coney . . . and how he looked up coney in *Hazon Garzanti* and there were the words rabbit, coward, aint-heart (not faint, aint), chicken-heart. Soon enough he was turning Latin phrases over in his mind, brushing up his memory because of the encounter that Krieger said lay ahead, and before he knew it they came upon him, the people of the village came out to greet him (as he saw it), saint Lupi on the side of the long mountain.

A number of logs were laid bank to bank as a bridge over the white spring-fed stream. On the other side they waited for him to cross, men and a few women, colorfully clothed. The men displayed pendants, necklaces and other jewelry, even geometrically shaped earrings and ankle bracelets, as ornamental as those worn by the women. Lupi at once put his hands behind his head, as Krieger had coached him, planted one knee on the mossy ground and waited momentarily in this submissive pose before getting up to walk the log bridge, the while hoping he would not lose balance and fall into the shallow brook, and thereby forfeit any authority he had so far gained, first by this ridiculous act of obeisance which Krieger taught him up in the rock blind the night before (laughing hysterically and coughing in the smoke of the campfire), and second by Carlos's delivery to a village sentry of a letter purportedly from Sardavaal that told of Lupi's immediate arrival. The letter was a mix of Spanish and Lenca—the dominant Indian tongue of the area—of which the fat man had some working knowledge.

It would have been better, of course, if the letter had been written in Poton—according to Sardavaal this particular tribe's tongue (about this Sardavaal had many theories, having referred to early missionary accounts and come to the conclusion that these people, this Poton-branch, were not some lost Maya group, but were refugees from Salvador, who fled the Spanish and ended up at the easternmost Maya boundary, where they resettled: a non-Maya group in the midst of Maya, an indigenous, displaced group in the midst of conquering foreigners—*chontal* (people time passed over). But Krieger—who had forged Sardavaal's signature on the letter, displaying originality in the flourishes, having never seen Sardavaal's actual signature, and so feeling very relaxed about free-forming the whole thing—said that some of the younger men in the tribe, whose occasional wanderings had put them in touch with the larger world and some of its language, were able to puzzle out the meaning of the communication, and pass it along to the elder.

"Hell, trust me it'll all fly like a bird," Krieger had assured Lupi. Krieger also said this might happen: as they caught him up in their arms once he had made his crossing they worked together to remove his clothes and brought him back to the clear grass-bottomed pool dammed above the bridge. He gave himself over to their hands. The women touched as frankly as the men. There was so much gentleness to the way they bathed him he did not cry out at the cold. His head was pushed under the sharp water and when he opened his eyes in its absolute clarity he could see feet stirring up the bottom, calves, the silver trails—rising beads of air, so many legs, the men in their breechclouts, the women's legs naked, the brown triangles between their thighs. Pulled out of the water he gasped for air and was led to the bank again. The women let their skirts back down.

Breechclout and a dyed poncho with what seemed to be a duck-down fringe (it was: Muscovy) were given to him after he was dried in a blanket. One showed him how to secure the poncho with a tie-belt around his waist. The women were gone, having turned their backs on the group so that Lupi noticed their hair tied in queues and greased. He was allowed to put on his brown shoes (several of them who wore tapir-hide sandals looked at these wing-tips with undisguised mirth), but the rest of his clothes were placed in a basket which he was handed to carry. No one uttered a word—they did not converse among themselves—but everyone smiled, including Lupi; instructions were accomplished in simple hand language. Three toted blowguns, toylike reed affairs, and when Lupi pointed at these, clay pellets were brought out of pouches with great enthusiasm, stuffed into the mouthpiece and shot with frightening accuracy at flat stream stones tossed away in the air. He was offered his chance to try one of these out, but declined, feeling somehow that indistinct tables of sophistication had been turned on him. How well would Krieger fare down here? he couldn't help but wonder. Maybe not so well.

The half mile they walked was a landscaped terrain that hadn't been visible from the stony perch where he had spent the night. Here over a low rise were rows of harvested corn stalks laid out with regularity. A system of irrigation, probably fed by another spring, was evident in a series of finely manufactured sluice gates of fitted lumber and with decorative sliphooks forged of silver and fixed like exotic mechanical birds atop each.

They passed other fields and orchards before turning through a dense stand of old trees and arriving at the stone wall that ran, much like a Roman oppidum or one of the perched villages in Provence, the boundaries of the village. He entered through an archway. The extreme declivity on which the village itself hung was unexpected. On leaving the cobbled plaza just at the entrance, he could see rows of humble dwellings and walkways, or streets. These dropped at angles so intense they made him dizzy. It was sheer architectural bravura, a cliff village formed in concentric circles. Across the gorge over which the village was situated ran a jagged rim of rock whose nearest walls stood in shadows except along the peaks of fractured stone. Because the village, down into which he was led along granite stairs worn smooth by human feet, boasted shade trees beside its crude fountains, while the cliffs not a hundred meters away were barren of vegetation and looked impossible to scale, he could see this site had been chosen both for its natural fortification and the sun's presence through the seasons.

Through a maze he was brought to a tiny dispensary. Here the scratches on his hands were dressed with (as he imagined) virgin wax, a kind of rosin or colophony, and incense that first had been melted over a flame into the other ingredients. And once this was done, he made his way across the plaza, up a narrow flight of stairs into the only dwelling that stood two stories, cantilevered along gables to provide a thatch-covered porch, where Olid awaited him in his sitting hammock. The old man wore a long tunic and a sash embroidered with crane feathers. An African gray parrot rested on his shoulder. A slight boy with a machete (and, Lupi thought, didn't it seem curious how factory-manufactured the blade looked?), its handle corseted with ribbons, stood away to one side. The parrot uttered a series of derisive clicks and squawked, "*Nonne hic facit ventum latrare et garrire?*"—this is he who makes the wind bark and chatter?

"*Ego? Non ego . . .*" Lupi began, but when he saw he was answering the parrot he interrupted himself and addressed Olid, formally: "Signor Cristóbal, Matteo Lupi *sum*," thinking that now for the first time since the baptism, or humiliation by water, or whatever it was they had accomplished back at the stream, he felt nervous. This might have been the language, however. He was willing to admit that as a possibility.

"*Nonne . . . hic facit . . . ventum latrare?*"

"*Non ego, sed alii*, others . . . the soldiers . . ."

A large earthen bowl lay at Olid's feet, brimming with what Lupi presumed were anathemata—consecrated objects (pair of bifocals, a mummified bat). Olid tapped at the lip of this bowl with his walking stick. He grunted. He cleared his nostrils, sucking back into his sinuses—and again, it seemed, the gesture, its purposive quality, dignified, distinguished.

"*Nonne epistulam accepisti a Sardavaal?*" You received the letter from Sardavaal?

"*Accepisti a Sardavaal*," the parrot talked as sparrows twittered in the thatchery, and Olid brushed at it. The blue-tipped tail flicked indignantly as the bird hopped off and over to a wooden railing.

"Sardavaal."

Lupi counted out a full half minute before intoning the name again.

"*Cur non venit ipse Sardavaal ad hoc narrandum mihi?*" Why hasn't Sardavaal come to tell me this himself?

He is no longer in this country.

Why has he left?

There were people here who no longer wished him well.

Sardavaal is a man of courage and would not run away.

He departed of his own free will.

The letter from Sardavaal? "*Quis epistula haec a Sardavaal?*"

It came from very far away.

"*Nonne tu emissarius eius?*" You're Sardavaal's emissary?

Yes, I am.

He would not come to save Olid from these dogs of wind himself, not his friend?

Sardavaal loves Olid. The chattering in the wind is not animals nor of nature but men in metal leviathans or dragons if you can imagine that have come here to kill themselves but they will kill you while they butcher themselves.

Mistake?

Incidental, not a mistake, and not not a mistake.

They kill me?

(Olid scowled, his whole face became glazed.)

"*Etiam, ad Olid interficiendum quoque*," yes, to kill Olid too.

Sardavaal says this? They are here to kill Olid?

Yes, Sardavaal says so.

You are this wolf, this wolf of Sardavaal's epistle?

Yes.

You shall take me?

Yes.

To Sardavaal, you will take me to him?

Yes, I will.

And what will happen to my families?

Your families?

All those here.

I . . . they will be safe.

Sardavaal sends an assurance they will not be harmed by the dogs of the air?

Yes, he does.

Sardavaal says they shall be safe.

Yes.

They will be safe if I go.

Because you go.

Olid nodded and kept tapping the bowl with his stick. An hour passed before they were brought *canjica*, a cornmeal porridge cooked in milk, fried green pineapple, broiled meat and afterwards coffee and cornstraw cigarettes. Lupi ate, choking on his food at the confidence he had engendered in Olid with his impromptus about Sardavaal. If Krieger had only seen the performance he had given, he thought, and then began to wonder why Krieger's approval, Krieger's ability to get through situations, suddenly mattered to him. He didn't know Krieger. And of course it was worth far more than they were paying him to be able to go through all this in the first place. He, Lupi. Not Krieger.

Olid finished his meal and sat for another hour. Finally, he spoke.

Prima ergo luce abibimus.

Which meant that they would leave at first light.

5.

THE coach of the bus was made of wood and inside it passengers sat on wooden benches. Neither the windows nor the windshield was fitted with glass and the driver wore goggles, an accessory which made his demeanor seem both menacing and *imbécil*. Jaw advanced under these goggles, speaking to no one and giving off an air of solemn authority, he reminded Krieger of—

"Boris Badinoff? the Rocky and Bullwinkle show? you know, flying squirrels? F-fan mail from f-flounders?"

His companion ignored him.

Danlí to Tegucigalpa usually required between two and four hours by bus, depending on how much time was lost with mechanical breakdowns, flat tires, luggage fallen off the roof rack, stops to siphon gas from the drum mounted on the back into the tank, or to show papers to local authorities. In a landscape solid and pale with the mountains falling away in ranges it seemed improper, wasteful, wrong to be thinking of old cartoons and foul little *jefes*—so thought Krieger, and as he did the bus crossed a ditch which tossed his companions against the seatbacks in front of them. He retied his laces, each sole placed one at a time on the knee of his trousers.

Three members of a marimba orchestra stinking of mesquite carried on at length and at the top of their lungs about the wire and rope that encircled the body of the bus to ensure its holding together over the potholed and occasionally muddy dirt road. Lupi and Krieger, in order to avoid them, had sat at the rear just behind a woman with baby in arms and her young son who brought with him a rooster in a woven basket. Olid, quiet, in the suit of clothes he had been given to wear, was seated opposite. A skinny soldier, beret tucked under his epaulette, had sequestered himself behind the driver, gently and vacantly to pick his nose in the soft morning air.

"I remember the first time I saw the ruins of Zaculeu in Guatemala I thought, Christ this stuff is straight Bauhaus," Krieger said. "You ever see any photographs of the place?"

"No."

"Clean lines all those lime-white vertical terraces mounting up and up and up with such regularity to the sky and how you can't help but stop and think all the atrocities that took place up there in the name of some indifferent boogawooga god, you say you never saw a photograph?"

"No," he repeated, noting they had already come to a stop so the driver could rewire the rearview mirror.

"Capital of the Mam Maya kingdom of pre-Columbia, couple hundred yards off the Río Selegua, etcetera, anyway United Fruit, like I was saying, UF had dug this place up as an expression of social responsibility back in the late forties and for each and every antiquity that ended up in the display cabinets at the Instituto de Antropologia y Historia how many more were spirited away for your Park Avenue marble mantelpieces? Let 'em keep the bird bones, the shells, all that crap their anthropometrists can diddle away with their calipers and their pocket calculators till the cows come home, whatever, but the really choice stuff? your basic Aztan polychrome vase, your Qankyak tumbaga and gold, your tripod bowls so gorgeous it makes your heart melt, your censers, etcetera? forget it! we're, what, twenty-five years later you think any of these fuckbusters can even donate these things to a museum admit all the stickyfinger shenanigans going on there?"

"They could do it *anonimo*."

"My ass *anonimo*, these guys don't do anything unless their name winds up on a brass plaque somewhere. Who knows how much priceless pottery's been fed into the garbage to avoid the embarrassment of the heirs finding out dear old dad was as smarmy a culture-rapist as Goebbels."

The bus started up again in a slow trail of dust.

"Say, Lupi, you ever eaten quetzal?"

"What?"

"Quetzal, the most beautiful bird on earth, psychedelic colors like you wouldn't believe, sacred to both the Mayans and the Aztecs, absolutely delicious. Roasted, broiled, not as gamy as quail. How's our friend there doing?"

Lupi looked at Olid's face and felt a quick pang of guilt pass over him. Bernhardt, he thought. Bernhardt, him and the landlord. Got to eat, got to pay your rent. Supply and demand. Food and roof. Olid's face drawn down into its peculiar silence, for he had said nothing since they left the village together before dawn, had refused the dried fruit and water Lupi had offered him.

"He seems to be—" Lupi began.

"Not that I take a dim view of it, of course, culture-rape I mean, so normal in the course of events it'd be like frowning upon the fact the sun insists on rising every morning. Still and all, but this Zaculeu project was United Fruit's great contribution to Central America and I was flown in to study the results."

"He doesn't seem very well to me," Lupi broke in, looking at the *viejo*.

"Oh, he's okay, little sleepy. But what was I saying, the results of this million-dollar dig—what do you think they came up with?"

Lupi shrugged, folding his hands in his lap.

"Syphilis, man. That is, they didn't get syphilis, well maybe they did maybe they didn't, but—hey, Lupi, d'you ever hear the one about the sylph named Phyllis with syphilis?"

"No."

"I didn't think so. You should read Woodbury and Trik's monograph on the thing, Goff's great treatise on pre-Columbian syphilis and it all came out of Zaculeu. Goff was able to use two crania found at the site to prove that the geographic origins of the disease which everybody had assumed were Old World were in fact New World so that the Guatemalans had this information passed down to them by good old Goff out of Hartford, Connecticut, insurance capital of the world, that syphilis ain't *our* forefathers' fault, ain't attributable to the conquistadors but instead to these grubby, infected little highland Mayans, among others, declared that Europe showed no evidence of the existence of *las bubas* before the *Niña* and the *Pinta* arrived back in port in Lisbon at the end of Columbus's first voyage with some sick Indians, lovely stuff isn't it? great Old World attitude displayed there, give the Guatemalans something to be grateful for like whether you should thank the guy who's only got one of his boots on your head and not both, but anyway Zaculeu was as well-integrated a job as I'd ever seen, seventy-four weeks is all the time it took to excavate and as I say a marvelous public relations number plus the benefits of keeping up the grand tradition of trafficking jade, pottery, etcetera, under informal if not formal immunity, and so I recommended the company strongly consider setting up subsidiary number one hundred and something, getting into the business of dry-season excavations, granted we were based mostly in Salvador and Honduras and a lot of the plummier sites were in the Yucatán, southern Mexico, Guatemala, around in there, but there was always Naco, pretty near San Pedro Sula a few hundred miles northeast of here, and we had warehouses and facilities there, so one thing leads to another and I'm liaison officer for the company on three of these projects simultaneously."

"But I thought you said you—"

"One not far from Naco, other two near Yuscarán, not to forget of course we could fudge like chocolatiers if anything seemed too flimsy, but I began to notice, Look Krieg you're making more in this collector market than you are on salary, learn a few of the basic tricks of the trade like mislabeling pieces, say like this necklace"—Krieger held his hands out before him, and rosaried the invisible jewelry—"this necklace, uhm, yeah this piece's, let me review my notes" (pretending to flip through a pocket-size notepad) "ah, yeah, this here's from Palenque . . . or wherever more prestigious site you can mark it up, say, well look this guy's a steady customer jack it up ten-twelve times its value, give the sucker a break . . ."

"The necklace?"

"Yeah, the price the price. And so I took a leave of absence, safety net against things not working out and six months later—"

"I guess it didn't work."

"It worked it worked fine, etcetera, but now recently the market has gone soft, harder to get good inventory profit margin shot to hell by these weaselly greedy subpar wetbacks on the one hand and your basic diminished constituency of buyers on the other, back in New York all these cokeheads snorting at their thumbnails in toilet stalls forty floors above street level get on the old horn push through some quick bond sales meantime you look down your phonecord to see you're floating over your desk and the only thing that's keeping you from floating away up to the ceiling is the cord which you hang on to with both hands for dear life and the guy at the other end's saying Morgan Guaranty what? these assholes with more grams in their desk drawer than gray matter in their skulls and you think they'll buy good pre-Columbian pieces these days? naw . . . like hey, wow, geewillikers man, aren't they really like crackin down on that now? and what does it matter to them that there are easy ways to get around it—the best one I know is you take your piece, a jaguar vase say, and you break it, ship it up in shards in separate boxes, bunch of valueless stuff there at customs right? and then you bring your restoration man in to put it back together again—naw . . . I mean like these asshole Wall Street types saying I . . . am . . . aware CDs flat as pancakes, so's money market, but like . . . insider trading's the way to fly."

"Seedees?"

"Hey, Lupi?"

"Yes."

"Whatever happened to Topo Gigio?"

"What?"

"Topo Gigio, the adorable little mouse on Ed Sullivan, oohh Eddie!— you never heard of Sullivan probably."

Lupi pulled on his lower lip. "I don't think so."

"Someday somebody's going to be able to tell me . . . so a few years ago I'm so disgusted by all this phony baloney I say to myself Krieger my friend you're looking unemployment benefits straight in the teeth unless you can turn this shit around and I have to admit I thought, Anything has got to be better than this. But I thought of half a dozen things all of them not suited to my delicate constitution, so I begin to look up old acquaintances, connections, etcetera etcetera, three of whom you find on your plate even as we speak."

As Krieger lit the cigarette he had been fidgeting with during the prior several minutes Lupi had enough time to arrive at the appalling conclusion that once one crossed Krieger's path there was no way ultimately to untangle it from one's own. "On my plate . . ."

"Uhm," he assented as he waved the match and inhaled vigorously at the cigarette, "yes, means to deal with what you've got before you, so I did some research did some contemplation on what I'd learned and *voilà*, here we are back in imports/exports."

The rooster had been anxious for some time to escape its basket and upon the boy's having fallen asleep made its move, departing the bus by a window in a cloud of luminescent feathers, red and yellow. When the bus pulled to a stop in the middle of the road the soldier leapt down to chase it. Krieger followed this activity with amusement, crying out "cockadoodle-doo" and laughing with the musicians, one of whom had worked his way down the narrow aisle to the back. "*Toma un poquito de eso, amigo,*" the frail moustached man offered, but Krieger, broadly smiling, answered. "*Gracias no.*"

When the soldier climbed aboard, the rooster dangled mortified upside down where it was held, clutched by its legs in one fist of its captor.

"*Aquí está,*" and he gave it back to the boy.

Krieger kept laughing, smoke bursting off his tongue, as if the laughter itself moderated his involvement with the others. "People, god. Certifiably crazy, just scratch your way a bit under the surface, and you don't have to go far, believe me and—look at that character."

The soldier settled down in his seat, his chin on chest.

"You shouldn't talk so loud."

"Oh hell, I'll shout it, you think any of these people understand a word of English, and even if they could who cares? Anyhow, where was I?"

"Topo—"

"—slightest fraction of an inch beneath the surface of their occupations or moods and what opens up almost without exception are vast wild alien worlds absolutely unexpected beyond anything you might have guessed at . . . it's not necessarily intriguing, I mean not even guaranteed to be all that interesting, sometimes it's just your favorite cousin turns out to be a squeeze artist or your girlfriend this sweet Marian-the-librarian type, you go out with the guys one night and you thought she was back home reading Trollope or something and you go into the club and you look up on stage and there she is, pasties flying, in this live sex revue . . . but more often than not I swear to god—wild vast alien crazy worlds out there, Lupi."

"Why do you say this?"

"If you'll just listen to me, I mean the two you're about to meet and your friend there—"

"He's your friend not mine."

"Whatever, but here I do a little work little snooping and . . . Pandora's box! pop the top and whadayaget? Worlds, worlds. Old Nicaragua'd come down some several notches since the polo-pony days private banquets at the lagoon Xiloa and some Argentine jockey has had more bubbly than he should've and here he is standing on the smorgasbord table, dainty as hell, trying to arrange a rendezvous with a huge dripping ice sculpture of Somoza's wife the problem was his amorous attentions were pretty god-damned funny until some big guys in brown suits pulled him down into the fruit bowl."

"Hey hold on—"

The rooster had again gotten free. Lupi grabbed it by a wing as it lurched off the back of the seat.

"Goddamn it," Krieger shouted, dropping his cigarette into his lap as he tried to wave off the mass of flapping feathers and sharp squabbling. The woman was screaming Thief! "¡Ay, Dios—ladrón!" and her baby began to wail. Lupi reverted to his first language as he tried to hold the angry bird away from his face, "Ma che cazzo da sei cosí stupido da far paura ma," none of which meant much.

Having come down the aisle, boots heavy on the loose boards of the bus's floor, the soldier got the rooster away from Lupi, who sat there dazed spitting feathers as the wild aaacking ceased although its legs continued to prance, dry and rubbery. With eyes empty, the soldier presented the bird to the woman.

Eat, he said, and shut up.

The woman continued to shout, and didn't hear him.

Ignoring her, he returned to his seat.

"Hurrá soldado," said Krieger, cigarette back at the side of his mouth. He relit it, offered a cigarette to Lupi. "Viva López Reyes, now where the hell was I?"

Lupi could not say. The flat green plains out the windows had begun to lose their definition in late-morning heat. Beyond, ranges of mountains rose away into pine green, shrouded by warm mist up into their valleys, mist that hugged fan-shaped anticlines and slid its ephemeral fingers through spiderwebs that spiraled up and fell like breath over the brown floor measured by its needles. Lupi thought of the fingers and how Nini might have liked to lie down there on a bed of boughs in her school uniform, and how after kissing her for a long time he might be allowed to roll her on her side and lift up her navy blue skirt, that scratchy . . .

"You're not listening, *caro*." Krieger put his cigarette out on the side panel of the bus.

"Yes I was, you were saying how that fat one moved his wife and seven? eight? children to a place a few kilometers inside Honduras near the village where I was."

Krieger said, "Okay. And so he's very protective of his family, good Third World trait, anyway it wasn't that difficult to locate him renew relations segue into what's doing for work these days and I find out his brother Carlos—"

"His brother?"

"Of course. All these people are related. You're a Catholic, aren't you?"

"No."

"But I mean, surely brought up Catholic."

"Yes."

"There we are. Well? the Eleventh Commandment? Thou shalt copulate like bunnies so to increase the papist warren. What the hell else is there to do in a natural state but hunt, eat, screw, sleep? Well anyhow these are all good Catholics down here, by-the-bookers even though they can't sign their own name on a birth certificate."

"Bautista, is that his son, too?"

Krieger's eyes closed, the lashes fluttered, lids opened again. "Question's rhetorical, right? right?"

"Not meant to be."

"I mean, of course he is, Jorge, Juan, who can remember all the names?—the whole lot, outside me, you didn't meet a soul back there that wasn't family, etcetera. And so I have these connections and this one gentleman requires any artifacts, literature, materials that have to do with longevity, fountain of youth and his self-image is obviously that he is exacting and scientific in his acquisitive procedures, mostly limiting his purchases to obscure offprints and old bones, I thought I'd test the waters with something Carlos had shall we say confiscated from the Cristóbal village—it was a figurehead, the kind of carved statue, busty gals, they'd put on the bow at the stemhead, and it was truly old could really pass for sixteenth-century without anybody getting fucked up or embarrassed and so I offered it by prospectus to this Berkeley, saying it had provenance that goes back to Cuba and Tampa Bay before where it had been owned by descendants of Carib Indians who'd stripped it off one of Ponce de León's ships in Florida . . ."

"And he bought it?" Lupi smiled despite himself, with a gesture that brought his hands forward, fingers drawn together at their tips, mildly flexed.

Krieger rubbed his eyes. "Huh?"

"This guy, he bought it?"

He looked down at his lap, up at the rattling roof of the bus, and finally at Lupi—a casual sequence meant to impart not disdain but ennui. "That's not all and he's not all. It's blossomed better than a hothouse orchid. Sure he bought it and I'll tell you he paid for it, too, just like he is going to pay for this one, the real goods, he wants an old man? okay okay, you got it. Now, the oldest authenticated man alive is this nip Strigechiyo Izumi but he's only a hundred and nineteen, and they talk about ones down in South America, you know a hundred forty a hundred fifty, no more than that, so I start thinking start thinking uhm, that malarky that Sardavaal was going on about and . . ."—Krieger thwacks Lupi's nearer thigh, all energy once more, and winks—"yeah! right! fine, okay: Gentlemen? start your engines!"

Tegucigalpa's lights and Krieger's voice were left below at the end of the day in the valley bowl as the airplane climbed sharply, precipitously, up in the drafty air, wings flapping birdlike but stiffly to Mexico City, where while they waited for their connection he stared at the photographs of the armillary sphere, then boarded a jet. When the airplane landed in Houston, it was the middle of the night. Lupi peered out the window at this country he knew only from photographs, television, newspapers, dubbed westerns with cowboys in chaps, spurred boots, leather vests, and sometimes black ten-gallon hats—these stuck up bank tellers and made demands of barmaids in Sicilian accents. But he couldn't see much, and the terminal (good word for it, he thought)—with its Muzak, its stale fuel smells, its pastel modular furniture and art panels, its taverns sunk in black niches and filled with damp smoke, and above all its faces, the faces and faces and faces canceled by harsh forms—had been just like any old terminal.

He sat down, twiddled his thumbs, closed his eyes. A brief rest. Bring something up to see.

Framed in the soft square what were those? smokestacks? the rim of a tide pool littered with molted claws of crabs? shorebirds slathered in spilled oil? No, he saw that they were hors d'oeuvres. Cut away to a colloquy between beefy faces obscured by Stetsons and double old-fashioned glasses of scotch. It wasn't long before he recognized the faces, for the show had been syndicated in Italy. Signor Bobbi restopped the cut-crystal decanter and handed with a look of oily empathy spread in his face the glass to sad signora Elli—beneath Signora's brow welled tears and as she contemplated this glass her eyes dissolved to clams on the half shell. He knew the episode. He was bored by Elli's troubles with her boys and husband lost in the jungles of South America and he was tired of her pissing and moaning.

There was a tug at his sleeve. Lupi opened his eyes. Poor old man wanted water. Lupi had to show him how a water fountain worked. You turn this metal stick here and the water comes up and you put your head down like this and suck it in.

When the airplane took off from Houston for New York, he peered out the window onto the receding runways and houses and streets below, all laundered by the vivid moon. Although he had flown before, any number of times, never had the earth seemed so far away, as the jet banked.

He was looking straight down at the ground. It was all pattern and points of star-white in the blanket of black. The snaking highways strung with headlamps; suburbs laid out in crisscross, their windows burning, their trees blots. The jet righted itself and the wing swung up again to block the view. He listened to the whistling, propulsive roar as he was carried toward an address written out in a childish script on a folded and refolded slip of paper in his pocket. The pill kept the *viejo* quiet.

6.

HANNAH came back in through the side door, switched off the set, didn't say anything. There was a rustling of paper and the front door opened onto fine drizzle. Only then did Lupi see her clearly.

Slight and strong as any cowgirl Lupi had ever seen in films, she walked out onto the roof. Even under the overcast her profile became visible for the short time it took her to turn and kick a rubber stop under the metal door. Her hair caught and gathered and reflected back shades from auburn to copper to brown and even to a dark coral color; it was dry now, and she had brushed its waves so that it fanned heavily around her shoulders, and came forward in bangs that curled over a broad forehead to rest along her thin eyebrows. Her lips were determined, cinnamon, the lower lip full, the upper a fine trace. What he noticed more than anything were her hands, as she reached to right the doorstop: long, elegant, spontaneous, grease-stained, swollen delicately at the knuckles—they were the hands of a laborer, an artist, a farmer, someone who knew how a cow was covered, a horse shoed, a stable mucked out.

In her wake, obliquely, a wisp of dawn penetrated the room, which Lupi could see was cavernous. A tint, the color of water strained through a used teabag, made its way into the interior. Ash, soot, bits of paper, leaves, plastic sandwich bags, other anonymous fragments of the city hesitated where Hannah had walked out across the tarred rooftop. These fragments Lupi watched as they floated clockwise, twirled, banked, collided, slith-ered; they raced out in her wake. Their movements were contradictory, even contentious. It was as if—having risen seven stories from the street only to be forced by their own weight to be carried back down, to be transformed again beneath a shoe or a tire—they could be consciously intrigued by the room's contents but chose not to be locked inside.

The bunkhouse (as Lupi would later learn this structure was called) stood at the southwestern corner of the roof. A rectangular construction measuring roughly thirty feet across its front on a north-south orientation, and perhaps a hundred and fifty feet long, east to west. Its door faced directly into the morning sun not quite two stories above the roof of the building, and its own flat roof was tarred and covered in gravel. During rainy springs, the drainage being feeble, pools of stagnant water would collect on this roof and serve as spawning grounds for the larvae of mosquitoes. Hannah never considered having this repaired, or altered. She liked the faint rotten scent of algae. Hardy mosquitoes, which carved lazy arcs around the floodlamps over the door in the summer night, she fancied, too. Hammond, Henry, Madeleine, the other three who lived with her here, all complained. But Hannah would slap away mosquitoes and sip at gin and revel—"Why in the hell not?"

Fashioned of corrugated tin and painted battleship gray, the Sixth Ave-nue gable, which faced Chelsea and the Hudson, Jersey City and Hoboken, had an enormous index finger painted on its surface, pointing skyward. The rest of the hand must once have covered upper stories of the warehouse building but was long since covered over by another sign advertising a car rental agency. No one had bothered to eradicate the finger. None of the oldest of the twine-and-paper men, the wholesale florists, the countermen who had worked in the district all their lives knew the index finger's origin. The nail was sharp with once-red polish, long, and hinted of having served a religious purpose as the finger, topped by an oval flame, pointed skyward.

The roof of the building was piggybacked by three other structures: a wooden water tank, an elevator house and a flight of architectural fancy they called the silo. This superstructure was built as a massive belltower. It had never been fitted out with bells but a tall, narrow, wooden cistern was housed within its walls. Its neo-Gothic body was decorated with oversized male heads which had curly (lumpy) beards, bulgy noses and recessed eyes. The effect (especially when viewed from the roof: telling from proportions meant to be viewed from a distance) was that they resembled comical Neptunes. Four of them, fabricated from the same mold, dressed the corners of the tower. A crumbling concrete stairway inside, trafficked by large and gentle rats, led to the highest point on the building where, from the archivolted clerestory over a tousled concrete coif, it was possible to see, on a sunny smogless day, the Statue of Liberty with Staten Island beyond.

Hannah crossed the flat expanse. At her back, the West Side Highway hummed where the rotten docks were abandoned to collapse erratic into the tidal river and an ocean liner moaned. Tankers, tugs, garbage and gravel barges, plied fore and aft its funnels. How was it possible, she wondered, that she had never been on a ship before?

She reached an oil drum which she used from time to time as an incinerator. She tucked the cassette bundled in newspaper under her arm, pulled a book of matches from her vest pocket, struck a match, touched the tiny flame to one ruckled-up edge of the newsprint. Once the bundle caught fire, she tossed it into the drum and watched the flames go from yellow and blue to green and red as they crackled, chawed through to the plastic. With a broom handle she flipped over the small burning mass, to feed the bottom fresh air; soon it was converted into a bubble of char. She looked out across the rooftops of the city and a shiver passed down through her.

Lights came on, dozens of them, to shine in this room so cluttered with paraphernalia that it took Lupi a few moments to pick Hannah out of the mosaic, a vision like the jigsaw puzzle of an alchemist's lab flung in a thousand bits, curved and irregular, overhead.

"How long has it been since the old man ate?" Hannah asked.

Lupi gaped. Objects of all varieties dangled from the ceiling, hung on the walls, stood in vast cabinets along the edges of the multistoried room. "I asked. He says he's not hungry."

"What is that you're talking to him in?"

"Latin."

"I used to know some passages, this one book, Lucretius, you know Lucretius."

"Personally."

"So did I."

"Personally?"

"Yes, I met him once, he visited me in Nebraska."

"I see," Lupi gave up.

At either side of the door, which Hannah closed, stood an antique cigar-store figure—carved in wood, brightly, grotesquely painted. One was a fat bald Harlequin, unmasked, with a green chin shaped like a zucchini slanting upward nearly to meet its nose; it wore a crooked smile, all tooth and angle. Its checkered blouse, pink and chartreuse, ballooned out about its belly, which was girdled by a silver cummerbund; its chubby legs were covered in white tights and blue bootees. Its hand was extended forward to offer a clutch of cigars. The other was an Indian chief with headdress of painted feathers white and with red tips, this hand stiffly saluting (or shading the savage eyes), in that hand a faggot of tobacco leaves. American gods, Lupi mused, like tritons or nereids standing vigil over fountains in Europe, like the sculptures of Apollo, Hercules, or successful commanders of troops that stood atop plinths in public squares.

Hannah made her way to the stove, lit a gas burner, selected a large copper skillet from the trammel overhead and with a clank popped the skillet on the grate. She spatulaed butter into it.

A griddle was taken down from a swinging crane that was hung with half a dozen griddles of various shapes and sizes. It, too, was slammed on the grate with a clang. She sprinkled a generous bed of salt in the pan. From the handles of both the skillet and griddle dangled tags with numbers. Iron, glass, wood, lead, stone, tinware; a sleigh, bicycles, stereoscopes, a loom, washtubs, hurdy-gurdies and zithers, a forest of calipers under glass, a collection of lamps (whale-oil, betty, wick-type, kerosene, a phoebe, crusie, electric), harvesting tools (hay knives, sickles, reaping hooks, rakes, hucking pegs, scythes), a battery of beat-up weathervanes.

"What is all this?" head thrown back, eye running the length of a metal purlin resting on a series of cross girders which supported the rafters. Hung from this purlin was what Lupi recognized, from all the numerable and fondly remembered westerns he had seen at the cinema in Florence, as a stagecoach: complete with oxhide thoroughbraces and iron stanchions, with metal-shoed wheels and ragged curtains at its windows and a bright red underbelly like that of a purple finch with "Abbott & Downing Co." painted on its sides.

Hannah glanced over at him, saw what it was he was peering at, and said, "Concord wagon, about 1840, 1850."

"But it looks, well I mean, looks real."

"It's original down to the driver's whip and the upholstery in the cab."

"What it's doing on your ceiling?"

Hannah looked up. "Where else am I supposed to put it?"

"But all this, is it some kind of museum."

Hannah whisked the eggs she had broken into a bowl. "It's my own, it's like my own crazy cross to bear."

Lupi hoisted off a rack a cylindrical object fitted out with a long thin nozzle and a plunger at the opposite end, and studied it. In its beaten-copper casement he could see a distorted image of himself. "What's this one?"

"Sausage stuffer."

"Sausage stuffer?"

Lupi sniffed at the object; an odor of antiquity emanated from it, the combination of metal mustiness and a stagnancy like hardened rubber baking under a noon sun. There was a small label, time-browned on the rack, with an inventory number written out in ink, matching the number on the label affixed to the sausage stuffer. The neatly drawn number was five digits long.

"What do you use it for?" he asked, slapping it in the palm of his hand.

"A sausage stuffer?" Hannah laughed. "Nothing, I mean, what would I use a sausage stuffer for?" The steak on the griddle began to spit and sizzle. "Mama Opal said you get the entrails, the organs out of the cow and all the sweetmeats, you grind those up and in they go and you squeeze all that down into a length of intestine, tie the ends. See that dent there? Uncle LeRoy caught a bull snake once, happened to be stuffing sausage, heard a commotion, sneaked into the chicken coop and this snake was half full of pullet eggs, hit him on the head with it. I never ate any sausage after that. I think he ground that snake up right in with the rest of the innards."

Lupi set the instrument down, swiftly, rubbed his hands on his shirt.

* * *

Her collection must have run into the tens of thousands of items. He looked at her where she stood at the stove, prodding the frying steak with a two-pronged fork (inventoried, no doubt), and wondered how Hannah could have the remotest connection with the fat man, with Bautista, Carlos, with Bernhardt—that man who first summoned him to Zurich, to the suite of cramped rooms in the Hôtel Eden au Lac, a grand pile that faced out over the smoky, drab water of the Zürichsee. Bernhardt, who later met with him in a café in Milan (noisy, bustling, the constant hiss of the big espresso machine, the clatter of coffee cups)—who had a job to offer Lupi and pressed into Lupi's hands a retainer. Three thousand Swiss francs he was handed in mint-fresh bills; just like that.

"*Questo è soltanto l'inizio, amico. Noi abbiamo tanto da fare con te,*" Bernhardt said. This is just the beginning.

The line was stale enough, but it was rendered somehow original by Bernhardt, made odd by the sight of this compact businessman who sat back in the overstuffed chair, his head shorn, his black shoes highly polished, his blue jeans new.

And from the first stroll beside the Zürichsee, mist rising off the water lapping at the pebble beach, coots, mallards, brown-and-white swans coasting the oil-blued marina, Lupi had found all that Bernhardt proposed to be like this: tinged with an affectation which made no sense to him. Somehow, it had been easier in the past for Lupi to accept work from those whose politics he knew—even when he sensed in them some manner of absurd idealism or ruthlessness or even backward thinking, in sum, when he saw aspects of his own youthful idealism—long abandoned—than it was for him to agree to travel that far away on Bernhardt's say-so.

America loomed ahead, however. Lupi's opinion of it remained low even after his days of political radicalism had faded away into mercenary opportunism (it was depressing to think of these things). This was one of the few sentiments which lingered on, a vestige of late adolescence. Another, quite the opposite, was his feeling for Nini—Nini, who stood for so much more than she should have, he knew, who marked the moment of his choice. But as he didn't know where Nini was, and did know, by globes and maps, where America was, the chance Bernhardt offered to witness it finally, the monster itself, firsthand, was too tempting to pass up.

He walked back alone toward the hotel, past the Henry Moore that shimmered insipid under the sallow Zurich skies, past the stands of neatly planted plane trees and manicured flower beds and tailored lawns. Thumb and forefinger rubbed, back and forth, the fold of francs there in his trouser pocket. The thought of marching straight past the Hôtel Eden au Lac— whose classical facade befitted the pomp and glory of another epoch— to the square several blocks farther down the lakeside promenade attracted his interest. He could catch a tram, he thought, a tram to the train station. He might disappear into its bustling crowd and buy a ticket for the first train north, up past the German frontier, money in hand.

Bernhardt, after all, had gone off to another appointment. They had agreed to meet three days hence in Milan. It had not been trust Bernhardt had shown in Lupi by fronting him this money and Lupi did not make the mistake of presuming it was. Rather, the money was all enticement, a hook. Bernhardt had known, as had Lupi, the tacit agreement between them was sealed by Lupi's acceptance of the Swiss francs. And he had indicated more of the same would be put into Lupi's hands in Italy with a balance representing four times the sum of these retainers to be paid upon completion of his "travels."

How the money warmed in his pocket, burned a little after its own degrading fashion. It wasn't, in truth, very much money given the nature of the job Bernhardt proposed; these jobs always take three times as long as they are supposed to, and Lupi was doubtful that only five days would pass between the time he left Rome and returned. Were it so, it would mean a thousand dollars a day. Not bad by any measure. Underground bureaucracies were no less gummed up than governmental or any other system of business controlled by hierarchies of subordinates, middlemen, chiefs— and experience told him that this is not the way things would ultimately work out. He took the money, anyway.

Furtively, Lupi glanced over his shoulder. A nanny with striking blond hair pushed a pram; she was daydreaming. Two children, behind her, ran into a clump of pine trees that edged the lake. They were about to throw bread, or stones, at the waterfowl. He saw no one else. He had quickened his pace until soon he came alongside the Eden au Lac. It was like déjà vu, the self-disgust; a familiar scape across which lay only old choices. One reasonable demon was heard to complain there were *no* choices, that he could only proceed, and at that, only by the shortest travelable route. Thus it was not so surprising to him as it was disheartening when he found his legs had carried him up the steps and into the foyer. He stood at the desk and requested the key to his room. In the oak-paneled lift up from the grand lobby he felt claustrophobic and queasy. In his room he lay on his bed and drank splits of brandy, champagne, gin, until his frustration twisted free of him and floated up like a swirling mass of detritus snatched off the comforter into a column of wind. If he could have wept, he would have. He even tried. It didn't work.

Sometime in the middle of the night he managed to stumble into the bright and elegant bathroom. He showered for half an hour, until the skin on his fingers and face puckered, but even so he didn't feel washed. Some weight hung quite palpable in his chest. He felt polluted. When he groped his way back to the bed he was surprised at what lay on the pillow. Bit of a bill, a Swiss thousand-franc note. He had eaten half of it.

Shortly after, the fat man directed Krieger to return to Danlí and place a telephone call to Bernhardt. Whomever he had discovered must be brought in immediately.

"Herr Lupi," began Bernhardt in his hesitating Italian, "I am proud to announce that the time has come to assist us in our project."

Mozart, Berlioz, Wagner: there wasn't a symphony wry enough to serve as background for the ambivalence Lupi's movie was shocked into sponging up: what was this? Bernhardt behaved as if this were some prestigious honor he'd just bestowed.

7.

THE telephone ringing loudly, mercilessly. Without its tape the answering machine had been rendered useless. For thirty, one, two, three, four, thirty-five rings Hannah stood looking down at the instrument not so much dumbfounded as defiant since she sensed who her caller would most likely be. There was a spare tape around somewhere, and she made a mental note to find it and prepare a new message, one that would make a caller think twice before leaving a date, time, and number.

She picked up the handset and gently, swiftly, set it back down in its cradle. The ringing stopped—but only long enough for the party at the other end to redial. Hannah allowed it to jangle along for fifty more rings before she lifted it and put it to her ear.

"I mean do you know what it costs to make, just to make the damn connection from down here, I mean really, Hannah, really wasteful, not to mention the bad manners of it, that first connection? you know how

long it took me to get a line through? two and a half hours's how long.
And that was using contacts through his highness the ambassador down
here, and what do you do? hang up. You know what you do? you worry me,
you make me nervous. You know what I am up to . . . nights . . . at
this stage? Hundred and fifty milligrams Restoril and for what, eke out
two, maybe three hours' sleep. This is not the way I conduct my life,
not the way I behave. We have a project here, a program, an important,
and of course I recognize that your participation is, that you're compul-
sorily—"

"What was the point of that this morning?" she interrupted. "No, wait,
it's so obvious, you're a lot less subtle than I remember you to be. What is
that, Peter, desperation?"

"Was what. What was what? Haven't been listening to a word I've been
saying—"

"That, on my machine, me, the accident."

"As you suggest just a passing reminder, nothing so desperate about it
and of course it was not meant in fact to be terribly subtle but I'm not
calling for, you're wasting my precious time."

"Krieger, what do you want?"

The briefest pause preceded his response, delivered in a mockish tone as
if he were addressing a third person, someone judicious and attentive, who
would be seen to nod slowly, affirmatively, understanding Krieger's reason-
able point of view (if he/she existed: he/she did not).

"Do you believe this stuff?" he began. "Do you believe what I'm
hearing here, as if this young lady has any pretext, any leverage, any
position of power at all to wield in the context?"

The line crackled, and Krieger felt he had reestablished to his own
satisfaction his prevailing authority in the conversation. It was not meant to
be a dialogue in the first place, but a monologue, punctuated by simple yes
or no responses to questions posed.

"There then, our friend arrived safely?"

"Tell me what he's doing here."

"There we go, that's the spirit, I must say that against all odds, and not to
think for a moment my colleague didn't entertain some serious second
thoughts about you, Hannah-pie, and his is a mind shrewder than which
I've never met, not in, you count the years, who has the time? and there
were moments in the earliest stages of the project, times when your name
was merely one of many."

Aware Krieger's hesitation was meant to prompt either protest or inquiry or some indication of ire, Hannah refused to capitulate. She repeated, "I want to know what these people are doing here."

"And as this person was ruled out for this reason that person for that, there were times my colleague's opinion of you, your not your shall we say situation which was, is, self-evidently perfect from our perspective, not your situation as much as you yourself didn't strike him how can I say it? equal to the task, but you know how macho some of these s-p-i-x can be."

Hannah hung up the telephone. She considered taking it off the hook. Half an hour elapsed before it rang again; she picked up before the first ring had ended.

He was calm. "You illustrate my point, that is I kept arguing your case with my colleague, this is not a suicidal person, this is not a person with much room to maneuver, either, to call a spade a spade, this is a person who loves her home such as it is—and do not think for one split second, one millisecond that we had not found a host of candidates for the job, people whose circumstances weren't far more incredible than yours, don't bother to flatter yourself for a moment on that count."

"Krieger, I'm going to put them out on the street."

"Hey, do you remember my shepherd's pie, Hannah? I've been wracking my head trying to think what it was besides the haggis you liked so much. Shepherd's pie, I just remembered, that's what it was. Sometimes I threw a bit of the haggis in with it give the base some character, you know"—he awaited a response, a flicker of hope, but none came—"the hardest part— did I ever tell you this bit?—the hardest part about making shepherd's pie is getting up at six in the morning to kill the shepherd," and he laughed rather too heartily before shifting to a descending scale, singsong: "No, no, no, this is not a suicidal person, neither is it a person who can go anywhere, not really, not in fact. That is what I kept counseling my colleague. Here is someone respectable in her own right, bright, attractive, an absolute perfection. Christ on a crutch, I would interject, here is someone who would be even, even sympathetic to the idea. My opinion, it is not that my opinion prevailed, rather it came to be seen as the, as they say the least of all possible evils. This quirkiness of yours is a mixed blessing."

Hannah felt at the back of her throat a tightening and her eyes were warm. She would not allow herself to cry. The most curious phrase came to mind, like an antidote somehow, and she said it as if she were reading it off a script. "Krieger, you bore the living shit out of me, why don't you just leave me alone."

Krieger said, "Incomparable girl, what are you trying to do, make me fall in love with you all over again? that's just choice, and coming from those delicate lips you ought to be ashamed, Hannah, but, living shit? it's choice, my grandfather Werner, I told you about him ever?"

"You don't have a grandfather Werner."

"No? well, he collected these things in translation, let's see in German what is there to match it? *lebende Scheisse*, no, *zu Scheisse gelangweilig?* just, just nothing comparable. Okay point well taken, and so tell me as I gather Mr. Lupi arrived safely?"

"Yes."

"And his sidekick, the older gentleman, he arrived with him."

"Yes."

"See how simple? So, Mr. Lupi and friend are honored guests. As I said they won't be with you very long. Your employee's wife, Henry's, she'll of course have to be brought into this matter as an ignorant cohort, she will assist Lupi in any way possible to deliver our brochure which he has on his person, and the chieftain himself to her father. This, Hannah, is so easy a thing to do. A request upon which the future of your silly sand castle rests, unstable a thing as it is, unstable—Hannah, you follow? I'm enthusiastic by nature but not one who resorts to threat. It's in my blood, enthusiasm, it's red and it's warm my passion, commitment to this. Were there another way to do it, but there isn't. Has Lupi said anything, that is—"

"Peter, your flaw is you overestimate, you underestimate. Lupi's been coy, hilariously coy, laughingly coy. You've chosen well, you and your friend. Listen, Krieger, while you gloat?"

"Listening."

"I'm doing this, I've never had a bit of real assurance that when it's done with, this, this your project, that I'll be left alone after, because I want you out of my life, understood, out."

Krieger was strangely sincere. "After, you are as free, that's shackled, hear shackled, Hannah . . . free as before. You don't seem to understand this is a project that is well, it's not your standard capitalist transaction, supply-demand, listen, you ever think about me? I already asked, but— Hannah you should have stuck with me, I am a Clark, a Lewis; I want West, want West, not its product. Not gold, West, man. Let these others develop, take their pans to the ore. I own West, I sell, I disappear get into something new like turn into a ghost and live under somebody's fingernail."

This time he hung up.

Hannah listened for a while to the dial tone.

* * *

Lupi had never seen such an enormous man before. He did not let his astonishment betray him. He appreciated he was becoming acclimated to surprise. He was reminded (by noetic twist) of that Christmas evening so long ago, poor old Milo, charlatan, minor-league politico who made it up into the ranks of an ambassadorial sinecure nevertheless poor old Milo, for no one need die in as miserable, claustrophobic, degrading a way as he had died. Perhaps it was the simple innocence which this big man emanated, the nice slow eyes, the smile? Milo was innocent after his own fashion, Lupi thought now, as is Olid, and here another, whose weight alone was warmly held in the sway of his arms as he walked, the ease of his sloping shoulders seemed to convey gentleness, thus innocence. Since when was innocence a point in favor? since lately?

This too was perhaps a pivot point for Lupi. Such a repository of evidence against social struggle he'd become, and at this his face was so covered with dejection Henry came directly up to him to state resonantly, "This one here got the weight of the world on him," turning a broad countenance to Hannah.

She said, "Henry, Madeleine, this is Mr. Matteo Lupi."

Maddie appeared from behind the back of her husband. Her face was like Nini's after they'd gone skiing in Limone that once, darkened under the sun burning down on the treeless alpine slope. Lupi remembered how he had broken his finger, by stepping on it with a ski. All that whiteness, the ice, and looking down to see the finger bent hideously backwards. He couldn't remember which finger it was now—index? ring? But he recalled with ease the precise rosy shade of his girl's cheeks, a shade he hadn't seen again until Maddie. All so awkward, though in the icy air not notably painful, popping the finger back into its normal line, edging himself obliquely, plowing sideways, down the mountain—all the while the finger swelling, going blue—with Nini's encouragement (she had a laugh, or two, didn't she? having decided it wasn't that serious).

Maddie, at whom Lupi managed in the midst of his remembrance a fuller smile than circumstances warranted, or allowed, remarked, "All we need now's the fan."

"Fan?" Lupi'd given up Nini beside the great turning wheels at the bottom of the trail, there at the lift. He'd missed a couple of exchanges.

"This might not be as bad as we'd thought, Maddie," Hannah said.

"Your Krieger's tied up in it, isn't he?"

"Maddie," Henry muttered, low.

"—so it's bound to be as bad as we'd thought."

She never spoke to Hannah like that; even Lupi could construct this much for himself.

"What was that about the fan?" Couldn't they discuss something else? Hannah tried not to laugh, but she failed. Lupi'd remembered that, then, too. His mother used to say it in English—the fan was what the shit hit.

She halved muffins with the tines of a fork, and crouched down to place them on the foil bed in the broiler. Lupi gazed up. The wall behind the stove was covered with brightly patterned rectangles, license plates, some rusty, some bent, some immaculate. Lupi stared at it; he was reminded of something, of—

"All fifty states," Hannah said, standing again. "A fair sampling of the different years, too. Nebraska and Oklahoma complete."

—reminded of Houston, its rectangular geometry. He was about to draw the comparison for Hannah but when he looked down from the decorative wall he found her staring at him, stiff-necked, unyielding, expression as unreadable as the symbols on the plates behind. Startled, Lupi stepped back.

"You're not what I thought you'd be."

A fire truck quarreled with the summary silence.

"What did you think I'd be?" Lupi asked, attendant to the prospect of catching a glimpse into the mechanisms of his dilemma.

"It doesn't matter."

Hannah sat at the long table and watched Lupi eat. Except for this end where he ate, the entire surface of the table was heaped with objects. Lupi would later learn they were principally her fishing and trapping collection: pronged spears, eel trap, mouse traps, traps for moles and bears, possums, martens, beaver, brown bottles of musk scents, and a host of fishing nets and shuttles to mend them with.

Lupi finished breakfast. He had never eaten steak for breakfast before, but addressed it with the same vim shown by the "dad" on the television set promoting steak sauce, half pretending he was in one of his westerns, one filmed indoors, say, painted sets and unshaven skinny actors, make it in Fargo, no Albuquerque, no Cimmaron City. This was what Americans did. It was tradition. He ate his steak, talking, glancing around at the eccentrically appointed room. It was morning, he told himself, this was breakfast.

"But, what I was saying before," Hannah resumed. "I was told you were coming. They told me to expect you." Her voice had grown faint, as if she were lowering it in order to overhear another conversation taking place between two other people. "Can I ask you a question? Do you know what you're doing here, that is, what they, or you, intend to do with that man?"

"Why?"

"Why . . . I think that's obvious. I don't want to get involved in something that's—it's just and this whole thing is beginning to feel over my head."

"Can you tell me something?"

"Well?"

"Can you tell me how you know Mr. Krieger? I might be able to answer your question."

"Krieger . . . well, long story."

"Have you ever heard of a Miguel Sardavaal?"

Hannah shook her head, yet Lupi seemed to have changed from sleuth-like (no longer the naïf) to resigned: it was the same kind face her father Nicholas pulled for days after he returned home from one of his fugues: somewhere between meek and deferential.

"You aren't in this, are you," he said, as if disappointed.

"What's that mean?"

"I mean you're not being paid."

"God, of course not."

"Well why are you putting up with—?"

"You mean Krieger didn't tell you?"

"Tell me what?"

"Did you meet someone named Jonathan?"

"What does he look like?"

"I don't know, I never met him, it's just that Krieger and I knew each other once and years later—it's like he's an inevitability, but of course you already know that because you know him—anyhow I thought I finally had lost touch with him but I came into this inheritance and it seemed like the next day and there he was again, doing me a favor, always doing me favors—"

"What favor?"

"He knew what I would do with the money, I told him once what I would do if I ever had any money, so he knew, and he already had found these people who could help me."

"Why didn't you just say no?"

"What good would it have done, look you're here aren't you, you think that's the result of me saying yes? They showed up here and they had nowhere else to go. What's more they're good people, Maddie and Henry, good people."

"But what were you saying about someone named Jonathan?"

"Jonathan's the one who led Krieger to Maddie, you see? Krieger knew Jonathan down there in Central America and got to his father who's so crazy his own daughter won't even talk about him and there was some . . . never mind, for godsakes it doesn't really matter, it's all just loops and loops, and in any case I can see how you're in it—it's not even that Krieger believes I owe him anything. He just likes things to be this way, knots and tangles, makes him feel safe, I suppose."

"Safe from what?"

"Himself, obviously, who else but."

Lupi took in a little city air through his mouth. Tasted of sulfur. "But what was it you meant you thought he would have told me?"

"Everybody has their favorite secret, their other life, don't they?"

"No."

"Come on, of course they do. What's yours?"

"Why should I say. Look, I've got things I'd better get to."

"You don't have anything you'd better get to. You're stuck. Now what's yours?"

"I don't have any," though when she pursued it Lupi felt the pressure build toward the projector's click, then subside.

Things begin to happen. They feel like movie, but aren't. Hannah comes out from the back of the loft. She has put on rubber boots and an oversize hand-knit sweater. She has brought with her another pair of boots. "Come on," she says to Lupi. "I want to show you why you're here and not somewhere else."

He considers refusing, figuring that at least some form of resistance to this flow might be worthwhile, or dignified, but settles for a brusque "What," knowing that it somehow impugns his authority (but what authority?—there is that delicate matter, too).

What to lose, nothing. He unlaces his shoes and steps into one of the heavy rubber boots Hannah has given him. It's too large.

"Here, hold on," Hannah says, goes to the back and returns with a pair of socks. "Put these on so you won't get blisters."

"Look, maybe I don't want to see anything."

"You'll like this."

Lupi pulls the boot off, slips wool socks over his own, pushes his feet into the boots.

The air was damp, cool, inert. The rain had for the moment stopped falling. Pools of fresh water had collected like mirrors in the various depressions across the flat roof. A fog settled over the city, dampening it. Lupi looked to his right, out across the street to the rooftops of other buildings, but the fog was dense, so what he could see was muted and obscure.

"This way," Hannah indicated.

Lupi trailed behind her. Together they circled around the north end of the bunker, walking toward the silo tower. The Neptunes stared blankly into the gathering mist above as they entered a door at the tower's base and, rather than climbing the staircase that led up to the large stone busts, turned right. Hannah pulled a set of keys from her pocket and unlocked a door and started down a set of concrete steps. That cock crew again, the one Lupi'd heard before.

Air that rushed up to them was warm and rich. At once Lupi was able to recognize that smell; it was as distinctive and familiar to him as anything from his childhood. It was the dark, raw, earthen odor of the farmers' meadows and feedlots, like those he visited beyond Fiesole, on the Pian di Mugnone or along the trickling Ménsola. The sweet, sharp scent of urine and manure and of alfalfa and hay. Lupi's hand traced the rail as they went down another flight to the landing. The smell was much stronger. Hannah paused, started to say something to Lupi, a word, a warning, but nothing came to her, and she opened the door and walked through.

A pasture. A hound dog, barking gaily, bounding across the artificial plateau toward them. The tin ceiling painted sky blue; and indicated here and there, a puffy white cloud, the kind of towering anvil-shaped cumulus that can throw half a county under shadow on the high plains. Several skylights in the huge loft like holes cut into the *trompe l'oeil* sky to reveal the grayness of the universe beyond. A red truck. An old berlin covered in silkies and Rhode Island reds, clucking. Half a dozen cattle, living cattle, cropping at scattered hay in a corral. One licks at barrel salt in a tub, flicks its ears. Windowless. Along the walls more painted scenes of the high prairie stretching away to an uncluttered horizon out at the earth's edge. The landscape gold with wheat and with neat fields of corn, barley, rye and other grasses. Timothy, orchard grass, smooth bromegrass. The realistic rendering of a white farmhouse, a clutch of outbuildings, a windmill standing on its frail legs, a barn and red silo centered in an oasis of oak trees far off.

The cattle are disturbed from their grazing. A half-moo; quiet. Their docile heads now individually lift away from the scattered bundles of hay and, while some continue to masticate, others blink, eyes like dark grapes at the centers of porcelain settings, each assumes a sidelong stare at Lupi and Hannah. Tardy black-and-white eyes each with long, girlishly curly lashes moistly take in these two intruders. A baleful lowing drifts from one dizzily into the air. A warm munching fractures the stillness. Sprigs of mullein foxglove, woolly and wan yellow, are fastened by brads to pillars and corral posts near the animals. These are meant to provide magical protection for the cattle.

Once Hannah speaks, however, having heard that familiar voice, they one by one drop their provident heads and continue to graze.

"So this is America," breathed Lupi.

Hannah dropped her hands into the pockets of her jeans.

"Yes, I guess it is at that."

Lupi's face was frozen and alive as he took in the land and the sky, smelled the air. He smiled. Laughed. "It's just the way I thought it would be!"

Envoi, that came to Lupi late in the first day, that came not as movie, but this time as a bit of dream. That was as if he could see it on the wall behind the bed where he sat, again, nursing the old man with the bad medicines. That seemed as if it had happened. Maybe he was merely hoping it had; though he couldn't see why. He wasn't mean enough to command such grief.

A boy off the road, his life in the balance. In a superficial way it is already unclear whether he is alive or dead. For while he is standing against the narrow trunk of the orange tree, a smile absurd and vacuous slit across his face, eyes closed, his chest is not seen to heave, although a prismatic crown of sweat stands in an oval around his forehead. He is fourteen or fifteen years old, shirtless, shoeless, his fatigue pants handed down from some bygone conflict. Five young kids hotly debate his future. His insensate body has been searched by them and no identifying paraphernalia, no tags, no papers, no uniform suggest which side it is he fights for. He must be fighting for either one side or the other, one of the kids has shouted. Not even his teeth, which are neither rotten nor studded with fillings, allow access to his background. He will not speak to them. He'll not tell them which side he is fighting for. It is infuriating. His features bear the high-cheeked nobility of rural boys descended through many generations of Indians.

He is anonymous but must be sentenced. The short, stocky kid slaps him diligently about his shoulders and face with the barrel of his rifle, shouting in a high, sharp, dry voice, "*¡Claro, claro hombre!*" The boy, informed by the jolt of the kid's rifle butt which tears heavily across his cheek, collapses on the ground.

The earth is like iron. He rolls on his belly. He makes no struggle. He makes no further movement. Only the breath passes in and out of his mouth, which is awfully cracked.

He must, they argue, be some deserter. It does not matter that his field glasses, his gun, his ammunition are similar to their own, for in the flow, the lascivious, unchecked, rampant, unmitigated flow of matériel into the area, it is not the origin of the weaponry but into whose hands it comes that is important.

Something has gone wrong, something premature, and the innate sense of ritual, a procedural dictate that insinuates into the blood from deep in the brain stem, from a part of consciousness that reaches far back into pre-cultural, preliterate mind, is offended: the boy is dead. This makes it less attractive to rape him before they mutilate him. Another basic kind of argument is incited by this mischance of timing, and words fly. The most nondescript of the young militiamen steps forward and without warning puts an end to all discussion by firing into the boy's neck.

His pants are removed. Tittering filters down through the forest before he is left naked, high in the pine mountains a few kilometers inside the border. He is abandoned to the shade of the orange tree, which plays over his ribbed back.

The kids descend by a path down the declivity of broken rocks. There will be another chance, perhaps later that same day, to set right the sense of ritual. Meantime, the stocky older kid, a self-styled *jefe*, has taken the pretty dragon ring for himself. He wears it on his thumb—admiring it every few steps, holding it up to the sun, where it glints—taunting the others with this bit of booty he has claimed for himself.

The voices fade.

They are gone.

There is only the sound of the birds. Later, a scorpion makes herself a temporary nest in the dead boy's gaping mouth.

III

Oz

1.

HOW was it that Franz's yawn from all those years ago seemed even now to be saturated in complicity with Krieger? Francis Wrynn's ignominious yawn where the jaw yawed and fell away flamboyant to one side, like a flesh-and-blood document that communicated to Krieger the interview with Hannah was concluded and it remained only that their discussion be brought to an end.

Maybe that wasn't right. Perhaps it wasn't fair—still, there was no forgetting that yawn, its false pearl-pink teeth, its shape at full extension like an inverted pear, overbite like an eave sheltering the narrow, feminine lower mandible. But to Krieger the evening was young. Be here now. There was far too much to talk about for Franz to start yawning. It was the last year of the sixties, Krieger might have protested, and the world would probably not survive long into the decade ahead, the emerald green of nuclear winter laced through the plumage of its rising wings. It didn't matter to Krieger that Franz, who at any rate lied about his age and the face lifts and fanny tucks he'd undergone, admitted to being in the region of fifty-five and, by his own assessment, was lazy, laggard, and not inclined to tag along to nightclubs and bars with his young friends (who did little else). Among these friends Krieger seemed to be his closest and was surely the most willing to accept the money Franz handed out with such liberality in exchange for those little favors he would ask, like running a parcel out to the island or taking a drive up to the lake district. Once in a while, more often than not at Krieger's insistence, Franz did condescend to step up to the low stage, draped in velvet bunting around its scrim and curtained behind with material which sparkled under the stagelights, in the club he himself seemed to own—Krieger had never been able to figure out how these thick, enmeshed nets of ownership worked, as they spun themselves around and about Franz's person—and sing a standard or two with the piano trio. The microphone lay in the palm of his hand. The low highhat splashed some, the pianist finished his intro and nodded over to Franz, who crooned,

> *"Something in the way you*
> *. . .* moo-*ve*
> *Attracts me like no other*
> *. . .* loo-*ver,"*

and the flesh along his Adam's apple twitched. Krieger whistled and applauded with the others when the song was over, but Franz could never quite tell whether his enthusiasm was patronizing—he understood how capable Krieger might be of such ingratitude; still, thought Franz, Peter was a good boy, he was good at heart, and if he happened to have bad taste enough to enjoy these stand-ins with the musicians, then bless him, and so be it. There was nothing evil in bad taste, unless you tried to pass yourself off as a connoisseur. Connoisseurship doesn't wash, Franz had told Krieger, in a free country. This isn't a free country, Krieger retorted. We're going to have to agree to disagree; end of discussion. What discussion? countered Krieger; it was just a bunch of tangents.

For Krieger's part, he had been on the road half the night before. He expedited the business at hand and drove through the day. He had done Franz a little favor, had to call into work sick in order to clear the time—but that was all right, he hated his job at the brokerage anyway, and there was already the prospect of moving on to another (parallel) field that would take him south, out of the country, consultant work in Central America, Belize; change of scene and (he thought) the chance to clean up his act some. Besides, Franz seemed—none of this was stated in so many words, but none of it was lost on Krieger, either—less and less enamored of his side business. He didn't need the money. He didn't want trouble. There was a hint, even before Krieger'd left to do this little-favor run, that it might be one of the last. Franz-the-frog had devoured enough flies and wished only to compose himself comfortably on his lily pad.

But he hadn't heard the half of Krieger's road stories; moreover there was the young lady, as Franz referred to her, with whom they had to concern themselves. One doesn't arrive in Manhattan with only a few hundred dollars, no contacts, and no place to live without eliciting some serious sympathy, does one? Krieger did not think so. Franz sniffed, not disagreeing, lay back again into the couch, and recommenced picking his teeth with the corner of a dollar bill which he had folded into a triangle (a bad habit he had given up trying to break). One doesn't, he said, true enough. What's that have to do with me?

Hannah was twenty-four years old but she looked like a teenaged boy, skinny, short hair the color of brownstone, a downward cast to the eyes. She thanked Franz for the money Krieger had given her for her car, thanked Krieger once more for having picked her up—a hitchhiker broken down short of her destination—and stood, as she thought she was expected to, extending her hand to shake goodbye.

"Nothing of the sort," while Krieger's eyes, uncautious, swept across her sweatshirt, "Franzy here and I are going to help you get set up, aren't we Franz."

"I don't know," Franz replied, unfolding the dampened bill and sliding it back into the parqueted wooden box which sat on the heavy glass of the side table.

"She's driven all the way from Kansas, straight through."

"Not Kansas, Nebraska," Hannah said.

"All the same."

"Where's that?" deadpanned Franz.

Hannah began to explain, but Krieger stopped her—it was just a joke. Bad joke.

"Consider it a favor to me," he insisted, sitting on the arm of a Sheraton chair whose upholstery was crowded with huntsmen, retrievers, bolting geese. The joints of antique walnut sighed; Franz lifted a finger. Krieger got up, straightened his lips until they were set, a line with two dimpled ends which deepened as he went on, "Or to Franz. He could stand to learn a little about the great outdoors, all the man knows is interiors."

"She can stay or go it's up to her, isn't it?"

"Nothing wrong with interiors," she replied as Franz spoke, and watched him as he began to comb the thinning strands of reddish hair with the arms of a porcelain figurine, a ballerina with glass-lace tutu. His scalp was gray, entirely freckled. She thought that he looked like a nice man despite—despite what he looked like.

"Stay or go you don't care? Come on, Franz, you're not showing Hannah here a modicum of that theater-district hospitality you're always telling me about."

"Theater district, what?"

Krieger answered, smiling at Hannah, "You know, a little Jew York, Jew York? little demonstration of matriarchal concern?"

Hannah did get up, and said, "I think I'd better be off, really."

"No please, stay, I don't care," Franz rose forward slightly. "Here, have a cognac."

"I don't drink."

"Of course you drink," Krieger said, pouring her wine from a jug. "This you'll like it's not so sugary, cognac's no good for you, but wine builds the blood, enriches the phagocytes, something on that order—you ever hear about how Satan came to Noah? Noah was planting vines, Satan came, slew a lamb, a lion, a pig, and an ape, and told Noah he said, Noah, these here are the four ways you behave according to the amount of wine you drink, drink a little you act like a lamb, drink a lot you act like a pig, too much you're a goddamn ape which adds of course considerable sympathy to the Darwinian approach but anyway—a little, a lamb. Give it a shot. Sit down."

"You don't have to if you don't want," added Franz.

And if you're a lion? wondered Hannah.

"You'd think we were talking about something very heavy here." Krieger poured for himself, and Wrynn—"Francis?"

"I didn't think that," she said to the window into the neon night darkening over the potted ficus trees and heard the uninterrupted rumble which gave from the streets—such noise, like the air mutilated—and the trains rushing on heavy track below the streets. The city was all vaster, more prodigious than she remembered it to be, which hardly made sense given that she had grown up in the interim. When she was small it seemed small. But now? "Why not, all right," she said, hoping she'd not come across prim.

"Why not?" Franz agreed as he reached into his breast pocket, pulled forth a coin and dropped it into the slot in the back of a shiny silver-plated pig that sat on the floor at his feet.

"Habit of his—if you own the bar you've got to buy your drinks or you end up with nothing but piss for property, right?" Krieger explained as he watched her take a sip, studied her with warm approval. "Not bad wine."

"Mr. Krieger mentioned your restaurant and the possibility of work," she started.

"Hannah, I told you to call me Peter, but look at this face, skin of a toad, I love this man and of course he'll be happy to give you a job, but as I was trying to say it's grunt-work that—"

"Peter?"

"But I do love your face, I'm being serious, I love this man. He's got a special truss, a liver truss—"

"He does?" she said, amiable, trying to like the wine, which she didn't think she did.

"I have no such thing."

"Like a fitted torture girdle from the fifteen-sixteenth century or something, the thing cost a fortune, you can't even tell he's got it on, see? and that's sheer fabric there, what is that shirt, Franz?" (turning to Hannah) "—old silk, I think it'd look better on you, do they have mulberries out in Kansas for the silkworms to spin in, funny-looking things, mulberry trees, twisty and ugly, but what those nasty worms do in them, very beautiful, hey Franz why don't you take that shirt off and give it to Hannah, it'd look so great on her."

"Peter?"

"Never mind, then she'd see the truss."

"Miss? what's your name again?"

"Hannah."

"That's a decent name, solid. Listen to me. When you get older you'll understand you look into the mirror and you say what's that? you say, that's disgusting, that isn't me, or it isn't supposed to be me, it's a horrid flesh-thing."

Hannah nodded. Looked at Krieger.

"But under the truss?—god, Hannah, just frightening—"

"Krieger."

"Francis?"

"So shut up, already."

There had been only peace and quiet when the car broke toward the shoulder of the road. Hannah slapped both palms against the steering wheel, turned off the ignition, and pushed the door open into the evening. The sun was low and brushed in a good hazel light so she could see that the independent front axle had come loose and this was why the car had lurched to such a precipitate stop, its left wheel, freed of the kingpin, having bolted toward the other lane as the right shot out to the shoulder. She gazed up and down the empty rural road in north Jersey and imagined the pleasure her uncle LeRoy—who surely had found the sententious note she had left for him before setting out on her journey back to New York—would have experienced if he were able to see her in this predicament. Off to see the wizard. Those were the last words of his she could remember. There was no wizard, ass-eyes. Of course she never said that, she seldom said anything to him. She just up and left.

She remembered thinking (it was a way to kill time—and she also thought, How deserted can a country road so near the metropolis be? where *is* everybody?): were this a cartoon on the big walnut-cabineted television in the front room of the farmhouse—that was left on all the time after mama Opal went away, the television, day and night, until they played the national anthem and even afterward there was snow on the screen to look at—the roadster would have split down the middle, each half careering forward, veering, zooming, zigzagging, kicking up great plumes of dust until in a cloud of curlicues and blurgits the two collided in a tremendous, orchestral racket, fusing each half back together, maybe, leaving the driver—a wolf or a big rooster with a porkpie hat—in a daze, stick-figure birds going tweet-tweet-tweet on her shoulders. But, later, whenever she thought of this it seemed more something Krieger would have said, and in time she would come to wonder whether the thought hadn't in fact been his.

Still, the car that had come around the curve in the dusk was a welcome sight. She had sat against the fender for not quite a full hour, her hands rubbing her shoulders self-consciously, and tried to crack her knuckles as the wind ruffled down into the deep pines. She waved her arms and the two beams crossed to the shoulder; she was about to meet Peter Krieger.

Such happenstance; then the ride into town across the George Washington Bridge and the extraordinary view down the west side of the island, the windows burning white in all the thousands of buildings which stood above the waterline and trees along the shore, down through the center of the city to a garage, a short walk, the marquees blazing in Times Square, into an anonymous facade and up an elevator to reach the highly decorated and overfurnished rooms of Franz Wrynn, there in his lavender pantsuit trimmed in lemon, and with a matching blouse parted like curtains to reveal a chest featureless except for the delicate St. Christopher medal. Franz, yawning and nodding. Uncle would have looked upon all this and perhaps he would have sighed, feigned disgust or alarm, but withdrawn somehow, withdrawn into some inner room where the noise could not be heard, gone to oil his rifles, or spit-polish the glass eyes in the heads of his trophy collection, the antelope, the wolverine.

Krieger had bought the car "on the spot" for three hundred dollars and paid her in cash. When he learned that Hannah was carrying a .44 Smith & Wesson revolver he'd bought it, too. Hannah was grateful he hadn't asked her what she was doing with it. She had taken it from uncle LeRoy, knowing the while she would probably have no real use for it, although she explained to herself that a woman alone on the road might need to defend herself. This had bothered her through three states. It didn't bother her now.

After, came questions. No, Hannah didn't have a place to stay in New York, she had driven through from Babylon but she was born in New York and raised there at least until she was nine-ten somewhere in there when she and her mother Opal moved out West. No, presumably her father was still living, she'd have no real way of knowing she guessed that that was one of the reasons she was here although now that she got closer, well, and her mother never talked about him much and when she did the story seemed to skip and slide, never quite fitting together. Always slipping around at its own pleasure, or to avoid its own pain. Her father's name was Nicholas and, yes, one of the reasons she had come to New York was to try to find him.

"Nicholas," Krieger said. "Patron saint of children, wolves and pawn-brokers—so, you're a runaway."

"What about let's talk about you for a while?"

"Boring."

"I doubt it."

"Believe me, very boring."

"You grew up in New York?"

"I don't remember."

"Come on."

"I mean it. I don't remember. It was too boring."

Hannah saw that the pines had given way to great flats, and that these were giving way to houses in rows and buildings side by side, up and up. Don't press him, she thought.

The wine was working.

"Yes, it's good wine," Hannah heard herself admit. She kept thinking that she ought to be asking more questions, but things seemed settled, even calm, as Franz yawned again. Krieger translated the yawn and Hannah's compliment, and didn't want the evening to die yet, so moved into an explanation of how Franz adored the movie *I Am Curious* (*Yellow*), how he had seen it seventeen times, although it was only released the month before, and was anxious for the "blue" version to be released—yellow and blue being the two colors in the Swedish flag—yellow being his favorite color after green, green being the color of Emerald City in his other favorite movie, the one Judy was born for, the one she could never again live up to and so began to punch herself (shoot up the smack) almost as self-inflicted punishment (Franz loved Judy and Dorothy, and saw in Lena, the star of this new soft-porn classic, a parallel and a friend), yellow and blue making green to finish out the three—yellow sun, blue sky, green earth.

He was coaxed back to life, as Krieger expected him to be, at the broaching of the topic.

"I followed that beastly obscenity trial blow for blow, there was poor Vilgot forced to defend himself by claiming that Lena didn't actually go down on Börje, I mean really, gosh did her lips actually touch his weenie? excuse me please do excuse me but that poor Vilgot had to say no at the trial, no ladies and gentlemen her lips were a couple of millimeters away from . . . me, it, my thing. But honey, I know. I saw it with my own two peepers. She blows him like a horn, believe you me."

"Like Gabriel?" Krieger smirked.

"I think he's had too much to drink," Hannah suggested.

"Franz here, he's a little direct, a little crass, you'll bear with him I hope, plus not much of a drinker it's true," Krieger whispered to Hannah, then said aloud, "Yes lord, Peter Lindgren, Börje Ahlstedt, Magnus Nilsson, Franz loves them all."

"I see," Hannah assented, wondering if this meant—in its own way— she had the job at the restaurant (they were being awfully open, friendly, whatever, weren't they?).

"Man alive does he get licked. I met one of those darling sound assistants when the trial was on last year, Tage Sjöborg, real sweetie pie," Franz continued, fingers flouncing at the starchy Byron collar.

"Franzy's made a special study of Swedish and during the war protest scenes . . ."

"Krieger here? didn't know a thing. I had to explain everything to him, *Vägra Militär Vämplikt!* you know what that means?"

"No," Hannah said. The room had begun to whirl, its details coming more pointed at her while the whole, what the details made up, became blunted. So this is why they called it tipsy, it wasn't so awful—she certainly wasn't going to let them know; closed her eyes, opened them, and matters were stable and restored.

"Refuse military service. And *Vägra Döda?* Defend yourself by non-violence. Ulla's lines at the Institute: negotiation, right? then meditation, demonstrations, sit-ins, lie-ins—"

"Lie-ins are Franzy's favorite kind," Krieger said, half wishing he had let him fall asleep on the couch.

"Shush—strikes, counterdemonstrations, hunger strikes, sabotage, economic and social boycotts, tax refusal, civil disobedience, paralysis of the entire society . . ."

"Most of all Francis here is in love with Lena."

"Lena who?" Hannah asked, surprised.

"First time he got me to go see the thing he got mad at me about it."

"Oh heavens, don't her tell that."

Krieger poured Hannah more wine: its acid was lessened, she discovered, if she drank it by gulping, as she might if it were water; also, this pleasant whirling sensation reduced the substantiality of both her situation and her companions.

"A toast," she said. "To my uncle."

"To her uncle," the older man echoed, unable to slow his friend.

"—Franz here is pretty up front about his odd proclivities but when we came out and he was going on and on about this Lena I said, But that delicious blond girl, Franzy tell me, I mean I don't get it. And he said, he said, Get? what's there to get? *Her*, I said, I mean you know? Like, so Franzy's defending her see, She's so beautiful, so brilliant, her consciousness, etcetera, and I said, Franz, no but I mean the"—Krieger cupped his hands at his chest as Wrynn choked, head thrown back—"you know, the uhmm . . . I mean, forgive me Hannah, but it's just the way it went down and here he is going on and on, Listen baby Lena she's the most—"

"That's not how I talk."

"Sure it is, Lena oh she's top-drawer."

"What bosh."

"And he won't listen to me, I'm saying Franzy they're out to here there's no getting around them I would've thought . . . and he says, Lena—and he's starting to get mad now, see—Lena can do no wrong. Puppy, I say, it's not a matter of doing wrong all I am saying is I would have thought Lena was just a tad zaftig for a man of your special and refined tastes, so you know what we do? we go straight back into the theater, see it again."

"And guess who paid for the tickets again?"

"You sure did and another tub of buttered popcorn. So I notice while we're watching he's pretty quiet this time, no translating from Swedish or any of that shit and when we get to the scene where Börje and Lena attempt to make love in a hitherto unknown position up in the Rumskulla oak tree, biggest tree in Europe, forty or fifty feet circumference, I see Franz bending forward in his seat to read the captions."

"She doesn't need to hear all this," Franz asserted, softening and having surmised the point of Krieger's story, or at least the object of its abstract direction. He'd spilled some wine down his front. Annoying, that.

"Börje is talking about how she's slept with twenty-three guys," Krieger went on, "and Lena answers, Yes but the first nineteen weren't any fun, Börje says, Why? and she answers, quote, I slept with them because they wanted to sleep with me, so that they could have orgasms. I couldn't believe that anybody could like me the way I look: drooping breasts, big belly, fat. Like, it was as if Franzy'd never seen the movie before. He was outraged. I thought, The man's gonna have a cow right here in front of us all but instead, he got up and walked out."

"This is such slander, I wasn't outraged I was tired," Franz said, suddenly weary.

Out the corner of his eye Krieger took in Hannah; she seemed unflustered, unmoved by the level of discourse tested on her. Was she wise and bored? or slow?—no, not with those fast-flicking irises she wasn't slow. Impressive, the eyes, nonpareil, almonds, like they are supposed to be, like he'd read they were supposed to be shaped, classic purity in this runaway's face. And the dirt under her nails was endearing. A soldier, she. To whom one might defer, under the erratic modulations of wine perhaps, elsewise. He quickly continued.

"Franz Wrynn tired of *I Am Curious (Yellow)*? Forget it. What'd happened was that he'd managed to watch it through all those times without once noting Lena's two most substantial—what to call them—baby's blessings. What is that great one about the phallus? America's favorite one-eyed matinee movie idol?"

"She's got beautiful eyes."

"Hannah?"

"No, I mean, but I meant Lena."

"What color are they?"

"The girl here doesn't care, and neither do I, it's getting late."

"It is," Hannah allowed, setting down her glass.

"Some more," Krieger reached to pour. "He hasn't been back to see it since, Franz hasn't."

"Well hell that was only last week, I think they're blue."

"What?"

"Her eyes, they're blue."

"You were going every night, though, and no, they're not blue."

"It's a great film and I'd go see it now."

"Why don't you take Hannah here?"

"Listen," said Hannah.

Krieger jerked his head toward Wrynn, while talking to Hannah, "I bet he can't sit through the whole thing sentient and alert."

"Listen."

"Those lovely young pouches wagging and all that soft female skin, why, you'll have nightmares for a month."

"Get your jacket," Franz instructed Hannah.

"I don't have one."

"Francis can buy you one on the way you know that leather shop get you a little something in suede with fringe down the sleeves?"

Hannah raised her voice, "Do I get this job or what?"

"You want that?" Krieger interjected.

"Well. Yes."

"You drive all the way from Kansas to New York so that you can become a waitress?"

"Obviously, no, but it's a—I need somewhere to start."

"Well then you've got it, right Franz."

"I don't care."

"You got it, Hannah. But we'll talk later. I've got a much better idea than you working in a sweat-job like that. It's like a noose around your neck. Look at me, upstanding white-collar corporate slug fresh out of college, foreign travel ahead the promise of amenities and promotion, and where will it all get me? absolutely nowhere is where and you think I don't know it. You have got to be born like Wrynn here have a little inheritance to work with not necessarily Social Register, not necessarily outfitted with fashionable equipment like family crest embroidered tuxedo slippers and a herd of polo ponies you slingshot from Saratoga to Palm Beach, summer, winter, summer, winter, up and down the pajama and cocktail circuit, but, do a little this little that to be free, stay outside the system."

"Krieger's got a thing about polo ponies," Franz said.

"That may be but meantime, as you know I'm broke and so . . . the job?"

"You heard the man, you're in, but as I say, we'll talk."

"Hey you, whatsername, Hannah," Franz called, having left the room and returned, his tone more serious, his face fallen.

Hannah answered, "Yes?"

"Let's do a raincheck on the movie."

"See there, he's already backing out."

"I've been up all night three nights running."

"What did I tell you?"

"You want her to see it so bad why don't you take her?"

"Here's a citizen fresh in from the Bible Belt, amber waves of grain, and you're telling me you'd rather put on that white-noise machine of yours and go beddy than introduce her to the big city? It's a total dereliction of duty."

"What about you? It makes more sense for you to take her."

"Can't. I've got something going and anyway I'll see Hannah later, right?"

"Oh, let's go," Franz sighed.

"There's the spirit. You'll love it, Hannah."

She had seen movies at the theater where she'd worked, but never one with subtitles, nor one where the screen was covered in so much flesh. There was the exhilaration of being where she was, the rush of the exotic, simply to be sitting there next to this stranger, and of being a stranger herself, come all this distance on her own, relying on fate and nerves to see her through—and there was the exhilaration too of watching Lena whom Hannah thought different from any character she had ever seen back in Babylon, Nebraska, on film or off, since no one, with the possible exception of mama Opal, had ever shown so much openness and will. She could not follow the sequencing, a difficulty exacerbated by the demands of shifting focus from caption to action, and so she surrendered to the actress and her mellifluous if incomprehensible Swedish, and knew that while she herself could never do some of those things that Lena did—it was sad to see her on the floor, lying there on her side, crying, sucking her thumb, while that man whose body looked thin like James Riding's took her from behind, his hips pumping with devastating insistence, some kind of sex machine— Lena was surely very much alive, was committed to being alive, and protesting against anything that might jeopardize it. So engrossed was Hannah it was not until the famous scene with the two-thousand-year-old oak that she remembered Franz was sitting next to her. His eyes were closed. From the grimace on the face it seemed unlikely he was asleep but Lena's anguished cries, made the more pathetic through the distortion caused by a tear in one of the speakers, distracted her. When Hannah looked up she saw Lena naked, rushing across an indistinct space, a rifle held waist-high, and she closed her own eyes against the violence which was about to follow.

Franz's lips fluttered as he snored. The expected explosion never came. Hannah glanced up; Lena was once again in someone's arms, it hardly mattered whose.

When the credits ran and the lights came up Hannah could see that Franz was indeed asleep. She tapped him on the shoulder but elicited only a shift of position and a faint groan; the diamond stickpin on his mackintosh rose and wearily sank, and she watched him for a while as the audience, talking and laughing, wrapped up in their own concerns, left their seats. She wondered how a person could come to this—not that he was destitute (as was she) or that he wanted pity (neither did she). The wrinkles which settled across the polish of his forehead were not unlike those she remembered her father Nicky having: these were city lines. The city clawed your skin right off you, abraded it along the planes most exposed to its invisible carbonic razors, the sulfur, soot, the particles that lay on your skin which when you sweated were not washed away but leached out, spread, and absorbed right back in. She searched the faces of all the others (most had gone—a few couples straggled) and saw how tired everyone was. That was it. More than the city working you over from without, it could exhaust you, within. She resolved at that moment never to be worn out by it, not at least within. Franz here needed a week's sleep. She pulled the stickpin from his lapel and, careful not to disturb him, slipped it into his breast pocket, so that no one would be tempted to steal it from him.

Out under the marquee the street dissolved inside a spring fog. Puddles to catch the prismatic abundance already gathered in broken sections of the sidewalk. The harbor smell—fishy and warm—revived a remembrance of her childhood here, and while her mother Opal never allowed her to wander unaccompanied in the city, Hannah found that she possessed an uncanny, almost innate sense of direction that led her to Krieger's door downtown, even though his instructions about how to come home from the theater were vaguely given, interspersed with more ideas about Lena, Börje and their tree. In the narrow foyer she pressed the button labeled PBK and was buzzed in without having to identify herself over the intercom. The apartment was on the top floor, a floor-through barbells flat—two rooms, one front, one back, and a connecting hall.

Krieger opened the door and smiled. Down the corridor inside the apartment Hannah could hear music. "I can come back later," she began.

"Don't be ridiculous, come on in, start getting it into your head that this is home, all right? this is where you're staying until you're set up."

Hannah could see the girl was dancing alone, singing along—"How sweet it is to be loved by you"—off-key, locked in vigilant conspiracy with herself to keep some emotional skin stretched between what was inside and what outside (or so it seemed to Hannah; once more, inside, outside). She stared at her, an apparition at the end of the corridor, and felt Krieger's fingers, as they had her by the wrist, "So did Franzy make it through?" Hannah told him.

"You mean you left him in the theater sleeping?"

"I didn't want to bother him."

"Love it, I love it."

She hadn't meant to sound as defensive as she did when she said, "I used to work in a moviehouse and Mr. Johnson my boss, he always let people sleep there all night if they needed," but the words had already escaped. It was perhaps her first indication of the goodness, or at least impassionate cool, Krieger was at any moment capable of, when rather than take advantage of this lapse (how quickly New York had her second-guessing herself, apperceiving her moves and words to measure them against all potential responses—what was this?) he let the matter drop, even digressed, to smooth Hannah's embarrassment.

"Who was it said, New York is not America?" he said, then raising his voice, "Hey, Mona?"

"Huh," she answered.

"Mona, meet Hannah."

"Huh?" louder.

The prudent choice, Hannah had already come to conclude, would be to leave, at once, even before another colorful if unassimilable piece in the Krieger puzzle was presented. Nebraska, its landscape of sky which could only exaggerate the events that took place beneath its great blueness, seemed sufficiently far away as to be on another planet altogether, viewed from the vantage of Krieger's place. What an insufficient villain uncle would seem here, she realized. Here all was amplified. Krieger was right. It was as if New York were an echo chamber and all the voices of America—perhaps all the voices talking and talking in the world—were thrown by some ventriloquism into this one place. Krieger was shouting. She had never seen eyes like his before. They were merry, fractious. The fingers had stayed at her wrist, which she withdrew once she'd noticed.

"Come here I want you to meet a friend of mine."

Mona continued dancing, shoulder-length ironed-straight hair flung erratic by her self-absorbed head shaking. She had bangs that lifted and dropped on her smooth forehead. Hannah thought of Lena, but Mona was the finest filament by comparison; her short sleeveless paisley dress twisted on the tall, pipestem body. Her arms were graceful, her fragile knees knocked as she dipped and thrust her pelvis to the bass line.

"Come on," Krieger said.

Hannah followed him into the front room, which was spare. A lamp in a corner, the shade crooked. Some pillows, a couch, oval table.

"Mona, this is Hannah."

"Huh?"

"This is my new friend Hannah, she went to see *I Am Curious* with Wrynn tonight left him there sleeping when the thing was over."

"Yall left him there?" she drawled.

"Left him there, comatose," he reiterated.

Mona pondered this, limbs caught in a tableau vivant. "Far out," she pronounced and began to dance again.

"I wasn't trying to do anything that would hurt him, just—"

Krieger fastened a hand to Hannah's shoulder, "Don't give it two more thoughts, Hannah. Franzy's a zoological study, protozoological study, ineradicable as a cockroach, creature Linnaeus would have paid a lot of shekels to get a good gander at under his microscope. Look; I've left him myself in places a hell of a lot worse than the theater, he always shows up next day unscathed. Anyway, you liked the movie? that's all that matters. Come here," and led her back into the bedroom, incense-laden with a waterbed illuminated under black lights positioned over the headboard and an even dimmer source from the tropical fish tank.

"Maybe I'd better go back and make sure he's all right."

Ignoring her, Krieger said, "You sleep in here tonight."

"The couch's fine."

"No, don't worry about it."

"I don't think so."

"Listen, I've got to leave early in the morning and there's no point waking you up. I'll take the couch, be back in a couple days, here's the spare set of keys, eat whatever you find in the icebox. We'll talk when I get back."

Was it possible Hannah felt disappointed? "What about her?"

"Mona? she's my friend."

What was the draw? she wondered.

"Business associate, really."

"What about the restaurant?"

"Twenty questions—you really interested in being a slave?"

"No, I need the money."

Avuncularly, "Give it a whirl. No substitute for experience, right? My aunt, she was the one who brought me up, she went overseas only once in her life and all she came back with from her travels was an ugly little ashtray, didn't even smoke, but the ashtray had the inscription in the dish— *chi non va non vede chi non prova non crede*—who goes not will not see, who does not try will not believe."

Hannah had been listening to the music. "Do I need special clothes?" peering back down at the other girl, and thinking that it would be something to be that uninhibited, free; no, not free, but—no, it was dumb.

Krieger scowled, then smiled.

"How would I know? They wrap a cute apron around your waist shove stacks of dirty dishes at you, you come home stinking somewhere between fra diavolo and pesto, and suddenly you're straight out of *Macbeth*— multitudinous stench of clams undined—you can't wash it off and the multitudinous seas really are incarnadined, but with tomatoes instead of blood. But anyway we'll talk, goodnight . . ." and after fixing her eye he left the bedroom, shutting the door behind.

The movement much later which broke in on her sleep passed underneath her body, thrusting in a solid wave first her hips, raising them as her head and feet dropped to configure with the reverberating bed. Her shoulders drawn she was lolled to right, level, and the silent mass returned below to resurrect her head and by cross-wave patterns sink stomach, buffet hips, then thighs and feet just as the torso began to rise once more. When this wave broke at the far side of the mattress a modest gurgling sound was heard before it surged back, swelling under her in more confused combinations. He was outlined against the fish tank (alive with yellow tangs and triggers) crawling toward her—wave-tossed—on his hands and knees.

"Hannah?"

She did say "What?" as she stretched her hand out to prevent him from falling on top of her, but he was immediately in her arms murmuring, kissing her along the hollow of her shoulder, her skin moist and sweet-smelling. He licked her forehead, smooth as paper, and his head moved down upon hers, his tongue exploring until it found her mouth where it drove in deep and anxious. Hannah tried to edge away. Her moaning like the water beneath them came in surges and his hands had both of her frail legs lightly under his own as he separated them. He maneuvered his mouth away and began to tongue her ear. She wondered why she didn't resist him more. The hands at her narrow back felt good as he pulled up her sweatshirt and lifted her up like a child, licked along her ribbed chest in search of breasts. But then the hands seemed to get rough, the teeth at her navel oddly abrasive, and Hannah began to withdraw in breaths, not words which Krieger could understand if he were listening (wasn't); instead, he acted against her own panic which had grown. He got her unlacy underpants down and was astride her just as she managed to conjure up an image of Nicholas, mama Opal, a skating rink—no, a roller rink, ruckus over that floor, worn like glass from the turning rubber wheels on the skates and drowned in a calliopelike music which bled from speakers hung from the ceiling in every corner.

No, it *was* a skating rink. She could see ice, and the blades slide over it. There was a sizzle, no, a scratch, no, deeper than that, the blue shaved metal against the frozen water. Skirts flew. Nicky's corduroys patinaed with a beard of white from falling. His wonderment at his daughter. His encouragement. His own slipping and tumbling to the hard surface like a clown.

Shutters closed, shades down, curtains drawn, when she woke up it was impossible to tell what time of day it was. Through the walls or windows she could hear someone practicing scales on a violin. She felt apprehensive (violin went pizzicato on a harmonic minor scale). She searched the apartment hoping to discover a note, but she found none (what could he have said? she wondered, in any case, or even more—what was it she might have wanted him to say? forgive me? or, I love you? or, don't be here when I return?) and gave up the search. Standing before the white glare of the refrigerator—empty save for the bag of brown withered alfalfa sprouts, box of baking soda, half-eaten pickle, empty wine jug—she shook her head, as there were no words she could say aloud even to herself addressing what she felt about the night. The cold air passed over her and she looked down at her flat front, saw between her legs the indefinite mound with its wave of hair and cupped her hands over it there, moving them in and down until she could feel the rush of liquid warmth, leftover Krieger. Unexpectedly, she began to jump up and down, first on one foot and then the other, to force the liquid out of her. She ate the half pickle instinctive it would work further against those little white fish swimming their way up inside her. The pickle was rotten, however, and she spat it into the sink. Water which she drank head tucked under the spout tasted like an old penny.

It was five-thirty before she found the restaurant shaded under its awning in the complicated streets over by the river. She was hastily dressed in blacks and whites, assigned her station, left to her own devices. By six the maître d' had summoned her back into the kitchen (hung with copper pans, pots, double boilers; garlic and fried organs defining the atmosphere) and told her she was fired.

"You got no clue what side of a plate the knife belongs at got no clue the difference between your soupspoon your teaspoon your dessert spoon, it won't do nothing personal, I am regretful, you may have dinner the cashier'll pay you, no hard feelings"—and to the Calabrese chef: "Got some of that baked scrod from yesterday for the raggaz' here."

"I can learn, man."

He was already walking away, "Okay no hard feelings I explain everything Mr. Franz and good luck? okay."

Slowly she walked back downtown. She counted out several coins from her change purse and bought a newspaper at the cramped smokeshop on the corner around from Krieger's apartment. It was dusk outside when she pulled on the cord to raise the venetian blinds, and the sun streamed in to form geometries that crept and hesitated at blue bats in the Chinese rug. Off came the pink dress and the odious white brogues that she always wore on special occasions (though they pinched her toes in their stout leather tips) and she replaced them with jeans and her moleskin shirt. She sat with a pencil just like mama Opal had always done and circled job offerings in the classifieds, feeling only slightly abashed at what solace she took in the simple repetition of a pattern her mother had set so long ago. The variety of possibilities that lay in those long narrow columns of type was as startling as what it represented from a child-adult's view; that is, from the view which is taken for the first time when work is equated with money, money tied to the ability to shelter oneself from the world's welter and to feed oneself, and those simple abilities touched by freedom. At once she understood that she was free, washed with freedom, inundated by it, and in turn daunted by it. There was no need to be a waitress or a secretary.

Something high up, literally, is what she would take, a job where she could see out over the entire city. This would be her criterion, and why not?

She had only slept with one man before Krieger but she had had enough experience to know he was not for her. She would get a job, independent of anyone, and would find a place to live. Before a mirror she began to brush her hair. She decided to grow it out. This was to be another start. She would not allow herself to feel guilty or disgusted with sleeping with him— she could do it again if she felt like it, nobody could tell her what to do one way or the other. Not that she wanted to, but it was her choice, hers alone.

The sun moved down into the cross streets and flickered out on the tips of the pieces and bits of clouds which could be seen from down in the concrete caves. The streetlamps came on and colored the uncurtained room with a fastidious yellow. She fell asleep reading a chapter in Krieger's copy of a thick blue volume which had been left open (not on purpose, she had hoped—again that tremendous pressure to interpret motives, his, her own, whoever's) to a page which discussed an event she had never heard of before, a historic betrayal:

> There are many ways of looking at sin, but from the universe philosophic viewpoint sin is the attitude of a personality who is knowingly resisting cosmic reality. Error might be regarded as a misconception or distortion of reality. Evil is a partial realization of, or maladjustment to, universe realities. But sin is a purposeful resistance to divine reality—a conscious choosing to oppose spiritual progress—while iniquity consists in an open and persistent defiance of recognized reality and signifies such a degree of personality disintegration as to border on cosmic insanity. . . . iniquity is indicative of vanishing personality control.

What was peculiar, she thought, as the book lowered onto her chest, was that Krieger had underlined the word *recognized*. Was it possible he could find it in himself to think that reality would cease to exist if he failed, or refused, to recognize it? She watched the fish tour madly through their liquid world and then regarded the room with a fresh eye—how, Hannah wondered, was it possible she could want him, Krieger, to be above a thought like that? No, she'd been on the road too long. The exposure to all this city madness come so soon after those years spent in country madness had bad results; the centerlines kept rushing over the insides of her eyes when she shut them, hoping to push away that word. Survival, that was all Krieger was thinking about, right? His survival, and even hers? That was a good thought, though it refused to settle in. Whatever it might have meant, the book left open to that page, the days she had been through—these and the other discussion she read about the blue men and women who walked the earth long before Adam and Eve fell from grace—palled like anything in the belly of this mendacious whale: I've come, she thought (though not in any words at all, but just down inside somewhere), like Dorothy, to a place at least of wonder, if not bewilderment. And mama Opal and Nicky and uncle LeRoy were enveloped in a dream, as was her dear sweet long-dead Vache, her pet whom Kitter had put down in the pasture one awful afternoon. This too came from Dorothyland, though in the morning was washed away as clean as shower-washed streets.

It wasn't supposed to happen, she had allowed herself to let it, but three nights later it happened again, although this time Hannah was led down the darkened hall by a hand more confident than the one she had felt tentative against the blue skin of her wrist in the doorway before. She, also, tried against tentativeness. Lena, she thought. She toked off the hash pipe whose ivory bowl glowed under the violet of the black light. Impetuous and prurient, and nothing she had ever done before. Her hips felt loose. She pushed her tongue into his navel. Krieger rasped breath even as he laughed when she moved her head down and closed her mouth around him, to bring him back up so they could do it once more. And how shocked she was at the physical pain and also with the beginnings of the sense of real debasement when she felt a canopy—him, his flesh—straggling across her and he'd gone ahead with forcing himself inside her before she was ready to take him—or, at least, he tried to, his efforts having come to an abrupt conclusion when she pulled away, fighting off his hands as well as the indeterminate, clenching water of the bed, her skin gone hazy and cold. When she had recovered her bearings, she began not quite an apology but an explanation—something that would be honest, and allow that she had never much tried all this before. He had nothing to say, because he'd fallen asleep. It was just one further matter they would never come to discuss, in part because she knew that through the way she had placed herself under him, thinking trespass, thinking bawdy, thinking maybe Lena all the while, thinking possibly other things, he could eliminate any protestation, and say simply he merely gave her whatever it was he had read in her movements she wanted; and that it was, none of it, really his doing.

Thereafter, Lena was exiled. Krieger didn't seem even to notice that in the morning Hannah refused to look at him full-face, and by evening she had moved from the bed in the back room to the couch in the front.

None of this (she herself noted) frightened her. But she had not finished. Frustrated by all the difficulties she came up against in her search for work, as the sentimental act of circling descriptions of jobs in the paper had also staled, and after the two bottles of red wine Krieger had bought to go with the take-out Korean, she was startled at how easy it was for her to agree to drive a panel truck to Norfolk, Virginia, without having any notion whether the action—by Urantian standards—was of sin, error, evil, or iniquity.

Registered to a Thorns Haggard, who was paying for it to be driven back down to Virginia, the truck was old, rust-pocked throughout, and the paint which covered it in paisley swirls went some way toward worsening its already garish appearance. The paisley was a statement, though, as his daughter had explained the day he came home from a football game to find it transformed, a social statement, and rather than argue, with misgivings her father had loaned her (Mona) the truck so she could move to an apartment in the city—where it all was, as she put it, *at*. Thorns's daughter—whom Hannah had had some difficulty seeing as a "business associate" of Krieger's that night when they met, although Krieger soon enough demonstrated that she was—advertised on a bulletin board at City College. Gas, all meals, return train fare, seventy-five dollars, drawn out in block letters under the words "Big" and "Bux," in a refulgence of Dayglo inks with a ☺ and the legend *Have a happy day!* running the circumference.

"You drive down you make just one little extra stop," Krieger proposed.

Hannah nodded and the wine relaxed the muscles in her neck so that her head tilted unwarily off to the side.

"There's five hundred in it for you, Hannah."

"To drive a truck a few hundred miles."

"For the little extra stop-off you'll make."

"What little extra stop-off," wry as she could manage.

"I don't know, search me, if I had to guess I'd say probably drugs taped under the chassis, but I don't know don't need to know don't want to know."

"Forget it."

Krieger quickly rejoined, "Hannah I said probably and then what did I say after that."

"You said you didn't know."

"So well?"

"What do you get out of this?"

"Another five, five you get and I get five."

"For what?"

"Middlemanning, of course, and this is where the middleman code of ethics comes to bear, see no hear no speak no evil. It's a one-shot enterprise, we both make a little cabbage and get out, and about the drug part?—I honestly don't know. I'm like you but probably even more strictly organic-macrobiotics, that hash business was absolutely an aberration, occasional foray into monosodium glutamate but I can't help myself this stuff tastes so good doesn't it," jabbing wooden chopsticks into the warm noodles, lifting a quivering brown bundle to his lips, then quoting as he chewed,

> " 'Courage is the price
> that life extracts for granting peace,
> the soul that knows it not
> knows no release.'

That's Amelia Earhart."

Hannah scoffed, "Amelia Earhart never came back."

"It doesn't mean she wasn't brave and anyway who knows?—she might be sitting down to roast pig and jungle juice on Papeete even as we speak, there're those who have their theories she simply dropped out of civilization, ditched the plane and the monkeysuit for paradise and pampas skirts."

"I miss the point."

"Point is what have you got to lose?"

"Well," she said, uncomfortable at the reference to women—knowing how shallow that particular vein in Krieger most probably ran—"I'll give it some thought," which Krieger took for yes, toasted, remarked how the humidity was up and summer was coming, old dead wet wearying summer.

Very early in the morning, night still, a taxi. This was a deep, smoky warehouse block, new moon, her face close to the red metal, unlocked the door then buffed the handle with her sleeve. It was a motion congruous with Hannah's resolve to be smart, but was so inefficacious it caused her to smirk. When she glanced up the moon too was a smirk, thin white smile between buildings. Inside, the cab was separated from the trailer compartment by a jerry-built wooden wall behind the seat. Hannah laid her paper sack with sandwich and carton of chocolate milk beside her. The recognition that what she was about to do would have sent uncle LeRoy reeling in anger made her smirk grow to a smile, cryptic, forced, but its self-consciousness was felt in the skin itself as it flexed across her face and fled. The fear was present in beads of moisture which collected under her nose; she locked the door and sat for some minutes in silence surveying the wind-borne fragments carried through the marble-and-limestone box canyon there before deciding she could not collect her thoughts, then fumbled for ignition, set off down Seventh Avenue for the tunnel. At every pothole the homemade godseye, another social statement, that dangled by a length of yarn from the mirror (glass cracked) swung into her face—she pulled over, took it down, opened the door. There was a stray cat feeding at a wire basket. She threw the godseye into the basket and thought what a good companion the cat would make on the trip, reached out to pet it, but it leapt down off the basket's rim and ran crouching low toward the shadows. So the plastic virgin on the dash with nodding wimple would ride as masthead and companion, she thought, the heck with cats, although the cat would have been warm in her lap.

Once she emerged from the tunnel, left behind the city and its southern boroughs for those miles of tank farms and oil refineries whose burnoff flames ascended, tongue-shards shot up into the orange sky, she settled down into the drive, studied signs and the blink of highway centerlines. Krieger, Wrynn (whom she was fond of—father figure? such a fruitloop), the stuff in the back of the truck, or underneath—whatever trouble lay there ceased to exist as the radio's yellow face came on to:

> *"I got a little red rooster*
> *too laazy to crow the day. . .*
> *Little red rooster*
> *too laazy to crow the day.*
> *Keep everything in the barnyard*
> *upset in every way . . ."*

and as the slide bar culled and begged, Hannah felt good to be alone again, here on the highway—

> *"If you see my little red rooster,*
> *won't you please drive him home?*
> *See my little red rooster*
> *please, drive him home . . ."*

and she said, aloud, "please, drive him home"—

> *". . . ain't had no peace in the barnyard*
> *since my little red rooster's been gone."*

She sang along, soulful, faking the words and guessing the rhymes. Somewhere (she did not know where) outside Washington she found an all-night gas station lost under a cloud of insects come to circle the fluorescent tubes secured in tin tents over the two islands. The vending machine inside was broken. She breathed in the crisp morning air that was to be found out toward the edge of the asphalt where there was a field that bellied up toward a house, outlined there like a child's drawing. Dawn stained the clouds behind the row of pink pumps as she turned around to walk back to the van and a diadem aura pulsed at the attendant's duckbilled cap. She must have been ten miles down the road before she realized that the attendant's comment about a cot in the back room of the office was meant to be an enticement. Although she flinched at the thought—picturing his bony face and toothy mouth, and the blue shirt unbuttoned to reveal a furry chest—it was not from prudishness but the unmistakable sensation of having discovered something for the first time.

This was what men did? what they wanted? she reasoned, as the music finished and a talk show came on. They were discussing the seven-second delay, as if there wasn't anything else in the world worth thinking about.

Nicky'd been the same way, within his sickness, after his own fashion—still, obstinate and unbending, and even unmerciful. Was that how it had come to pass she had been in New York over a week now and hadn't begun to search for him yet, hadn't put three minutes into it—even though this was part of the point of coming back in the first place, so that she could tell him about mama Opal, tell him his wife was gone, tell him she knew he'd left them because she turned out to be a girl instead of what he wanted? Pretty damn monstrous to assume all the blame because there wasn't that nasty little Freudian doodad down there—oh, god, could she tell him a few things if she could find him. Maybe she never would, though. Find him, or tell him? Either one. Woe all sewn up in it.

It was like the road, this business—just there is all, just something made to travel on, make use of while all the while leaving it behind and allowing it to perform its function of simply stringing out mile after mile, moment after moment.

"Why don't you jerks cool it?" she cried at the radio.

But it *was* there, to be reckoned as something firm and durable, hard to adjust, even callous, and while it didn't make her angry it did make her curiously adamant. She would finish what she had begun here, take what was hers, move on. She had the quickest feeling, as the sun cleared the tops of the billboards and trees, that she could do anything she wanted to do and that nothing could slow her down, let alone stop her. Buoyed by this, she drove on, bare toes curled heavy on the accelerator pedal while, as with most euphorias, the strength of that moment skimmed, flittered, and lapsed behind like a powdery dust whipped into tiny cones on the paved shoulder. Cars began to appear on the road; everybody's day began.

Soon enough the outskirts of Norfolk were upon her and gone were the meditative cocoon of road before her and background from radioland its blues and country voices strung out end on end to make one democratic fugue (she saw) punctuated by the midnight preachers, the faith healers out there smoking cigarettes and drinking coffee all night in their little home-made studios, all scat-hollering and saving people.

She parked at the curb. It wasn't too late to turn around. The spare set of Krieger's keys was hidden in her change purse, the rough-hide purse mama Opal had bought for her so many years ago at a county fair in Red Cloud. Krieger would have to leave the apartment sometime during the day, and she could slip in, take what few possessions she had stowed there in the front hall closet, and escape. How hard could it be to disappear into a land of so many millions? She'd never see him again, would she.

The money represented a little security against her having to return to the farm, beaten so soon by the city. It waved like a membrane between an empty space and a void. Hannah squeezed her hands between her thighs (the jeans were worn to white there) and considered the membrane and what treachery she and mama Opal had traveled through because of Nicholas and uncle LeRoy, the one an empty space, the other like a blanket between stars.

Little Miss Nancy. Hannah's uncle made it one of his habits to call her that. She asked mama Opal what it meant. Little Miss Nancy—it meant an effeminate or overprecise man. She knew what it was he had intended as he pulled on the turnip of a lobe which gave off his magnificent German ear, rolled up his shirt sleeves, and left the kitchen by the screen door which closed with a slap. Her value, she was being told, would never exceed that of oleo or beef tallow, neat's foot or offal, the throwaways, secondary orders of what butcher could make of beast—and to uncle there was nothing that couldn't be measured by cattle and land.

Hannah understood there was no direction but forward. She unfolded the map against the steering wheel. Written on the back were addresses, and Krieger's number in New York. In case something goes wrong but nothing will, he'd said. In case something goes wrong, she thought, disdainful—something goes more wrong than what?

She memorized what was written, tore the map into small squares, released them one at a time out the vent as she found her first destination on a quiet enough street where there were trees and houses and, as often in neighborhoods at the outskirts of a town, no sign of any people under them or in them.

The accident like all automobile accidents was a sort of excerpt, like the paroxysm of a millisecond where time itself gets bunched up and folded back for just an instant, so immediate and present that no crumb or component, no remnant, absolutely nothing subdivisible could be found in it, for its being over and its beginning were a single factor, an element of a piece: that is, the whole moment was over exactly when it began.

It began like this. A deep crunch. A shrill screech of balded rubber. The peal of glass. These were all one.

Hannah's forehead popped lightly against her knuckle on the top of the wheel. No scream, no hysteria. She was convinced she'd fainted, as there was no memorable sequence between her having started to pull the truck up the gravel driveway of the small clapboard house (front yard cluttered with swingset and some tricycles) and what she could make out now.

She heard the siren—it was above the nurse's head, a reference point. It began to hurt, then. The siren did. She tried to ask them if they wouldn't mind turning it off.

"Almost there almost there now," she heard but, bliss, the siren desisted, some doors fell open, the passionate blue sky appeared above, bluer than usual and not chastened by clouds, as Hannah was lifted out onto a gurney and all the stimulus seemed to withdraw so she put her whole soul into just keeping the breathing going, the beloved elasticity of the breath into her, good old trustworthy air, high-air, heady stuff.

"She's just fine," someone told someone else.

"She's in one hell of a mess," someone else contradicted, but of all the silly things, how could it be that the overriding feeling which followed her into the emergency room was neither fear nor the pain of her injuries—which proved to be more dramatic than dangerous—but the knowledge that she, the same woman who just a few hours before was reveling in her solitude, had never felt so lonely? No, that wasn't so hot to feel that lonely. It's the kind of thing that can push a person into plights like this, just the kind of thing. That was a shame, wasn't it. How far down can someone get.

"So the fucking rearview mirror ends up on the floor and well the universe that thrives behind big teeth chomping chomping to the tune of the old natural selection waltz, and out of nowhere comes this car smashes into her rear end stop me if I'm wrong, right Hannah?"

Krieger set up the story for Franz, who lay back in the doughy sofa and listened with less interest than his countenance of pragmatism might have suggested, which is to say his mouth was drawn down at the corners under the first evidence of a pencil moustache he had decided several days before to grow (it would be shaved off by evening). Hannah drummed her fingers on her hand cast, wandered down the hall to the bathroom. She noticed the curtains were drawn back in Krieger's bedroom, allowing light like cognac to filter in on the fish tank. All the fish in the tank were gone. She studied her blackened eye in the mirror. No matter what Krieger told Franz about the excursion to Norfolk, she knew she would have to spend that afternoon finding a room to rent, and a job. She flushed the toilet for the distraction its rushing water would create and came back down the hall—a parolee walking down a hall, she thought. She still felt like the same Hannah that walked down this hall only days before all this happened. Krieger was wrought-up.

"Right, her rear end, the rear end of the truck, and who climbs out of it egos bruised but a rookie cop and his partner warned five times, lawyer says I'm telling you five times, about his hitting hooch on the trail, we're talking the kind of sump wakes up three in the morning downs the pint of apricot brandy his daughter's saved away for her slumber party, moral rectitude of a game-show host right? for the love of god, you got these guys flying out the screen doors out back of the house for no reason whatsoever that's at least obvious to these blues and what the hell you expect them to do?"

"What, what?" asked Franz. He rubbed his nose.

"It's instinct, it's bred in the blood, they pull their pieces out of their holsters and go running after these deer sprinting down the alley, I mean you don't dash unless you've done something wrong right?—here she is, Hannah, sit here," and he caught his breath when she came back into the room.

Franz thought to ask her if she liked his moustache and ran his thumb over it.

"Now listen, and so, one of them, the sober one, has enough of god's good sense to go back call in for an ambulance and backup happens to notice that as a matter of fact there was a girl at the wheel of the vehicle these assholes have just back-ended, but once the ambulance pulled in pulled out with Hannah in tow, attends to the more immediate and paramount concern of agreeing with the goddamn police dogs, as I understand this monster German shepherd? right Hannah?"

She shrugged, and glimpsed away out the window into the street.

"Sniffing like crazy against the tires and not in search of a place to piddle, real pro this mutt and without doubt and obviously the only professional within a country-mile radius, sniffing sniffing etcetera until your drunk rookie crawls back not having successfully shot anybody in the back, says, Hey whatz Snuffee zo dern innurst in? Snuffee? hey gal? and having noted the remote possibility the Norfolk Police Department might through the olfactory cells located in goodole Snuffy's snout have discovered the avenue whereby charges of negligence and extreme misconduct and who knows what else against the officers aforementioned might well be avoided, they proceed to dismantle piece by piece the entire blasted panel truck until you know what they found, I mean, for the love of sweet Jesus you know what the fuck all they found?"

Franz raised his eyebrows—began to raise his hand. Krieger was talking too much. But it was too late.

"Quarter key cut snow, lousy quarter kilo most of it cheap sugar and here's Dick Tracy going—You cain't get ya a lobster in a four-star restrunt weighs this dern much, I mean that's with claws included, no sir you cain't. And here is all this glee among the good buddies, scored themselves quarter key of snow so proud of themselves buttons flying all around in the air and you can bet the Norfolk PD bowling team this week'll be hell to mess with, the pins will just drop from the pride of it all—hey Hannah, you remember that tune, 'Stairway to the Stars'?"

Hannah looked at the Jefferson Airplane poster on the wall and without success tried to integrate its brilliant oranges and yellows which were familiar in shape and sense but whose volatility burst and collapsed forward.

"My aunt used to play Roger Williams's arrangement of it on the Lowry organ—"

"Whose?"

"Anyway, oh hey that's pretty good Francis, whose organ, that's rich, so anyhow they arrested Hannah went over her with a fine-toothed comb but of course no record and she had no idea that stuff was there, so the bail was pretty minimal, I guess she's supposed to go back down there at some point, but I doubt Franzy'll let anything like that happen—"

"Anything like what happen?" Hannah asked.

"No, I won't let anything like—" began Franz. He wiped the back of his long hand across his mouth. Krieger kept talking while each of the others spoke.

"She always, my aunt, she always tried to get me to play along with her, play the melody of 'Stairway to the Stars' I mean on a comb with toilet paper or something on it, have you ever seen that? I never did, though. Too weird."

"Regarding Hannah," Franz continued.

"I knew Hannah was clean, or I never would have proposed she, what I'm saying is she was competent, clean as a whistle, no record, nothing" (turning to Hannah) "except for that insane call you made from where? nurses' station? the nurses' station, okay etcetera, but check what Franzy's done, old beneficence." Krieger passed Hannah five hundred-dollar bills folded in half and held together with a paperclip.

"Since when was I supposed to be competent at, at what?" Hannah began, ignoring the money. Her face was beginning to color. "The only reason I even made that call was because of what they found in the truck. There wasn't supposed to be anything in the truck, you said."

"I said who knows?"

"That isn't what you said."

"Don't act like it was news."

Franz mediated, "It doesn't matter now that Hannah's back safe and sound."

"So what's this, then?" pointing at the money. "I thought you'd said—"

Franz shifted. This was it for the little favors.

"That's yours."

"Why?"

"That's right, but it's not like you didn't give the business your all and Franzy, ever-living-loving saint that he is—"

"Peter, please, that's enough, Hannah's home, everything's fine."

"No, I mean it."

"I don't understand," Hannah said.

"Francis recognizes where the blame lies, blame . . . call it that, blame, not that you or I had any idea the van was transporting illegal merchandise across state lines."

"Peter, please," drifted more firmly from Franz.

"You knew." Hannah had placed the bills on the coffee table where they fluttered butterflylike.

Krieger's face settled into temporary ambiguity.

"You knew all along."

"Knew what?"

"Peter" (Franz).

"I mean, I suspected that the van was some kind of transportation of course I suspected, I told you as much didn't I? Suspected is the correct terminology suspected I was born yesterday thinking they'd offer you a thousand me a thousand."

"A thousand?—but you said five hundred."

"Five hundred, a thousand, whatever, just to drive some college girl's transportation I mean little Mona, a little short on the stuff upstairs but nevertheless a fervent item."

"Peter," Franz asked, "who's Mona?"

Hannah put the money in the breast pocket of her cowboy shirt.

"Fervent, almost religious in her particular penchant for the great god Cock, if you'll pardon me, and there she is up at college studying what studying Comparative Religion can you believe? you think you're having some kind of special like even mystical experience when you're with her but as a matter of fact, no wait a minute don't interrupt matter of fact whatever in hell you experience is I am told nothing compared to the Song of Solomon behavior she's capable of . . ."

"I'm going," Hannah announced.

"You're quite welcome," started Franz.

"Nevertheless so, Hannah, you took a ride, there were admittedly a couple flustering snafus and here before us is the compensation for our wrongs and what the hell otherwise than, well, welcome to New York, right Francis?"

Franz said: "Hannah, before you go I think it's important for me to note that I had nothing to do with any of this. It's very kind of Krieger here to suggest that I've been a saint in this, but I deserve none of the credit."

"Francis?"

"Yes, Peter?"

"I believe we need to have a few words in private."

"I believe we do, Peter," and as they stared at each other in disconsolate silence (was this one of their games?) she collected her rucksack out of the closet and only remembered after she quietly threw the lock and opened the door that her toothbrush was back in the bathroom but dashed down the stale corridors and creaking steps as quickly as she could, chest pounding, yet despising the manner in which she was making her escape. They did not follow her out into the street nor had Krieger come to the window to look down through the tangled ginkgo where she crossed between cabs, made the far sidewalk, glanced up, ran toward the corner. She chose turnings through the Village into streets whose names she had never heard of, and tried to be random in her choices. Eventually she came to the docks which jutted out into the river at the end of Horatio, and walked out to stare in the choppy water. Later, at a drugstore far downtown, she bought a fancy French toothbrush and paid for it with the crispest bill she had ever held in her hands. I didn't think those people ever brushed their teeth, just maybe rubbed Brie around on the gums or something, was what Krieger would have said; she heard the words so plainly she recoiled, turned, half expecting him to be there behind.

The toothbrush was paid for and she owned it. She ordered an egg cream at the long, sticky counter just to be able to go to the ladies' room and try it out. It was the greatest toothbrush any person could own on earth, she thought, clowning in the mirror, pulling her hair back and sucking in her cheeks so she looked like mama Opal, which made her wonder whether she ought not catch a bus back to . . . but *where?* . . . and the *where* answered the question even before it could be asked.

2.

"**P**ATRIOTISM is the last refuge of a scoundrel."
Krieger quoted Dr. Johnson to Lupi. Hadn't that contradicted something Krieger'd said earlier? Maybe so, maybe not. It was a bit of a fog, but what matter. He was leaving Honduras, leaving Krieger. The old man had revived a little.

"Last refuge of a scoundrel—" were the final parting words he offered under the burned reds of the range of mountains which embraced the capital. Made in reference to the "other branch" of their operation, as Krieger had come around to calling the fat man.

Lupi anticipated his being finally reduced to a nomenclature of twigness, and a dry twig perhaps at that, one which might be pruned away if it were to the tree's best advantage. He recognized it for the seduction it must have been and yet it was less clear why Krieger would bother speaking contemptuously of the fat man, especially after having puffed him some just the day before, affirming his credentials as a clever historian, wasn't that so?

The turn, as he thought back, all seemed to begin out of thin Sierran air, with "People who talk about what they call *callchore!* by which they mean a smattering of the two dead languages of Greek and Latin, and yes we know how important it is you happen to have currency with one of these tongues, but anyway a smattering of them and maybe some ability at finding a patroness, maybe a Venetian for you, no? and one with a great big goddamn palazzo with central air so in the summer the rot-stink of the Canal doesn't make you the more nauseous when you have to do your annual servicing of the old cow," and at that Krieger had slapped his— Lupi's—knee in a great gesture of friendship. Lupi joined reluctantly in the laughter but stayed aloof as possible to note the next turning. "No, but anyway, what am I saying, nothing really, just that, and to you I can say this with impunity and trusting at the same time you'll go ahead with what we've devised here because as I mention if for no other reason than it is significant and purposeful, right? it's just that our other branch has as I always used to say a *Vichy personality.*"

Dangerous material, Krieger. Lupi felt along his neck and ear to find if they were warm. He did not want to blush nor did he think it wise to display any sort of emotion at the moment of their parting. He continued to nurse along the idea that the passport might as readily get him through Italian as American customs, and suspected that while the fat man had only provided enough cash to transport them from the airport in New York to the city proper he could exchange both his and the old man's tickets, and apply them toward a transcontinental flight. It would of course involve abandoning Olid, and Krieger's confidence that Lupi could never do it was, as ever, reproachful and delicately, surely true. There was no going back now, anyway.

"Hey Lupi?—you ever hear of a guy named Tony Shafrazi?"

"Toni who?"

"Compatriot of yours, right? Shafrazi or something or other? maybe not, but anyway this Tony, you've heard of Picasso, right?"

"The artist."

"Good boy, so Picasso painted this huge canvas when you're up in New York if you've got a few moments in the afternoon tomorrow go by the museum check it out, *Guernica,* you know the image the town in Spain being bombed those minotaurs and the women and children all running for shelter their faces stretched out into Play-Doh tragedy, real statement this piece of art—but of course Picasso'd long since moved to the foot of Mont St. Michel, Mont Parnasse, whatever it is where Cézanne painted all the time—by the way, he bought half the mountain because he was crazy with envy he could never paint as well as Cézanne he's got a huge fortress of a mansion there, they buried him there in the mountain and he's probably still weeping bitter tears into it, etcetera etcetera, so anyway here comes this Tony character waltzes into the Museum of Modern Art past the guards and spray-paints the goddamn *Guernica* a few years ago and you know what I think?"

"You think that's a good thing, right?"

Krieger paused. "Lupi, I like you. I tell you one thing it's not."

"What," he said, resistant.

"It's not Vichy personality."

3.

THE whole island had seemed so balmy—something Hannah had dreamed must be West Indian—the afternoon she put down first and last months, and a security deposit on a furnished efficiency not far from those docks where she'd made her first escape from Krieger. The floor overhead was occupied by her landlady, a wispy woman who kept her own counsel and whose movements could never be heard through the overlapped piles of old oriental rugs which covered her floors; beneath was an auto-body repair shop which meted out a constant bouquet of gasoline, oil, diesel and which, in contrast to the other neighbor, was a source of constant noise. Inside the apartment itself the furniture was dated and worn, property the widow had grown tired of and put down here rather than discard. Hannah rearranged the table, chairs, rug but couldn't dispel the feeling of transitoriness which pervaded the space even into its chintz curtains, its broken cylinder desk, its whistling, iron-black airshaft (her "city-vu"). She told herself that in time the room and its furniture, having absorbed her through routine and touch, would come to feel more permanent, more her own—the photograph of mama Opal holding hands with her very young daughter, standing on the deck of the Staten Island ferry, smiling, which was placed on the mantel (the fireplace had long since been bricked up), threw the first possibilities of this conversion over the walls and floor.

The job she at last found met her criterion but was not what she might ever have expected. As on all her applications she was forced to misrepresent her qualifications.

"You suffer from acrophobia?" she was asked.

She said that she didn't, and the man gave her the job because she was the first person who had ever applied with the company who didn't ask what the word meant. She had a good set of worker's hands, too, had good height, and though she had no portfolio like some of the other applicants she sat down with Conté crayons and pad and could reproduce copies of any image placed before her.

Simon Deutsch was her boss, and the master painter. After Hannah and another painter had fleshed out (to the master's cartoon) drapery and scenery, Deutsch mounted the ladder along the great cylindric leg of the billboard—himself looking like a worker out of a WPA fresco or a Diego Rivera—with extension rods dangling from his belt, clanging their hollow aluminum ring, muttering, "Eh, Hannah, *wenn nämlich die Sonne im Osten steht, ja?*" squinting into the dawn out over freeway and highrises, commuter trains and the tangle of television antennas, dead trees and smokestacks, cakes of sooty ice down in the estuary, and set to working up the face and eyes.

"Hannah have you gone and seen Coit Tower?"

Where was it?

"Simon's never been wester than Piscataway," the other man said.

"This is true, Hannah, but I seen pictures, I got one of them albums full of the pictures of the great Coit. On the top of the highest hill in San Francisco. My father was one of the last of the Wobblies, you ever heard of the Wobblies?"

"No it's not," the man interrupted.

"What's not?"

"Coit Tower's not in San Francisco."

"Nicanor, it is. Cut me some more slack on that left leader, we're sinking down here. Hannah, pop us that chalk green there."

"What for the green?" Swarthy, bright-eyed Nicanor was about twenty, Hannah guessed. He wore his hair in a moderate, but proud, Afro.

"You tell me, mister know-it-all, the screwdriver, Hannah."

Nicanor gave the matter some thought. "You're changing the guy's eyes to green."

"Hannah, the thermos." The morning wind buffeted the scaffold into the flat surface of the billboard, and Nicanor mildly cursed. "Hannah, I've been working here with Nicanor for what five years going on now and he still refuses to learn the basic lesson about skin. It's why he's still painting trees, bobsleds, toilets for me, and not the beautiful faces and hands of the people out here. Skin, flesh, Hannah, listen to me, it is green. Okay?"

"Green," she repeated.

"You know Hannah here doesn't even know how to clean brushes," Nicanor offered in his own defense.

"Hannah is brilliant. She'll learn," and offered the thermos across to Nicanor, who took it and drank. "But, Hannah. The skin. I learned it must have been forty-five fifty years ago when my father took me back to the Old World. All your medieval painters knew it. Sassetta's Saint Francis? green. Giotto's madonnas? green. They all knew—chromium oxide green is absolutely inert, absolutely permanent. It is like god. The tinctorial power of the color, the range of color properties. Goya's Jesuses? green. They're all green as grass, I'm telling you. The Old Country is all churches and cathedrals you know and they're all filled with beautiful pictures. Flesh, first coat, green, this is Deutsch's cardinal rule. Learn it and you'll be fine."

"People ain't fucking green," Nicanor finished.

He held the thermos out to Hannah and while she didn't really want any coffee she took it anyway, seeing it as the chalice it must have been in this communion. She wondered how many times they had run this discussion through, the younger man always gently refusing to give in. It must have been his way of remaining in the position he wanted to hold just under the other, unburdened with business responsibilities, and notions of aesthetics. She held her hand out and looked at its long fingers and rounded knuckles and the tributaries of veins that ran across the back from the wrist, and she saw that he was right, that there was indeed a green cast to the flesh.

"It's green," she exclaimed.

"See that."

"Hannah here is green in many ways but that ain't one."

"*Hör auf damit*," Deutsch said, seriously. "See the shadows on the face as if they was light. See the reflections as if they was shade. Blend out your green with white and yellow for the shady patches, and just green with yellow for the light. After that we go over it with the color of the race. People don't understand that race-color is only semiopaque scumbling, that the background color, the deep-shade you scumble over, is green. Now here give me that tray, no the deep one, right."

"You mean you're gonna let *her* work on that arm?"

"Nicanor, you've got the entire grillwork, the whole front end on this car yet to do, let's move, it's cold." Deutsch turned to Hannah and said, "No one knows chrome and metals like Nica here. He's the top in that field."

Satisfied, Nicanor moved down to his end of the scaffold, hooked the safety catch to his belt and turned on the portable radio he kept in the pocket of his windjammer. Earplug in, tuned to a lite-rock station, he sat down, legs dangling freely out over the planks, and began to work quickly. Hannah listened to Deutsch and watched each move he made, but caught herself glancing from time to time down at Nicanor to admire how deftly and rapidly the image was coaxed up off the blank surface. Then she looked at Deutsch, a good man of the old school. For the first moment since she had come to New York, the first time in months even, she felt things were going right.

She learned on the job, prepping the masonry stories up, taking the blowtorch to greasy spots, pointing up loose brickwork, checking the porosity of the surfaces they were to work on, leveling mortar joints which protruded beyond the face of the brick, furring and hacking the walls, hosing them after the wire brush had circled the entire area, January wind singing across the rope rigging of the scaffold, the gentlest to-and-fro sway of the planks underfoot, and below the indifference of foreshortened pedestrians and pulsating hum of traffic to gaze up here where image and a few words promoted the purchases of some product.

In the beginning it was daunting, the height. Instructed by Deutsch never to look down, Hannah still felt the sensation like a morbid plastic that the heart passed off throughout the limbs which was only neutralized by concentration on the work. She excelled, however. Within a year she had apprenticed at locations up and down the island and at billboards near the Jersey mouth of the Lincoln Tunnel and past the Triborough Bridge. The advertisements were for cigarettes and cars and liquor, and required backdrops of supernal snow-capped peaks, fresh lakes, autumn leaves, carefree couples.

It was a simple life. She would return to her apartment hands, shoes, face, hair splattered with paint and dust. By the time she cleaned herself up she was too tired to go out, or so she told herself. She sometimes wished she had friends, but she had no way of knowing how to meet anyone. On weekends she would go to see a picture. She read through the discarded books from the library of the widow's husband, an odd assortment that ran from popular mechanics to bird-watching. She strolled nearly every evening down to the West Side docks to sit in the glow of the chemical sunset and watch the couples lean together and talk in low voices and leave the boardwalk to filter back into the streets and buildings. She missed walking barefoot on the dirt in the fields.

For all her solitariness, however, Hannah explained to herself that yes, well, she felt happy. She could do whatever she wished, whenever she wanted. That in itself was like having come into a wholly different world after the straitened and overdisciplined and what she later came to see as unforgivably perverse life she had led back on her uncle's farm outside Babylon, on the dry yellow plain of Nebraska.

Also, it was a life from which for a time Peter Krieger seemed to withdraw, and for this she felt a sense of gratitude which was only occasionally broken by the strange caller who telephoned her after midnight irregularly from month to month and said nothing but only played bits of music, recordings, early rock and roll, from albums she was sure she remembered having been in his large collection, songs to which Mona had danced and shaken her hair during Hannah's brief stay.

An afternoon some years later. Bitter middle of August. The lawn without graduation of color composed of synthetic blades and perfect as a putting green edged in foxglove, golden marguerite, daffodils, day lilies, lupine whose pale pink spikes nodded under the humidity, giving off none of the fragrance of flowers, as each was made of silk and stood on wire stalks wrapped in paper. Above was only a flat gray city sky pierced through with vague bars of white. The soft lamb's ears, planted in sod tubs sunk into the roof, bobbed exhaustedly as a butterfly faithful as the foliage to the wind's whim fluttered over it. On the terrace twin pots of leggy geraniums. In the miniature Japanese maple the male cicadas buzzed, pulsating and monotonous, testaments of the friendship of one who had brought them in a jar from a village on the north shore of Long Island, captured there in the garden. Hannah sat for a while, watched the gnats swarm in a furious milky ball over the rose garden, and could almost hear what they reminded her of, the creaking of swings, children flying back and forth in long arcs squealing, as a jet withdrew into the frontier above the rain gutter, rotting finials, tar vats. It was midday. Deutsch was going to be upset that she was so late.

Franz lay there, cottonballs on each of his eyes, dozing on a chaise longue in the sun, and the houseboy had told her not to wake him up. And where, she wondered, was Krieger?

She went inside where the air was drier and cooler, and pulled down a book from a set on a shelf in the living room: Nathaniel Hawthorne. "One afternoon, last summer, while walking along," she read from the story called "Howe's Masquerade." She glanced up at the bookshelves with their rows of volumes fronted by knickknacks, trinkets, and saw in a frame under glass on one of the higher shelves a cut-out silhouette portrait, a profile, its dimensions no greater than a prayerbook. While the artists who produce these works, scissors flying this way and that through the black paper, the ribbons of waste falling away as an outline takes its shape, generally have reduced their science to a pattern they simply repeat—no matter what their sitter looks like—Hannah knew who this was the moment it caught her eye. So, then, where was Krieger, indeed? She put the Hawthorne down and went back out on the roof terrace.

Krieger was somewhere in Belize, was what Franz heard—wherever in the world Belize was, he was obliged to add—and whatever he was doing there Franz did not want to know; it slowly emerged that he had fallen out of love with Peter (Franz volunteering this in just these words). Forbidden and repressed as Franz now painted Krieger to be, that was that. Vulgar, unstable, contentious, were other words he attached to the memory of his former favorite, but Hannah was one who would know all about that; right? contended Franz.

Disquiet was only one of the reasons Hannah didn't answer that question. Krieger had called so many times before, with news he had seen Nicky near Gramercy, and then proceeded with a perfect description of her father, an older Nicholas to be sure, hair thinned over the scalp, flesh collected under the chin, but Nicholas still. Hannah had, as ever, a difficult time separating one Krieger from another.

"After all, you and he were lovers, weren't you?" Franz went on, pulling the cottonballs from the shallow dishes of his eyes.

Hannah lied, "No."

"Of course you were, and you know how I know?"

"You don't, though."

"Hannah. Know how I know?"

She tapped the heel of her boot against the floor.

"Because he told me you weren't and he is terrible at lying."

"Krieger's one of the best liars I've ever met."

"You're wrong. An obfuscater, an operator, maybe, but whenever he lied you could see it, it'd come over him like a panic. But who wants to talk about it?"

"That profile in there, in the library? That's him, isn't it."

"What profile?" Franz frowned, pushed himself up on his elbows, squinted at her. "No, that one? no, that's somebody else."

"You're a pretty bad liar yourself."

"It's part of my rehabilitation. Lying poorly, like a bad rug."

How was she supposed to take that? she wondered; but Franz anticipated the response, since he'd at least in part set it up.

"Everybody changes at some point, don't they?"

Well, that was true enough. "Not for the better, not always, but you were already—"

"Changing? back in the Krieger days?"

"That wasn't what I was going to say."

"Well, I was. I've been out of all that shit-kicking for years. Who needs it."

"Hey, just out of curiosity, what was it you were into?"

"Just out of curiosity never mind, main thing is—and you know what, you can thank yourself some, you were partly responsible, the combination of getting rolled that night, and your accident down in wherever it was, down South . . ."

"What do you mean, rolled?"

"Krieger didn't tell you?"

"Tell me what?"

"*I Am Curious,* you remember—well, they released the blue version and I went to that same theater to see it, I fell asleep again. Little plastic surgery later here I am. You got a man?"

"No."

"Everybody needs a man."

"What for?"

"I believe that's obvious."

"Right—to destroy things."

Franz got up, dressed in a swimming suit under a djellaba. It was one of those hot days when the air retreated to another place and what wind there was lolled about like a kind of skeleton, without body or breath. He pushed the gate aside and Hannah followed him through the pavilion and out onto a sandspit under a dome of glass. A long, very narrow swimming pool glittered underneath. Wrynn stripped and slid into the calm green. Hannah watched him, his long back and thin thighs, and the splashes of white he made on passing through the water. The float rocked, then coasted, when he climbed on it out at the far end of the pool. His wrists bobbed along the surface as beads drifted over his chest and face.

"Come on in why don't you?"

"Oh, no, thanks Franz."

"Hell, come on."

"I don't feel like getting wet."

He readjusted himself on the float. "Here's the reason you have no man."

"Very funny, card," she smiled.

"What did you want to see me for anyway?" having drifted to the side. The water was like honey under the tinted dome, and it ran from both corners of his mouth.

Hannah thought, Interiors—she'd come to the right place.

The person on the other end had sounded marvelously relieved when to his question "Is this Hannah Burden?" she'd said, "Yes." It was her uncle's attorney, whose voice croaked like rubber stubbed against warm asphalt, "I was beginning to think I'd never find you."

She hadn't had the chance to ask him how he had in fact found her, not that it mattered, since she had lived in the same apartment since she got to town, for when he told her that the redoubtable, detested uncle LeRoy was dead she could hardly catch her breath.

(Wrynn listened quietly as water slapped the raft's edge while Hannah's memory of the conversation evolved.)

"In what event, what?" Hannah had asked the lawyer. "You're going to have to slow down."

(This was when? Wrynn interrupted—Just before I called you, she answered, and went on.)

"In, the, event," but now it appeared the lawyer was going to read too slowly. "In the event the beneficiary named herein shall, directly or indirectly, you with me Hannah Burden?"

"Directly or indirectly."

"Under any pretense or for any cause or reason whatever, oppose the probate of my last will, or institute."

"Excuse me?"

"Yes," exacerbatedly.

"Probate means oppose the validity of the will?"

"Probate's the process of establishing, officially, that the will is valid, yes. That's, yes, now if I may, can I go on? Institute, abet, take or share, directly or indirectly, in any action or proceeding against my estate to impeach, impair"—

Hannah thinking: peaches, pears . . .

—"set aside or invalidate any of the provisions of my last will, I do hereby revoke any and all devices, bequests, trusts, or other provisions to or for the benefit of my niece Hannah Burden, is that much understood, then?" and the lawyer excused himself to fetch a glass of water. As desk, papers, telephone were left behind the beneficiary imagined this country lawyer's office; humming ceiling fan, its birch blades paddling; bookcases glass-fronted to jurisprudential sets all brown, black, red-rowed behind; the filing cabinets, photographs of his family.

I, LeRoy Mann, of the city of Babylon, county of Webster, state of Nebraska, being of sound and disposing mind and memory, not acting under duress, menace, fraud, or undue influence of any person whatever, do make, publish, and declare this my last will and testament, revoking all previous wills and codicils. Whereas I am a widower and formerly married to Berenice Davis Mann who died on 8th July 1954, and whereas I have no children living or dead, I hereby give and bequeath all of my possessions, properties, stocks, monies and holdings to my beloved niece Hannah Burden, of New York, New York, provided she survives me, moreover provided she satisfies the conditions set forth herebelow.

"Hello? sorry. Better, now where were we?"

"The conditions," said Hannah.

"Yes, well, we were getting there, perhaps we'll simply move on ahead to that portion of the will, since it's that upon which all this seems to hinge in any case, right? *Hereby authorized to execute in such manner*, no wait a bit, let's see, yes here we go: *Furthermore, it is understood that the conditions precedent to my loving niece's taking possession and becoming sole owner and proprietor of the generous gift of my entire estate are as follows, that (one) she shall neither sell nor give away any of my personal chattels, nor purchase any other such chattels, and that she live just as I have lived, with precisely these objects I have passed my own life comfortably enough surrounded by, and that thereby she might come to understand, appreciate, cherish . . . skipping ahead here, uh . . . .*"

"I don't understand."

The lawyer excused himself, took another call; a bluejay scolded from the maple outside his window, and Hannah listened to it dazed. A click and the lawyer was back on the line.

"The significance of these conditions we might traverse briefly, then, at this time since I'll be sending you a copy of the full document, and since it was found, was deemed appropriate that all these conditions be met with the purest fidelity and that in their, their intricacy be fully understood by you before you begin to benefit in any way from these considerable resources."

"Spell out what you mean by appropriate, fidelity, considerable and—" embarrassed, in a way, to interrupt, yet it was as if the tardy, deliberate cadences of the lawyer acted as a vise, compressive as her father Nicky's summer migraines must have been (she remembered them, the packs of ice mama Opal applied to his temples, how the man ground his teeth and shouted, the front of his shirt soaking with melted ice).

"Goddamn it all if your uncle didn't have some reason behind these here precautions he took with you," veering, as Hannah understood, from the script. "If you would listen, stop gloating and just—"

"I resent that," she said.

"To be brief."

"Please, fine."

"The farm, the land, stocks, monies, all holdings are given to you under the requirement that, in order for you in your own lifetime come through labor and fitting circumstances to understand first and eventually to appreciate the man your uncle was, you take as your own responsibility the maintenance of the farm. Your beloved uncle kept half a dozen head of Guernseys, two dozen poultry, kept his own silage and provender for them, in essence ran his farm by himself and in his last years without any assistance whatever, certainly without the help any number of people might naturally expect of their only surviving kin, the last of his kin left on earth who, rather than following the most common of familial strictures, to respect and keep, chose instead to abandon this poor man to his own devices—"

"Wealthiest son of a bitch, I mean *the* wealthiest in that whole county . . . poor man, sick bastard, he wrote all that crap, didn't he."

"Hannah Burden?"

"He could've hired the whole town of Babylon, Blue Hill and Red Cloud thrown in, to come out every damn day and feed his poor hens one grain of scratch at a time, by hand."

"Hannah Burden, I'd like to finish. You certainly have available to you the option of refusing to abide by the conditions, as I read to you before. You would thus forfeit any benefit under the provisions of the will, the estate will be liquidated and all the proceeds thereof will immediately be transferred into a trust for a certain charity Mr. Mann has named, and it would further be provided that you receive the sum of one dollar a day for as long as you live, one dollar issued, under the direction of this codicil, where is it, yes, right here this codicil, one dollar each day as long as she shall live to be issued from these offices by check, and posted to your current place of residence. But this is skipping ahead, just to finish the conditionary items."

"Go on." A deadweighted sinking sensation.

"That you must, further to come to a closer appreciation of your beloved uncle, eat your food from his plates, using only his utensils, sleep in his bed, in those selfsame linens he slept in, sit only in his chairs, cook all your meals on his stove, tell the time by his several clocks—this itemized chapter of the will continues for, let me see, well, roughly sixty-five, seventy pages, which I will be posting you, as I said, so there is no reason to read it all here, it would take several hours, maybe more, long-distance . . . but I believe you have a sense of what the what? the spirit of the will is, at least in these directives?"

After a few moments Hannah's voice crackled: "But he was clearly, absolutely insane. There's no question. I mean, you can see that, surely?"

"It's not my place to agree with you on that."

" 'Being of sound mind,' it's a joke, any judge in the country, I'll move to have it overturned."

"That would be very difficult to do, very difficult. I've seen this kind of thing before. Frankly, it's more common than you'd think. I had a client years ago left his house, two cars, a sizable life insurance policy, left it all to his pet bulldog. As disgusting an animal as I ever saw. Beautiful new wall-to-wall carpet in this house and saliva trails everywhere. Ruined, just ruined. The family of the deceased spent two years litigating. Ran it all the way up to the state supreme court, but nothing doing. As trustee I had to assign a curator to the dog, somebody who would watch out for ground glass in the dog chow."

"This is ridiculous."

"Courts and judges these days have adopted a very liberal approach in assessing competency or capacity. Until proven otherwise, a testator is presumed competent to make a will. Originally, he, your uncle, had made out a holographic will, just written it out himself and signed it, brought it in for me to file, but when I told him it wasn't worth the paper— that is, holographic wills are authorized for mariners at sea, for members of the armed forces serving in combat, that sort of thing, he called me out, said he wanted to do the thing up right, in accordance with all the formalities prescribed by law. I can agree with you there are . . . elements to it—"

"Venomous—"

"It's none of my business, that is, whatever problems there were between, but to get back to your notion about turning it over it's my opinion, if you'll pardon my French, this here thing's solid as a brick shithouse."

"That is exactly what it is," said Hannah.

"That determination you can come to at a later date, after you have read it through carefully and discussed it with your own attorney."

"I don't have an attorney."

"I advise you to get one."

After she hung up she had called Franz, with whom she hadn't talked for years, and asked him whether she could see him immediately. Pulling the door behind her, its heavy mass closing temporarily in the frame, she prowled through the hot streets for a time feeling at once victimized by the past and the future. She hailed a cab, and gave the address of Franz's new penthouse on the Upper East Side.

He paddled with short strokes to the side of the pool, careful not to get his face wet, and rolled with studied delicacy onto the Mexican tiles which lined its perimeter. He walked past her, fastening the tie on a fresh terry-cloth skirt, without betraying his thoughts about what he had just heard. Hannah followed him through several rooms, each of which faced out over the park covered in heavy leafage and reservoir which lay like a blinding mirror within its banks, until they had come to his study. Here was the ballerina figurine and there the piggy bank, arranged to face one another on the low glass table. As she took in the room she recognized it was laid out in the same manner, with the same furniture, curtains, rugs, as had been the apartment where she first met him. He opened a low walnut door, concealed in the paneling along the wall, and ducked into the dark for a moment. When he emerged he had a bottle in one hand and two crystal glasses in the other.

"What's this?" she said.

"To celebrate."

"But you didn't understand. I'm not going back there. I have to turn the thing down."

Franz shook his head, grinned, drew the cork from the gold foil. "You know how you told me about that Vache, what was it, you had once and how I mentioned it was better for an animal to die of disease than be force-fed cement for three weeks before it was shipped off to slaughter? well, it so happened I checked with the stud ranch I have a little bit of interest in over in northwest Jersey and found out I owned a small herd of cattle, can you believe? So I told them, honey forget the chemicals, forget the cement, leave the girls in the pasture with salt lick and straw, or whatever the hell it is they eat, let them die of óld age, and all that gets me to thinking about your problem with this will, and I start wondering, now what are chattels? Aren't they things that can be moved, i.e., like through a loophole? For instance, can cattle be chattels?"

Hannah smiled.

"You with me?"

"I am."

He lifted his glass. "To the whore with a heart, Our Lady Francis of the sacred cattle."

And she came over and embraced him.

4.

WHEN Madeleine Work and her husband, Henry, first arrived in New York they came with bundles as tatty and tied-together as those seen in so many photographs of immigrants at Ellis Island who stood there in the great hall filled with a billowing echo of languages, enmeshed, one woven through the fabric of the next. And they may be said to have felt as alien and disquieted. Each had been here before, though rather than ease their passage, earlier exposure to the vertical city produced in them more dread than hope. The man named Ingram—and neither was certain this was his surname or given—met them so briefly at the train station, was all an endless ravishment of talk as he helped them gather their baggage on the ramp. Madeleine, who was always the one instantly to form an opinion, later told Henry there was something queer about that Ingram, something slippery. But of course Henry, while he was predisposed to trusting his wife's intuition, as it was more often than not proved right, argued against bad thoughts, for it was Ingram who had made all the arrangements so they could finally escape the South, the camp, the shack.

"I've got a letter here from your brother, by the way," said Krieger as he lifted a bundle of what was presumably clothes, tied into a quilt and bound with scarves and rope, into the back of a cab. It went through Krieger's mind, what kind of motherfugger could Owen Berkeley be to allow his daughter to continue this way? the man Henry Work he sized up as decent, one who would feud with nobody—he'd claim he was constitutionally incapable of arguing with a woman (a matter of body, the disposition of its fluids and spices, no doubt)—as his eye lit on the big brass safety pins that gathered the straps of his overalls. This guy was a string saver, collector of buttons, magazines, marbles, and he could fix radios, appliances, car engines with eyes closed. Brittle old pipe tobacco could be made damp and aromatic as fresh-mixed by sealing it inside a pouch together with a wedge of green apple. A cardinal struck by a car found dying on the shoulder of the road in some high grass, etcetera, out there by some wild sumac, say, he would know to anesthetize it by a bead of gin touched to its beak at the tip of his little finger then drown it in a puddle of rainwater and bury it in a bank of dirt, even leave a stone to mark its place. Call him Abraham just see what kind of rise there is to be gotten.

"Abr'ham? your old lady hard of hearing?"

"Maddie, did you hear what Mr. Ingram here says?"

"I heard."

"Well, take the letter."

Krieger handed her the blue envelope. "I just saw him last week down in Guatemala, he's doing some fine work there, fine work, you all must be very proud of Jonathan, right Abr'ham."

"My husband's name is Henry."

"He pretty near stopped a polio epidemic or something all on his own in one of the northern departments down there, it's made him into kind of a local folk hero."

"Maddie, aren't you going to open it?" Henry went on, having loaded the last of their baggage into the front seat of the cab.

"Actually, as I think it may pertain to some work I'm currently involved with and I don't have much time, etcetera, I really would appreciate it if you have a look at it, let me know if Jonathan wants me to do anything for him before I go back down, hey—who's your favorite boxer like, Clay? Joe? Rock?"

Madeleine opened the letter and read it, trying to imagine what Jonathan looked like now, thinking of him the last time she saw him in that barber shop when he was thirteen, up at Berkeley house on the Hudson.

Dearest Maddie, how does a person start a letter like this after so many years apart? First off, I love you, sister, and of course I miss you, and also it's important to let you know right away that (how silly this will come off sounding) I stand with you, I support what you've done and Look—look at how you were right from the very beginning, Look at how long it's lasted (that doesn't sound flippant or prejudiced I hope). Well, it's my hope that someday soon you'll let me see you and Henry again. I don't blame you for taking the decision to make the cut a total one. But whenever you decide to start making exceptions—remember I'm still the same devoted boy you left that afternoon at Schiavellos, right?

By the way, Mr. Ingram, whose idea it was to get you two set up in this new place—he hasn't fully described it to me but it sounds great—is a good man, someone to trust. He's doing this partly as a favor to me and partly, I guess, as a favor to an old friend of his. Be nice to him, for my sake? If he needs any help or anything, well there it is.

I think you would be proud of me and the work I am doing down here with these poor people. I know it sounds bleeding Liberal, but what else is there to do but try to put back in some of the endless, vast masses of things we have taken out of here—food right out of these people's mouths, timber off their forests so they can make grazing land for fast-food hamburger-chain cattle, all the rest of it, it's all genocide of the first order. If only you could see what we have done. I'm ashamed to be American.

Maddie, when do we all meet? Ingram swears he will not say how he found you and where exactly you're going, and I respect that in him. I gather, for his work he needs to be in touch with Owen. And, as you, I'll have nothing to do with that if I can help it, though he claims it is all in a good cause.

But I've run out of paper and this lamp's fluttering, must be low on kerosene oil. I send you hugs and kisses and regards to Henry, and still hope that one of these days maybe soon you'll relent so we can all be together again?

Love,
Jonathan.

"Anything in there for me?" Krieger asked, pleasantly, if a bit oversure of his forger's skill.

Madeleine was distracted by something she could not quite place her finger on; the handwriting seemed so different, its rounded letters almost like a child's. But then, she thought, Jonathan was always the baby in the family. "No, not really," she answered.

"I understand this is touchy? but, as it turns out I have some business to transact with your father and I left his address back in Toncontín of all places on earth. Jonathan gave me the address, I'm going to have to telephone him, won't be able to see him this time through."

"Jonathan's explained to you that—"

"I know all about it, no, not a word from me, not in my best interests in any case, Jonathan had mentioned you a few weeks ago and well, turns out our paths crossed just right, etcetera and thus there you have it. Don't worry about it, I'll get the address from another friend, but meantime here this is Hannah Burden's. I would love to talk, Jonathan is such a fine field man down there, you all ought to be proud of him, and good luck," Krieger had turned away, taking several deliberately tardy steps, and was rewarded for his patience when Henry caught up with him to name the river town where Mr. Berkeley could be found. "I'm obliged," he said, softening his gratitude with as thick a Cajun accent as he could muster.

Hannah Burden, who had never known a man named Ingram, understood Franz Wrynn's having had a role in this generous gathering, and when Maddie described features pale as someone who had emerged from months in a ship's hold, the slender nose, corn-colored hair, khaki suit wrinkled and the perfectly knotted red silk tie, she knew that—like a chilly puff of air blown off the hearth in the middle of summer, maybe carrying a feather from the one dead hatchling in the chimney nest—Krieger had just brushed past.

That evening she showed them what the cartons in the loft contained, and began the long story, how they had come to stand there in these large dark rooms. Later, after Hannah had retired, Maddie asked Henry was he happy. And Henry, standing outside the ruckled siding of the shack in which Hannah lived, said he was.

Matteo Lupi stood there now, in the same place. He knew so little. Time to visit the *viejo*. The cigarette the man Hammond had given him, with a shrug and a grunt following, burned at his lips and in his lungs. He tossed it away, aware how awkward the gesture would have looked on the big screen, fingers flung open and the palm turned up. That wasn't the way you did it. You filliped it, palm down, from the middle finger, with a subtle flick of the wrist, and kept the fingers close and tight, if you wanted to do it properly. No, he knew so little.

He would resolve, then, to observe quietly. Absolutely. *Res ipsa loquitur,* whereby in law as in the mercenary jungle, the thing must speak for itself, came to mind. It came in the form of his father's subtle courtroom voice, for it was one of his father's favorite legal Latinisms.

His father—even here, today, Friday, the memory of his voice payed out a wave of sickness over him. Not dread or fear, for his father made it a habit never to punish him physically whenever as a boy he had done something wrong; but a kind of sickening, sinking disgust just at the tone of that voice, its perfect diction, the smugness it betrayed as it moved—repetitious and in its own good time—to its point. It was unshakable. But what matter? Gabriele Lupi (Gabriele not in honor of the annunciating angel but the poet D'Annunzio, an acquaintance of his grandfather, who was likewise Pescara-born) was gone. *Mal di fegato,* Lupi mused. A rotten liver, all that sherry, and two lungs black from chain-puffed cigarettes. And in his courtroom periwig and robe he had seemed unassailable.

Lupi grinned and his eyes were reflected, distorted, in the mirror. Behind, he could see Olid. Later he would ask Hannah where the bath was. It would be good to wash the old man. It would be good for that matter to wash himself, and his eyes flashed back into his own image. Heavy lids and long, benign lashes contributed further to this appearance of sleeplessness. His eyes were such a deep brown their pupils almost vanished, the contrast of raisins to pumpernickel in a dense loaf. How could he still be hungry after Hannah had just fed him? He ran his finger over the fine thin bridge that trailed off his forehead and extended down into an aristocratic nose. The straight edge was interrupted by a bump, put there by the well-aimed blow of a French billyclub in spring 1968. High cheekbones were pronounced—Olid, in this, was an ancient ancestor—where they rested under rough skin kept always in restless activity by muscles strung beneath. His lips, nervous, delicate, were the most obvious legacy of his father—conveyers by their very form and manner of a sense of urgency. They now moved.

He said to himself, "Okay, great."

Things weren't so great. He ought to get busy. This dead time was the worst kind of torture. It couldn't hurt to help with the animals downstairs. That would put him more at ease. Also, it might make Hannah see he was, as she, more of a country child lost in the city circuits, and relatively—no, more than relatively: clearly, absolutely, utterly—in over his head. No, he wasn't in over his head. There was the old man to take care of. There might be something to be learned from the experience. He was in America, after all. He'd hated it from the outside for so long, perhaps he'd best examine the matter more closely now that he happened to be on the inside. He would offer to milk a cow. He left Olid and made his way back into the front room of the bunkhouse to find Hannah.

The television was turned on again, and the man Henry sat in front of it bathed in malevolent color.

"Doncha get into that hamburger rut,
Tendermoist' ll liven up most any cut,
Pork, veal, beaver, beef bourguignon?
Tendermoist' ll give those blahs a whole new tone—"

Lupi regarded the screen, where a slab of meat (a bit blue) was being smothered under a tide of a viscous brown substance. A knife speared this piece of meat once, twice, two clean angles, a fork deftly found the heart of the portion, the questioning face of a man good-humoredly skeptical over the flesh he was invited by his wife to partake of, then came the bite, a fine manly chomp, the consequent satisfaction, beaming as he chews, beaming as he lifts a stout squarish bottle and kisses the proffered cheek of the wife . . . but, wondered Lupi, had he really heard the word beaver?

He was wary of Henry, who'd been studying him all the while, and suddenly realized he couldn't offer to help with the cows because he had never milked one before, had never so much as looked one in the eye. And he certainly had not studied that oddity, the udder, which they carried along with them between their back legs. So much for the country child.

"Hello," he said.

Henry watched him, his face betraying a kindly curiosity.

"You know you shouldn't sit so close to that box. Causes cancer. Cancer in the eyes?" gesturing, thinking maybe the Negro couldn't get a grip on what he was saying because of his accent?

Henry stood to face him.

"I," Lupi decided not to pursue it (reconsidering, now thinking, He ought to pick me up—and don't think he couldn't—and throw me off the roof) and retreated to the smaller room, confused by the demeanor of Henry's face as he had begun to leave although he might have lingered, might have felt gratified or certainly less perturbed to see that Henry moved his chair back away from the screen.

Olid was awake, humming the song they'd sung, the women, back in that valley, a few days ago. When he saw Lupi he sang a couple more notes and stopped. Lupi sat at the end of the bed, wishing he were tired enough to sleep, or more exactly that he wasn't so tired that he'd become too tired to sleep. Don't stop singing. It's nice, that song, it's like an aria, pagan aria, he told the old man, in Latin. What is it? the song.

"Sardavaal," complained the other.

"Yeah, yeah, I know, I know."

* * *

They had begun to view things differently from an early date. By the time Matteo celebrated his twentieth birthday each had agreed never to speak to the other again. Yet Matteo had—despite all effort to the contrary— learned certain lessons well from his lawyer father. The laws held within the chambers of civil men were, he discovered, eminently applicable out in the "jungle." His father moved easily in the small upper echelon of Florentine society (a parochial crowd, the boy always sensed)—Matteo couldn't recall a time when dinner wasn't served by a butler with white gloves. From adolescence, however, it became clear that son would apply those lessons learned by the example father set, those insights into law, government, human nature, to the destruction, point by point and brick by brick (or so he thought), of just that society which engendered and championed them to its own benefit and fixed continuance (to use the law's language, and he knew it by rote).

Lupi became a fledgling radical, disgusted by the politics (—*siete soltanto piccolo borghesi,* of the petite bourgeoisie) of his family. He chose to display his newfound political conscience in a particularly dramatic manner. The American consul from Turin was passing the night at the Lupi villa on his way to Rome for a meeting with the ambassador. A strapping Texan, boisterous, graying, loose-cheeked heir of an oil fortune and armadillo farms, a neighbor of the architect of the Great Society (whence his sinecure), chinless and with a runt wife, was seated at Gabriele Battista's right addressing himself to a plate of gnocchi while talking amiably with assembled local dignitaries. The discussion at the head of the table was about prospects of effecting a quick end to the war by detonating a hydrogen bomb over the center of Hanoi. This was a theme popular with the rustic consul, and his wife strained to follow, although the conversation was in English, since neither she nor the consul had as yet managed to learn Italian.

In walked Matteo, aged fifteen. He heaved half a bucket of pig's blood over the Texan, dropped the tin pail and raced out of the room before anyone seated at the long, candlelit table had recovered enough sense to scream. The *carabinieri* searched three nights and two days before cornering him up in the dank nave of the San Alessandro above the public gardens in Fiesole. Tired, hungry, but mutely defiant, he was taken home. A request was passed down to the editors of local newspapers; thus the disruption at the Lupi's dinner never surfaced. The farmer who leased several acres from the Lupis, to keep chickens and other small livestock, was quietly paid triple its value for the pig whose throat the boy had slit. Having delivered

Matteo into his father's custody, the police assumed matters would cease there.

At the Liceo Scientifico his presence had become burdensome to his professors—the notable exception was his philosophy teacher, in thick tinted glasses, who loaned Matteo Mao's red book and urged him to make a closer reading of *Il Principe*. He did reread Machiavelli, though all of it was forgotten now, and organized Le Volpi, a dissident underground society which would empty more clotted maroon-brown blood into file cabinets and on porches of churches and offices. Matteo had graduated, precipitous, from family and classmates whose response to social injustices, to issues from imperialism to apartheid, was anything less than rigorous and committed and, if it came down to it, violent opposition. He learned how to fashion Molotov cocktails, and owned a doctor's bag of stiff black leather in which he could discreetly transport them. By the time he turned nineteen he could make a pipe bomb eyes closed—it was, after all, he told himself, much easier than memorizing the names of all of Dante's damned in hell.

Time passed, allegiances fluctuated. Friends who had stood with him on the lines, arms locked as they marched, friends who had taken tear gas together and made serious bonds of conscience, who had become friends out there in the street, pitted against antiriot police, seemed to disappear, a few at first, and then nearly all of them. Le Volpi disbanded and its founder became vagabond. He worked in a bookshop in Milan, reading novels in its ill-lit, cavernous interior. He lasted as a clerk in a Parisian tabac for the better part of an afternoon before being fired. A job waiting tables at a tourist bar in Rome with a view of the Vittorio Emanuele, which resembled, he pointed out to his customers, a massive, hideous wedding cake, lasted for some months before he quit in disgust. There was nowhere for him to go but back underground. The attraction was slight but was nevertheless more potent than any other. Nothing else seemed to interest him. He made a telephone call and was soon enough on a train, plagued only by the polar distance he felt between his own errant apathy and the fervor and bright anger he detected in the voice of that old acquaintance he had reached in Siena. The tour which followed through underground flophouse laboratories and slum arsenals in the cities up and down Italy became analogous to the way in which his mind had begun to function. What had begun in ideology metamorphosed into a simple job, earning him enough to keep moving from apartment to apartment, city to city. The girlfriends (each of whom attenuated before the image of Nini) had begun to get married, or get jobs, move away. He had to keep working simply to stay alive in the underground. The looseness of his associations gave rise to two unhappy developments. First, among the tiny networks of the truly committed he began to make fast enemies for his own lack of a stable politic. Second—and it was this, like a disease that worsened day by day until it had spread and assumed predominance—because Lupi was now resigned to a life on the move, and one in which his identity must be a chameleon's, he found he was obliged to take whatever jobs came his way no matter what they were or who was behind them. He moved through depression from morning to morning.

Rarely did he chauffeur kidnap victims. Usually he would tap telephones, steal documents or destroy them, place anonymous calls (a threat, a demand, a declaration) or shadow people: photograph them, tape them. He would manufacture bombs and timers if he had to. He was considered by those who knew of him quite expendable in the service of whatever presently required his expertise.

Cara Nini, he would write from Venice, in hiding: My sweetest girl, what I do now, how I have got from those days of you and me together to these days, I just cannot say, I cannot piece it together for myself in reverse so improbable even impossible a road it has been. It's all twisted, and I too, I sense I am all twisted. I miss you. Do you understand that? I'm not happy. I'd rather not miss you. You see, I know that you think badly of me, you simply have to. But don't think that I have changed so much from the man you remember because I haven't, except that the foundation maybe of beliefs on which I built this life seems to be something weaker than originally I thought it had been. I would come anywhere you want, wherever you told me to meet you, to talk, even for an hour in a restaurant for lunch, not that I would know what to say. Once something is started it seems it never stops. If you've gotten married I wouldn't want to get in your way. Just to talk. We can't get back to where we began, but there is always some way to move forward. Isn't that so? Whether your parents will forward this to you I don't know, wherever you are now, I hope they will, but wherever you are and whomever you are with I send you my love and all my hopes.

Christmas 1974 had him at the wheel of a stolen Peugeot, racing across the bleak, snow-dusted hills near Siena, the bound and gagged body of the retired ambassador to Cyprus bouncing heavily in the trunk. Dottore Milo need not have remained tied up and the scarf gag served no effective purpose, as the man had been dead for several hours already.

It was early afternoon. Lupi had been driving all night. Important things happen in cars, he thought—people are made, people born, people die. The kidnapping (important, considering their prey) had taken place in Calabria, and the former ambassador was to be delivered to an address in Bologna. Lupi had no thoughts regarding what it was Le Brigate Rosse, perpetrators of the crime, intended to do with poor Milo, whether he would be put up for ransom, tortured (teeth were sometimes pulled, an ear removed, vintage bayonets run up anuses), made to confess secrets against the state in a kangaroo trial, or be butchered and left at the end of a blind alley with a note—*Tutto il potere al popolo armato, niente resterà impunito!* All will be punished, no stone shall remain unturned, all power to the people, the power which will reside only with those people who arm themselves for the struggle—pinned to the chest. He couldn't think about it. His contact with the man had been confined to an unhappy registration of dull, muffled thuddings six or seven feet behind his head as the automobile tore around an icy curve.

When the car was first placed in his custody, he was given a map marking the route he was supposed to take up the peninsula, but Lupi, after following its directions through the provinces of Campania and Lazio, had decided around midnight to bear ahead through Tuscany rather than veer east into Umbria as he was instructed. It was not that he mistrusted the contact man from whom he had received the map and keys to the car (who could as easily have delivered a copy of the map into the hands of the police and obtained the objective of shocking a certain segment of the Italian government—Lupi tried always to understand his personal expendability in these matters), but the roads through Tuscany would save time.

Dilapidated trellises, rusty wires attached to rows of poles, litter the winter-fallow fields, running in loose parallels over the white asymmetric land. Vineyards; frayed traces of blue smoke out over the sparse chill. A magpie, maimed possibly, limps ahead on the shoulder. Up ahead a sluggish bus halts to deposit a woman with chartreuse boots in a town that immediately falls astride the car and as quickly becomes a rectangular fragment reflected in the mirror. A crow whips, dives through the frost out before the hood, lifting on its wide wings just in time not to be blown into an explosion of tattered feathers. And he thinks, Crows may eat magpies.

Lupi imagines he can hear Milo coughing, or is it laughing? It occurs to him that no one would be the wiser if he stopped and offered his captive something to eat, or drink. It must be very cold back there, he thinks. It is, after all, Christmas morning.

He comes up with the idea of dropping in on his parents. He has not contacted them for four years. By driving through Tuscany, and on through Florence to Bologna, rather than following the Adriatic coast as the map proposed, he would have a few extra hours. He has no idea why he would want to pursue this idea, nor is he sure his parents will even allow him in their house. He's not sure of much of anything, is he? Not sure whether his grandmothers are alive. Whether the family is together for the holiday. What has become of his younger sister. Perhaps he might find out about Nini, whether she ever married Claudio, and if not, where she is and if she completed her degree in medicine, where is she practicing, is she a mother, is she happy, would she ever be willing to think of him in a special way again?

He believes that he could turn himself in, present Milo to the authorities. Only in the precincts of Florence could he hope to do this and emerge, through the influence of his father, with a moderate, even commuted sentence. He has years of information to trade on. Too, he's tired, all the time tired, more tired than when he had mononucleosis after leaving school and home the first time.

The road is quiet. Christmas and the dead chill have banished all traffic. Holm oaks, towering naked chestnuts, and firs zip by. Arranged in columns to rove over rounded bluffs are tidily pruned olive trees. Familiar landscape, to make him feel warm inside. The town of Greve, its river clotted along the banks with black ice; l'Ugolino, in the undulant hills lined with cypress; Grássina; Ponte a Ema; Badia. The snow is beginning to pick up as the Peugeot crosses the Arno. There are more people walking in the streets of Florence—dressed-up, strolling under the fine pellets of hard sleet—than he might have expected. Not that he would be recognized by anyone (this bothers him, he has to admit, a little).

It is as if the decision is being made for him, as if the hands at the wheel inform the car by instinct to follow the Arno past the Ponte alle Grazie and San Nicolò, by the spectral high-rise apartment buildings huddled like a dozy mirage around the Campo di Marte, and up the hill toward home. The Peugeot comes to rest alongside a stone wall covered in denuded branches of vines and rosemary bushes that topple like tumbleweeds over its edge. Lupi's fingers locate the key, turn it, and at once the enveloping whine of the engine, his constant companion these past hours fallen into the night, dispersed on the kilometers of road behind him and his helpless companion in the trunk, coughs into a muteness. He sits for a moment. Twenty feet ahead, up to the right, gates open to the gravel drive. The snowfall accompanied by a frozen sleet is crystalline and makes a series of multiple pitched taps—pings—on the roof of the car. He pushes against the door and climbs out into another world, and his exhaustion, a hazy confusion unto nervous delirium, folds in over him. The door snaps shut, configuration of thin steel colliding. An indistinct recollection of his own extinct childhood, his youth, is conveyed by the simple smell of this snow that wavers through the familiar air. Florence burns like so many cats' eyes below. It comes as a pleasurable shock to the homecomer, all this tranquillity. Lupi traces the city line from the campanile of Giotto and Brunelleschi's dome up over roofs, hills, faint rises, whitened treetops as he leans against the side of the car before gathering his senses.

Head thrown back, mouth agape, he drinks in bitter little flakes that smack on his tongue. What was it he had done here as a boy, beside the granite wall with its irregular rows of cleats pointed like so many square fingers at the sky? Merely thrown snowballs at passing buses which wound their way laboriously up past the Medici villa to Fiesole's square? Had he hidden in the thick hedges across the road, face and hands blue and his lips eelish, eyes withdrawn and terrified blebs caught in the flashlight beam before he was commanded to come forth by . . . by who had it been? his father? the family's manservant? What had he done then that required he hide himself in the juniper hedges in the middle of winter, terrified but openly defiant? It was a memory summoned by a perfect scent of sleety rain over the hard grass (dead grass) and in the foliage.

He opens his eyes, walks around to the trunk of the car. He has decided he will release his captive long enough for him to walk a hundred paces down the road and back. It was not stipulated, after all, that he had to act inhumanely toward Milo; he was entrusted to communicate the victim from one point to another: no more, no less. He opens the trunk and sees that he is still there, yes, motionless, silent, before he hears the deep grind of a camion rounding the fork in the road below. The trunk is slammed shut. He ducks down behind the Peugeot as the camion, its open bed filled with children, singing, shouting, lurches by. Lupi peers from his hiding place at this strange vision of the truck with its load of children, all bundled in coats and wrapped in scarves and shawls, bright smears of color against the bowing sky. He continues to watch until it winds around the bend of road and disappears up toward Fiesole.

The intrusion has made him apprehensive; he wonders, what does he possibly think he is doing?—

The police are looking for him throughout the central and southern regions of the country. By evening the newspapers and RAI will have christened him *Rapista di Natale,* the Christmas Kidnapper. Isn't it so tragic—each will mourn—such a horrid thing could happen during this holy week, this religious period, a time of pacific introspection and prayer, hardly a time of taped wrists, ugly demands. They will have taken telephone calls from extremist organizations as diverse as the neofascist Ordine Nero and the Sinistra Proletaria (on and on and on), and all will claim responsibility for the abduction, all will denounce the Christian Democrats as charlatan and Dr. Milo as the merest threadbare puppet—shelved but symbolic—in their stupid show.

The temptation grows to throw himself at the feet of his father, and to confess that he had been right—no, not right, but had made points which should have been better taken, listened to—and beg his forgiveness, hope that he as well would ask his son to, well, if not forgive actually, at least understand the stiffness that can come with habit, and then of course turn freezing Milo over (Milo out in the trunk, it was preposterous—this was the way to save people, save the country—), hope for immunity in exchange for names, locations, activities. It seems so plausible. The prospect wells inside him. He is, he rues, hungry.

He decides to leave Milo where he is. It would be too dangerous to let him out of the trunk. Someone might spot them, might identify them. He locks the car, shoves the key into his jacket pocket, walks up the twig-covered shoulder to the front gate. There is a brass placard, eaten green at its edges, beside the buzzer at the gate, beautifully incised with serif lettering; Andrea Gabriele Battista Lupi.

Turning up the drive, hands pushed low into his trouser pockets, the familiarity of the landscape deepens. Pace quickening, he walks up into the grove of pines where he would be enshrouded in evergreen branches and bushes heavy with berries as he approaches the house. Lights that shine in the windows of the villa spill out across the blue-white lawn. There are cars—heavy, new, expensive cars—parked before the front door, which is decorated with a sprig of holly tied with a red ribbon. Through the windows along the north corridor of the villa, behind wrought-iron grillwork and framed by shutters, Lupi can see a group of people seated around the dining-room table . . . and he begins to think, *Questo non va.* This is not going to work.

Christmas dinner is under way. A fire burns in the stone hearth. Bottles of champagne stand in ice buckets, white linen tied at their necks—things tied, he begins to imagine them, strangled, everything being choked, the holly, the champagne. He sees his mother grayer, heavier than he remembered her, more brightly dressed, perhaps to make up for it in some way—her gown, red as the berries in the holly sprig, backdrop to the shimmery bracelets that encircle her forearm. As she speaks she waves her arm and the bracelets tumble where she defines an extravagant S-curve, emphasizing a point. She engages a man seated at her left, diminutive, whose dark head seems outsize for the paltry shoulders beneath it. He follows the course of her animated talk with politeness. Lupi does not recognize him; most likely he is a barrister, a judge, or local administrator—he and the others, several with their backs to his shrub out in the forlorn world hung in sleet, are seated at their supper (his supper? no), beneath the chandelier (also not his, he is quick to tell himself).

The table is presided over by Gabriele Battista, face contorted in laughter. Not an atom in his body seems to have changed in the years that have intervened; he appears inexorable, ineradicable. All at once, as son observes the fork carry lamb into father's mouth, it becomes evident the shrewdest, most violent, most sophisticated and committed collective of radicals could never hope to arrogate from this man a single fleck of power. It would be possible to murder him, slay the whole smug group of them where they sit eating their magnificent Christmas dinner, burn the villa down. Nothing would be accomplished by it.

Lupi's face exhibits recognition. It is a mixture of the pain that has cropped up out of what he stares at through the window and reaction to the idea that has just dawned on him. One thing is evident: he cannot change the course he is on, cannot confess, cannot come home.

He slouches across an octagonal stone piazza, at the center of which stands a fountain with three granite dolphins, each capped with white, and enters the villa by the servants' porch. Voices imperative and rushed he hears in the kitchen. A pan clatters as it is placed on the burner. The maid, her Tuscan accent softening each "c" into tightly clinched shushes, is scolding someone (who?—has his father come so far, done so well, that there are submaids, underlings under the underlings? well, telling from the voices, yes, it's so, as she is scolding someone) for burning biscuits. He smells the scents of lamb roast, gravy from the drippings, cooked arugula, of vinegars and olive oil, warm and winy, which fill the hallway. He rubs his hands together unhappily, breathing into them, and glances around sees what he can see, which isn't much. The kitchen falls quiet. The maid's voice, that was it, the maid pecking down the pecking order on yet another housekeeper, or a cook, or whomever, stops. He makes up his mind what he is going to do. In three steps he is down the short hall, and reaches a door. He ascends by way of back stairs to the second floor, where, in his mother's dressing room, he proceeds to fill his pockets with brooches, earrings, bracelets, pendants, necklaces. Hidden behind an ornately framed daguerreotype photograph of his grandparents, whose cheeks are heightened in unlikely rose and flesh tones, is the wall safe. He tries his memory on the combination. Faintly, from downstairs, a wave of fresh laughter filters up. A clunk (heard through the burglar's bones, so soft was it) is registered; exhilaration, and the square metal door comes away. There is no alarm. Down the front of his shirt he stows hundreds of thousands, millions of lire, in paper bundles. A gold fob watch, lapis-studded gold cufflinks, rings, an antique cloisonné snuffbox which later would give up several unset diamonds. He takes everything that will fit in his pockets. On the wall is an eighteenth-century pencil study for an expulsion from Eden which the thief thinks too befitting the circumstances to leave behind. He breaks into the frame, removes the drawing, rolls it up, pushes it into a coat pocket. The bastards, he thinks.

Laden with the jewelry and money he shuffles back through the hallway and downstairs, breath fluted, lungs a burden. He is tempted to risk a foray into the kitchen, as he hasn't eaten since afternoon the day before, but a lull in the chatter from the distant dining room and an unexpected arpeggio from some ghostly *pianoforte,* perfectly tuned and suddenly accompanied by a strange, overly vibrato soprano voice, discourages him. Who possibly is singing? and what? A shiver runs through him as, disconcerted, he plunges out into the sinking afternoon.

The storm has let up again, the temperature has fallen. The engine must be turned over three times before it finally catches. He is halfway to Bologna before he remembers the man, sad Milo, his grim charge prostrate in the trunk. For the first time it occurs to him the man might have frozen to death; he will not, however, stop the car to look. He can't do it. Let someone else see what there is to see back there.

In a trattoria at the outskirts of Bologna, Matteo has a warm meal. Prosciutto, red peppers. Polenta, chicken; spinach in oil and with hard-boiled eggs. Coffee, and grappa. It is a good meal, and he feels well satisfied, sitting alone in the chair next to the window, facing out on passersby in the street bundled up in their winter coats, stepping quickly along their way no doubt to somewhere comfortable, their homes, the houses of friends or relatives.

He asks the waiter for his bill, pays, and goes out to join the others in the cold streets. As he opens the door to the car it strikes him that he might never see his mother or father again.

One thing: that boy, Claudio, the only other person who had touched Nini, Claudio had once called America the corpse of Europe. "The death of Europe in America," he had said. Okay, the death of Europe in America, fair enough, wise idea. Even dogs and stable cats and pet geese are known to find a place—some favorite haunt way out in a field, or in some secluded closet in the house—where they may die in solitude and in peace, with dignity, perhaps; many animals do. Why shouldn't an entire culture enjoy the same simple prerogative?

So, there was that. And, also, as he looked out across the street at a collection of five cylindrical chimneys each with conical caps which lent them the appearance of a Chinese family huddled up together, and beyond them, this family group in the melting pot, out at watertowers, eaves, setbacks, curtain walls, skeletons of buildings going up, skeletons of buildings toppling down, roofs, windows closed, opened, cracked, boarded, the infinitely intricate collage that was New York, he knew there was something else.

He knew that Hannah was dissembling on one matter still. While she had come around to telling him that this was the only one of its kind, this pasture, this ranch, and that by the weakness of the way things were she was weakened to the outside world by having it and keeping it (though strengthened in her inner world), he could envision hundreds just like it, thousands of others—not like anything movie could make, nor even anything he had thus far seen with his own eyes—and so he knew that they were there, hidden behind ruinous facades, each resigned to a certain secrecy, perhaps.

But there, there. Out there.

IV

Hung Storm

LeRoy

JULY 1955

BABYLON: a puzzle of buildings arranged around a central spine, a backbone laid out long on the flat, dry ground, which rises up two stories over the Nebraska prairieland. Men and women dwell within the hundred-odd houses that crowd like so much squared scree fallen from nowhere to rest around the main street as if defensive against a nameless threat that lurks out over the parched lip of the horizon. The people here work in small businesses in town, as tailor, grocer, tobacconist, barber, liquor salesman, cobbler, pharmacist, or hand to the farmers whose spreads extend in the outlying grassland. Babylon's two most unusual businesses (they are unusual, at least, for such a small town) are the movie theater and the slaughterhouse. Both are owned by the same man, Mr. Johnson, who is fond of saying he makes money on the one so he can lose it on the other. He is devoted to picture shows; they take him places he might never go otherwise—exotic huts of the South Pacific in which men like Johnson himself might touch virgin skin the color of seared butter; bordellos of Mexico City out whose balm-breeze-blown windows lean black-haired sinyereetas; boodwars in hot Paris; night alleys of New York. A businessman, Johnson knows the movie house is frivolity. It does not run in the black. There aren't enough quarters in the county Saturday afternoon to begin to pay off the film distributors. The paint on the marquee is faded, chipping; the screen wants retaping. It constantly sieves money. Johnson doesn't seem to mind. He feels he can afford it and it has had the not inconsiderable effect of making him both a prominent and popular citizen in town. He is an industrious, clean-shaven, pleasant individual with no remarkable aspirations beyond keeping both his enterprises running efficiently and being seen—personally—by his fellow townsmen as hale, substantial, trusted. This was, as he understood it, good business. The abattoir, owned and run by Johnsons for over a century, is the largest, most venerable firm around. His pioneer forefathers were aware of the power of good public relations and its connection with the profit-and-loss factor. This had come to them, as it had to him, by intuition, but as he was fond of saying, charity is not best learned from books or church, but side by side with other men doing the work they were put on the earth to do.

A set of railroad tracks had been laid at the turn of the century for the purpose of transporting cattle, hogs, and sheep to and from the yards of the Johnson slaughterhouse on the outskirts of town, and by turn to ship weighed head, butchered meat and by-products back out to the markets east as far as Beatrice. In the 1930s the tracks, owned by Chicago Burlington & Quincy, neither continued into town nor ventured farther west toward Harlan or Furnace, but dead-ended in the stock-crowded yards, and so never attracted the services of a passenger train from the county seat or capital until Bloomington, the next town over, developed the need for them.

Bloomington's mayor was a shrewd gentleman, whose eye was trained on the governorship of the state, and whose ambition even touched upon a seat in the Senate. His town needed the services of the Chicago Burlington & Quincy. Bloomington must be connected by rail to Hastings and to the rest of the country from there out. He appealed directly to the railroad, proposing that some matching costs of erecting a station could be undertaken by the town of Bloomington itself. Unknown to the men who advised him, Chicago Burlington & Quincy had already drawn up plans to pursue marking a route that more or less satisfied his designs, so they readily accepted his terms, and within some months began to lay track. Though Babylon was miles north, and off a direct course for this connection between Hastings and Bloomington, it was decided that money might be saved by using the prelaid tracks and continuing them across the golden azimuth (as the mayor nicely phrased it) into Franklin County.

This the majority of the townspeople of Babylon disfavored. Some threatened at a town council meeting to move their families away if such a thing took place. They believed a passenger train would cast open gates for strangers, like those they had seen at Johnson's picture shows—cutthroats, vagabonds, foreigners—to flow in from the outside world, bringing chaos and heartbreak. Even the freethinkers among them pointed to history, saying, Look what happened to the native Americans, the plains tribes, peaceably living off the land until the explorers came, and behind them the hordes of settlers—why allow this second wave? why risk it? Several farmers parked their trucks and tractors on the rails in protest, blocking for an afternoon the progress of a swing train with a full load of ties. The work went on, however.

While, as a good businessman, Mr. Johnson understood how the railroad could benefit him, he was the most outspoken against its construction. He liked Babylon the way it was. The underbelly of too much convenience is disaster, he proclaimed. He used all the civic power he could muster to stop this proposal from going forward. But the matter was out of his hands: Chicago Burlington & Quincy was not to be stopped. The tracks were continued past the stockyards, on through toward Bloomington, which awaited with excitement all those things that the many voices in Babylon decried.

In the end the Babylonian isolationists had overestimated how appealing their town would be to travelers looking for employment or a new place to put down roots. A few people moved in, but more left. Indeed, if any passengers happened to arrive in Babylon when the wind was gusting in from the Johnson yards they were only too anxious for the conductor's cry of *Allaboard*. As soon as young men and women came of age—some the children of the most vigorous who had fought against opening Babylon up to outside influence—they found the railroad by far the best way of escaping home and family. Chicago Burlington & Quincy contributed, in the end, not to the corruption of Babylon but rather to the slow shrinkage of its population.

Still, many of Babylon's citizens remained content, whether by design or fate, that almost without exception the only travelers come by train to town were poor dumb beasts, arriving there to be weighed and either shipped or slaughtered on the spot.

LeRoy Mann's sister, Opal, and her daughter, Hannah, were to arrive on the Chicago Burlington & Quincy on Saturday, midday.

LeRoy had never before seen his niece, and had not laid eyes on his sister for nearly a decade. Since the death of his wife a year earlier, he had sunk into reclusiveness broken only by the necessity of fetching supplies from town. To be left alone for days at a stretch was a wish easily come by where LeRoy lived. His farmstead was thirty miles from town out on the great yellow plains of wheat—vast enough that there were directions on the compass one could follow in a straight line and still not reach the rambling fences that marked the boundaries by sunset, a skittish-edged fire over the crackling tracery.

Weeks could go by during which LeRoy would not be seen, but when planting time came and went, and it was noticed that he did not hire the usual small collective of Irish, German, and Scandinavian itinerants to help till and sow, town gossips began to speculate about what was really happening out at the Mann farm. Gone round the long bend, it was conjectured. Who could skip planting time?

His sister's cable was received with disbelief. He read it twice before walking outside with it, absentmindedly pinching and ripping its edges in his stiff fingers. In the short message,

> HANNAH AND ME COMING STOP/
> RIVE TRAIN SATURDAY NEXT STOP/
> LOVE SIS/

he concentrated on the word "rive," searching it for any other meaning than *arrive*.

But there was no other possible meaning. She had taken him up on his offer. He glowered at his boots, shook his head. His had been the right response to her own letter, the one she had written from New York mentioning that Nicky had left her again. He'd offered, in his reply, what he usually offered—that she and niece Hannah could come stay with him on the farm if things didn't work out otherwise. But then, this?

"Nicholas," he told the pickup truck, drawing out the "s" like steam from a pressure cooker. He was always leaving her, Nicholas, it was all he was good for was leaving her, coming back, leaving her again. "Nick, you son of a bitch."

She would never take him up on his proposals. He made them out of his own sense of family politesse; it was what he felt ought to be said, and in any case New York was so far away.

They were grounded, the offers of help, in his knowledge of his sister. She had been the more independent, even the prouder, of the two, and whenever difficulties arose she confronted them with disarming grace. Grace was her middle name, he scoffed. She forbore, and forbore. Crises were moments to be gotten through, though not necessarily to be learned from; suffered, not studied, at least that he could say against her. Nicholas was like two men: one she loved, the other endured. But the forbearance took such a form that it was impossible for those around her to know, from day to day, year to year, whether all was right with the world for Opal Burden or just the opposite.

Fugue was the word she was given by Nicky's doctor to explain his behavior. A tough, tidy little word, pretty, resonant, with its counterpart in music, that glorious and logical tangle of tone. Fugue; it was pathological. Nicky had no conscious choice. Unlike the musical form, Nicky's fugues were bitterly illogical. He might step out for a short stroll along Greenwich Avenue to buy some ice cream—pistachio for Opal, for Hannah chocolate—or cigarettes, or simply to clear his head, but would keep on walking, not to be seen for months. He would wake up the next morning in an unfamiliar mews and wonder at the two paper tubs of ice cream that lay in puddles beside him, dotted with ants. Chocolate, pistachio? While he had no concept of who he was, what his past was and how they possibly wrapped together to deliver him into just this alley behind a restaurant, a seafood place if one were to guess by the stink that bloomed in the ash cans, he did retain certain instincts that helped him to survive during fugal periods.

Hotel restrooms were where one best washed, if one could get past the doorman unseen; janitor's closets in office buildings, if they were equipped with a sink and mirror, were viable options.

Parks were pleasant to sleep in during the long, dull days when he found himself out of work.

Nights, when he seemed most to come alive, were better passed in bars where he could dance. He was a skilled dancer and the music seemed to carry him out of his body and float him away from anxiety, those flashes that rushed down through the flesh of his neck, bristly, crude, voluptuous as a blade, swirling across some sense he—Nicholas—was not himself.

It was in these clubs and bars he met his women, also. This was what hurt Opal the most during fugues. But he was helpless, she knew: it was a disease, this bad fire which scorched his mind.

When Opal finally did find him, some women did not easily give up their Nicky. He was a handsome man, thin, compact, with a clean jaw and face of fine angles, delicate, veiny hands, straight auburn hair that lay back across the crown of his head. He wore his shirt sleeves rolled up and his black string tie knotted loosely at the neck and the effect was of carefree elegance rather than slovenliness.

Nicholas Burden had been gone half a year and Opal's determination to keep her marriage together had begun to slacken. She was worried about Hannah. Hannah was so precocious. Opal felt that she couldn't bring the girl up by herself. Other women in the typing pool at work thought it was crazy of her to spend every lunch hour out in the city, walking, eating her lunch out of her paper bag, looking for him. What would she do when the fall came, and the snow, later?

When she finally did encounter Nicky he was sitting on a bench in Central Park, his arm casually draped around the shoulder of a young woman. At their feet sat two girls (twins?) in matching pinafores, who played jacks. Across Nicky's face a beatific smile spread. Squinty-eyed, cigarette with a long ash at its tip hanging at the corner of his mouth, he coached the girls, teased them and chuckled. The woman, whom Opal thought pretty, glanced up to see the unhappy face of the other, staring at her man with such an ashen look. She attempted a smile, lips closed, pleasant in the way strangers passing in the park acknowledge one another. Nicky didn't notice Opal as she turned away. The sighting smeared into oblivion.

By the time she got home her cheeks were dry. Nicky had a new family, for the present. Nicky would have many other new families. His fugues would get worse or better. She couldn't afford to care any longer. At least on her brother's farm Hannah would have a man who would behave more or less like a father.

A day later she cabled LeRoy. The cablegram, creased, lined like a muddy bank marked with bird tracks, now rested in his shirt pocket. Opal was coming with her Hannah. He half expected another letter the next day, setting straight the mistake, or simply canceling out. But none came. That left only a few days for LeRoy to prepare.

His farmhouse was clapboard, a two-story structure. It rested, in alternately fallow and planted fields, at a position of modest prominence on a rise that fell away down into a southerly depression, at the bottom of which snaked a gulley where an erosive stream ran in the spring, or after a good rain. The house centered a traditional assortment of farm buildings—stout barn, sheds, outhouse, coops, stable, a dump of rusted tractors, plows, equipment so weathered it seemed to rise from the earth and weeds which overgrew it, poking through every chink and crevice, and pulled—under an explosion of morning glories and nasturtia—a spring-tooth harrow into a sculpture, its burnt-red extremities coiling high, ready to snap down upon a crop of poppies, each new April. Mice and snakes made in this nest of metal and weeds their homes. From time to time he considered burning this dump, but whenever he came down to survey it, the project seemed too much. The building closest to this site was the bunkhouse, a large cabin, the oldest surviving structure on the farm, which he had restored for the hired hands. This had been used less after his wife was stricken. She'd no longer had strength enough to cook meals three times daily for a crew of harvesters. Each year the number of men got smaller and area of fallow fields got larger. After she died LeRoy managed only to plant subsistence crops, and accomplished most of the field work with the help of just one or two men, neither of whom lived on the farm.

He had thought he might be able to put up his sister and her child in this bunkhouse, but a quick tour through its spiderwebs and ruin dissuaded him. The place, he had to admit, was a mess. He felt defensive about it, but that passed.

Two bedrooms upstairs in the main house were readied. One was at the end of the hall, facing east toward Babylon, whose smoke could be seen curling into the atmosphere on a winter's day, though the town was too far away for any spire or gable to be seen. Out the windows of Opal's room there were three weeping willows whose branches reached down into the still brown water of the pond, at the center of which stood a makeshift duck house, driven into its mud bed at a precarious pitch. During droughts the pond evaporated, leaving a wide baked-clay shore cracked by the sun into a patchwork of unreadable characters, cuneiform. Animals rambled to the banks of the dead pond during these dry months, by habit, and stared for hours at the dirt mosaic as if, once its meaning was deciphered, some spell might be broken and the sky'd gather up in a shroud of clouds and drench them under sheets of water.

LeRoy's sister-in-law had come out to help. She made up a bed for Hannah in the room at the head of the stairs, a long, narrow room situated between the other two. This room presented her with a problem, for in it her brother-in-law kept his collection of heads, a motley assembly of trophies representing a lifetime of avid, but not very accomplished, hunting. Mrs. Mann had refused to allow the heads to be displayed downstairs in the main room. She considered them vulgar. So he took over this odd-shaped room upstairs, where he came to pass half an hour in the evening, breathing out pipe smoke over the coats, bristles, horns, and marble eyes. A gunrack, fancily carved out of a light oak, cradled half a dozen rifles and a two-barrel shotgun. The gunrack was mounted on the wall over a daybed. Around the four walls ranged the heads of an antelope, a whitetail buck whose three-tined antlers were a maze of silky webs cast by wolf spiders, a gray Virginian fox who'd been caught stalking the chicken coop, an elk, a puma hide and his prize—a big, dusty buffalo head whose rigid countenance combined a sense of savagery with indifference, the master of Hannah's new room.

They stared, these trophies, with black eyes in deft, frozen alertness. The antelope was seen to glance left, graceful head erect, ears pricked, studying a sound, the distant tick of a .30-30 Winchester, carried by a lilting breeze. The sound had a decade ago vanished into the last of her personal history, which, with it, slumped into the earth, and was lost in sport and a little smoke.

The sister-in-law cried out when she first opened the door to this bedroom. She'd never ventured into the room at the top of the stairs before. Its door was always locked. As her cry, a sort of shocked nick on the air, reached him downstairs, he laughed to himself, simply couldn't help but laugh. He bit his lip, awaited more, but when nothing further was heard from above, he was disappointed. The sun popped under a heavy cloud, and came back out, strengthening the shadow's edge thrown across the carpet.

"You need any help?"

Just the quiet. The clock ticked in the kitchen.

When she finished, an hour later, she came down.

"How old did you say Hannah was getting to be?"

"Never said," but after a pause he allowed: "She must be eight or nine, now. Hasn't been easy to follow from a distance, also being as I've never met the girl."

"Impressionable age."

"I wouldn't remember what it was like to be forty let alone nine."

"That might be."

LeRoy observed her coming around, sure and slow as a buzzard hawk, to her point. She said (or meant to say, but didn't), tossing her shawl over her shoulders (for now they were out front, on the porch), Don't you think, don't you reckon a child that age oughtn't be made to sleep in a room full of dead—

During the drive back into town not a word was exchanged between them. LeRoy dropped her off. Her husband bade him hello from the porch swing. He drove away.

The days passed, neither slowly nor quickly. Early evening, Friday, uncle went into Hannah's bedroom and sat in the periodical light sprayed by a sun falling in and out of a string of long, high clouds.

It occurred to him that he ought to check the guns to be sure they were not loaded. No need for the girl to shoot her head off. One at a time he took each piece off its rack, weighed it fondly, knocked back the bolts with quick open-palmed flicks of the wrist, drawing the cool lever knob toward the butt of the rifle with his fingers and checking for unspent shells. He took down his N. R. Davis double-barreled, side-by-side, 12-gauge, bought from the Sears Roebuck catalogue after he and Mrs. Mann were first married—heavier than he remembered, cradled in his arms. He looked over the Winchesters. The first, his .22-caliber pump, he used for woodchuck and rabbit; the other was a Model 94 dating from the end of the last century. Face close to the lever, the smell of it so nostalgic time drew in—

1937 it was. His Springfield clutched in hand. World War I surplus issue. Built in 1903, .30-ought-6.

Empty; he raised the piece to his shoulder and sighted out the window down in the weedy lot in the barn's shadow. He cocked, pivoted in deliberate slow motion, rifle quivering in his arms, the skin at his sighting eye clamped to the slit where he aimed, searching out the heart of the make-believe prey. He stopped the arc and spotted his phantom target. Adjusting an aim toward the breast of his object he steadied his hand, swallowed breath and held it, rock-still, squeezed.

Cluck, he pulled the trigger. Missed.

Again, Cluck.

Yes! it went down hard on its knees, the legs simply buckled under. Its face bore an uncontorted look of sensation beyond hope—firmly lodged in some dense kingdom of peace at the far side of the struggle. He looked at it, blinking. It was there. To LeRoy this face registered in its look a kind of gratitude. As he lowered the Springfield he could almost smell the burnt powder in the room and it sent down through the fabric of his body another sensation, one that perfectly mimicked a lust whose impulse was sated.

The sound behind his back startled him. He stood still, hushed. The strength in his loins decayed. How many hundreds of years would have to pass before the house might finally reach down into the ground to find its bedrock and its level so the snaps and creaks and pops its structure made upon sinking farther into the ground finally faded away? This discussion among casements and walls and doorsills, would it ever reach some conclusion?

Cunningly his finger felt for the trigger as he listened for the sound to come again.

He turned on his heel.

Cluck! as the hammer kicked he broke into an unvoiced laughter, for the room was empty.

He walked to the window, gazed out across the lot into the fields: all this was his land for the span of his own lifetime. That was good. His own. He decided to go outside. He was tired of the pantomime. He would take the

.22 and stroll along the road, shoot something, maybe a prairie dog, a squirrel, a fox. Whatever started out of the vesper bramble.

He replaced the Springfield on the bottom rack and lifted down the rifle. A box of cartridges was kept on the high shelf of the pantry. He loaded in the kitchen, slipped a jacket on, and stepped out into the dusk.

The world was a muddy pink. Half an hour of fair sun was left. He walked up along the road. Its surface was solid as glass, the result of rain followed by warm, baking days. He reached a crossroads, not quite a quarter of a mile southeast, away from the house. Here the county line ran, and his land was divided by a series of leaning posts grayed with weather and age, along which were hung several strands of old barbed wire, woven with the green beards of purslane, awn of grasses. Years ago the posts held the wire up. Now the rows of wire themselves, hardened by seasons of rusting, held the rotten posts up with their red, corroding strands.

Crack! crack! his rifle reported as a pair of blackbirds paced the shoulder of the road ahead. Lazily their large wings carried them up and off toward the west away from him. Except for the calls of birds out working the brush for food, and for the softest rush of the evening wind in his ears, everything was held in an unscathed, emblematic silence.

He shot a brown bottle that was perched on top of a fencepost, and it shattered before him. Its neck had already been shot off by somebody else, leaving only a squat glass crown, the whole of which burst as the bullet ran through it.

"Good," he told himself.

He turned to walk back to the house. The sun was sinking into the long horizon, cloudbanks still pulsing with a refractory of colors. The earth's air, the density of its very atmosphere along the ground, pulled the bottom of the sun's sheared sphere north and south, and distorted its base so that it was fatter where it submerged itself along the slight curve of the land's edge.

The sun, huh? shoot it, he thought, and propped the butt of the gun against the hollow of his shoulder, and unloaded the three shots left in his five-shot clip directly at it.

The sun down, to home. New moon meant the sky would turn black quickly. The rifle rode handily tucked underarm. Evening star was already up there, twinkling. The thud thud of his footfall sounded on the baked road. It made the earth feel hollow. The familiar hoot of the barn owl now. Light shone out the kitchen window, breaking in a bar across the lot. Insect buzz at the side of his head slapped at, quiet. Meringue clouds lost their color. A range of stars building in the east, over town. Bats wheeling around the barn, intermittent peeps, diving, jutting. Upstairs he put the rifle on its rack. He sat again in the chair in the room, surrounded by mute partners in a mortal dance.

Woke up, dawn-light in his eyes, having rounded the world. Morning, and time to go into Babylon.

The train ground to a halt, wheels screeching on the blue tracks, mad squeal of metal moving against metal, track stubborn, wheels locked. The slide terminated after a buck, in a stall, a hiss, an utter calm. Cinders fell, heavy hot pellets, into the fields. Smoke puddled in the air. The cabooseman clung to his handle bar. Passengers peered out windows, hoping to see what was causing the delay. The seasons of Bonus Marchers, striking farmers who had laid threshing-machine cables and spiked logs across trestles to derail trains, were long gone. Pickets winking in dust-bowl wind, the chants, the echo of gunfire and of men yelling angrily—all that was over now. Enough milk had been dumped from cans into ditches here in this part of the country that some people claimed its rancid odor could still be smelled as far east as Cleveland on hot days when the wind blew hard enough. The plains were a peaceful place now; plains wars were over and, as Nicky said, all the wars were moved to the city. Since 1874 barbed-wire fences crisscrossed it. That settled people down, kept their cows separated. The Indians had been dispersed to reservations, and buffalo had been eliminated from the frontier: the vanquished pair were minted into limited immortality on either side of a nickel, the nickel Hannah rubbed anxiously with her thumb as she looked out the window with the others on the train. She studied the coin. This was what you bought stuff with in America. It was sort of comely. You could buy land with it, a home, or a train—you could live in a train if you wanted, see lots of places. The word *Liberty* was stamped on the coin over the forehead and nose of a profiled warrior. His eyes were shut, she noticed, and over his face was a mask of grief. It made her feel sorry for him, poor early-man with his braid. On his shoulder the number 1936 was stamped, like the number on the back of a prisoner's pajamas. On the nickel tail was the buffalo with *The United States of America* emblazoned, a silver rainbow over its silver body. Its tail swished, but its head had to be bowed for it to fit on the round form of the coin. Well, things fit or they don't and if they don't somebody makes them fit. On the buffalo's head George Washington's periwig sat, a helmet. The buffalo also wore a beard on its chin. Hannah knew this was

Abraham Lincoln's beard. She killed time by flipping the coin up, catching it and guessing heads or tails.

Alarmed by the silence, a baby starting crying. The crying carried down the corridor from the car ahead. Gratitude for a break in the monotony was now expressed by a stream of confident complaints the travelers offered one another. She looked to mama Opal, "I thought there were supposed to be mountains here."

"You've got to go hundreds of miles west for those."

"Mountains, with snow on them."

"One of these days we'll take you to the mountains."

"Tomorrow?"

"Hannah, did I tell you that all this used to be under the ocean?" and mama Opal began to explain to her the inland ocean, fossils, the waves lapping the mountains' edge, and her daughter listened and imagined it all, and heard behind her, "I didn't pay twenty-three dollars to sit here in the tracks," and another, saying, "Time'll pass, may I introduce myself name is Grant."

Coffin.

Retail.

Physician.

Sun-glint snapped off someone's belt buckle.

"You ever hear the one about Dr. Coffin and Nurse Graves?" Hannah had no idea what all the laughter was about. She turned around and saw that it came from the man who was in retail. Retail was a kind of thing her father Nicky said crawled with the scum of the earth. Retail, he would say, and spit.

Opal
AUGUST 1956

UNDER the aegis of a darkened cloud the tornado churns like an inverted serpent in sly summer. Winding, wind draws down into an orderly coned funnel blocking off the brightness of the sun. The chicken hawk and the crow are pulled like helpless rags out of flight into the swirling snake of air. The dun cloud is dense as a wandering island floating over the rolling geometrical fields. The twister dropped from the cloud like a chain that seeks mooring in the unexpectant earth. Grasshoppers along the set rows of wheat and rye desist from their songs. The voice on the shortband has interrupted music to establish the cyclone watch. The dragon of dark wind drops its stinging tail lightly into the loam. Asphalt is eased from its flat soft base running straight for miles across the great plains. Sunlight is shielded from that swath of land where the tornado begins its hellish harvest. Planks, shingles, frames, tarpaulin, shutters, grates, brick, tarpaper, rain gutters, glass, stones are rearranged within the circling wind one hundred feet over the earth, above where a yawning rectangular hole shows the dimensions of a structure that once stood. A shaft of dried hay is driven at such speed that it lodges headfirst in the stone-solid trunk of an elm. A tractor and its plow are lifted far above the ground and deposited gently intact and operable upon the mansard roof of the grange hall. Within the blast's bowels a roan pony is impressed against the side of a washtub inside which a bantam rooster roils and riots until the pony bursts like a bag of blood. The crooked and ambiguous air, running scales on the metal tines of a springtoothed harrow, mimes a folksong sung by frightened children who are hidden in a storm cellar tunneled beneath the barley shoots. Alfalfa, bromegrass, bird's-foot trefoil, soy, timothy and clover are pulled from broadcast and banded fields. Barbed wire and tumbleweeds dance flibbertigibbet like greased lightning. Spittlebug flies with wheatstalk, sweet clover and hourglass fagots. Leafhopper twirls like a screwy zozzlestick in the sorghum. Aphids and guidoing crickets cling to the peeled ground in flight. Even the two-rooted white clover is yanked aloft from its insistent lime-struck pod of turf behind the rickety century-old farmhouse, oddly left unfazed by the growing gale. Turn and turn about the tornado weaves across the rolling yards and dells northeast toward the sprawling clutter of town where men and women and their children crouch against the oncoming whirlwind. Like a clotted dervish it marks a course to the dust-paved streets. The minimal contents of a trickling stream named after a forgotten settler are partly sucked and ascend in gyres around the central core of the glutted monster. Suddenly in a wrenching single monumental twist the roaring spiral veers away from its northeastern ray simultaneously disgorging itself of countless unnamable bits and fragments of what lay in its three-mile path. The ascendant walls of the turning column hard as stone now gain new velocity as the snake dances quickly over the petroleum depot and slaughterhouse and three grain silos west of the huddling clapboards saved from demolition by the change of course. To the accompaniment of voluminous groans the beamed sheet-metal roof of the howling slaughterhouse is ripped like onionskin off the top of its walled structure. Halved carcasses of swine and cattle and sheep sail as massive forklifts tumble easily into the upchurning twirl. In instants the arrangement of men, machinery, and beasts is tossed into wild shambles by the rocky air. At the end of the central chamber in the roofless building a bandsaw is now toppled upon a man whose head is lightly blown against the concrete floor, concussing him. The woman who was standing at his side is miraculously elevated into the middle of the violent vortex, and suspended fifteen feet above the man lying beneath his bandsaw on the floor. Her arms are raised tenderly by the rushing fingers of invisibility and her pink dress and slip are lifted as if by the ginger touch of a lover anxious to run his hands over her naked and motionless body. These clothes are sent high into the sky before the hindmost swift-flown edge of the funnel snags the sparking end of a powerline and introduces it to a thousand gallons of petroleum that send a percussive flash exploding low across the horizon. Hung thus in the storm the woman's substance is drawn up in microscopic particles and sent to the topmost mass of jet-black thunderclouds rocking overhead. Just before retracting its tongue off the shocked sod the tornado throws three grain silos together momentarily into a curious tripod and then tosses them out into cornfields. One is carried up with the receding cone to the thunderhead but is casually cast a quarter mile east to collide with a turnstile on a grassy knoll where Guernseys and a black Angus graze.

Hannah
JULY–SEPTEMBER 1955

GIVEN words say it was me speaking now I'd say mama Opal and I looked out the window, streaked with the dust of a dozen states. A bitty wind made the fields, so thick with what the picture books at school had taught me was wheat, rise and fall like waves in a dry gold sea. Such clear air crawled over the crops in streams making the blue out at the fences wiggle. The passengers had gone back by and by to talking. We were near Babylon, a man with a black hat like a pancake said. It was probably cows blocking the tracks up ahead, his woman said. Cattle's what it must be, someone agreed behind us. I watched mama's eyes move nervously. I had put my buffalo-head nickel back in my pocket. Mama had told me to and I minded her.

A bell rang way off in the distance. I knew that mama Opal wasn't nervous over the train stopping in its tracks. She was tired from the long trip that began it seemed like years ago, in a drizzle that splashed over the big house with all the walkups and windows where all the women could look out into the streets to see us children. It seemed we were locked in the train forever. So many towns and trees had run one into the other that any church or courthouse, lumberyard, river, borough hall or garden, any arch, stone-walled prison or museum, had melted for us into one great blur of prettiness.

Just the greatest beauty it was hard to believe it could be real out through the window.

It was our country. It was our land. I had never hoped to see such a thing in my life but there it was. And time during the trip had been swept away into a flatness. Something we could not count on. I would wake up in the middle of the night and think it was noon. I was able to mistake towns for stars and stars for lantern bugs.

The bell rang again.

So slow you couldn't feel the difference, the train started forward again and picked up speed a bit at a time. I looked out the window to see the cattle that blocked the tracks but didn't see them. All I saw were the soft fields that stretched away to the place where the clouds came down to touch the land.

As we came up to uncle's town, there were more fences we could see that marked off squares and other shapes. I said something to mama Opal and she said to me, What a smart young lady you are.

She was proud of me when I said things like this. I loved to make her happy and to make her proud of me. I was always on the lookout for smart things to say to her, to show her I was her young lady. That's what she called me when she was proud—her young lady.

Today was Saturday. Come Sunday, she said, everything would be glorious. Home someday? I asked, I'd have my own room? Maybe I'd be able to see the mountains out the window. I must have heard her wrong. She said, Come Sunday.

Tying up land with poles and lengths of wire or slats and drawing lines with sticks or surveying instruments, plumb bobs is what they're called and tripod-mounted scopes and demarcations, and settings-off, making some sense of the wild by all these things that were called ownership. This is what our job was on the green earth, divvying up being the birthright of every pioneer, that's what uncle LeRoy would come to say. It reminded me of sidewalks in the city, chalked up for hopscotch. Crosswalks, the boys' baseball diamonds, stripes on the blue of the policeman's uniform, lines on the bum's socks, wrought-iron fences out in front of brick houses marking off the front yards with the ginkgo trees between stoops. Marks that all by themselves made up the silhouette like the kind you can buy in summer from the artist on the sidewalk, a silhouette (I've got one of me) from childhood on through life toward when you give up your ghost and they stick you right in the ground, that too marked by sunken grass and a gravestone. I know. I've been to a cemetery before. That was when mama Opal's own mother passed. It was bad uncle LeRoy didn't come. Everybody must go to the graveyard when their mama dies.

Say it was me speaking, I'd say the town appeared on both sides of the train. We were here. The noisy talk of the passengers, our temporary family, filled up the car. Babylon, Nebraska, pop. 334. Now, three thirty-six.

We were the only passengers getting off the train at this stop, though you'd never know it from all the loud talking and moving going on. Wind through wheat'd make for sounds more understandable than all the talk these people built up. People talk most when they've got nothing in their head, or too much in their head. It's a natural thing. I've noticed it. I'd be quiet myself except that right now I've got too much in my head.

So this was Babylon? Why would so much lumber, mortar, brick, glass, stone be dragged here, just to this spot, to be lifted, hammered and pulled together to make a town? The towns we had passed through seemed to have at least a river, or a bluff of hills ranged about with cottonwood trees or maples, a rise, a ring of sand around a lake's shore—something that called to mind a reason for settlers to build a first home and for others to want to follow. Yet so far as I could tell (and after months of wandering around Babylon and environs I would come to realize my question was fair) this town was not nestled beside a low-flowing, majestic river, not even a gulch. No plateau edged it, no hill crested beside it, no valley of luscious vineyards stretched away at its feet. Its character seemed defined by no character at all.

Months later, I learned that Babylon lay outside the known alleys of the tornadoes that spin their way across every other quarter of the state—it was for this the land was homesteaded. Babylon had a reputation of being a hex on twisters. Even the Indians held that its grounds were possessed of fortunate powers that kept the winds at bay. Ever since, it spread out its streets and structures, unprotected from the winds' forces by either land or trees, it was as if the town and all its inhabitants stood out on the high plains in defiance of that part of nature.

Two men stood on the platform. One was smoking a pipe. The purple of the smoke was funny against the red paint on the side of the station house and all the yellow everywhere else. The man with the pipe was my uncle. He didn't look very happy, did he.

There was so much to learn!

Hens lay eggs. Lambkins are born with long tails that must be docked isn't that crazy. You can do it with shears or an ax and block. There are different kinds of earth. Some kinds of earth you can walk on, some earth gives birth to plants. These can grow. It is hard to believe. Words stick to each different thing. Knee-high by the fourth of July besides sounding pretty has its meaning. What grows out of the earth. Corn does. So does wheat and weeds do, too. Rice, it grows out of the earth but requires more water. Apple trees come up out of the soil, they make flowers and afterwards apples. Green and red. You can climb up an apple tree more easily than up a willow tree. Up in the branches of an apple tree you can eat raw apples. They are tart on the tongue and the meat is crisp against the teeth. Too many of them and your belly will ache all night. At night there are stars in the sky, in the day there are birds. Both birds and stars have names because there are many different kinds of the one and many different positions for the other. Bats like the sky, too, but in between day and night. The sun is a star. It's so big and warm because it's closer to us than any star. Some of the planets are there, also, they look a lot like stars you have to be careful. The moon seems to get confused once in a while. It drifts like a sliver of nail in the daytime sky, milk-white up in all that blue. I couldn't tell you why the sky is blue and I don't know why uncle keeps saying once in a blue moon. I think the sky might be a reflection of the oceans but this is what mama Opal would call an educated guess and my uncle would call cockshit. The world is mostly oceans. That is where the fish go. People live down there probably. They have gills. They lay eggs just like birds do. Fish lay eggs I mean. The underwater people I don't know what they do. They probably lay eggs, too, otherwise water would get on the babies too soon and they would drown. If you shoot something with a gun it stops moving. That's because it is dead. We die all of us, even apple trees, wheat. Stars, bats, corn, planets die in time too. I saw a banty rooster die. I held it in my lap. I knew just when its ghost inside flew away, I could almost see it. Time's something that moves but not in such a way you can see it going. It moves inside people and things. The earth is round. This roundness can be seen along the edge of the horizon from up in an apple tree, or on the roof of the house. It's not easy to see but once you've seen it once it is always easy to see after that and also it is easy to close your eyes and imagine the curved line of the horizon sweeping away in both directions downwards. Then you get a sense of how very grand the earth is. It may be shaped like an egg or a marble I don't know. Some people are born with mean temperaments just like other people are born with crooked noses or flaps on their lips that make them lisp. There are words, names for these folks. Unkind, unhappy, cruel. They hurt other people. It's their nature. Some probably run out of people they know to hurt and then they have no choice but to hurt themselves. They're crying inside, these people. They're crying in the same place where time lives. You can't see it. No one can. There are other people whose souls are sweet. Sweeter than the stem of the honeysuckle you can draw out of the flower and suck. They cry too, these people. But their lives are made up of atoms sparked and borrowed from the spirit of a blessed one who alone knows the nature of all these things. I will tell a secret. I have seen this spirit once. Like a dull gold, it walked out under the great elm beyond the porch. I never told before. It was majesty.

Hannah's uncle didn't bother to pretend he relished the prospect of their living with him for a long time. She overheard him explain to mama Opal how his "responsibilities in life had come to their proper conclusion" at the moment his wife died. The subject came up, mostly by innuendo, from month to month as summer elapsed into fall, but when his sister announced that she was taking a job at the Johnson plant, LeRoy shrugged—he had made his position known. He professed unwillingness to adjust: if Opal and her daughter were able to work around his habits and needs there wouldn't be much for him to say.

For Hannah the experiment with school was not a success. She started in the first week of September. The schoolhouse was too far away, east of Babylon, for her to walk, and class let out too early for mama Opal to pick her up. Uncle made the trip, driving her there and back, for a week, but by the weekend he had come to his decision. He had relished, he said, the chance of being left alone to his own routine during the day, and so long as Hannah continued to pull her weight by doing her chores before and after school, he had no complaint about her continuing schooling—however, he would no longer drive her. I'm not your private chauffeur, he told her. He had not come this far through life only to arrange his entire day around Hannah's personal schedule. If she and her mother could figure some other way for her to attend, she could rest assured he wouldn't stand in their way. His contribution'd reached its conclusion, though.

With two extra mouths to feed, Hannah's helping out at home was more practical than anything she could learn in school. He said this, too. And so the decision had been made.

Where did his meanness come from? don't know. Does he see me as some kind of bastard-girl? don't know. I am to blame for something, maybe for mama Opal's having to marry Nicky, but it wasn't my idea to go and make me, was it? no. Maybe he loves mama Opal (I think he does) but he doesn't love me. He hates Nicky. He won't discuss paying for somebody to find Nicky and bring him out here away from the city and put him under someone's care, someone who can fix his mind problems.

We didn't do very well in the day, uncle and I, when she was away at work. Here was the best of all, the best uncle and I would ever do together—

It was supper, or breakfast. Supper. He drank his coffee out of the saucer instead of the cup anyway, but here he was eating his peas on his knife. Neat row of wrinkly balls on the silver.

"Hey," I said. "Look at that."

He didn't like the word *hey*.

"Hey that's good," I said, and tried with my knife. Peas down my front. I gathered them up with my hands and ate them. Mama Opal wasn't pleased. I was acting up.

"Hannah, the hey story," she said.

I didn't want to do the hey story.

Mama Opal said, "Hannah."

Uncle hated *hey* and she knew it.

"No."

Mama Opal and I never had words. It wasn't something she and I did. We were together. We faced the world together.

So, I did the hey story—

> *"Hey is for horses*
> *which live in the stall.*
> *Hey ain't the right word*
> *for polite folks at all."*

She did smile, though, at my "ain't." She knew I put it in on purpose.

"Pretty good," uncle said. "Here's how you make peas stand still on your knife."

It had to do with gravy.

Gerald
DECEMBER 1955

CHRISTMAS Eve. Hannah has made a minor discovery. If her uncle were to catch her here in his bedroom she would be stropped and put on double chores.

Uncle has warned her about not "transgressing the sanctity" of this bedroom. But uncle and mama Opal are not in the house. Mama Opal has driven the truck into town to pick up last-minute surprises for Christmas. Uncle, who is of the opinion that women should not be seen at the wheel of automobiles or trucks, and who had argued with her about it as always before she took the keys and left, driving swiftly away in the constant snow, is down in the pasture. He may be recognized as that bent figure in overalls and earmuffs observed from the northeast window of his bedroom.

He is some distance from the house, in perspective not taller than Hannah's thumbnail held out at arm's length. Each frequent breath is visible as a small puff.

Hannah crawls cautiously across the plank floor. The planks are wide and rippled. She glances again, from the depths of the room, to assure herself he is not lumbering back up toward the house.

He is not. He appears to be studying something in the lower field, through the curtain of snow. Hannah now feels safe, but her heart is beating hard. It would take several minutes for him to reach the house even if he started up the long, gradual slope right now; there would be plenty of time for Hannah to sneak back to her own room.

There is, in the bedroom, a fractional scent of mildew. She thinks this is strange as the room is immaculately clean, austere. A red-and-white Navajo blanket, an eye-dazzler, serves as a rug on the left side of the double metal-framed bed. Every object seems to have its place in the room. Nothing appears to be mislaid and nothing is askew. Physical rite, mode of worship in the right angle. The wallpaper, whose design is an incongruous pattern of blue and gold flowers gathered into fagots, is badly faded, and probably is the victim of the mildew.

The girl hasn't the faintest notion what she is doing here, what her curiosity has led her to; it seems natural, however, to begin to open drawers and look through their contents.

Shirts, underclothes, long johns, stockings. Tidily folded and arranged. In the bottom drawer blankets, extras for the bed when it gets very cold. Underneath these blankets she comes across something interesting. Photograph in a rosewood frame. Looking out the window to make sure he is still at safe distance from the house (he is), Hannah lifts the photograph out of the drawer and stands up to examine it more closely. The image is browned by age, is mounted on a light beaverboard that is chipped a little on one corner but has prevented it from curling. There are three children in the photograph. A boy, an adolescent, on the left, standing, thumb of his right hand inserted self-consciously at the corner of his trouser pocket, outfitted in a double-breasted suit with a cravat and formal collar, a precocious smugness on his young face. It is uncle LeRoy. The eyes are telling. The lower lip, which curves neither up nor down, trails forward into an appreciable pout and makes visible a fine line of teeth. His dark hair is parted on the right, combed forward into an angle, cut at precisely forty-five degrees to the eyebrows, across the forehead. Below the brow, wide-set, iodine-colored in image as in life, these eyes gaze out, unperturbable. His left ear, hidden save for its tip, because of the camera angle, is much higher on his head than his right.

Opposite him, in the right of the frame, leaning against a shapely table, is mama Opal. She cannot be more than five or six years old. She is kneeling (possibly crouching? it's hard to tell, for her legs are shrouded under the drapery of her clothes) on a plush chair. Her pale leg-of-mutton sleeved pinafore is starched and ruffled. On the table is an open book. Her right hand rests delicately in the gutter of the book, holding down its springy pages.

Whose idea was the book? the photographer's? their mother's? And who, or what, are they staring at intently, behind the apparatus that faced them in the studio? a funny stuffed monkey hung at the end of a stick? And that carnation there placed on the page of the opened book, did that act in the photographer's imagination as a simple symbol for the freshness and promise and purity of youth? Who was this third figure, posed in a reclining position atop the table, his lanky legs dangling off the end on the left side, torso propped up on his left elbow, his shoulder leaning affectionately against the puffed sleeve of his sister's pinafore? He, too, wore a double-breasted suitcoat, but of a lighter color than his brother's. Is that a ring on his finger or a flaw in the print? Who could this be if not a brother? But uncle LeRoy did not have a brother, and mama Opal had no brother other than uncle LeRoy.

Why was this boy's face scratched out with many bold strokes of sepia-colored ink? The face once depicted here is almost eradicated. Who would have done such a thing to a family portrait?

Careful not to disturb the hairbrush, the hand mirror, the inlaid box of cufflinks set on the top of the chest of drawers, Hannah leans forward on tiptoes to look closer at the vandalized photograph. The ink failed to blacken the eyes out completely—the eyes of the older boy are still visible, even though the lower half of the face is actually torn away, gouged off by the pen. The eyes are clear and light, like those of mama Opal, and around the irises a fine dark line traced a circle, kind and rapt, perfect circle.

Sharp pain melted into the sound of a solid slap: it is felt at the back of Hannah's head. Her ear popped while her hand caught the side of the inlaid box which tumbled with her to the pine plank floor of the bedroom. The first kick was just between her bony buttocks and she lay on her side. The second kick of such force it actually propelled her forward. There was a darkness of shadow cast across her field of vision, which she could not understand, as she stared at the wainscoting and floral wallpaper that abutted its fluted ridge. Her body coalesced. Involuntarily, it awaited the next kick. She heard her blood up in her throat and her breaths that came short, shallow and irregular.

Hannah could not locate his voice. It asked her what she was doing here. Uncle stood over her, one stockinged foot placed on his niece's hip. The foot, heavy in its gray wool, gave a nudge forward, insisted upon an answer. Toes worked off Hannah's hip and dug deeper into her soft, narrow side. They bore down. Hannah could feel her face getting hot. Uncle's hand picked up the photograph.

"Do you know where you are?"

Hannah coughed. The foot rolled her over onto her stomach, then rested its weight on her back. Hannah closed her eyes and kept her face turned away from where uncle stood. He must have taken his boots off downstairs so she wouldn't hear him, she thought as she cradled her head in her arms.

"What would your mama think of you?"

"What?" so small it seemed to be the wallpaper speaking, or the in-laid box.

"Breaking into other folks' rooms? That's the way you been brought up, is it?"

She was jerked light as fluff off the floor, one hand yanking her head up sharply by her hair and the other dragging her by her leather belt. The girl flailed ineffectually, and screamed as her uncle tossed her, face down, across the room, where she landed on her knees and chin. Quickly she began crawling on all fours toward the open door. Under the lintel uncle caught her up by the back of her shirt with such force that the buttons were torn away from its front. What'm I doing I'm going too far, he thought, but it was as if he himself were just a component and not in control of it.

"I didn't mean to," she said.

By the collar of Hannah's shirt he marched her down the steep staircase, thin arms dangling like the stick arms on a scarecrow to either side, hung aloft by the fabric of the torn shirt, walking her across the front room to the kitchen, both of them crying just a little, perhaps, and him thinking so what if she knows about Gerald so what if she brings all that business up out of the cellar again, her mother knows now, they all do, that it was not his fault, not mine, and there was no need for Opal to go like that, look where it landed her after all, and look at this little sidewinder—"You little son of a bitch," even then realizing he got the gender wrong, even then realizing that was part of the problem, somewhere.

She is not thinking. She is afraid of his hands. They seem to be slapping at her face. Her shirt is open at the front and she is thinking about wiggling free and making a run for it, but his hand is over the flat pan of her ribs holding her back.

Opal entered by the kitchen door, bags in both hands.

"Hannah?"

Uncle LeRoy let go of her, turned, hurried out of the kitchen.

"Roy?"

They heard him climb to the second floor in a few long strides, skipping two or three stairs at a leap.

"Roy?" she screamed, and quietly, "Hannah?"

He was directly overhead. His footfalls preceded the sound of his bedroom door slamming shut with such force that the panes of glass in the kitchen window rattled in their frames.

"Hannah, what's happened?" She dropped her bags and pumped up fresh water onto a linen towel to clean her daughter's bloodied chin. Hannah's shoulders heaved and her face was so contorted it seemed she was screaming with laughter.

Mama Opal began to cry, also. Shrill beyond anything Hannah could remember, mama Opal started to shout her brother's name.

"Roy . . . Roy . . . Roy . . ."

As suddenly as she began crying she stopped. She told Hannah to hold the towel to her chin, and to lie down on the table. The towel was frosty cold with the well water.

She was at the foot of the stairs calling his name, over and over.

Hannah looked at the blood in the towel. Outside the snow seemed to have let up. She tried to roll over onto her back but found she couldn't. Her face ached. She wondered whether uncle meant to hit so hard—she was sure he didn't.

The same semiblackness she suffered upstairs darkened the view before her. It was as if a blanket had been laid over her head. It was frightening.

"Mama?"

"Roy, you get down here and go get Doctor."

"Mama?"

Uncle LeRoy left in the pickup truck without saying a word. When Doctor arrived mama Opal explained to him that the girl got bucked in the snow by a young filly. He knew she was not telling the truth. The snow had let up. There was no reason for him to ask any questions. Uncle LeRoy stayed out of the kitchen. He lit a fire in the front-room hearth. The snow started to fall again in earnest. Mama Opal let Hannah pop the corn to string with the cranberries (they had a nicer color than gooseberries, but you couldn't string a gooseberry anyway) for the tree uncle had cut that afternoon in the field. She was not going to let Hannah's Christmas be spoiled. She did not invite uncle in to help them trim the tree or drink the eggnog. This had to be somebody's home, and tonight it would be theirs.

Butcher
AUGUST 1956

MAMS—Now everything was going hunkydory before I started up work here in this town Babylon its near Blue Hill and Red Cloud you can find it on one of your National Geographic maps. But now this here sleepiness started to bothering me so much after the accident I dont know whether I'm coming or going. Thats because everything blew sky high. But I guess I'm getting a little ahead of myself. I believe I told you in my last I settled on coming to this place partly cause as I got such a fear of them cyclones you know and part because I got the offer to work here at this meat plant its one of the biggest and most modern in the whole state. So I got me a nice little place in town living on the second floor of these spinster ladies house, started up working here and the job pays good and have taken a considerable liking to the town. At the plant is where I made the acquaintance of the broad. The broad is what they call her I should say. I dont know why they call her the broad. I wouldnt call her that myself if it was left up to me but I was still pretty new here at the job and she was already going by that name when I come on. She's prim and proper but she's got a wild streak on her too. You know she reminded me first time I saw her of when we lived in back on Grove Street in Lincoln, remember? Remember that girl there I met that young girl there she was from Wichita Kansas. She was good looking. She had got her a good bookkeeping job short hand and the works. She roomed three doors east of us staying with that widow lady. She would come and sit in the swing, those were the days. I asked her once if she knew how to play bridge and she said no so I taught her how to play bridge. She was such a nice girl I wonder what ever become of her if you know let me know would you? Anyway I know the broad her real name what it was but thats just because I looked it up in her purse one afternoon a while back when she werent around I dont believe I recollect where she was but she werent in the front office where she works for this Mister Johnson he owns the place. Maybe she went home early she has to tend to that nutty gal of hers. I know that gal drives her brother to drink sometimes anyway thats what they say. She dont have no husband because she lives over with her brother Roy Mann on his ranch. They say her husband run off quite a piece back. She may not really be a bastard, the gal

I mean, is that how you call them and well I dont have no way of knowing myself for sure but thats what the scuttlebutt been. I seen her once, skinny tyke, both knees with scabs, awful cute. Cant imagine what a young sprout finds to do with herself out there in the middle of nowhere like that out on that big spread, three maybe more thousand acres they say he's got. Uncle of her is a queer one, worst temper they say youd have a time finding. It has to do with that he lost his wife premature. She got cancer bad. They all say he started acting peculiar right after that maybe took to drinking some too. Opal I called her one day a few days back I guess. She didnt hear me least I dont believe she could have heard me being that she didnt answer me back.

Point I guess I'm driving at is that it used to be when me and the other boys was working I always felt just fine and didnt give one iota about the broad not two hoots. Dont get me wrong I didnt treat her wrong or anything, just didnt pay her no nevermind. I come in in the morning and go on into the yard behind the stalls and talk with the other boys for a time over ours all coffee. When the boss comes in right after that we all go ahead and set to working. Now some people probably wouldnt want to work here at the plant but everybodys got to eat and somebodys got to break down the sheep and pigs. Otherwise you can forget your beefsteak your bacon and your rumproast.

Sure could do with a spread of your fine cooking right now, makes my mouth water just to think! So when they bring down the days stock laid out in the crutch, that's when I go to town. Its honest work and hard work too. You got to be like a medical surgeon only stronger. Oh, I tire so easy just now, didnt quite get to my point in writing. I think I'll just let my eyes rest awhile now, Sweetie, okay?

Johnson
APRIL 1956

"WHAT brand hawk is that?" queried Mr. Johnson, index finger pointed straight up at a big turkey vulture.

"That's no hawk," I contended.

"Sure, it is, Hannah. Look at the wingspan."

"Not a hawk, not close. It's a eagle."

"An eagle?"

"Yeah. A eagle."

I thought, *It's a big black turkey vulture and it's up there just circling circling waiting for you to drop and then watch her corkscrew down pretty as you please*

"An eagle!" Mr. Johnson had caught on. Hannah was joking. "Ho, ho."
perch and start up pecking your eyeballs out

"A eagle, or a redtail."

Mr. Johnson smiled, self-congratulatory. "Your mama's right to be proud over you. I grew up in the city, too. Bloomington's not New York City, granted. But my, you do pick things up fast."

first that one then the other

We had strolled so far away into the mild-rolling fields that the house, the barn, and uncle's collection of broken-down tractors and rusted-out cars, tireless, perched on the half-sunk reddish rims of their wheels, engines hoisted away long since for replacement parts, were no longer visible. A flock of savannah sparrows trilled and chipped yards off to the south, invisible in the short grass that runs along the dry, eroded ravine.

A late April afternoon. The sky a pallid dome high overhead. Cloudless except for the whitish puff that formed itself into some recognizable shape, like an ocarina or a jawbone, before it disappeared again. The fields where the crumbly soil had gathered sun-heat were only now giving up their storage of warmth back into the air. It was so exquisitely subtle you could sense it spread upward from the shallow ground into the soles of your boots. It was good to be outdoors. The winter had been so long. I had done my best to stay out of uncle's way, but when the snows came one after the other, piling in layers gray on top of gray, this was hard to do. He seemed to be angry with me all the time. It had to do with his brother, the one he killed by accident, the gun accident, the one that made mama Opal go away with her mother. The one where if it didn't happen they wouldn't have gone away, right, and Nicky'd never have come around and there wouldn't have been a Hannah. Mama Opal and he talked about it. I know because I listened to them through a door. His temper seemed like a disease.

"Hear that?" I said, pulling the field glasses up by the tired leather strap.

"No," Mr. Johnson squinted.

someday this strap's gonna break and I pray it won't be me that's carrying the glasses when it happens

I scanned a stand of bushes but could not see it. We walked along. Mr. Johnson was talking, mostly about mama Opal. I watched his face. Crow's-feet spread at the corner of his eye like a delta in a geology primer. His squint exaggerated these wrinkles so they furrowed deep into his skin; the bottom wrinkles of the crow's-feet reached down in a curve until they looped back forward and joined the creases that trailed from his large mouth. His nose, creased too, was blotched as the back of a brown trout. Or the egg of a turkey vulture. It seemed to me by its shape that it had been broken once or twice. Those cobalt-blue eyes. I'll bet they had as much to do with his success in life as anything else. So much can happen by fate, by a thing not to be fought, because it is not there to be fought—there before you are given fists to fight with.

Uncle thinks this Johnson owns more than just the theater and slaughterhouse. He says that he secretly owns most of the businesses in town and half its citizens, too. *Uncle . . .*

Mr. Johnson is pointing out the direction where the sparrow song came from again. His brown hair jostled.

"Out over there."

"Prairie dog town."

"No, there, over there."

I handed Mr. Johnson uncle's field glasses.

when this strap breaks the lenses of the binoculars will shatter and it better not be me carrying them

The sun was lowering in the sky; it always, I noticed, seemed to move faster when it was setting, or rising. You can see it rise by degrees, swelling from a flat sliver until its entire orange body is squatting like a fat old lady on the horizon. It slows down as it climbs higher in the sky, then speeds up when it wants to set. I've watched this happen. I have a theory about it, too. I think it is an illusion and that it seems to move faster because you can see its movement relative to things on the earth, trees, a hillside. I told mama Opal about this. She said it was a sign of growing up I'd figure things like that out. For example, the song of the vesper sparrow? It is almost the same as that of the song sparrow. It's much easier to distinguish them from their markings. The vesper sparrow? She's got a set of white feathers along the outside of her notched tail. No other brown sparrow's got that. Some things in life are easy.

Mr. Johnson trained the glasses on the bird. "There't is. Song sparrow. To be young and have such good eyes."

It was a vesper sparrow.

Mr. Johnson was very kind to me; tonight was the first time he and his wife had ever come out to uncle's place for a visit. Uncle had said it was not proper for mama Opal to invite her boss and his wife for supper, but here they were. We left mama Opal and Mrs. Johnson back at the house. Mr. Johnson suggested he and I take a walk in the fields before dinner; he wanted to see the land. Uncle LeRoy was at his Utopian Club meeting in town.

"You like it at your uncle's?" he asked.

"It's all right."

"Don't sound so enthusiastic."

As he spoke he ran the binoculars over a treeless ridge behind which lay the county-line road that chased out into the great plains straight as an arrow until it reached its vanishing point. Killy killy killy, came the brisk call of the hawk overhead. It bickered with the vulture, chased it away. Then it hovered low, picked out a fencepost where it landed, raising its broad wings before bringing them in to its side. That was unusual, hawks don't act like that. Its back was rust, same color exactly as uncle's old harrow; I could see its dull yellow claws grip at the pole and its two-whiskered neck ruffle above that white throat. Mr. Johnson let me look at it through the glasses.

"What do you do out here in the days?"

"Lots."

"I mean besides chores. What do you do?"

"I don't know, lots."

"I see," he said. "Hannah, I have a proposition t'make you. I haven't talked about this with your mother, or your uncle yet. Before I did, I wanted to see whether it would interest you. You know I run the Bluebird in town. Well, I need somebody to work weekends, ticket taking, this sort of thing. Of course, you'll get paid, start a little savings of your own that way, maybe even start your own account at the bank. That'd be fun, wouldn't it? Maybe you'll meet some kids your age plus you'll get to see all the movies you want, for free."

what's he want?

"Shall I put the proposition before the powers-that-be?"

he wants something from me

I shrugged, and said: "If you want."

Mr. Johnson frowned. "But what do *you* want, Hannah?"

folks own folks that was something Nicky always said

"I doubt uncle's going to let me."

"But you, would you like to? You'd meet some of the kids in town and so forth, have you ever seen the movies even?"

"No," I admitted.

"You leave it up to me. We'll see what we can do."

tell him no right now

We had reached the top of the rise and the lights were already burning in the windows of the farmhouse. A red-winged blackbird now called, kong-koree, and flew up over our heads, with three-four others, out toward the night part of the sky.

Sun was easing down. Mr. Johnson, for all his movie houses, didn't know that the sun was a god and was putting his horses in for the night. Four immortal restless winged horses whose breaths were flames. And the sun himself, his rays still working their clear and golden streams out over the plains, reddened a bit in the evening dust, he too was tired, and would go now into his princely palace built high on burnished pillars.

I let Mr. Johnson in on this but I don't think he believed me. When I looked up into his eyes I could see he was waiting for me to say something further about his offer, but I thought, Let him do the talking.

"I don't mean to be pushy or prying, Hannah. You know, your mama she worries about you, worries for your happiness. And, of course, if it worries her it naturally concerns me, being that she works side by side with me every day at the plant."

I could picture mama as she worked in the small office next to Mr. Johnson's, deciphering bills of lading, or making out payroll. Her fine, good, wide-set eyes going through the figures.

"Did she ask you to talk to me?"

I hadn't meant to sound suspicious.

"No," he answered. Mr. Johnson was rolling a cigarette as we walked. "I like you, Hannah. And I like your mama. I want you to be happy in your new surroundings, that's all. No crime in that, right?"

"Guess not."

"Guesses not, right. Well, so. Appears your uncle's home."

"I'm hungry," I said.

Uncle was drunk. (Mama Opal would say it like this: "Uncle was drunk drunk drunk.") We walked in the door he came right up, face flushed, and took Mr. Johnson's hand: "Hallo there, Johnson."

"Evening, Roy, your niece here and I have had a nice walk down into the fields. A wonderful girl too, you're lucky to have her around to help."

Uncle looked the other away. Mr. Johnson winked at me. I winked at him.

He must not have thought I ought to have winked at him, because he frowned. Uncle pushed forward into the breakfront and backed away. Then he seemed to get undrunk, just like that.

In the dining room was the steamy smell of sauerkraut and caraway. Mama Opal told me to wash up. Uncle was already at the head of the table honing a carving knife over his long whetstone. We congregated around the table and sat where mama Opal told us to, uncle at the head, facing Mrs. Johnson at the other end, Mr. Johnson between them on the far side, because he said he needed elbow room to eat good food, me between uncle and mama across from him. Uncle said grace. The bowl of mashed potatoes, the kraut and peas, and the gravy boat filled with brown gravy from the drippings were all passed around. Uncle speared slices of roast beef, put them on the plates that were handed him.

"The snakes's quite a problem last year," announced uncle.

"This cabbage is just marvelous," Mrs. Johnson told mama Opal.

"Thank you."

"Quite a problem yes. You have any trouble with rattlers down at the slaughterhouse, Johnson?" he continued; he was chewing with his mouth open, and I was dying to say something but I saw mama Opal send me a look. "Give me some pepper."

salt your tail, birdie

"Not with snakes, no."

"Come haying time the snakes's so damn—"

"Roy," she sent him a look now.

It was comical but it was not meant to be comical it was meant to be tragical—

"So prevalent the prairie's literally crawling with snakes."

"Don't say."

"Crawling snake, that is correct, crawling snake, diamondhead snakes, you can take it put it in the bank and draw interest on it. I used to hire what, six, seven boys for mowing, sent 'em out, and by noon three of them'd be bitten."

"Three."

"Three, at least, sometimes more."

"Heavens," exclaimed Mrs. Johnson.

"Hannah, chew fifty times," mama Opal said to me.

fifty? usually she says a hundred

"It's true," uncle reiterated. "I had me a pair of boots made of bull's hide double-thick like, still have 'em I believe, don't I, Opal?"

Mama didn't know.

"That's right. I believe I do. Want to see them?"

"Oh, don't trouble yourself, Roy," said Mr. Johnson.

"I heard a snake the other day," I began. No one listened. *heard a snake the size of a train*

"Well, fine. But as I was relating I had these good boots and I put them on that same afternoon that these three boys come in snake-bit, and I took a scythe out into the meadow and started up mowing along the fenceline, and these here snakes come at me a dozen at a whack, coming and coming. But whenever they'd strike see, why then their fangs'd get caught up in that tough leather of the boots, and it held 'em, hanging. I didn't pay no attention to 'em at all until the weight of the animals, and there must have been dozens hanging on, started up to bothering me, so I'd stop mowing and cut them off with my scythe. Pass me the spuds, would you, sis."

I noticed how often Mr. Johnson would glance at mama Opal across the table, and smile. It was a closed-mouth kind of smile. It was not good. I drank down the water in my glass.

"Uh-uhm. I had to stop at least once every hour after that to cut them rattlers off my boots, and when I was done and come up to home for supper the boys picked off enough heads to fill a peck measure brimming full. After about a week of that, I can tell you that them rattlers become quite a scarce commodity down there in that hay field."

After the table was cleared and coffee brewed, the custard pies were brought out from the kitchen. Having concluded his story about the snakes, uncle had eaten his meal in silence. But with the arrival of the pies, he began singing to himself:

> *"Come all young men*
> *and my warning take,*
> *Don't ye never get bit*
> *by no pizenous snake.*

You know that song, Johnson?"

"Well, can't say as I do."

"Roy," said mama Opal. "You don't look too good."

"Aw fooey:

> *Carse a pizenous snake*
> *is a . . . horrible beast,*

> *'Twas poor Adam's . . . fall*
> *and 'twas . . . Eden's decease—"*

"You do look a little peaked, Roy," just as uncle collapsed face forward into his slice of pie.

Mrs. Johnson shrieked. Mr. Johnson leapt up and held him steady in his chair by locking his hands under uncle's arms. Mama Opal cleaned the custard off his face with her napkin. His head slumped, rolled in an arc above his chest, humming, groaning. He pushed Mr. Johnson away, jumped up, walked a few steps to the front room, crumpled straight down in a heap, beneath the carved crossbeam of the alcove.

"Help me get him upstairs," said mama Opal. "Hannah, keep Mrs. Johnson company. I apologize, Mrs. Johnson. This isn't like Roy at all."

"Here we go, now," Mr. Johnson urged.

Mr. Johnson and mama Opal got uncle upstairs.

"Isn't that a shame," Mrs. Johnson offered.

A racket upstairs preceded silence. Mrs. Johnson didn't listen to me; she was staring at the ceiling.

"Do you think he's going to be all right?" she said.

"I don't know."

maybe he'll crack his head open and out would run black gunk

We sat in quiet for a bit. "I'll go up and check," I said, finally, not waiting for her to say yes or no.

"Why don't you, Hannah."

The house had narrowed into noiselessness, like when a person is swimming in a pond underwater. Wheeling around the smooth banister at the head of the stairs I walked down the corridor. The door of uncle's bedroom was ajar and a yellow glow gathered in a narrow strip on the opposite wall. For a moment I stood, listening.

A man was mumbling. It was Mr. Johnson. Through the crack along the doorsill I could see uncle LeRoy on his bed passed out. I saw mama Opal, in profile, standing with her face looking down at the Navajo blanket. Mr. Johnson stood close behind, his chin resting on mama Opal's shoulder, arms twined around her, gathering in his palms her breasts which were nearly as ungrown as mine. Neither of them saw me in the blackness of the hallway. Mama Opal closed her eyes as he ran his hand down the front of her belly and let it come to her hip. He pressed his fingers into the folds of her dress. Their skins were yellow in the yellow light. There were pinpricks in between my legs as I saw this but they made me mad at myself.

Suddenly, Mr. Johnson dropped his head back, eyes closed, the front of his hips pressed firmly into mama Opal. His face was strained, as if he were in pain. His jaw gnawed like a goat nibbling sorghum or at a tin can, and the crow's-feet fought like an accordion against his cheek. I almost burst out laughing he looked so silly.

I could've screamed.

Then mama told him something in a voice so soft I couldn't make out what she said.

A sound, below. The scrape of a chair against the floorboards. Mr. Johnson let her go. He whispered. Mama Opal kept on looking at the rug. Quickly I moved, and quietly, back along the hall and downstairs. Mrs. Johnson was sitting at the table.

"Is he going to be okay?" she asked.

"I don't know."

We ate our pieces of custard pie.

snake the size of a train

Gerald
MAY 1956

SEVEN-thirty by the sun's long shades.

The dun mule she let loose from the stables, and out he trotted into the dewy meadow. The chickens she freed from the coop. She spread feed at which they began to peck. She collected eggs. She mucked the stalls and milked the Guernseys. In two heavy pails she brought the steaming milk up to her mother. By walking in steady steps across the lot she never sloshed a drop of milk on to the ground.

In half an hour her mother finished with purifying the milk in the double boiler and it was time for her to go to work. Uncle had set off early with two men who were surveyors. They were going to the area farthest away from the house, a remote section of land referred to as the pells. No one knew why it was called the pells. They had set out on horseback. Besides their surveying equipment the men carried rifles. Indian squatters sometimes camped along the creek that ran through the pells. This region was not so much open range as it was plateau scrubland and eroded short cliffs.

Mama Opal told her to shelve Ball jars of mincemeat, preserves, tripe, marmalade, down in the storm cellar. All the jars were carefully labeled and dated by hand. She looked at her mother's profile caught in the morning sunlight as she untied the apron strings with both hands behind her back. A stray wisp of hair hung down in her face. It was afire in the rays that streamed through the window.

Her breasts hung fuller in her blouse than Hannah remembered them before. She stood staring at her as she unknotted the white bow. "Did you hear what I said, Hannah?" she said. She hung her apron on a hook. "There's a mouse that's got into a sack of meal down there, too. Why don't you clean that up while you're at it, okay?" She sat at the kitchen table to tie up the long laces of her boots. "You're quiet this morning," she said.

Her shoulders drew up.

Mama Opal was hugging her. The girl was shaking; "I've got to go to work now," she said, her words spoken over Hannah's hair. As she clung to her mother Mr. Johnson's hands came into her imagination, and she wondered what things they did with her body, under her clothes. Hannah pushed her face into mama Opal's shoulder. Hannah's eyes were closed, mouth open for breath. Mama Opal allowed her to hold tight for a few moments, then placed her hands on her shoulders, backed away and squarely faced her.

"I hate it here," the girl said.

The woman pulled her to her again, partly in order that Hannah not be able to see in her face her own confusion.

"I hate it," she repeated into the fabric of the blouse; the fustian smelled clean, was crinkly with sun.

She released the girl. "Hannah, we don't have any choice. You know that. It won't always be like this. I'm working saving every penny I earn. You're just going to have to try a little bit harder." She was gathering her things for work.

"I hate Mr. Johnson."

She stopped, looked at Hannah. "Mr. Johnson's a good man."

Hannah bit her lip: she knew now that mama Opal knew.

I hate uncle, too, she said. Or, she thought she had said it. She heard the words, heard them as if they had been spoken, but mama Opal's response made her wonder whether she had only imagined it.

"That's more like it," mama Opal was saying. "There's my little lady."

I hate uncle and I hate Nicky who had to leave us too

"Mama loves you too, darling," and she kissed her on the forehead and went out the door.

Hannah followed her. The door clapped shut behind them, pulled by the tight spring. At the slap of the wood in its frame Hannah heard the cocks crowing and the mule began to bray, thinking it was about to be fed again. Mama Opal climbed into the car. As she pulled away Hannah raised her arm through force of habit and twisted her hand back and forth on its wrist, waving goodbye. The Chevy faded into the field—gears grinding, as she had trouble with the stick shift—and Hannah let her arm drop to her side.

The jars of pickled meats and fruit, vegetable preserves, she began to transfer down into the storm cellar. She had to stoop (she'd grown to be taller than her mother since they first arrived—good food, uncle said) to avoid butting her head on the fat, hewn-wood crossbeams that bore the weight of the house overhead. It was cool, and deep-dirt-smelling. Every jar, every tool and utensil, five-gallon barrels of fresh water, extra clothing, blankets, medical kit, benches, tins, lamps and oil, the rifle and magazines of ammunition, steamer trunk—everything was arranged meticulously.

Mama Opal had continued to can preserves and pickle meats at uncle's insistence, even though there seemed to be more supplies set by down here than there were even upstairs in the cabinets of the kitchen. Back in darkness, walled along an edge by the foundation, was a root cellar fairly bursting with stored vegetables. These uncle rotated by season, removing the spoiled carrots, potatoes, beets, and replacing them with whatever crop was in season. The aged vegetables, the unused, went into the compost heap.

After she finished storing the jars, she swept up the cornmeal that had been gnawed at by mice. She put the good cornmeal into four one-gallon jars, and set mousetraps. Grain had spilled under the steamer trunk, and Hannah turned to pull it away from the wall by its leather handles, but it was heavy and would not budge. It was locked. She looked around for a key to open it, to remove some of the things inside so she could move it. The key she found on an old square-head nail.

What she found stacked in tissue inside the trunk was not what she might have expected. Photograph albums. Dozens of them. The mildewy odor reminded her of uncle's bedroom and reflexively she glanced up the stairs. Two pullets had strayed up to the rectangular opening, curious; they began again to peck. Hannah lifted one of the albums out, and opened it. Inside was a bold signature written in black ink. The surname was the same as uncle's; mama Opal's maiden name. Gerald Mann. Dated 1928: Yucatán, where was that? She turned to the first photograph, careful not to break the hinge on the old leather binding, which colored her palms with dust. The silver had begun to come up on the plate.

In the photograph two men stood side by side, facing the camera. They both were dressed in light-colored clothes, and wore old-style hip boots. In pencil an arrow was pointed at the man on the left and his name was written, lightly, Henry Mercer (and on the back: "H.M. inventor of poured concrete, American original, a fine fellow"). Flanking them were small-statured, dark-skinned men, each of whom held a large heavy knife out at shoulder height in a kind of formal salute. Spread out before this group in the grass were various objects which appeared to be tools, primitive tools, and they were arranged to make a nice display. Everyone was smiling. Behind them Hannah saw blocks of dressed stone that were partly overgrown with vines. Birds and square heads of men ornamented with curlicues for hair and with rough misshapen noses had been carved into the stone. It must've been a foreign land; she had never seen such spiky plants before.

She turned the pages of the album, and there were more photographs of similar scenes. She thought she recognized something familiar about the eyes of one of the men who appeared in many of the plates. It was surely Gerald Mann.

There were also three books. A squat volume, the size of her hand, cranberry red (the good red) with a green ribbon and the edges of the paper painted like an exotic bird's plumage. The cloth was frayed, water stains flowered the bottoms of pages. *United States with an Excursion into Mexico*. Handbook for Travellers, edited by Karl Baedeker, Leipsig, 1893. With maps that folded out.

The first map was of New York City. Home. The city looked like a flattened, sandy-hued centipede, complete with legs along both sides of the body that stuck out into the water. It was water because it was blue. The legs were numbered. They were docks. Extending back from the centipede head there were—she counted—forty-eight legdocks on one side and on the other, seventy-four. Its grayish snout was called The Battery, and digestive organs were similar to a trout's, so that, if one were gutting New York City with one's pocketknife, midway between gills and tail were stomach, heart, liver, the rest. Broadway was a spinal cord; there was a heart labeled Washington Sq.; stomach, Central Park; a liver, Croton Reservoir.

Then there was the what was this? xv. Bookes of P. Ouidius Naso—what a name—entytuled *Metamorphosis*, translated oute of Latin into English meeter, by Arthur Golding, Gent.—

"Hannah?"

She restacked the albums and grabbed the third book off the pile,

Lucretius. *De Rerum Natura*, ed. H.A.J. Munro, 1st edition, 1865. This she hid by wrapping it in the burlap sack the mice had chewed through. She stuffed it into the pail of cornmeal sweepings.

"Here," she shouted, easing down the vaulted lid of the trunk, locking it.

"What you doing down in there?" uncle said.

"Putting up bottles like mama told me."

"Well, that's enough."

She came up into the light.

Uncle ignored her; he gazed down into the mouth of the cellar, hands on hips, thumbs looped into the leather thongs of his suspenders. He descended the narrow steps, crabbing some as he made his way, peered in, closed the inner tin-covered door at the foot, came back up, pulled closed the double doors.

Then he stared hard at Hannah. He said nothing. Hannah saw his eyes were red as the binding on his brother's Baedeker—*that's right your brother Gerald the one that's the ghost*

The pail got heavier in her hand. She looked down at the pail, half expecting it to say something, too, like loosen your grip on my handle little girl, or, get this cornmeal out of my tub or I'll tell him what else you got in here. Wash me, polish me with the chamois, treat me like I'm silver not tin, hang me on my peg and be careful about my constitution for I easily dent, now get on with it there's a good girl to make a pail proud.

Lucretius
JUNE 1956

HANNAH'S a-dreaming. Up in the hayloft. She is conducting a symphony.

These things, not ripe, and hidden still to others, are read by me. Vesper star, emerald star, shepherd's star, hardly before the sun has set you twinkle, and all of us that ever lived in the wonder-working earth have watched you in your progress from ships, mountains, plains, and islands. You are a goddess, too, morning star, star of generations that make other generations. Who wards away all the winds. Who the vesper sparrow and sparrow hawk and all the birds of the plains discuss every day from morning to night and without ever getting tired of saying your name and talking all about the many things you have done and can do. And you who are the one all the cattle low for, and horses neigh and jenny and jack bray for, whose light can be seen through any telescope even at noon. All these things of nature copy you they like to pretend they are you just like I like to pretend you're my sister. You, the one the mystery words were named for: quo magis aeternum da dictis, diva, leporem.

A ripe black fly buzzed slow and fat in the rafters, creating the only sound in the loft except the regular rustle of paper as she turned the pages of uncle Gerald's volume of Lucretius. She worked systematically, her imagination burning, reading first the translation, then whispering the Latin with a mystic reverence, and with no idea of whether her pronunciation was correct. It did not matter. Only the resonances of their possibilities mattered. And the process of pronouncing the words. It was all a mysterious incantation. Beautiful things now and then revealed themselves to her: magis aeternum, magic eternity; diva leporem, diving leopard. These conjoined with *grant to my speech everlasting charm* to lift the charm into real magic, picture-music, the groundworks above which her leaping mind might leap even more—

For you the dogwood, bunchberry, pipsissewa, creeping buttercup, crocus, ponderosa, milkweed, cattail, cottonwood, sumac. For you the witch hazel that pops like a little bomb, the climbing boneset in the margins of swamps, the sheep laurel of hummocks and knolls, for you the tumbleweed that rolls across the plains windy as the preacher on Sunday mornings, huffing and puffing. For you the blue sparks of the morning glory!

Hannah had read with horror about the ritual slaying in Aulis of the maiden Iphianassa. The killing knife was wielded by her father as weeping worshipers solemnly looked on, and the spiritual leaders of the town Danai shook their heads yes and spilled their tears on the soil; tantum religio potuit suadere malorum. Hannah could see the smirking acolytes in their schoolboy excitement fondling the sacrificial knives under the folds of their robes, leaning each against the other like young wolves, anxious for the terrible fun to begin. She was reminded, too, of Abraham in the wisdom of his hundred-some years, at Jehovah-Jireh, his sword at Isaac's throat, the glint of his madman's eyes, his son dumb with fright, his face pulled into a great frown. Blood always, always the blood stuff. Blood of the lamb, blood of the cross, blood about which uncle spoke with his own book, the black one he read every night by the fire. Hannah'd tried it, but—blood blood blood. Her own book was best. Those other people were crazy and all they cared about was killing.

For you the rooster's cockadoodledoo, the piebald mutt's yipyap, the wasp's buzz under the eave.

Nothing comes of nothing. Otherwise what would happen? Apples would bloom in the lilac bush, roses emerge from the butter churn, a mosquito'd be born out of snowflakes, a man from empty air. Neither can things that exist be reduced into nothing, but are changed in time. So that raindrops tumble in the ground and planted crops grow to bear their vegetables, so the trees are heavy with fruit. In this way nature restores itself. Not all bodies are visible. The wind that can carry houses and people sitting at dinner in them and whole towns at a sweep away into its funnel: you can't see that. You can't see the racket raised by rain on the tin roof of the stall in the pigsty. Banjo's thrum, scorching heat, supper smell, river chill, whistle of the dove wing, toothache. You can't see those. Also unseen is the emptiness where masses move, called the void. The pages of this book wouldn't turn without the void to turn them in.

Somebody says that sheep are made up of countless perfect little sheep. And a sheepbone is made of sheepbone seeds. Sheepbone seeds are not visible to our eyes. But they're there just as sure as "Blue-Tail Fly" frailed fast on Mr. Johnson's banjo. There as the hornet in your eyes and nose, there as the skeeter bites you through your clothes, there as the gallinipper flies up high, but wusser there yet? well, what? the blue-tail fly, silly.

The night sky is infinite since it has no boundary. The sky has no boundary since there would have to be something beyond to bind it. But since there is nothing greater than the sum of all things, and since the sum of all things is what is outside the sky, the sky goes out and out forever. And has no boundary. No barbed wire, no post-and-rail.

For you the slapping waterfall and the sleepy Platte. The sun pillared behind the cloud, and moon's halo before the frost.

There is no middle in a universe, no center. Except the point from which we see it.

There are many middles, and so there is none.

Hannah held her breath, and concentrated on watching the motes float across the beams of sunlight that fluttered across the air in the loft. Someone was downstairs in the barn.

It was her mother's voice calling her.

There was the sound of someone climbing up the ladder. After a few steps had been mounted this sound stopped. Then, a hollow thud resonated quietly—jumped back to the ground. A door opened, closed. Outside Hannah could hear her name called. Her mother was looking for her; she would soon have to hide her book and sneak back down.

For you the green ash and red cedar which resist the drought, green for Venus and red for Mars. For you sandbur and cocklebur. The sunflower that tips its yellow head, tall's a man.

For you the cirrus that look like mares' tails, the bigger-than-twenty-moons cumulus in banks over the shadowed peat. For you the dust devil.

All things are moving. All that moving is what makes things so as you can touch them. The secret war that rages within an apple core. The hurricane that storms inside a single shaft of buffalo grass, tempest in the honey locust, apocalypse in the mulberry bush. Restlessness of a hand its flesh and its blood and its bones. Falls like the cards of a cardhouse, drops like the row of dominoes from uncle's dominoes box. First beginnings. A setting into motion by the blow of an atom set into motion by the blow of an atom set into motion by the blow of an atom.

Johnson
JULY 1957

BELLE Star Farms and Equipment. Dearborn, Michigan. Johnson in his suit, rather forlorn-looking, shopping. The insurance money in his pocket. A ferret-faced salesman taking the group of cowboy executives on the grand tour. This gentleman seems to know everything on the subject. He is a real kicker.

"Prototypes, boys: Wackett punch, Blitz instrument, Greener patent killer, the Bruneau and Baxter masks. Indeed, any of these hammers, humanitarian devices, may render a sheep or young calf insensate for the twenty-thirty seconds required to completion of . . . procedures. The stunning of pigs, our committee recommended, oughta be insisted on in all cases, and not, as sometimes at present, only practiced in the case of large swine which give trouble or with a view to the avoiding the noise. There is no doubt legislation oughta be forwarded to this end. No animal need suffer before he's made meat. It is, however, true and undeniable that, even after the stun-hammer is utilized in your modern plant, the animals are by necessity hoisted into the showers before butchery may commence and that this process sometimes stimulates the beast in such a way that he regains his consciousness. The larger kine can on occasion put up quite a fight as you all know, even though they're hung upside down, as you are aware, by their hind legs. It is my personal conviction—and I cannot substantiate this scientifically, although we have scientists working on the problem even as I speak—the meat must be, shall I say, negatively influenced, qualitatively, by the premonitory consciousness of and consequent struggle against what is about to happen to the beast. The chemical constituents that must be dumped into their circulatory systems cannot in any event have a salutory influence upon the tissues."

Opal moved then, as she had for months, nightly, daily, across Johnson's imagination—

"It seems to me and, gentlemen, I hope you'll agree, that outfitting your house with the most effective stun-hammer available on the market today is something you'll want to pursue, even if you felt that the humanitarian aspects of using the instrument were of small concern. We know that there's an art to what we do here, and our art cannot be as tidy and regimental without it. Furthermore, the end product's of a perceptibly higher taste quality if you do use it. What I refer to is the FlumpBlin Velvet-punch. We have heard of some clients who have gone so far as to incorporate the very fact they use this newest pneumatic, high-impact stun-hammer as an integral part of their advertising campaigns. Your little old ladies are very touched indeed by any indication of industrial humanitarianism. It can, we believe, result in increased sales. I don't possess particular knowledge about each of you gentlemen's markets, of course. But take you, Mr. Johnson, just for instance. If the area your house targets in Nebraska is it? Yes, if the area your house specifically targets has at its boundaries competitors who overlap your own distribution network, market analysis would show that by adopting the fact you make use of the Velvet-punch, which is demonstrably the most technologically advanced such device made in this country today, you can put quite a cramp in their style. Well, then, if you will just follow me, we would like to demonstrate exactly how the FlumpBlin Velvet-punch works."

Advancement of learning in the new world, Johnson thought, and the salesman reminisced as they walked through the showroom: "Important feature of the Chicago houses is the adaptation for rapidly dealing with the premanufactured merchandise which they receive. See, in Chicago the cattle are driven up these winding viaducts, by which they eventually reach the roof. It's a sight to see, state of the art. Each of the prebies passes round and round and into a narrow pen where they give them one quick blow to the head, drop them through the trapdoor on down into a room. That's where they start to make the real rounds—round steak, ground round, you get the picture."

And the group laughed, uneasily.

Opal
AUGUST 1956

FIRST the cuckoo came out and sang eleven times its chirrup. Then it disappeared again behind the double doors. After that, the band of painted cows, horses, pigs, goats and a one-eyed goatherd paraded around a winding track set in the second-story balcony posed along the perimeters of the clock house. Heavy cast-iron weights shaped like elongated pine cones dangled at the ends of brass chains. They hung from the cuckoo clock down along the papered wall so low they nearly touched the kitchen floor. And at the end of eleven strokes the clock played its tune:

Bone-white, the moonlight got caught in segmented spines of a cloud, a vertebral column across the starry flatness. Where was mama Opal?

Cepheus and Cassiopeia were framed high in the window, and she said their names out loud. She leaned forward in the sloped seat of a red wicker chair, placed her elbows on the kitchen table, craned her neck so that her head was almost upside down, and peered up at Cassiopeia. The sky was as much blue and gray as black.

There was a man shouting in the next room, his hysteria muffled by rag rugs, deep-cushioned furniture, doors, the wall. The voices of several others counterpointed and interjected to fill pauses left by the first man, uncle LeRoy. Deep musical vibratory resonance filtered through the kitchen, the cuckoo song done.

The girl sat quietly. Her hands were firmly cupped around a porcelain mug filled with warm cocoa. A whitish film had formed on the circular surface of her hot chocolate which, when she placed her index finger on its center, lifted like a hoary skin away from the pale milk. She pushed the chair away from the chrome-legged table with its painted metal top and walked now over to the window above the pewter sink. Along the length of horizon was a taffeta of blackish and yellowed clouds. These low banks were all that remained of the thundercloud which spun the tornado down from its base earlier that day and came right through Babylon, just where it wasn't ever supposed to go. She couldn't help but think all her Lucretius and her invocations and prayers to the vesper star and all that up in the hayloft had something to do with breaking the hex on the twisters. It had come down, she was convinced, looking around for her, not any of the others. But it seemed it mistook mama Opal for her. She turned and tiptoed to the door adjoining the front room, where the men were talking. Cupping her ear to the door she eavesdropped.

"It's just too early for you to go drawing those kinds of conclusions."

"No sir I feel it here," came uncle's voice, "I sense it, it was bound to happen, she was fated. I never figured this was what would happen but a body never knows." His shuddering clipped words into staccati, lending them the kind of grandeur that preachers sometimes display while terrorizing their congregations. The girl froze when they were quiet again. She was prepared to jump back into her chair at the table, where uncle had told her to sit while the visitors were in the house.

"There's only one eyewitness swears she was even within ten miles of the plant, Roy, and he's flat on his back in the hospital don't know which way's up. Got a concussion left him unconscious for who knows how long, they didn't even find him in all the rubble till late this afternoon."

"That's right, said he got plowed under by a couple of steel girders and a bandsaw. Was lucky he didn't get cut in two. Not too reliable a source I'd say, poor bastard, brush with death like that."

"All I know is she went to work this morning and she never come home after the storm hit," uncle replied. "If this man says he seen her at work, he seen her at work."

Mr. Johnson cleared his throat, then entered the conversation. "Now, Roy, listen to me, this man didn't exactly say he saw Opal."

"It was Opal."

"I came into the back room and sent everybody home the minute they put up the alert, Roy. There was only a couple of the boys decided to stay on. Now I know for a fact that I told her to go on back here to be with you and the girl till the storm passed through, and I'm damn sure she set out to do just that. We searched the whole damn place high and low well as the surrounding countryside, and all we come up with was these couple of men who stayed on when they shouldn't have. One of them is dead because of it, and the other one thinks he's seeing angels in his hospital bed."

"She might be helping out back in town still, she'll be along in a bit."

"Johnson here says they called everything off for the night. That was an hour ago. She would have been home before now."

"I'd have thought Johnson would be the last man in the county willing to call off the search."

"Just what do you mean by that?"

"I think you know what I mean."

maybe mama left Johnson to go find Nicky and'll send for me

"Look, Roy."

"No, you look I don't think you want to hear what I'd like to tell you, in front of these men."

"I don't know what you're talking about," Johnson declared.

"I think you do, sir."

"Listen you two this isn't a bit helpful in finding Opal."

Johnson cleared his throat.

"There's no finding Opal if Johnson's called the search off," LeRoy said. "Maybe he doesn't want to find her."

"I didn't call the search off, the mayor did."

"The mayor did," scoffed uncle.

"It's true, Roy," said a man whose name was Shau.

"A snap of the finger here on Johnson's hand and what would happen? I'll tell you what. The search'd be on again."

"Don't be absurd, Roy," Johnson said.

All the men spoke at once in Johnson's defense. After they quieted down, uncle LeRoy added, "It's not that he doesn't have his reasons."

"That's enough," announced Johnson. "I'm going. I've lost half my plant today, my business, I've had a man killed, others hurt and Mr. Mann's sister is still missing. I've got better things to do than sit here and take this man's abuse."

"Patience," Shau said to Johnson.

"Worst part about it's she deserved what she got," uncle LeRoy went on, talking to himself. "There wasn't no choice in it."

"Everybody thinks the world of you the way you've taken Opal and the girl in," Johnson said. "Not the least myself. She's a fine woman, hard worker. But it's not me that controls the sky. Putting any blame at my doorstep in this is wrong, it's evil. We'll look for Opal, keep looking until we find her. You should rest now. Take care of Hannah, and rest."

"Her? She's a curse, that's what. She's the very devil in my life, that's what she is. And her mother with no husband. Now she's finally paid for it, they decided to take their toll on her this time. Now I'm left with the curse."

"Don't blame troubles on the girl."

"Not in my house you'll not instruct me what to say and what not to say," uncle shot back, his chest closing and voice rising.

"Listen to reason, Roy."

"I think you'd better be on your way now. I appreciate your coming but there's nothing more to be done here."

The three men left in a chorus of false encouragement as Hannah slipped back to the kitchen table. After several long minutes uncle came into the kitchen, and saw that she was asleep, her head propped on her hands, resting sideways on the table. She heard him grumble, smelled the whiskey, emptied her mind so she could sit perfectly still as he came up close behind her and with his rough lips kissed her—he hardly knew how—on the back of her head, straightened her hair a bit, extinguished the light in the kitchen, and returned to the front room. She spent the rest of the fitful night sleeping, then waking, then sleeping, curled on the hook rug under the table. This was where her uncle found her the next morning as the cuckoo sounded nine strokes. She was going to find why the wind came for her—it was going to be in the book.

Mama.

Vache
OCTOBER 1958

WHEN blackleg brought down his prize young Angus, uncle fell mute and refused food for three days before openly assigning the blame to me. After mama Opal's disappearance things hadn't got better between me and uncle. I'd have been happy to go somewhere else to live but there wasn't anywhere else to go. The death of this Angus, and how each of us reacted to it inwardly, drove us further apart than ever. And without mama Opal to reason with him and to console me there wasn't much to do. Of course, we both knew it wasn't my fault Vache got sick; she was my girl, but of veterinary science I was innocent as any child of thirteen, especially one who had been raised in the city, might logically be. After Kitter came out and lanced her leg, uncle began to eat and speak again, and to drink. He confined himself, as he would confine himself generally thereafter, either to ordering me about or rehearsing his long since unshakable concept of me as the cause of everything bad that befell him, as the single reason things, anything, went wrong.

He wheezed and had both hands dug down deep in the back pockets of his gabardines. The disease had a mysterious name. Charbon symptomatic.

Vachel (spelled Vachelle by me who had registered her birth, named her) I had led across a rough sumpy clearing of brownish brambles and gray-green nettles, sharp stones and rachet-edged brush, swordy ryegrass, mud. I'd left the gate ajar. This was the marshy field she'd come down into, where the animals were not allowed.

It was then, I suppose—low-lying, mucky from rain, rough, brambly, the uncut field—natural infection set into her torn hind leg. I soaped and washed all her cuts. She seemed to get better. But two months later I came upon her in the unmowed lower field again, breathless and gaspy, her pulse firing.

"Bacillus chauvaei," Kitter said.

"What's that?"

"Shushup."

"But, Roy, this was inoculable."

My uncle LeRoy pulled his hat off and ran his forearm across his wide brow.

We stood over poor Vache, her loins, flank and breast swollen grotesquely. Dr. Kitter shook his head, philosophically, bent over and fetched out the scalpel from his black morocco bag in the grass. A sour-smelling, sour-red and frothy jam spurted up the fine blade and spattered across his wrist and fingers when he lanced the tumor.

"Blackleg, all right, bacillus chauvaei, charbon symptomatic. We're going to have to put her down."

"No."

"Hannah, I said shush."

Kitter wiped his hand back and forth in the deep green grass. A glint of light caught against the scalpel blade. He pinched his handkerchief along its base, pushed downward toward the blade tip. Uncle drew his hands out of his pockets, rubbed his wrinkled neck with one agonizing movement, coughed.

"Well," and he glanced at me but I looked away across the field. "You need any help then?" he asked.

"Let Hannah stay down here to help me out," the doctor said. "It'll be good for her to learn about these things. You just go on up to the house, Roy. We'll be along in a few minutes."

Uncle replaced his hands in his back pockets, smacked his lips. It was a disconcerting sound. "No, no," uncle answered, matter-of-factly. "She's coming up with me, here's enough damage for one day." Then he made an odd whimper, which caused my chest to tighten.

"Now, Roy, it ain't Hannah's fault."

"You need any help then, or not?" uncle replied, clearly.

Dr. Kitter turned his head, looked away from us, toward a grove of white-barked quaking aspens, their rounded leaves quivering though there was no breeze. Mama Opal used to tell me aspens quaked in the still air and that's how the wind got started sometimes.

"You just go on up to the house," Doctor said. "I'll be along shortly."

"Get to home, gal."

I looked down at Vache's head, her eye black, clouded, strength gone. Turning away, I started up the hill. Kitter put her down while I climbed the quarter mile up the slow incline back to the house. Uncle followed me, quiet except for his labored breathing, ten paces back.

Hannah
NOVEMBER 1959

I DECIDED on my fourteenth birthday that I would go to work at Mr. Johnson's movie theater. This is what mama Opal would have done if she were in my place. She was gone, she never was coming home again, I knew that now, I'd cried and cried, knew the whole time that that wasn't what she'd want me to do, cry. I telephoned him and told him I wanted to take him up on his old offer. When the words came out of my mouth I could almost hear them as if they were words spoken by mama Opal. They had adultness to them. He asked me whether uncle would consent to allow me to work there, and I told him yes. But I hadn't asked uncle LeRoy. I was too old for that kind of malarkey. And if uncle LeRoy knew what my purpose was in wanting to save up money he might have just given me the money and told me to go. I don't know. Maybe not. But it had to be my money to go away with, and not his.

On the first Saturday I was going to go into town to work I told uncle what I had done. Just so there would be no questions that might come up later in Mr. Johnson's mind, I even told him that Mr. Johnson understood that I had taken the job with uncle's approval. I knew he wouldn't argue with me. We seldom argued anymore. What point was there to it? he complained. He was right, there wasn't any point to it. He wasn't my mother. I could hear his elephant-slow boots mount the stairs and he called down, telling me never to mention Mr. Johnson's name in the house. I know that uncle cherished his solitude, and this is part of the reason he allowed me to work at the Bluebird. But this was a giant step, and if he had argued, we both knew he would not have won.

Our relationship had entered into a new phase, had arrived at a new kind of silence, as if there were nothing more to discuss and our arguments, when we did have them, were waged with eyes. He had never touched me again after that night in the kitchen. Whenever he came near me I had a way of looking at him. I could almost feel my eyes become electric, and I could square my shoulders too. Who knows if he even noticed this thing I did or, if he did, if it made him scared of me like it was supposed to? But when I gave him "lip" these past three years I did it knowing, more and more, that

I had an invisible glass around my skin, unbreakable by him or anybody else. I was my own father and mother and there was nothing he could say to change it.

Mr. Johnson was tolerable—a little, as James Riding would put it, lightweight. I didn't blame him for what had happened. Maybe he loved my mother. Maybe he was of two minds. Maybe she was pregnant and she went away to have the baby. All fantasizing, but it's okay. He took it upon himself, even when she was still alive (dead, you see, it *can* be written, so—even before she died he took it on himself), to look after me. He thought of me as a tomboy with my hair cut so short (I cut it myself with scissors and a bowl)—but he said, "Hannah, there's a whole world to fill with people, and somebody out there's got to be a tomboy."

I stopped wearing dresses. Not that I had so many in the closet. Uncle LeRoy's sister-in-law commented I had filled out enough that I could wear mama Opal's dresses, her silk organza with the stripes like a tiger, or her white organdy that went so well with the navy bonnet. But I was cool to the idea, I don't know quite why.

At the movie theater there was a projectionist—James Riding whom I mentioned—who wore cowboy boots, blue-jean shirt and pants, and a Navajo buckle he had bought during his travels to the pueblos in Arizona. Except for his sharp, red-black beard spotty as lichen along his cheek, he was tolerable-looking, and told stories of his travels to places as far away as Buenos Aires and Lima and the Panama Canal. James Riding had a low opinion of Mr. Johnson and of just about everybody else in the county, but he had great respect for me. He said I reminded him of himself, how my independence was pronounced, how I had my gaze trained toward great adventures.

James Riding was learned for a man of twenty-one. He said when the time had come some years ago for him to work he went to work—like all the boys in Babylon eventually did—in the Johnson plant. This was the only place where a young man could come in to build a career on something substantial. He lasted only a week. There were three jobs. They were horrible.

One, slaughterhouse. Two, the processing plant. Three, the butcher shop.

One, death dolled up in whites for the beasts. False bottom door pops wide open and descent into hell in a hurry: age-old, no sweat. No thanks.

Two, quarter-ton semifrozen slabs of bone and muscle hung from hooks along the sliding ceiling racks, stained aprons, special bandsaws, cleavers, the meat now still and without stench. This is where they make bacon, where the jerky is made for all the jerks. Nope.

Three, the sissification of a once-live beast, trudging to and fro in damp sawdust spread on a cold marble floor behind the showcase, summer's humidity attracting black bugs, paper doilies and a cuts chart, promote and push the tripe and mention menudo as a curative for hangover, brains tart and tasty with black butter, the heart of a calf stuffed with prunes may win a man's compliment, hocks and a chuck swell, epigrams of sweetbreads, calf's head à la terrapin, fort lincoln and frizzled beef, the exchange of smiles with unimaginable vulgarians. How do you like your lamb? Re-demptive.

Impossible and impossible, said James Riding.

Other things James Riding did not like: preachers and Jesus, war, politicians, the rat race, the race to space, race discrimination, lime rickey, and root beer.

He liked my ears, liked kissing them with his tongue. He did this up in the projection room while the movie ran for its hundredth showing. I liked the feel of our blue-jeaned legs all wrapped around each other up there on the narrow couch, and how I would get so wet it soaked straight through my panties. There was a lock on the door, but I was the one who always locked it. Otherwise, Mr. Johnson might have walked in on us. James Riding didn't care if the door was locked or not. Let him come on in, he said.

The first time James Riding went all the way with me he hurt me, but I believe he hadn't meant to. I was so slick between my thighs when he pulled off my jeans and he ran his palm up along my leg there that he thought I was more ready than I guess I was. He was too big for me. I couldn't believe how big he felt. I wanted to look at it, but I didn't dare. I gritted my teeth because I wasn't going to let him know how much it hurt. But fortunately it didn't take him long to finish. Afterward he seemed grateful to me for letting him do it. I told James Riding I loved him more than any man, and that was why I let him.

He started talking about what we had ahead of us and it was always so exciting to hear him talk. We were going to run off to the Baja Peninsula where we would have our own little ranch and take good care of the animals. There would be, say, fifteen or eighteen children, at least, by my count.

I don't know what happened to all these plans. They sounded so great. Poor James couldn't hang around waiting for me. He had to keep moving on. You can't spend your life running movies without going batty. I forgive you, James Riding. The children would have been very happy, though, all of them at the table speaking in Spanish.

Butcher
AUGUST 1956

WELL there now Sweetie I got me some shut eye much better now. I got my mind back home in my head. Where did I leave you off telling? Oh, yes. Anyways I dont know how it all got started what I was telling you about before but a couple of days back the weatherd gotten worse than I'd ever seen it in years and years. There was tornado warnings put out all over the county and the sky was dark as a hole. I recall I was very skeptic about it all even though the sky was truly peculiar. I was skeptic because as I said this area is famous back as far as the Indian times for being a blessed ground and not a cyclone alley like most of the rest of the state. Now the plant works full shift so it never really shuts down day or night. We just come on work when these here tornado warnings was put out and the boss Johnson come around the freezer and tells everybody that they'd put up tornado warnings. Now he said the safest thing to do would just be to go on here at the plant since there werent no use trying to get home when the watch was up for twisters. Now a few of the boys decided they'd go home anyhow and the boss let them go home to their families. I thought I'd better go ahead and get back up to home myself but Mister Johnson he took me aside after he went and made that announcement to all the other boys and he told me that he didnt have much patience for weather predicters and that he'd lived in these parts for most of his life and seen plenty of skies even darker than this one and no tornado ever come of it. He told me seeing as I was the only man working the saw and that without me the plant would pretty much be shut down he would see his way clear to paying me time and a half wage if I'd keep at it. I thought about it and told him okay I'd stay with it. He was very happy about that and I figured he knew more about these things than I did anyhow. So I just sat tight in the plant and stayed on wage. The broad kindly brought us back news she heard on the short band in the office kept us updated whether they had sighted any tornados which they hadnt. I guess Mister Johnson decided to go on up to home himself since I didnt see him around no more after he come to talk to the boys earlier but the broad she stuck around and I figured that was pretty nice. Thats about when everything just blew up in our faces. Here we heard this roar like an engine more like about one hundred engines to tell the truth deep like and I thought this must be it. I pretty near died in my tracks when I heard that rumble outside the plant. Whooom you could hear it over the noise of the saws. Whoohooom, just like that. Then the saws they all shut down the lights and everything shut down all you could hear was this deep deep rumbling roar. Thats when the windows blew through and the roof started up shuddering over our heads. The poor broad she screamed like there was no tomorrow and I got down on the concrete real quick like. Then it all it all just I dont know just happened. The roof tore off at the far end of the plant. I think it started coming up at the far end of the building and off she went just like that. But it werent any brighter in the plant when the roof come up like you might think. It was pitch dark just black as night. Things flying around in circles there was whole shanks of fresh killed meat come scuddling across the floor. Undressed carcasses. Chairs tables knives cleavers chains. A pig head I swear come flying straight at me its entrails hanging out behind like the tails on a kite. I could smell gas right after that. My sawtable come down on top of me afterward I think and then I just hardly recollect anything at all after that.

What happened they told me was the plant caught fire and the gas depot next door sprung a leak and powerlines was knocked down. They tell me I was saved probably by that bandsaw that got blowed over on top of me.

The one thing I do recollect is this. I'm sure as God is in his heaven before that saw come down on me I saw the broad hung up about fifteen twenty feet in the air. You dont have to believe me you can say I dreamed it up. She werent flying or shuddering around or going up or going down, she just hung there. I swear she looked down with her arms spread out very beautiful and she didnt seem frightened sort of had this strange smile on her face. All these tools and slaughtered beasts and bricks and things was blowing round and round and round her but she was hung up there perfectly still. I suppose thats when the plant and the depot blew up because they never found her after that. One of the boys was killed in the accident too but at least they found him not too far away in a field. The broad they never come up with. And that'll always bother me because to tell you Gods honest truth I dont care that some of the boys never thought too much about the broad one way or another or that they called her the broad in the first place but I always thought she was polite and pretty and sweet. She never bothered me none on the contrary. And as long as I live I will always remember her up there in the wild air like that. She was like some beautiful angel hung there before the end of the world.

But I cant go on anymore about it because I'm starting to feel a little bit sleepy again and the doctor tells me when I get to feeling a little drowsy the best medicine is just to nod off for a while. God speed, your son.

Gerald
JUNE 1956

THE moon acted as cynosure. Hannah lay awake in her bed, situated directly beneath its transparency. Funny how the moon turned everything gray. Its vast reflected light aborted within the confines of her bedroom and through an unshuttered window concluded in an irregular rectangle, thrown with delicious sentiment across her face, and spilling in more fastidious geometrical shapes over the sill, floor, wall, bedstead. The concerns of a dog that froze in a field, its foreleg gracefully suspended, its damp nose working before a crumpled snout, displayed in a single abundantly echoed yap the lunacy of an animal's cycles. Prowl, devour, sleep: mindless round robin into perpetuity. Prowl, devour, sleep. Another, fainter bark ripped into the illuminated night. No birds sang. There were no other sounds.

Hannah twisted under the bedclothes. There was no sleep to be had. The thought of getting caught in this defiant venture, caught by her uncle, whose cycles had seemingly narrowed to two, with regard to her—prowl and, when possible, devour—kept her mind moving.

Hannah's stubborn friendliness in the face of uncle's harassments served only to rile him up more. Uncle LeRoy exactly interpreted his niece's compliance with his rules for the intractable defiance it really was. Not in a position to retaliate, Hannah waged war with her uncle through a scheme of complacency. An insult propped up every quiet yessir; vanity of fulfilling some menial task assigned by uncle with every intention of breaking her spirit was restructured by the girl, sometimes through her mime of strange grins, other times through feigned shyness, sometimes by a crooked frown, sometimes with an unwitting and spontaneous blink, into pure hokum, into insolence. Mama Opal could not have intervened even if she understood the nature of their conflict.

Getting caught with no ready excuse in uncle's bedroom last Christmas had been the first false move Hannah had made since she and her mother arrived. Uncle's overreaction served by inadvertence to even everything up between them. He had gone too far. Mama Opal refused to speak to her brother for a week after the incident.

Hannah cried, in bed, under the closeness and warmth and privacy of her pillow for many nights after it happened.

Death; the death of uncle's wife. Abandonment; the loss of her own father. Uncle finally apologized. To say, he came as close to making an apology as he possibly could. The apology, as only Hannah knew, was riddled with lies. Hannah had rifled his drawers. A silver dollar was missing from his coin collection. She had damaged a favorite family photograph. With no other father available, uncle had taken it upon himself to discipline the child. Who would, otherwise? By the time he'd finished, through a process of democratizing all fault, even mama Opal was made somehow responsible for what had happened. The three of them stood side by side on equal ground in his imagination, like figures in a primitive painting.

But Hannah suspected the rage she would encounter were she caught with Gerald Mann's books would be much greater. In the first place, Gerald Mann did not exist. Only the books remained. Remnants of a ghost. Hannah would claim Gerald Mann for her own. Those faces of brothers, one youngish filled with smugness and life, the other an obliterated apparition, with eyes that matched mama Opal's, as empty as a field awaiting the seeding machine. If Hannah could take on at least bits and flecks of Gerald Mann's being through these books, what would happen?

She got out of bed and slipped on her clothes, shoes, and a light jacket, walked downstairs and soon was outside in the yard bathed in moon. It was a warm night and dewless. The signatures of the million stars overhead were nearly washed out by the bleaching light. Its intensity was enough, Hannah thought as she strode to the barn, to keep a hen from laying. Inside the barn beams shone through cracks that ran where the roofing wasn't joined. A chiaroscuro played over the forms, some familiar, others not. Hannah didn't need much light to locate the pail. There was a sputter from a stall, then silence.

Lucretius tucked under the waistband of her pants, she set out toward the rocky meadow carpeted with ryegrass, brambly and stony, where they never bothered to mow. Here uncle never came. Only the dogs ran down here. She opened the gate, hurriedly made her way down. It occurred to her as she went that she might not be able to see the pages clearly in the moon. She stopped, pulled out the book, opened it up. The paper had an eerie glow, but the type was distinct. Hidden from view of the farmhouse, with only the roof of the barn outlined against the starry backdrop, Hannah sat down on an outcropping of rock.

She flipped to the opening pages. The text was in Latin, with English translation facing. On the front endsheet, beneath Gerald Mann's signature of ownership, was drawn a diagram. Hannah fixed her eyes on this diagram, squinted, straining to focus, and saw in it a radiance of some kind of possible magic, or an explanation of everything from the commonplace to the divine.

Beneath the diagram were the words: *turned to whole*. And in pencil on the pastedown: *out of Duff*.

Hannah traced the lines in the figure, to memorize them by touch, and stopped, hesitated, wherever Gerald Mann had written in a letter of the alphabet where certain lines met.

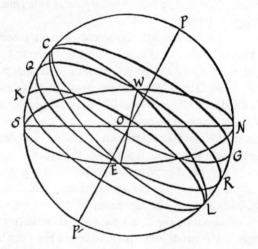

In the center of the circle there was an intersection of lines. Across the middle ran a straight line, halving the pie, marked on the left "S" (*sun? south? star?*) and, on the right "N" (*night? north?*).

Cutting diagonally downwards, from the upper right of the circle, through the center, ending at the lower left, was another straight line. It was marked "P" at the point where the line connected with the arc of the circle just right of its apex, and "P′ " at the left of its nadir. The point at the center of this circle, where the lines intersected, was marked "O."

zero? orbit? ocean? ourselves?

Zero made some sense.

Opal?

Opal, yes, she was the littlest circle, the O in the center, okay.

A series of ellipses, one two three four five of them, was traced on different axes, intersecting the edges of the circle at different intervals, starting from the midway points "S" and "N." Hannah's eyes followed the first ellipse, through the rings of confusion, around its perimeter. At each of the intersections on either side of the circle there were other letters.

None of the letters suggested anything to her.

Drawn across the "O" at the center of the circle, at an angle not as great as that of "POP′ ," was the only line in the diagram that did not connect with the outer circle.

Was the drawing unfinished?

That was a question that didn't count. It was as finished as it was going to get, right. Everything up till now was as finished as it was going to get.

The drawing was finished. Try this.

Hannah rubbed her eyes and studied the page, one eye closed. In a moment some of the structure fell backward into the page while other lines, other arcs seemed to lift off the paper and hover over it. The drawing had metamorphosed into a motionless gyroscope. It was wedged halfway into the physical body of the book itself. She noticed that at the top, actually at the back, of this shorter straight line, which was as long as the line drawn across the middle of the circle, was the letter "W" (*surely, west?*) which ran through the central "O" and terminated along the front edge of the ellipse, actually itself a circle, where it was marked "E" (*earth? east?—no, east, of course*). Around that circle born from the ellipse Hannah now ran her finger: S, E, W, N.

South, east, west, north, these were—

sewn into a bundle, all sewn up

—points of the compass at whose center was the observer, the compass with its cracked glass face, and the needle shivering as she walked across the fields in the daytime, twisting and whirling whenever she spun, the compass held out before her face where she watched it, until she fell down, head spinning and her stomach fluttering. The points of the compass were subdivided into two poles. The "P"s were poles, but she saw no equator in the sketch, since the "E" meant east. Counterclockwise she traced the circles to find herself an equator.

The moon had sunk some, its light not as brilliant as when she came down into the brambly dell. She might have heard the first dove, behind her in the twisted scrub, close by. The sky was still cast in gray-blackness. She heard a faint coo whose hollowness was like an invisible encyclopedia of mourning, its every aspect. Its solemnity was matched by the paradox of its distant-nearness. A strange, dry chill blew over her face and hands. It came from nowhere. She turned around on her haunches in order to see the dove. With patience she studied the hillside, looking across the area from which she thought the sad song had given. Nothing moved or made any more noise. Her breathing, which had quickened and become shallow, slowed, and she looked across the rise for the morning star. It was, she thought, too early for doves to call and, as she settled back down, she heard the homonym: mourning, morning.

Hannah looked down at the diagram again. Its perspective had collapsed back to the flatness of the page on which it was drawn. Her heart fell a little at this and she tried to will the drawing back into its optical-illusory three dimensions, but couldn't.

The land, the sky, everything now pulled away from her, but arbitrarily. Arbitrarily, because in its big starry regions, expanding away and away, she felt the outrageous certainty that she herself had no place in it, the land or the sky. In the simplest act of sitting in this field under the night with a book, with its diagram, mysterious, in her hands, she understood her absence would be regretted by no one and nothing.

In that moment another prospect became clear. That the power to forgive her father for having abandoned them was at once a possible act and, being possible—that is, having a meaning unto itself without ever being communicated—could be rejected, could be a power beyond the virtual.

She could, she knew, in a flash of knowing, withhold forgiveness from her father, forever, and that act would generate real force in the world. And because her own place in the world was, by every evidence, arbitrary and without much point, this evil, so generated, could in no way circle round to its source. There was no such thing as spiritual gravity.

Here was an "N"—for Nicholas, saint Nick.

A twig clicked behind her, up the rise. She turned and studied the thistles and stones that riddled the declivity. Nothing was there. She stood up. The book dropped into the dirt. She stared up the hillside, picking over each detail of it; finding nothing, she sat down and took up the book one more time, opening the covers and turning to the drawing.

It meant nothing, she thought. The noises in the night meant nothing. Her own way of distracting herself.

Just as she moved to close the book to give up on any rebellion against ignorance before mystery, she saw the word where she had begun, precisely where she'd begun, the word which denoted her place in the universe, depicted just here, in the diagram. Three letters shone in the moonlight and she ran her finger across them, directly across the straight line that traversed the center of the circle.

It read: SON.

The abstract melted into the concrete by a strange process of language combining the two hemispheres, south and north, linked by an observer who stood midway between them, at their threshold, and who became their flesh-and-blood counterpart. Possessed, Hannah's eyes darted around the maze of letters and lines, as she mumbled aloud whatever word combinations the symbols might render. Then she read it, astounded as much as anything by the sense that even mysteries have a logical, even linear, order to them, once some initial premise is reached. Three letters, in perfect counterpoise to the others. WOE, she read.

"Woe."

It fell across the path of SON and found at its center the common zero, the mutual *oh*, right there the *oh* of Opal and the *en* of Nicky and the terrible "S" for Hannah, all the big mistake. And the circular mark fashioned in the ink on the page, the circle which gave each point of the compass a letter to anchor it and give it life, served as—more than a symbol—a perfect sketch of how the rest of the diagram worked. The "O" was observer, was perfect, was the "oh" of exclamation and love, was the antique "O!" of address, the true first word of the world which at once circumscribed everything, began everything, ended all; it was a self-sufficiency, an eye, a mouth, an egg, a sun and a moon. It was the zero that preceded the first natural number and the zero that followed whatever final number might indicate infinity. And surrounding it, as if it were the axle, and the four points of the wheel the compass points, were the ways this universe might move. South-east-west-north, whose anagram too meant closure and spelled out a kind of zero. The wheel had two spokes which extended from this zero-axle out to the points of the rim, and these were the results of that universe set into its spinning motion.

One was progenitor. One was its product. The other was fate.

She traced with a twig the other lettered bands that swung around the circle, filling in possible vowels, hopeful other words would further solve the puzzle. Gibberish was all this exercise produced. More and more the diagram began to resemble a child's sketch of a ball of yarn. As helpless as a baby waking from a sweet dream, against its will, unable to fall back into a sleep so that the dream may go on, Hannah now began to try out the three words in combinations.

"Sewnson, woesewn, woeson. Woesewnson."

Each word gave up its own strict meaning which, when mingled with the others, suggested a sense: the son sewn in woe. Or, woe sown in the son. Pop made son for woe . . . son was sown by pop who was sewn in woe.

Hannah lay back and took in with her eyes the high ceiling of stars that flickered overhead.

She picked out the Dippers. Lucretius had looked at that same moon and it had looked just the same so long ago as it looked now. The earth under Hannah's back was warm, but prickly.

Her thoughts were all confusion, but their patterns twirled still around the words, wobbling, faltering, straying a little, gliding further and further off center like a top whose gyrations slowed and whose instability gained, its fat bell racing side to side and threatening to topple.

"Woe, woman, womb, woof, worm, work, wound."

It came like a moan, this incantation, so slowly made. And as she inscribed each word on her lips she noticed the stars were turning blue. Several turned reddish, or pink. The moon remained and the space between the countless stars stayed black-gray. The face in the moon was restless and stony. It did not spring to life as the stars had. Hannah blinked. When she opened her eyes once more the stars were white.

Then the dove called behind her again, although its cry was oddly guttural. This time Hannah refused to acknowledge its presence, or nonpresence. The shooting star that burned overhead was only extinguished once it had traveled far down toward the horizon over an island of sunflowers, their heads bowed. They looked like monsters, drooped and groggy on their stalks. She shut her eyes and smiled to herself. Yet this time steps were taken and the thistle crackled. There was a scraping of pebbles being dislodged. She bounded up and turned to face the hillside and what she could see was so radically different it was just as if she had tumbled out of her own life and into another's.

There it was, glaring at her, its eyes muddy yellow, luminous from within, stationary and aglow in the dark that hovered in the brush. It was not ten yards above where she stood.

A goat? but—

Hannah gagged on the scream that broke in her lungs. Nothing moved, nothing sounded. The head of the goat was very stiff, almost statuesque, shorn of any locks. Its flesh clung to the convex forehead and stood out like marble. From its poll two thick scimitarlike horns swept backwards, undulant, marred by knots and bosses, culminating in points jagged, sharp as arrowheads. They were a corrugated filthy white, and beneath them were pendant ears that tapered into its pied shaggy coat. Sunken nostrils and watery black lips were at the end of its narrow expressionless head that began to toss.

Now its head stopped moving and off its back rose large wings—they extended to their fullest reach, and they resembled the webbed structure of a bat's wings, filmy membranes stretched between the delicate elongated bones of four or five fingers. The wings rustled like paper as it brought them back into its sides.

Hannah stumbled backwards tripping over her book as the goat flexed its jaw as if to speak. She snatched up Lucretius, holding the creature's stare, began to walk sideways up the hill, giving it as wide a berth as possible. The barbs of weeds brushed against her pantlegs. It made no move to follow her but only turned its head to watch her as she crept away.

As she reached the gate she glanced back down into the rack of weed and rock.

Considerable shadows. The moon had gone down.

She ran toward the huddle of buildings colonnaded on the flat ahead, ashamed and angry. She had wet her pants. Her eyes were full of tears. Again she thought she heard something, whipped about, expecting anything, expecting to see it bearing down on her, its black wings careering: only stillness and far away the drowsy performance of different birds passing to matutinal songs. She hid her breeches under a pile of hay in the barn loft and walked, clutching the book in her hands, across the shadowed clearing to the farmhouse, half naked and still shivering.

It wasn't for a day or two she remembered the nature of the dream (and against the physical evidence of her cut feet, and the musty book itself under her pillow, she knew it must have been a dream, a nightmare)—it was a—

son was what she should've been, the dream was right, a son for Nicky, not this Hannah whose name even turned around upon itself like the mirrored folds she had looked at between her legs, for if she had been a son then Nicky would have had both mama Opal to love, mama Opal who shared the same blood as Gerald, whose blood was all like angel hair now, tiny Geralds all set loose around the plains, and he would have had the boy Nicholas to love too, instead of this Hannah, whose name folded in from both ends on itself and began with a kind of laughter before your mouth or anyone's mouth came down closed to make the other sound, like an uh, and—?

Yes, she wished (half believed) it had been a nightmare. There was nothing in the front of the book, right? No circle, no letters. The book was a primer that covered all kinds of subjects for school, the three Rs. Oh, and there was no signature. It might have been there in the night, but this morning it was gone, right? No south, north, east, west, and no spheres running around like bracelets and, but for the photograph of a gawky man in a funny old-time suit standing there in a faraway place with pointy plants all faded and brown as the water the sheep pass at the Texas gate when the truck goes by too fast, there was no ghost of Gerald either, or the goat, who he must have gutted to climb in its skin and chew at grass in the night with its picket teeth and rimple gums. Ah, day.

She got up. The smell of flapjacks. Uncle LeRoy would pile them high and drown the tower in syrup. Hannah, she liked plum preserves. For mama Opal, marmalade, sparingly.

"Hannah?" cried her mother. "Come eat."

Hannah—spell it backwards and it still comes out the same.

Fathers Mothers Sisters Brothers Others
AUGUST 1956

A ND afterwards? after the storm that afternoon?
In a circle tykes play. Hunker over a game of marbles, aggies, cat's-eyes, clay marbles. A dust devil toys with Russian burrs, driving them lightly across a barn in shambles.

Chairs, an ottoman with green velveteen upholstery, highboy, a mahogany breakfront its glass shattered, gateleg tables of varying size, an armoire whose treble-beveled mirror is cracked, rolled rugs set in the tan sun in rows, bric-a-brac broken and spared both by the wild wind, a leaf-and-floral-patterned chamberpot, a player piano with tubby putti inlaid on its sides sans its rolls and bench which might be a county or two over—these are set with other things, lifetimes of objects, of stuff, by men in lines in the road before a house that was destroyed.

A baby is crying in its bassinet out under the dusty sky.

Catch a grasshopper and it will spit brown tobacco on your finger before you are able to slide your fishhook down its gullet. Two young men know this. One is catching hoppers and putting them in a jar for bait; the other is fishing the brook for tonight's fry. Everyone is going to share. Browns and brookies twist in the creel, a rainbow lies in the shallows, gills caught in a forked branch set in the water to keep it fresh and cold.

A group of women stand in a circle where the kitchen of the house once was, its simple order hurled to kingdom come. They are picking through rubble salvaging whatever is usable. Here is a butterbox. There is a fork. There a gravy boat with a scene in delicate blue on its sides of Venetians poling through their Byzantine waters and blue ribbons fluttering behind their blue side-cocked hats.

The crowd at vespers gathers in song then silence: ritual mimetic recollection of the deadest silence before the storm. Outside, the children still crouch together at marbles in the falling light facing each other around the ring traced in the dirt with a stick: the power of sphere and circle. And of omission.

To hunker upon the plains of a new hybrid pagany. To hunker in the newest africk of savage midwest America the newest Old World knocked out of the old Old World's bowels. To feel tragedy obscured and at abeyance in this posture of pure surety. Aboriginal laze, and to rest comfortably with hams on heels. Squatting with haunches, knees, and ankles acutely bent so to bring the hams near heels and throw the whole weight of one's life on the fore part of the delicate feet: not the best posture for the untrusting, the cowardly, the faithless.

Hunk
honk
honcke
honck
O house, place of refuge or safe abode.

V

An Observance
of Hermits

1.

P.S. (the letter ended) What, without divulging secrets scientific or theoretical, is it you'd propose to do with It once It comes into your possession, for as you must understand we cannot afford to be cavalier about such matters.

"It" being the term Krieger insisted upon using for the old Indian, the old Indian being through some rite of conjury the same Cristóbal de Olid who walked away from his would-be executioners so long ago, like a saint out of any martyrology. The postscript Krieger had added to the first epistle, the one which gave the historical sketch of early Spanish enterprise in the New World, may have been just the touch which lifted the whole matter out of the realm of the possibly grotesque into a more benign reality; and here the saint seemed almost sprung from his own mythology, willing to climb down off the stone facade of his own cathedral—jaunty little miracle fated for encasement in the reliquary, a jewel-encrusted box in the shrine. The question was purely custodial and on the surface could have no impulse other than good. Addressed to a man of science who had over the years lapsed into an increasingly impoverished connoisseur and collector, the thing came as a bit of a shock.

It never really occurred to him, from the first epistle forward through their negotiations, that he would pass on the opportunity to have this living, breathing specimen come take up residence with him there in the house over the Hudson. But experimentation, and study? Owen had not considered it. At least, not deeply, and not practically. Materials were to be had, findings, answers to the half-formed queries he had assembled, disassembled, and reassembled through the years which had shot by so quickly. But how to get at them? Here was the first instance in a career (he could still bring himself to call it that) given over to pure nervousness, defensiveness, staring out windows, where he might be challenged and then rewarded with some sort of disclosure. He had to face it, this was exciting. The mysteries locked within It could not be drawn forth by surgical procedure; anything remotely hinting of anesthesia hinted also of autopsy, either of which would defeat the point of the venture. And besides, Owen was neither inclined nor set up to undertake any such thing. Yet the answer to Krieger's inquiry came more easily to him than he might have thought; it also would force him for the first time to accept a premise in his son's research that he had never admitted to liking. As a collectible, Olid was a *pièce de résistance*. The acquisition involved a greater outlay than the mere money, which in any case he barely had. It was all getting a bit complicated, he understood, but it was also enlivening. He sat down to pare his fingernails, and answer Krieger's postscript in his head.

The orthodox approach would be to observe the subject, just like the Frenchman who sat in the cabbage patch under the moon all night, watching the cabbage grow, hoping to discover some essential pattern there, a cabbageness within the garden. Here he could control diet, and he could note results. Here he might vary UV-light intake, observe the behavior of suppressor cells (autoimmunity was surely a key, the body's unwillingness to reject the cells of its own tissues). Here allow minute adjustments of the subject's environment to stimulate in it—It—effects which could be measured against its earlier condition. Here, here, and so forth, but what Owen thought was to make his study more from the inside than the outside. He'd create an environment which would ensure the subject's continued health, say, working with the subject as closely as possible, and then progressively introduce himself (a not too perfect, Northern member of same species) into that environment. The maximum (known) obtainable results of the experiment were already achieved within the physical being of the elderly Indian—it was merely a matter of adaptation, or bridging assimilable chemical balances, modes of behavior, ingestion rites, all life patterns. Come midwinter should It want fresh venison, they would go hunt down by the Hudson and kill deer. When the weather got warm, corn and squash could easily be cultivated.

If it wasn't working, the time might come, Owen foresaw, to abandon everything and journey south himself to be absorbed into whatever power, what water and earth, what vegetable and meat, was there to produce continuation. Successful survival within a hostile environment, wasn't that the very definition of youth? He would go south only as a last resort because among other things it'd be seen as an admission that some of his son's techniques—which had never produced very substantial results, for all of his third-rate anthropology, his conventional rebelliousness and high jinks—were still worth trying.

"Continuation is a self-fostering state," he began to write Krieger, having finished with his manicure and sitting at his desk, "It is like the old joke about the egg. Such perfection of form, an egg. Such natural beauty. Durable, a house full of life. So perfect that the chicken—that hideous and cretinous mass of feathers—is only a necessary aberration which must take place between an egg and another egg."

But he didn't send that. He was paying good money, the concessions to Jonathan aside, and the many risks aside. There was no need to clue Krieger in on his proposed methodology. He was under no obligation to clue Krieger in on anything. A man may buy a Rembrandt, or a Renoir, take it home, spread mayonnaise and mustard over it, and eat it for his supper. One owns one's body; one may throw it off a roof. Privacy of determination is one of the great prerogatives of ownership. It was heartening that Krieger (whom Owen knew as Corless) asked what Owen intended to do—otherwise his Honduran correspondent would have seemed too much the merchant. However, Corless's surface humanitarianism would not trick Owen into sharing secrets.

Esteemed Dr. Corless, the letter began, Yours of November third to hand, for which many thanks. Indeed you are correct in assuming (and no, it is not presumptuous of you to have indicated your proposition in such frank language) that this would be of interest to me. I say "frank" with some reservation naturally since *frank* may not be precisely the term for those several instances in your letter where you couch our subject matter in codewords. I understand fully and am perfectly sympathetic with your need to be cautious, but if we are to do business, you and I, then I think it will become necessary to define our terms. As far as I am concerned you may continue in the contract you draw up to use these obfuscations, which in theory might legally protect you, but before any transfer of money can take place, before we can proceed, I feel that a code key must be established at my end. Therefore, let's say that if you do not contradict and correct the assumptions I make here, in your next letter, I can rest assured that I understand what it is we are in fact discussing. A hundred and fifty thousand strikes me as a reasonable compromise.

I appreciate that the supply-side resources are thin, yet so must the demand-side be weak. This splits the difference. Please agree to this by return, or I'm afraid I will have to bow out. And as we both want this transaction to occur, and also in light of the fact I will agree to every other stipulation you have imposed, I hope we can settle on this sum now, not wrangle over it, since for each of us it is the least important aspect in the deal. You have convinced me of this in your letter.

I confess I don't know exactly what *hanging paper* means (phony bills?) but you can be sure it is nothing I would be capable of doing—I wouldn't know where to begin. Arrangements will be made for the money to be wired wherever you wish or, of course, payment can be made in cash if you prefer, though you may or may not be aware that carrying more than ten thousand cash in or out of the country is against the law (I think). Not that that measures up to *kidnapping*, to call a spade a spade—kidnapping being my gloss for your "shipping"—*It* meaning, I presume, our patient. *Shipping It*, kidnapping the quadricentenarian and spiriting him across international borders being naturally a crime of considerably greater gravity than smuggling more than the allotted number of hundred-dollar bills (or whatever denomination you require, let me know) through customs. But in any case, as I say, let me know what form of payment you require and I will take care of it from there. I should add that because I am permanently situated and you are, it would be my guess, transient or at minimum mobile, I think it is unnecessary for you during the rest of our negotiation to worry about my dependability and honesty, about whether I am going to *hang paper*. I don't deceive myself into believing that the post office box I am using for this correspondence in any way affords me real protection from you, or any real anonymity (for example, I'm sure your name isn't Corless, and a little research has turned up "Corless" as the special agent in charge of the FBI office in Miami who broke up that assassination plot on President Córdoba earlier this month, so I can see you don't even feel sufficiently threatened to throw up more than transparent protection for yourself). You could find me, I think, with relative ease, if you wanted. I know that I could not find you, though. So spare me gratuitous insults in future communications, if possible. I would appreciate it if only as wasting less time.

Now, as regards It. I do not have extensive enough facilities to house more than one and therefore I won't be able to take you up on your offer to ship these lesser patients you have access to. Were the world a more pragmatic, less vicious and insipid place, undoubtedly by now all my work might have come to "more." It's hard for me to imagine what actual progress could have been made with proper facilities. I myself now am far too old to leave this country, at least too old to undertake such an adventure unless I have to, a sorry indictment in itself: family responsibilities, if not a poor education, one which circumstances forced me to undertake on my own and with no professional help, the restrictions of a repressive government—these and so many other things combined against my studies. It is no wonder all the serious research on cancer, at least all of the imaginative research, is being done elsewhere. And now you have idiotic youths blowing up laboratories and setting lobotomized monkeys free in the streets! The priorities are turned upside down, or even worse drowned under so much neoliberal milk toast that nothing can be seen for all the dead white of boiled bread and confectioners sugar. You can understand my frustration, especially at your kind offer, and believe me I would like more than anything to take you up on it but as you see I cannot. But what I can't have in quantity I would want in quality, so, yes, it is that oldest one of all I want.

Of course, of course, of course; he will not be harmed in any way while he is here in my care. This would be counter to the very nature of my own research. I will be willing to sign any document you wish, confirming this. Humanitarians' first principle is the preservation of that which we find most precious of all, life itself.

Now finally to answer your question, yes I would be honored to meet with your representative and examine the documentation which I understand will include photographs along with other verifying materials, but am only prepared to do so at a location that we both deem to be neutral, and safe. It's not my intention to sound mistrusting of either you or of whomever you might send, though I think you'll agree it might be wiser to do things in this manner. Somewhere in or around Manhattan—a place already crawling with so much questionable activity that a conference between us regarding our own projected peccadillo would be unnoticeable—might be best.

I hope this will not create too many hardships for you. If it does, I am willing to listen to alternative strategies, but do keep in mind—and I say this not to lean on your good nature, nor to curry sympathy—that you're not dealing with a wealthy man (indeed, I'm not eager to sell off prized family portraits, antiques and other possessions to come up with funds to make this lease-purchase, though I am ready & willing), and so my suggestion that we meet in New York is well considered. I know of several possible places where we might without any fear of being discovered, meet, go over your papers and, if all is in order, proceed with this transaction. Before I indicate where these are, I should like to have some reply from you regarding various points made above, and until then I will remain, Yours faithfully, Owen Berkeley.

"Jesus god," Krieger chortled, dropping the four sheets of neatly typed paper onto the table. "A few dozen of these guys you're looking at enough to fund a first-class private army down here, swank pad, naked maids, maybe a chalet over in Switzerland for a change of scenery from time to time and if the revolution heats up, live like a king."

"You wouldn't know what to do with yourself if you were rich."

"Working with great idealists, men of vision like you I'll—" (pausing for a retort which did not come) "probably never get the chance to find out, but still, they don't make them like this Berkeley anymore. You said there's another letter?"

"There is," said the fat man.

"Well, let's see."

Krieger looked over at him and saw the scowl had returned; the envelope, pale blue edged in red swatches, he waggled, before releasing it into a wispy arcing flight that ended on the floor at Krieger's feet. Krieger picked it up and read:

Corless my friend, Far be it from me either to question your sincerity and graciousness or dispute your preeminence in matters scholarly having to do with It, its history, its actual age and any other details concerning the presumption it has acceded to the not quite Methuselahean age of between four hundred sixty and four hundred eighty years. I am not an irrational man, and I have no pretensions that would lead me into misjudgment of your aims in this matter. Before I write another word here I want you to rest assured my interest in pursuing our transaction remains constant. No doubt there is some logical explanation so simple I can't see it, like the forest-for-the-trees type of problem. Everything in your proposal made perfect sense to me but for one small detail. By nature I am not a critical person (except when it has to do with matters of physical science, of course), but something struck me as queer when you mentioned Its ownership of an armillary sphere and a kaleidoscope. Now, I recognize that the former article must well be genuine, carried over to the New World in one of those quaint caravels used by Spanish mariners in those heroic times, but the kaleidoscope . . . and the supposition Mr. Olid (can we call It, *him* I mean to say . . . by his proper name??—at least, in my half of this correspondence

I intend to from this moment hence, assuming you will destroy my letters as that would be expedient and wise, and understanding you best proceed with the *It* mannerism for reasons mentioned in my last)—the supposition Olid himself manufactured this as a toy for his children: well, this bothered me. I have looked into the matter and discovered that the kaleidoscope was first invented by one Sir David Brewster who indeed coined the word, as I gather from the Greek *kalos* which means beautiful, *eidos* which means form, and *scope*, that is *the watcher*. Both the kaleidoscope and an instrument called the teleidoscope, whose clear uncolored lenses broke the world into kaleidoscopic images when manipulated in the same manner as the kaleidoscope, were all the rage in Europe in the early nineteenth century. Now, unless I have completely misunderstood the chronologies involved— reviewing your letter this doesn't seem probable—a Spanish (not British) kaleidoscope dating from the period when our man first settled in the mountains of southern Honduras would predate historically the earliest known example by nearly two centuries. This is not impossible, to be sure. But its improbability does not seem to me to bolster any allegation that may be made about Olid's antiquity. Indeed, I assert that if anything this kaleidoscope business throws those claims into serious question. I think you would agree? As a scientist I am willing to postulate any number of reasons why the little toy—and it sounds from your description as if it is a primitive example—is in his possession. A traveler might have brought it to him as a gift. And the inscription you say is on the burled wooden barrel in Latin, Xtobal me fecit anno d. MDLXXXVI, may well have been carved on later, as a joke perhaps rather than with the pernicious motive of forgery underlying. Nor is it out of the question that he *did* have this idea independent of the known course of history, independent simultaneity of various inventions such as, say, calculus (Newton and Leibnitz) or the wheel not being so uncommon, that he found shards of colored mica or quartz, or agate, jasper, etc., and tinkered with these until he found a way to make them work. This is a loose Planckian model for all research. I'm sympathetic with an immethodical, even chaotic view of the history of all the sciences: chaos seems almost a pathognomonic sign of human progress.

I don't like the kaleidoscope. Rather than substantiating the assets you claim for your product the kaleidoscope merely clouds and corrupts the issue. Have you got it wrong do you think? In any case, I for one should like to forget it and, as I say, my interest remains strong, and unsullied by this curious anachronism, and in the meantime still remain yours, anxious for response to mine of yesterday. Truly, Owen Berkeley.

"Crackers, a loon," Krieger concluded. "Talk about your loose planks."

The fat man sniffed. "Pathognomonic, characteristic of a certain disease. Write him back, Corless finds terms compatible, representative to be dispatched to any address he—purchaser—deems suitable . . ."

"I don't know why *I* have to write these things all of a sudden, I thought you did such a great upper-crust job on the first one."

"You do it, I'm tired of your commentary on my work."

"The kaleidoscope, what about."

"That's your problem," he said and, as he might have expected, Krieger had finished the second epistle to Owen Berkeley within the half hour:

Dear Sir, Thank you for both of your letters. Your attention to detail and your erudition are equally breathtaking. Before I proceed to address the details of our transaction let me address the problem of the kaleidoscope. I have no reference books down here in the mountain forests which I could use to double-check your points. Even if I had, I doubt I would bother since so obviously you know whereof you speak. Instead I have examined the thing itself with a fresh eye and find that I agree with you. I have interrogated It on the subject for fifteen minutes this evening and It continues to insist that he made the thing himself—Itself—and more or less at the time the inscription gives. What more can I say? It—this—is a small point in the end and proves little one way or the other. It may well be that It is remembering wrong or that he is having some fun at our, mostly at my, expense. I have replaced it in its teakwood box, the top of which has some lovely marquetry work in darker-colored woods of a scene that looks sixteenth-century to my untrained eye. The image is of ships anchored in a bustling port that could be Genoa or Naples. The case easily might predate the kaleidoscope, you'll suggest. See how well we have gotten to know each other? And again I would agree. So this item, exhibit "K" call it, we withdraw, and insofar as our concerns are with a larger view of matters, good riddance. Indeed, if you will allow me I'd like to make a present of it to you.

After mature deliberation we've decided to accept your offer of a hundred and a half. We feel this is a fairly low wholesale price for what we offer but in light of the importance of your research we think it would be derelict of our own duties to go ahead and make the sale elsewhere, even though we might realize a higher price. We would like to look on it as our own small contribution to the advancement of your work.

We're ready to send the packet of supporting materials via messenger to any address you name. I hope you'll agree that our request of reimbursement of this messenger's traveling expenses (should you elect not to go ahead with the purchase) is fair and reasonable. Sincerely yours, Corless.

"Done," and after placing the draft on the bottom step where the fat man's daughter would see it in the morning and copy it out with her own untraceably childish penmanship to be sent along to Owen Berkeley, Krieger walked outside, kicked off the switch to the generator and listened to it wind down as all the light bulbs were extinguished and the dark woods in turn began their trespass into the *bolsón*.

The letters are good, he thought—only two impediments were out there in the dark. But Hannah had something to lose. Jonathan Berkeley?—it was open.

How's your road?

"*Bix a bel?*"

This was the question, put in Yucatec, that once. The group in this lovely old Spanish cloister garden behind the golf course, air scented with orange and lemon, stone benches around the walls, ghost of a breeze through the humidity. The greens were, as ever, unoccupied, though the links were kept up nicely by gardeners from the embassy; only sometimes were they ever used, and at that the soft grass was less often brushed with an iron than flesh encumbering itself in the comfort of this semi-natural setting.

Krieger'd coughed at his cigar.

There was this guy, this Berkeley kid, and he was down here mucking around, some kind of brat anthropologist copping scads of attitude, his hair grown down to his chest and cropped tight Maya-style across the forehead, his nails curling, his feet dirty, left his robe back at the milpas and managed to get into *guayabera* for the occasion, though to Krieger's eye he still looked like a dime-store Jesus, just not as threatening. The guy was a long way from home.

The Lacandones, what about the lousy Lacandones? and whoever could give the first flying fuck?—but there he was talking Indians, this kid who was green, a pup, a cub, his long hair and the "gone-native" politics aside. He was arguing, cordially it had to be admitted, with someone about some promising data which might come through infiltration into the tribe.

"You lose your dialectic that way, though," it was proposed.

"Right," Krieger said. "Peyote button now and then, all right, but unless you're prepared to do a Castaneda trip, make everything up, I mean the worm's best left in the bottom of the bottle. Drink the tequila. But the worm's already dead."

"Worms are rich in protein."

"You'd fare better eating cirrhosis and onions."

Jonathan wasn't listening, was saying at the same time, "This's the only way to get inside, penetrate the purple haze, you've got to live through to your scholarship, you can't be a good mechanic and keep your hands clean."

"That's different," Krieger recommenced. "Mechanics work with known systems, finite engines, like osteopaths. You come from one world to observe the behavior in another, unknown systems, infinite injuns. Why should the scholarly community pay any attention to your findings? that is, aren't you seen as a traitor? I mean, you ladies, don't you consider him a traitor, a when-in-Rome sort of tourist?"

"I'm afraid I don't know his work."

That's right, be delicate, go soft, you can never tell when some colleague is going to end up on a grants panel cradling the family jewels in one hand and the sword of justice in the other.

"Specious bunch of philistine crap," Jonathan said, breaking in on the inner dialogue.

Which took Krieger aback. He acquitted himself by repouring wine around the table, thinking, Jonathan, wimpy sort of name, and like most every Jonathan since the second war named after the famous General Jonathan Wainwright, great hero, great American, yet still the only thing he's remembered for is the death march at the Bataan Peninsula where instead of winning he was forced to surrender, was even taken prisoner by the nippers, who stowed him in Manchuria until the war was over. Jonathan, he nearly snarled it.

But, *bix a bel*?—dinner conversation, some pretty boring fare at that, and Krieger looked around the table: the fat Nicaraguan; the anthropologist Sardavaal up in Tegucigalpa to raise a little money for some lost community; a couple of ladies from Tulane (the one on the far side of the table warming more into the discourse with Jonathan, having perhaps gotten the upper hand with her last query); the whole lot of them decadent (Krieger averred), dissolving into the landscape, the one woman cross-eyed behind her glasses which was at least to Krieger's mind sexually inviting—cross-eyed women being especially attractive to him, drawing the man into their bodies in some fashion he couldn't explain. And yet, everybody in this particular group knew that *bix a bel* meant "how's your road," "how's it going with you," and that the proper answer would be *toh in wok*, "straight is my step."

But this Berkeley jerk, thought Krieger, having to show us that he knows

Yucatec, kindergarten-level. Hard to cut slack to such negative space.

Toe in wok, no (Krieger was thinking fast—he had to say something that would bring the conversation back to Sardavaal's tribe. Krieger sensed there was something there, something possible, with that tribe. He hadn't yet figured out what. But something), well, tried-but-true he offered, "Straight up your *Az*-tec."

No one laughed.

"*Käläx t' an*," Sardavaal smiled. Obscenities.

"Anyway so tell me more about your father's work, Jonathan," Krieger'd gone on. That was choice—hated his father. No memory this guy, either. Hadn't there been that time on MacDougal? Ranted about the establishment, pissed on money, very garden-variety utopian and, plainly, how much easier to piss from the comfortable height of financial security than from down, say, in the gutter?

"He doesn't interest me."

Turning to the woman in a flannel suit, which seemed so out of place in the setting, "He interests the rest of us, though, a gerontologist, admirable discipline, I think."

Sardavaal was back to talking earthquake relief by then.

Time flies, and the ground flies, too. Krieger almost said it aloud.

"What we've done is suggest that by putting barbed-wire armature inside the adobe walls the thing holds together better when it starts rocking."

"That's interesting, barbed wire."

A tedious bunch, Krieger thought, turning to the cross-eyed woman whose irises were deep brown flecked with marigold. What color was she between her legs? he wondered. What taste? what smell? what feel? There was, apropos the itch in his fingertips to test out the resistance of the cotton of her skirt—so gaily patterned—another Lacandon saying that came to mind. When the party began to break up and the dinner guests said their goodnights, Krieger managed to get her off to one side. "*Ki' wenen tech. Ki' l(le) bá (al) a wilik*," he whispered. Sleep well, you. Take care what you dream.

She got the message.

2.

BERKELEY house sat on a knoll where it surveyed the long lawn, the rolling irregular grounds that extended to its northwestern border, and the sea of trees which sparkled and waved, a sinuous and torrid expanse out beyond the combination of hedgerows and post-and-rail, long since collapsed in desuetude, that marked the property line at one border. Locusts, birches, lindens, maples, merged to make a carpet whose nap would change in the gentlest wind. In the autumn, when the leaves were at peak, it seemed at times as if the entire forest were constituted of embers. In winter, under the slow snow during the short days, it had seemed to Owen—who gazed out over it from the relative security of his second-floor rooms—to be the gloomiest conceivable stretch of earth, like a desert, a wasteland of interest only to the complaining crows that lit at the tops of branches. Many birds made these forests their sanctuary and others passed through on their way from Canada south toward the West Indies, the Caribbean, to quarters in Costa Rica, Panama, Colombia, Venezuela and beyond each fall. But of all the seasons summer seemed kindest here when the leaves were green and meaty, and the trees were caught up in ceaseless song.

The house itself where Madeleine, Alma, and Jonathan had grown up was a sprawling immensity, too grand for the family ever to have occupied more than a small number of its rooms. It had the appearance and the magnitude of a mansion but these, the last generations of Berkeleys to live in it, never thought of it as a mansion since the family could never afford to maintain the grounds or the structure itself. An accretion of Palladio, Williamsburg, Victorian, the house was fitted out with clerestories, three turrets, two widow's walks, many balconies. Dormer windows jutted from all angles of the slate roof. At the peak of every gable stood a finial or weather vane, painted ships and tin cocks long stuck in place, pointing beak north/tail south, or bow east/stern west, no matter which way the wind blew. Tall chimneys were each finished with decorative brickwork. Fashioned in part of river stone, clapboard painted white, and later of brown brick, the house had been added on to by succeeding generations of the family since its cornerstone was laid in place in 1775 by the chandler and fur trader Theophilus Berkeley.

Diversities of architecture reflected the changing tastes of the house's owners through the centuries of its history, and the varying qualities of workmanship and materials represented a chronology of their fates. Theophilus Berkeley's son and grandsons lived comfortably in Berkeley house through the first decades of the nineteenth century. Thousands of acres were kept in seasonal rotation and what land the family was unable to utilize was profitably leased. But already by the end of the century the great-great-grandchildren had begun selling off acreage in large parcels along the borders of the farm. This was a process that proved difficult to halt. What remained in the hands of these last descendants of the patriarch was their small private cemetery, walled in and lost under the darkness cast by great willows whose roots pillaged its caskets and crypts, and Berkeley house itself, situated on a fraction of original land that remained—about a hundred acres along the river, many of them overgrown with trees, berry bushes, and wild vines.

The arrangement of rooms and passageways within the house was no less quirky than that of its exterior. Corridors wandered off to terminate at doors locked half a century ago. One balustrade led up a stairway which ended at molded ceiling where architects and carpenters had run out of ideas or encountered an unresolvable problem and been forced to nose the topmost riser of a staircase in where a chandelier were better hung. False windows and false doors abounded. A ballroom described the shape of one wing, and it had a grand staircase which led down to a lower foyer and a series of glass doors that gave onto a terrace. The parquet was now covered in a fine film of dust; the floorboards on the small raised bandstand were wildly warped owing to a leak in the roof; glass in the bank of doors was cracked.

The Berkeleys' nature had always been industrious, bright, eccentric, nepotic, isolationist, and until their latest manifestations, practical and unspeculative. It was a proud family as well, and that pride was a quality passed from generation to generation so unerringly it seemed almost a genetic process. Their isolationism contributed, over the years, to the very undermining of industriousness and led to the dispersal of the property. When Owen was married and became the head of the house, the lands that protected Berkeley hermeticism were so broken off and scattered that this trait became more a function of the imagination and will. In so many words, the house itself had become the land.

*   *   *

Late fall. Gables sunk in coral, shadows making mischief over the lime-moon lawn. The leaves crackled crisp underfoot. The berries in holly bushes the only objects a brighter red than the flash of the cardinal through their prickly spines. Summer had been dry, nearly drought; a freak frost had tricked the leaves into turning early, but the birds had still delayed migration. They flitted everywhere and, far above, a red-tailed hawk beat its broad wings three times then glided into its circle, eye trained on the open country below for the movement of a rabbit, or a mouse.

This abundance of bird life Jonathan first gladly remembered after being away so long. If it was true that his father was entangled, after a lifetime squandered in the pursuit of ridiculous impossibilities—alchemical conversion of dry ice to diamonds, vacuum-carriage urban sewer system, biologic codes of immortality—and all at the expense of his family, year after endless sinking year, now in something that would finish him, finish the "Berkeley line" (for Jonathan himself had no intention of continuing it), then Alma's telegram in its typical Alma-panic and Alma-mother tones would not be as farfetched as it seemed when Jonathan first read it.

If not—though this time it sounded as if things had gone too far, Owen always having gone "in and out of it" but was now more "out" than ever—he had explained to himself that some days could be spent on his project, an old project, one which even he had given up much hope of ever completing: to find his sister Maddie who was still in exile—find her with or without Henry, and this would make the trip worthwhile. If not, he would pay homage to dear sweet mother Sophie and poor brother Red and maybe fill his pocket notebook (bought especially for the purpose) with lists of some new sightings, and return to his fieldwork before the culture shock, to which he was susceptible, settled in to wreak havoc on his conscience.

Barefooted and toothlessly whistling, perched awkwardly on an old bicycle jerryrigged with a steering wheel for handlebars, a man had brought him Alma's cable on Tuesday, *gracias doctor*ed him with teeth like Indian corn cutting straight across the lips. In his small house in Lejamani he locked his notebooks, tapes, and all his medical supplies in a file cabinet, packed up and left in the truck, feeling slightly guilty at leaving Manuel de Jesus Díaz behind with the generator only half rebuilt.

Lejamani had served as Jonathan's base for a year. He'd come to Central America first as a graduate student, working on human ecology and agricultural biology in developing nations, but in fact had never yet reduced the masses of notes and figures into a doctoral dissertation. He had worked for the OAS in Salvador and Costa Rica for six months here, seven months there. He dropped everything when natural disasters took place, and flew with other volunteers into sites to help the dying, those burned by volcanic ash, or crushed by falling beams in an earthquake, the homeless after a flood. His most important published paper was about the Carib Indians along the Atlantic coast of Nicaragua who—unlike the Chorotecs, descended from the Aztecs who settled across the inland plains and had been subjugated by Cortés in the sixteenth century—had lived in not quite unobserved primitivity and autonomy until the end of the nineteenth. Primitivity carried with it a fundamental honesty, he believed, and the thrust of his argument was that socioeconomic conditions among individual tribes unerringly and in every respect had deteriorated ever since. In the early part of the eighteenth century the British turned Moskitia into a *de facto* protectorate. Both the Christian barbarians, led by the "butcher-bishop" (his term) Bartolomé de Las Casas, and imperialist Britain—seeing the need to establish a command post for military discourse with the French and Spanish—had played key roles in destroying the "simple" (meant to be ironic, that is: complex) societies they had found there in Latin America. And what the Spanish and British neglected to do, the United States, the good old homeland, undertook to finish:

> *"Land of the crow-juanist's pride,*
> *Land where the Tacho-shafted died,*
> *From every big-booted kick to its neighbors' underside,*
> *Of thee I sing."*

His father, sent a copy of Jonathan's typed notes back when he was writing them in southern Mexico, responded responsibly, with a letter that called him on several points. First, this was not the language of academic dissertation nor was it one which seemed to him very special, or new, however clever. Second, contrary to what Jonathan may have thought—even hoped, as children can often hope in their quest to see well over the shoulders of their elders—he, Owen, was not fundamentally in disagreement with his son's findings, his opinions, his moral outrage. Third, this was especially nothing new, this outrage, and even Maddie in her running away with the stableboy (Owen refused to call Henry Work by his name) showed more basic pluck than anything he was doing with his Maya studies and simple readings in post-Columbian literature and art (or whatever you geniuses locked away in your ivory towers, or mud towers, down in the middle of the jungle call it).

Jonathan was so surprised by the letter that he spent several days drafting his response. He didn't want to seem like a child. He didn't like what his father had said, but saw there was something to it, a care Owen usually reserved for Alma, or Red. But the letter came out—gushy, full of love and again, all wrong, too far the other way. He sent it anyway. There was never an answer.

It was with an obscure anthropologist named Miguel Sardavaal that Jonathan had spent his most rewarding month to date in Central America. Sardavaal enjoyed the reputation of both pioneer and outsider (a combination Jonathan cultivated like bamboo and reeds). His work was concentrated in the remotest areas of the most backward districts of southern Honduras and northern Nicaragua. His materials (Sardavaal's colleagues knew of piles of undigested notes, and remembered when he attended meetings to give eccentric, impromptu papers which were recognized to be the richest stuff to have come out of the area) remained for the most part unpublished. He hadn't the time and was always giving his typewriters away. His research was therefore enveloped in a kind of mystique. Jonathan came into his temporary employ under false but not dishonorable pretenses. They met, through a mutual acquaintance, at a soccer match in the loud dusty stadium in Comayagua. The day was white in its heat but the players were fast, out on the shabby yellowed grass, and the crowd was enthusiastic and loud.

The man who worked his way across the bleachers to make the introduction was someone Jonathan knew he had encountered before. A corporate type of the kind Jonathan had run up against in the OAS and even in his tour with the Peace Corps—Jonathan, indeed, continued to think of all Americans down here as either rapists or saints—but clearly this man, approaching jauntily, all smiles, was some fresh brand of renegade. Jonathan remembered his name even before he reached out to shake his hand because, during the last discussion the two of them had had, the origin of the name Krieger and its having to do with the German term *Blitzkrieg* came up. A party for the medical volunteers Amigos de las Americas, at the *campo de golf* at the shantytown edges of Tegucigalpa, proceeded with its bartenders in white, stained waistcoats and pennyloafers?—was it? maybe not. There might have been an earlier meeting back in New York? that was plausible. There was also something about a very bad joke: up your something or other.

"Here's your man," Krieger announced to Sardavaal, whose own smile was one of forbearance. "I was just telling Dr. Sardavaal about you."

"Telling him what?"

"Telling him what we talked about, don't you remember?" and he began to whisper, close, softly in the crowd. "There was something about that drought where was it now down in Alabama? chickens shrivlin' away, the fish all justha drying up in they ponds, corn poppin' right in they stawks, blessed catfeesh djaw member that one just come boxing long the road just popped up into the pan to cool off in the bacon grease?"

"What?"

"Ya still like Prez?"

"You know what, you must be remembering somebody else."

"No, no, I never forget anything. Hey, wait: you cut your hair, man."

"Of course I know Dr.—" but when did Charlie Parker ever come up between himself and Krieger? or was Krieger guessing? yet it was true the Parker albums had caused trouble at home so many years ago, as did the trips down to New York to the jazz clubs, all frowned on by Alma in the ever-present pro-Henry, anti-Henry climate of the days after Maddie left home.

"Looks great, the hair I mean, that mop must've got pretty hot out in the canoes, no?" Krieger gestured to the other man, "I believe you two have met before, Dr. Sardavaal? This is Jonathan Berkeley. That's right isn't it?"

"Of course I—"

"Inside joke," Krieger offered as an aside to Sardavaal, "bacon grease."

Sardavaal's attention was called away to the field as the crowd rose to its feet. Legs pumping, the Honduran worked the ball down toward the goalpost, shot wide. Krieger groaned, then continued. "Well that's fine that's clever, Mr. Berkeley, Jonathan, I remember *trabajo garantizado*, all work guaranteed, right?"

"*Trabajo garantizado*—what kind of work?"

"What kind of work? This is Dr. Sardavaal I'm sure you must know who he is for godsake, you've been down here for a while haven't you?—no, I remember now, I think we all had dinner once, remember, after the earthquake? and maybe back in the Village?"

"Which?" Sardavaal asked.

"Uhm, Managua, maybe? can't remember, faces and names even some ideas yes, but earthquakes no." He cleared his throat.

"Yes I—" Jonathan extended his hand, which was taken, a cool bony hand, then turned, "Your name is Krieger, isn't it?"

"Why not," he winked, "but in any case it's all arranged, and if I can be so bold without embarrassing Dr. Sardavaal, you owe me one. 'A man should not mean but be,' so okay?"

Jonathan's gratitude—which ended, after Sardavaal left, in a tour with Krieger through chambers of an Iglesian brothel, "raven-haired" women with "volcanic" eyes (the descriptions seemed appropriate at the time), waist-long tits, tattoos, caterwauling babies left in dark corners ("etcetera")—was at first grudgingly offered. But the gratitude was premature, also, and, as it turned out, some of the skills which Krieger claimed for Jonathan were extravagant fabrications. The tequila had blown the evening out of proportion, though. They ended hugging in the street.

Jonathan had no expertise in epidemiology and yet so many miles outside the already far-removed village of Huanquivila, Sardavaal—who had need of an epidemiologist—could hardly send his young intern home.

"Dr. Krieger," Sardavaal reasoned, "is an enthusiast."

A liar, thought Jonathan, doctor? *doctor* Krieger? Trying to remember what it was Krieger had said declining the mulatta in the whorehouse, joking in his perfect Spanish, a Spanish so adroitly rendered that he sometimes sounded "international Spic"—upbeat, oily, spiced with so much ingratiation the words themselves seemed commerce. He had, however, talked Jonathan into taking her. He wasn't in the mood, after all. It was something Jonathan'd never done but the room had gone into a hole by the time it came around to deciding so that before he knew it he was naked, in a feather bed which smelled of aspic, warming to all of it—how did people live? how did they go forward from day to day? life was okay, it wasn't all that bad, no matter what the circumstances, right—while Krieger (as it turned out) sat at the table in the room, writing letters. One of the letters (in the morning, it seemed as if he had produced enough to fill a postman's satchel) was that which made an ultimate link—that is, in Jonathan's life, though perhaps in Krieger's too.

Krieger would from time to time, with capricious irregularity, write Hannah. A letter would come and she would put it aside for a day or two, even as long as a week, before opening it to read. Some were tangential and chatty, others she found unexpectedly sweet—"So we finish with this hemp-and-slat bridge, wobbly-looking piece of work, but it spans this forty-fifty-foot gorge, Hannah, handsome slithering creek down at the base of the thing and a falls so far down you can't hear it roaring, or spitting, &c, and so I'm yelling at these ignorant little bastards who I catch stuffing carnival explosives, a cherrybomb I expect, down some poor frog's throat and chucking the poor beast out over the gorge's edge just to watch it blow in this muffled burst. Just the insanity of it. But they insist that I be the first person to walk across this bridge. Celebratorily, you know. And I think of all the lashing I helped with on it and the boys at my sides sitting there for days along the banks slapping mosquitoes and flies, all of us trading advice and lashing timber, only the Peace Corps cat here whose handiwork I don't trust, &c, and so well yes, I go them one better grab my favorite kid in the village here, bright brown-eyed punk, and up he goes on my shoulder and we set out together to make the far bank, and midway across there's a mighty strong surging swing to the thing, the water so far below and the wind playing with the loose vegetable strutting, I wish you could see this bridge Hannah, but in the end there we were at the other side and all the villagers were screaming, walking back and forth across for the rest of the day, marveling at their accomplishment. I missed my calling, I should've been a funambulist, join the circus, ride a unicycle up on the highwire. As fine a day as I've ever seen. So it goes."

After his internship with Sardavaal, which continued for many months longer than Jonathan had thought it might, the return to his own work was difficult. Primitive cultures ("fundamental" was Sardavaal's term) in the upper-mountain regions were more interesting to Jonathan than the introduction of literacy or higher-tech agricultural methods to cooperative farms. Astronomical determinatives in the lashing of cedar branches to construct a bridge . . . six monkeys on a morning branch to judge the gender of a pregnancy . . . the salted fingertip in the shaman's hand to draw off a cataract . . . prophetical readings that might be made from the puke of a firstborn son . . . the persistent reference throughout the most alienated communities to the superiors or gods-of-the-silver-heads (who Jonathan suggested must be conquistadors, though Sardavaal demurred), beings who had flown between stars from the farthest worlds in the night sky to devour the men and women of the ground-world, and how some of these gods still lingered among animals of the forest, ancient beings, wizards, cow-headed girls, brutes, ranting apocalyptics—through Sardavaal Jonathan had glimpsed, in the veils of translation and peyote, another layer of mind. He'd begun to think of his own as the bastard culture, one where the very act of walking across the land was an act of surveying, reducing the clods of dirt to measurements of abstract value—purchasable, and thereby powerful only if owned. Here the land and earth was still motherly. He thought these things. They felt clichéd, sentimental—but in his gut he sensed he was on to something.

One morning Sardavaal left. Jonathan was disappointed but not surprised. This was how he behaved. It was known throughout the anthropological community. It was why tutelage under Sardavaal was good and bad. You learned, but he disappeared as he saw fit. Jonathan was handed a pouch with money in it, a map, the briefest note thanking him for his work, acknowledging how useful it had been, wishing him good fortune, expressing impatience against the day when they would meet again.

He reestablished affiliation with the university—having taken a leave of absence—and communicated in letters to colleagues his continued intention of pulling all his notes together into a book, but privately he had come to wonder what real purpose there would be in it, other than securing for himself a temporary niche in the publish-or-perish world he embraced from the farthest possible remove. One thing he did know was that no monograph, article, or dissertation was going to better the fortunes of Manuel de Jesus Díaz (who could be seen waving, battered straw hat tipped back on his dark head, in a cloud of dust left in the wake of the truck), or of any of those skinny, giggling children caught up in the whirl of terrified hens and cocks.

The truck, affectionately if wryly nicknamed *El conejo*, had neither horn nor brakes, but since the exceptionally agile hog that ducked its crap-caked snout away from the front fender and careered wheezing down a red embankment was the only traffic Jonathan would encounter until he reached the outskirts of the capital, these were not necessary. He parked *El conejo* in the lot at Toncontín airport, removing the distributor cap from under the hood. This was a precaution against the truck's being hot-wired and stolen. It was an old move, one he'd learned from others in the fieldwork years before. Still, the odds were at best even that *El conejo*'d be there on his return. He should have asked Manuel's brother, who knew how to drive, to ride into the capital with him and take the truck back to Lejamani; but it was too late now—although the flight was delayed five hours—because there was no telephone in the village and so he had no way of discussing *El conejo*'s fate with Pablo Díaz. Bored, he watched half a dozen air force troops roll dice across the cracked tarmac in the shade of a transport helicopter. Over the mirage and heat of the runway Radio 15 de Septiembre propagandized and played Menudo—biggest band since the Bey-atlas, he mimed Díaz. Defiant and a little reckless, Jonathan rummaged through his knapsack to find his portable receiver, which he tuned to Radio Progreso, a Jesuit station, for while he disliked the Jesuits as much as he did the anti-Sandinistas, he figured the two ought to at least share the air space that was only rarely filled with the roar, windows snapping at their frames, of a flight taking off, or maybe landing.

* * *

Grand Central was more stale than ever, rank, gamy, teeming with people, people whom he couldn't help but see as *gringo*, even knowing he was one. Awkward—didn't feel great. And what lay ahead was a bummer unless he could reinvent it even as it took place, as an anthropological exercise in some manner. It was, he knew. And so he would have to think of it as such. It was the truth, wasn't it—the reversed Descartes bit, I am therefore I think, had not escaped him, nor the internal discoursing's defensiveness. Nor even its silliness or show of exhaustion. Tight belt, man. Little day-after-Thanksgiving spirit, eh?

The train hugged the riverbank. He knew each stop by heart from having made trips to Manhattan as a youth; they ticked by as the train passed their outskirts. The Jersey shore was concentrated into a long skyline sunk under a film of filth the shade of sepia seen in old photographs, the ones in which all the men and women and children are long since dead, the flowers turned to dust and the vase that held them there broken and discarded, or hidden on a back shelf of some antique shop. Yonkers, Glenwood, Greystone, Hastings, Dobbs Ferry—old man Dobbs and points along the river his ferry served: these were things Jonathan once knew but the details were lost as he watched the shoreside houses, bushes, what he used to call shields, shields of granite, burst by the window. Ardsley. Irvington (what was it about the headless horseman that never got through to him as a child the same way it had his sisters? Even Maddie, who was never afraid of anything, had been known to wake up shouting, having seen him, a white halo in the woods, a hem and a haw of wind rasping at a sill).

His ears rang; involuntarily he gave an unsteady toss of the head, as the train pulled out of Croton.

With this new development, which frightened Alma but which Jonathan was sure she didn't understand, the family would be dispersed and all its history gradually forgotten—he guessed he had to face that. *Non compos mentis*—as if a mind could ever reach that state of composition until it was dead, done with, composed, like a garden in November, like gardens he could see out the window.

He sensed this might be the last time he would spend in the house, before they would be forced to sell. Alma had already taken it upon herself to evict the boarders their father had allowed in. There would be the matter of dispersing hundreds of heirlooms, antiques, rugs, books and papers, the controversial collection of "longevity memorabilia" (which had cost the family more money than anything else Jonathan could put a finger on)—of setting loose the poor little caged animals, ferreting out the forgeries and shams from any legitimate artifacts he had accumulated (by sheerest good luck, Jonathan thought). Alma hinted that these debts were enormous, and that their father had assumed them with singularity of purpose. Whatever chattels could be auctioned to help offset them would be. There would be the matter of convincing Alma the time had come to have him put in a nursing home—he knew she would resist. The whole trip was nothing but a tremendous pain in the ass he told himself and then recalled how they used to call Rhinebeck Swinebeck and at least that brought his spirits up, made him less grouchy there in the train, alone, feeling somewhat ridiculous about his continued adolescence.

A young man, about Jonathan's height and build, picked him up at the station, just north of Kingston.

"Jonathan?" Dill guessed as he looked up into the face contracted into a disoriented yawn; he recognized him by the similarities shared with Alma: that clear, flat brow, the eyes receptive, opalescent, the face narrow, the skin taut. Together they collected his bags—old duffel and nylon pack— and climbed a set of chiming metal stairs from the platform to the lot where the car was parked.

"Long trip, you must be tired."

His shirt sleeve flapped in the open window as he looked out on the strange surroundings, the Victorian houses, the gas stations—thinking, Are they stealing *El conejo* now?

"I'm sorry about your father—" Dill began, and broke off.

He was a strange sort of a person. Jonathan looked at his hands. Impossible to imagine those upon his sister. "How's Alma?" Jonathan went on, but didn't wait for an answer. "Say, what time is it," and feigned considerable concentration over resetting the hands of his watch. "I always forget whether it's two hours forward or back."

"She's all right, she wanted me to tell you that she wasn't able to tell him about your coming home until, well to tell you the truth she's at the house telling him now."

Jonathan lifted his fingers to his eyes; there was a sign that drew up and was passed whose message painted in crude, red, block letters spelled out COUNTRY LIFE CONVENEANCES SUPPLYS INJOYMENTS—and as these letters pressed away into the gauzy world conveyed behind, deep in his wavering sight, just what he wished to gather up of memory replaced those words half-hidden in their stand of shabby, gnarled, twisting vines and his father was there, there, hands laid across his chest as he asked why, Alma why this now, honey why'd you go do this to me?

He unpacked up in his old room on the second floor, dressed, came down for dinner. Alma had made a special occasion of his homecoming, the table set with the heavy silver, the tantalus liquor cabinet unlocked—to which Jonathan went immediately, lifting one of its decanters to the rim of a glass.

Owen had not come down to greet him. Alma said he was asleep. Her voice telescoped up from the grassy parapet as she rehearsed for Dill (whom Jonathan could see sitting near her quietly, noncommital, a little sour plucking at his lower lip with his fingers and staring out over the rampart into the field) her plans for the first days of the "reunion." As he peered down at her, her sweatshirt violet and with Japanese calligraphy printed on its front, her hair was alive with motion, fingers probing the air before her. He drank the balance of scotch and set the water glass on the sill. Jonathan, always bad boy, always the schmo, but he thought he would have to rise to this if for no other reason than it did seem to be near the end of something—most likely the last tenure of any Berkeley at Berkeley house. Big fucking deal, he thought.

He focused his attentions elsewhere. They took him from the parapet to the maple tree out another window where a mockingbird, flashing its pewter-banded tail, rendered calls of warblers. He was reminded of a Gatling gun . . . where had he ever seen a Gatling gun? Family trip to Gettysburg, Pennsylvania.

He took the booklet he'd brought for the trip and a mechanical pencil out of a side pocket of one of the packs.

Note that. Something to blanket the scotch, or whiskey—same thing.

In the book he wrote, *Remember the mockingbirds here so many of them Id forgotten completely. Their songs endlessly varied or has some ornithologist somewhere figured out some number of finite variations? Their flicking tails Id forgotten as when they perched themselves on the eave or at the end of a limb they look like nasty little Gatling guns but then as a note Im just in here in old room and all the rest the bird is beside the point and have to face dad and Alma acting like Alma acting like Alma is this all my fault no it is not my goddamn fault and Owen is going to act like Owen acting like who cares. Gatling guns they used back in Civil War our Civil War of course that is?* while outside, the mockingbird would continue to sing all night.

He could've sworn it spoke a phrase to him in Spanish, but there was no way for him to interpret what the bird wished to say. He scratched, further, in his notebook, what he had thought before the bird drew his attention away—*big fucking deal*.

Owen is about to feed the troops. The cages along one wall of the room he occupies hum and squeak, by fits and starts, with activity inside. Excited little feet paddle, pink feet, and they give, it is true, quite a joyous and comfortable feeling to the office.

He is thinking that it is a shame his daughter Alma's seen fit to bring her brother home, to ask him to come home, because she's frightened (young Jonathan, escapist into the past with his balderdash about moral restitution—who's more alienated from his profession now? father or son?—and all his bunk about civilization as toxin, and the rest of it). Frightened about my mind, well she doesn't know the half of things. She and her Dill, her fellow. What I want is future here, not present, not past. Is it so much to ask? Bad time of year. No leaves, no snow, nothing.

A road leads up to the house, loops in back, leads back.

3.

OUT the window a few high threads of cirrus were frivolous details in a sky otherwise as chalky green as celadon. Dawn, and already warmer than usual for the time of year. Jonathan was up before sunrise, having slept heavily after the rich food. Recollecting the events of the evening he wished he were back in Honduras. He'd finally excused himself from the table, saying that if he didn't go to bed he would fall asleep in his chair. And as he climbed the stairs he'd felt guilty, since Alma had gone to the trouble of making dishes she knew he liked: paella with lobster, mussels, baby clams, monkfish, shrimp, three times the measure of chorizo the recipe called for—chorizo in honor of the Tropic of Cancer, or something along those lines. The feast was presented with great enthusiasm. Their father had come to the table late, dressed formally and moving stiffly in shiny old glen plaid with a woolen tie thickly knotted at the neck. He moved brittly but with grace.

"Alma neglected to mention you were coming," he'd said, as he sat in his chair at the head of the table.

"Well it'd been a while, Owen, and so, on a whim, why not come up and check on the family," Jonathan answered. Using his father's given name was a risk. A further visit to the tantalus had helped loosen him up.

"A nice gesture but not necessary."

"Thank you, too." (What did that mean?)

"How go your efforts at saving the world?"

Already drifting into their usual exchange. In order to compensate for his feelings of defensiveness he leaned into his response a little hard. "Alma told you I'd been down into Nicaragua helping with the harvest?"

"Don't bait me," his father broke in, which left the table silent, but Jonathan proceeded—

"The CIA's brewing up another mess and just like I told you we're going to fuck up just the same way we've continually fucked up since, since before there even was a CIA."

"I'm sure the Marxists appreciate your assistance."

"They're a democratically elected Socialist-oriented government which replaced an American-backed neo-Nazi dictatorship."

"I see."

"One of the most callous, brutal, bloody, venal dictatorships in history." As Jonathan lifted his spoon to his mouth he hesitated, then ate, swallowing harder than he knew he ought, feeling awkward eating food after making such a pronouncement. It hurt his argument somehow, to talk about injustices while feeding his face. "And yours?" he said.

"My what."

"Your efforts to save—"

"Alma? what's this in my dish?"

She had been listening from the kitchen, and answered a bit too quickly, "Paella."

"Looks awful, smells fishy doesn't it?" asking Dill.

"I understand you're involved in something, some sort of project," Jonathan interrupted.

Owen smirked, scratching his temple gently. "I'm not at liberty really, contractual commitment to discretion and besides this isn't dinner conversation is it, you came all the way from Nicaragua—"

"Honduras."

"—to talk shop? Let's have some wine, teaspoonful can't hurt the blood, Dill?—what is this concoction again? meant the wine for you, accelerates my blood sugar—this soup reeks."

"It's a fish stew, Mr. Berkeley, so I guess—"

"I don't want fish soup, it's deleterious flesh."

"Fish is good for you," Jonathan asserted, thinking, baited, and took it hook, line, sinker.

"What do you know, you don't know anything about it, fish is deleterious to the alimentary canal, sodium chloride, like drinking the worthless product of micturition."

"Gandhi drank his urine, considered it beneficial to health," countered Jonathan, wishing immediately he hadn't said anything at all from the moment he sat down.

"By-products give death, and how old was Gandhi when he died?"

"Old."

"He was seventy-nine when he died you call that old?"

"I should live so long."

"Wasn't Gandhi murdered, Mr. Berkeley?"

"That's right, by a fanatic Hindu," Jonathan agreed with Dill.

"You people weren't even born what do you know. Gandhi died of recycling the highly corrosive urea produced in his kidneys and micturated from his body for one reason only, because it is waste, and no longer wanted by the system. Should have ingested olive-green seaweed, from the Sargasso, inhibits cretinism and myxedema. Paella," he repeated quietly, then, raising his voice: "Alma? Bring me my milk, please." And then he had a good laugh, to himself.

Having a pretty good time with us, Jonathan thought, abashed at how easily still he was drawn in by his father, drawn in by the false sense of having outgrown him, in some way, and half the time drawn in only to be set up for some laughter. Alma might have been wrong, he seemed awfully capable. Owen was quiet again.

Alma came into the dining room, "You want to eat your paella first."

"You don't listen to me—" turning to Dill, who focused on the tufts of black and gray hairs that grew out of Berkeley's ears. "Neither one of them listens to me, they never did."

"Of course we listen," and she sat down next to him, pulled the napkin out of its ring, snapped it and placed it in his lap.

Jonathan watched her; she had assumed the mother's role—the catering, the babytalking. She handed him a soup spoon and nodded at the bowl. Tentatively, he brought a small shrimp up to his lips, which were curled in disgust.

"You're acting like a child," she said.

The soup spoon clattered in his dish, and brothy rice carried a shrimp over the lip onto the tablecloth. "Burnt my, goddamn this stew." Hands shaking, he pushed his chair away from the table and with some effort rose to his slippered feet to shamble out of the room.

Dill smiled, a misplaced attempt at conspiratorial mirth, but Jonathan's face was wrapped in anger, and Alma caught the look and interpreted it for what it was: a display of just that anger he had grown up under, a bleakness she could compare to any of the disused, wrath-embedded rooms in the house they had explored together as children, warned by their mother to be quiet, and to stay as far away as imagination could take them from the suite of rooms on the second floor where their father worked. Worked, Jonathan said to himself, and felt as if he too might begin to rock with laughter. Fathers and sons, mothers and daughters, damned if it isn't the most tedious war of them all.

Jonathan showered, put on fresh clothes, and went downstairs and out into the morning.

The fields were still blanketed in dew and a fine steam sat over the river below. An ultramarine line ran along the western horizon but the brown sky so quickly bled to the pale green spread across it now he had barely perceived its transformation. As he walked down through the grass, long and each spear of it wet, toward the field, he could see the moon huge before him, hanging low and dissolving. It looked like a cement medallion, pocked and genial. Then it was gone. The morning star had already burned out into the blue. His *babouches* were waterlogged with the dew that had collected on them and when he came back up to the house and walked into the kitchen he slid them off and carried them dangling by two fingers of one hand.

"Good morning." He tossed the slippers on the stone floor by the door and sat down at the old refectory table and Alma brought him a cup and saucer, the same china they had grown up with, Blue Willow stamped on the reverse. The bone china painted with its familiar cubist pattern of lotus tree, bodhis crossing a bridge over a brook, quirky vessels sailing in the sky littered with cherry blossoms, the central palace, the woman in kimono on the bamboo porch of the pagoda, and the indecipherable geometric shapes, like op art, that ran around the edges of the plate. He knew the pattern without studying it—less recognizable in an immediate way was the hand that laid it on the table. Jonathan smelled his coffee, the scent of the kitchen itself.

"So—"

"So," she agreed, "I feel like for some reason I ought to apologize for his behavior last night but I know, of course, that, well obviously it isn't my fault."

"Alma," Jonathan frowned.

"I mean, I know it's not. It's just I hoped we'd have a good talk, everybody would get along, it's not very often we're together anymore, all of us, but on the other hand John you could have been a little more tolerant."

"I didn't come all this way, look I don't want to talk about it, what I want to know is are you going to tell me about what's going on here, why the telegram."

"I don't know, exactly that is; I'm not sure what—"

"When I got in to the station, Dill said something funny, said he was sorry about Owen, what did that mean?"

"He shouldn't have said, I mean maybe you misunderstood."

"So what's the problem?"

"I'm not sure. He's going in and out more, I guess you could see . . . but it's less that than, well, there are all these telephone calls, different voices, the mortgage on the house—"

"What mortgage?"

"He's taken out some mortgage on the house if what I understand is right, a second mortgage third mortgage, the whole property, there seem to be these bank managers calling, some loan officer, always angry."

"Calling about what?"

"I don't know what they want, people coming around peeking into the windows, and some consultant shows up the week before last at Dill's in New York with insurance papers, saying he was looking for me, next of kin."

"Did you sign anything?"

"No, there hasn't been any paper presented to me to sign, I'm just saying this has all been like spirits, and it feels like somebody's trying to upset, I don't know, a balance somewhere, but—"

"He is in trouble, you know."

"What?"

"Owen. He's in trouble—inside. There's something wrong with him."

"You always say that, I think he's been pretty good recently."

"Alma, listen. Why did you ask me to come? Anyway, I agree, he seems good to me, call it good, but look, how long has this business of people peeking in windows been going on?"

"About a month ago I think it started."

"You know what it probably means?"

"What."

"Nothing. Some pervert. Some joke."

She shrugged.

Jonathan looked into his sister's eyes. They were the same as his own: blue, and sprinkled with flecks of black and gold. As he began to talk she found she wasn't listening to him. She worried that the night before he'd excused himself and retired early because he was angry at her for asking him to come. She'd gone to bed despondent, dozed off after midnight, and dreamed fitfully (room of biped antelopes, suits, gowns, cocktails cocked before them in hoofed hands—cut to a warehouse bazaar where a vicious cavalry was intent upon breaking down huge aluminum doors—how was she supposed to interpret *that*?) and got up to smoke a cigarette by herself. The bedroom overwarm. She smoked sitting in a chair by the open window looking out at the graphite lawn as Dill breathed noisily, asleep under the sheets. She remembered thinking, Jonathan's not going to be able to fix this. "I thought Jonathan? I thought what would you like to do today, do we have to go into all this on the first morning because I thought first we ought to go visit ma before anything else, I'll take you why don't we go ourselves this morning, can't we do that?"

Jonathan watched her. She had the same sweatshirt on as she had worn the evening before. Her breasts were defined at the flourishes of the white calligraphy. Very Berkeley breasts, full and plump, ready to nourish. She felt she was more unstable than she really was, he thought. She needed his approval but it was not for this he felt a strong sensation of affection come over him. Not a bullshitter; maternal, and of good heart.

Fifteen minutes, he figured. If his father were true to his old habits he wouldn't be out of bed until ten-thirty, two hours hence. Alma would come looking for him, within ten or fifteen minutes, so he had to work quickly. This might be his only opportunity.

But the bolt was frozen in place. It resisted with such steadfastness he was afraid he would end up breaking the key in the lock. Deferential to the racket Jonathan made by cranking the handle, a mouse—albino, whose pink eyes fathomed the rubble labyrinth of its circuitous residence—scurried away to the wall. He jiggled the key in the lock again but it would not be coerced. There was another door, he remembered, through which he could get into the offices—the place where Owen had worked, hidden from the world, passed his days, often nights, where his research, everything that defined him, had gone forward.

He went down the hall and found another door that led through a corbeled passage to the top of a back staircase. Up several steps, across a short landing, down several steps and he reached a door painted pink. It was unlocked. He went in.

The sewing room was cramped. It had served in the past as a dressing room, or a sitting room, ancillary to the capacious master bedroom which Owen had converted in the 1950s into his laboratory/study. The door—also pink—by which the two rooms were connected was locked, but Jonathan managed without trouble to open it with the thin steel of a table knife, brought up from the kitchen, wedging down to meet the lock at the angle that compelled it to give way. The door closed with a click behind and he was immersed in steam-thick light sieved through damask heavy as hide. He slid the knife into his back pocket.

"My god," he said.

The air was oppressive. He threw back the heavy curtains: the light spilled through in harsh blocks. It seemed as if it had not penetrated into the room for years. The chair, arms threadbare, cushion a shabby concavity, seemed pathetic, bared to the world. An army blanket, of a nondescript color, an artifact of its owner's tour in the service, lay crumpled beside it. Jonathan thought, This is outrageous, it's . . . but his frustration burgeoning, unfurling itself, did not overtake his attentions which were summarily wrested from the sense of his father here, alone in his laboratory, sitting up stiff as a mannequin, breathless and bloodless, to the clutter that lay before him, a proud mess shining in silken webs of silver. Strewn about the room, besides the books and papers covered in Owen Berkeley's notes (hypotheses, equations, autobiographical outpourings), was laboratory equipment. He walked over to his father's desk—or desks, rather, as he had taken two tables, each with all of its leaves added so they were extended to full length, and arranged at one end of the room perpendicularly, one abutting a wall and stacked to the ceiling with bookcases. Their shoddiness notwithstanding, he could see at a glance that the collocation of books, offprints and monographs that stood in these crates was as highly systematic as ever. The other table extended out into the room and faced the windows. Stacked on it was a year's worth of mail.

Jonathan began to sort through the pile. Catalogues from Carolina Biological Supply, form letters from the copyrights office in Washington, magazines, a partially completed 1040 tax form, bank statements, missives from three real estate firms expressing continued interest in "handling" Berkeley house should the property become available, a birthday card from Alma. Piles of more paper, parcels on the carpet in vast uncertain stacks, books caterpillaring along the wainscot and heaped on top of them more books.

It looked as if there would be too much to go through. The trick with the knife, jimmying open the door from the sewing room, was a remnant from childhood, something he'd once figured out (and never told anyone about), which remained simple as swimming; but to find his father's address book in this litter would take luck.

Awkwardly he shuffled through the stack that spilled from a wire basket on the library table at his immediate left. There was every possibility the booklet would not have Madeleine's name listed in it anyway. The light in the room seemed to harden as he narrowed his eyes to the words, names, numbers, codes, colorful stamps, dust jackets, a wild mélange of scrawlings from a woman in Liechtenstein, named Lüchinger. Written in a broken English it read:

> In response to the your Query I have One Hundred and Seventeen years old and it is my Diet to eat plain Tripe and Wasser and to kept my Body Pure on the Seventh Day of God's Week. If you please make out your Money pay to me in DM Cash this shall appreciated be. PS: Gewürztraminer is also benefit Health.

Jonathan put the letter back into its envelope, and opened another:

> Aunt Tillie here and my second cussin by my ma's line her name of Mildred who is elder yet, & also Mildred she got a freind on the Bingo team down at Elks Clb. has a quaintans down there at the nursing Home who's got her a brother fought in the Little Big Horn and all he ever ett afore they got him in there in that there nursing Home was black beans & shredded cow beef. Mind, strict beef of a cow body, no beef of lamb, pig, bull or any other beast of four foots. Cow, & mind you, shredded. This manner is which the natural health giving Erbs and Spices may enter the Blood flow. In respect & Advance appreciation for your bursement in respect of these advisements.

There was this:

> Collard green, the fresh raw milk of a chevron, no flesh of the animal, amaranth grain, kale, limabean, much buttermilk, no egg nor any Rocky

Mountain oyster, considerable root of the cattail or if that not available to the sickly body considerable sweet spuds. My personal age 114, verifiable with authorities of the State of West Virginia.

He put these back on the stack, looking quickly at the documents on top of piles which rose out of other wire baskets, but all he could find were more letters, postmarked from around the world, each of a similar nature. The correspondence was massive, but it looked as if few of the letters had been answered, and indeed Jonathan came across a box beside the table on the floor which was filled with letters complaining that Mr. Berkeley had not lived up to his part of the agreement.

Prominent at the center of the green blotting pad which seemed to be the central writing area was a long letter which began with the words "Dear Berkeley, your letter to hand" (which seemed a rather stilted old phrase given that it was very obviously written in a child's script). A number of words in the letter had been circled in red ink, and transferred in Owen Berkeley's hand onto a separate sheet of paper attached to the letter by a pin. The words were:

Chocolate,
bowl of saltwater,
crow,
worm,
birds,
fish,
game,
bananas,
lotus,
turtle,
horse,
ice.

Another recipe for immortality.

Behind him a wall of cages came alive. The mice in them began to stir. Several started running with such speed inside their basket treadmills that Jonathan was certain the sound could be heard all over the house. He tried to shush them, but his movements only made them more excited. One of them depressed a small plunger that was fixed at the base of its cage, and this set off a crisp, faint beep. Immediately some of its fellow inmates enacted the same procedure. Jonathan did his best to ignore them, and continued looking frantically. The phrase *give it up and get out of here* had visited an instant before the book, tucked inside its unbending leather covers, emerged and was in his hands.

Under M, nothing; nothing under W for Work. He turned to the beginning of the alphabet. None of the names was recognizable. Aaron, Abouassi, Almeda, Anderson, Ayer read like alphabet soup in a melting pot; at the end of the Bs and seemingly out of place was "Daughter" and a number.

The clicking sound the telephone made each time its wheel revolved back to its original position seemed deafeningly loud. He wondered, would he be able to recognize Maddie's voice after all these years, if she answered? or would Henry answer? Instead, it was a recording and its deliberate message, a woman stating she was not willing to come to the telephone but that a name and number accompanied by a substantial reason for her to return the call might or might not, as circumstances dictated, prompt a response. The tip of Jonathan's tongue slid up over his piltrum, then wetted his lips. There was the smell of antiseptic in the room he noticed in the instant he recradled the handset; that, and the odor of decay—some hapless mouse decomposing in a vent no doubt, or a squirrel that had wintered in the attic and had got itself trapped up there, just the kind that can gnaw through the electrical wiring and set a house on fire.

It was the stack of odd-shaped letters, written in childish script, in pencil, on sheets of thin salmon butcher paper, and with envelopes whose Honduran stamps were familiar—presidential profile, Caesarian and torpid, engraved on their faces—that caught his eye as he reached across the desk to replace the booklet. The letter on top—they were stacked with comparative care, and there seemed to be four of them—was disarming in that its tone, its language, and its import were completely out of character with what age the writer surely must have been, if the handwriting were to be trusted as a measure of such matters. As Jonathan read, feeling both angry and silly at the same time, a host of problems began to formulate themselves before him, and that grown-up inner world, that sanctum which the offices had always been since he was a child, suddenly began to open up. Phrases like "and if in the course of your custodianship It happens to pass away or in any manner be disabled or in any way injured, it is understood that the full responsibility for such accident shall fully be borne by you, the custodian"—"so many examples of breakthroughs both in the applied sciences and even the arts that have taken place not in industrial think-tank scenarios or, god forbid, in the groves of academe, that one begins to wonder is there any other possible way in which to proceed: that is, just to think of all the credit Edison gets, while Nikola Tesla, who is still considered a madman, a freak, something suitable to a carnival sideshow, we acknowledge, men such as you and I, to be the real pioneer behind electricity, radio, radar, the electron microscope, vertical take-off aircraft, TV, solar energy, etcetera etcetera—and what did his neighbors at the foot of Fifth Avenue, just above Washington Square, what did they think when his windows exploded blue flashes, exciting the laughter of delight from friends such as Mark Twain, echoing across the dry summer cobblestones and down into the park, as he tested a cordless, phosphor-coated bulb, or blew two million volts of electrical ganglia around himself for no other reason than to demonstrate his own genius? what did they think? they thought well how in the hell can we deport him to Yugoslavia whence he came with a few pennies and some horrid verse?—this, and I tell you as a comrade and in sympathy with what anguish your reclusivity must sometimes breed, is your lot, or might be, also, and this is why we feel your project worthwhile, and are willing to throw ourselves behind it to the degree we have and do"—"so happens that in our research and utterly by chance we discover that the place we have chosen safest and most comfortable for It and the diplomatic escort who will accompany happens to be the residence of a relative of yours who we assume will be ready to assist in directing the final leg of the long journey, and whereas, per our earlier communication, all responsibility once It has reached American soil is transferred to you for the period of inspection and, it can be assumed without overbearing assuredness & certainly without any hint of pressure, custodianship, we assume this decision will meet with your approval and intend to proceed immediately with our arrangements"—phrases like these were Gothic to the point of hilarity. The offices were wrenched open, indeed; it was as if it were a physical thing, as if it could be heard.

And and . . . *and and*. Where had that come in before? He could picture the wink, the "etcetera, etcetera."

What he found last, before drawing the curtains shut again to allow the room to settle back into its former reddish darkness, was a letter, its hand spindly and wiry, with great crests and flourishes, its lines as errant as Krieger-Corless's (or whoever's):

Dere mister Owen,
This heres a kinda tempt to let you no me & Maddy are ok & how she sometimes miss you & the family something bad. We come here where I got

work working for a nice gal still pore but we are doan ok. I spose theres awways goan be some bad blood over what happen afore but someday I hope things can be better for Maddy sake. Pleese rite if you want. (Maddy dont know I sent this)

                                                          Henry Work
And may God Bless

There was no stamp on the envelope, marked *Postage Due*, and the letter was dated the year before. The return address was in New York.

It was as if the tantalus had taken on lungs, a throat and voice, the way it called him . . .

4.

T HE family plot was not contiguous with what remained of the land that surrounded Berkeley house. Until the end of the last century one made one's way from the house to the little walled cemetery by any number of paths or the carriage road that ran to the northernmost end of the property. When at last the acreage that surrounded this plot was sold it was agreed in the terms of sale the Berkeleys would retain ownership of this piece of land and have an easement to it by the bridle path that ran along the river until it veered inland and up past the cemetery's gate.

Since then, in the 1920s, the land that separated the plot from Berkeley house had been sold, resold, and resold. Roads began to cross the subdivided hills in a pattern like a trestlework bridge fallen into a gorge. What had once been Berkeley farm, and after, O'Donnell farm, was reduced to a stitchwork of houses, streets and a small, already run-down shopping mall. One of these streets, Case Hill Road, soon enough ran within a dozen yards of where the remains of Theophilus and Susanna Berkeley rested undisturbed for nearly two hundred years. From time to time the developers who owned the parcel of land along Case Hill Road—and who had been able to build and sell houses across the street but not adjacent to the ivy-covered walls of the graveyard—approached the Berkeleys with offers to buy. Hats in hands they appeared at the front porch, a real estate broker anxious to pay double its appraised value, a licensed gravedigger prepared to disinter generations of bones at the former's expense ("—after about thirty years?

Well with all respect, in a climate like ours? frankly speaking? all gone to dust down there anyways, box, the whole kit and caboodle"), the minister who would clear his throat in discomfort, invoke in a raw whisper words like deconsecration service, municipal cemetery, right and proper. None of them would have expected what came from grandma's lips: "All dust? Well, the earth is greedy but not so greedy as the men that walk it." Once, the city council attempted to sue the Berkeleys to give up the small gore, but as it turned out there was no legal way to make them sell. The law provided that all surviving heirs of those buried within the precincts of the plot sign a release allowing for their ancestors to be reburied. This no Berkeley would ever do.

When Jonathan and Alma emerged from the shadowy bridle path there were no neighbors stirring. A Saturday morning. The grinding drone of a leafblower somewhere, unseen behind brick and glass, picket and chain-link fence, shrubbery, blocks of the neighborhood street. At the edges of Case Hill Road, viewed from the primitive tangle of trees and weeds, Jonathan felt he was standing at the brink of an alien world. The two-story, clapboard houses in a tidy, close-set row each with its porch, each with its glimmering storm windows put up more or less simultaneously—and all this year prematurely—differentiated ostensibly by shades of paint (white, peach, pale green, forest green) and modest landscaping: trellises, there a sickly stick of maple held firmly in place by a metal brace and three cords tied about its trunk and staked. In the driveway of one house were five cars, two tireless and up on cinder blocks, one a shell of rust covered in melting dew.

"God," he said. "When did they build all this?"

Alma walked around to the length of wall facing away from the street. She pushed open the iron gate that gave into the yard.

Jonathan followed her into the enclosure. It was darker here, owing to the overhanging branches of the willows. He tried to imagine his mother's body there, under the brown clay; he wondered which way her head was pointed. His brother William's place was buried under the rubbery black of a trash bag, formless heap itself covered in the leaves which rain had transformed into a mucky rug. "Poor Red—"

Alma came up behind him, wedged her hands between his arms at his sides and embraced him. She mumbled into his back, into his shirt, between his shoulder blades.

"Look at this fucking mess."

Headstones lay akimbo in the high pale grass. Some had tottered over forward or backward, several seemed to have sunk to the side. The stone chapel, built into an angle where the walls joined, was in ruins. Its slate roof had caved in, the wooden crossbeams having rotted through. Broken bottles (beer, sour gherkins, juice, tomato catsup), paper sacks with garbage spilling like a cornucopia's fruit from top and torn sides, cans, a tattered kite were scattered. Jetsam? wondered Jonathan, from vandals or the anonymous neighbor, his sense of decorum slackened after a multitude of pink squirrels, daiquiris, grasshoppers, white-wine spritzers at a cocktail party, moved not to foxtrot with his hostess on an autumn night but to demonstrate his offended sense of dignity at having to live with a burial ground within view of his kitchen window. "Look at all this. Like it's the city dump, the bastards."

Jonathan came back that afternoon and in (modest) defiance parked the car on the street across from the plot. Dill, who came with him, helped set the gravestones right again, collect garbage into a burlap sack, scythe and rake away the knee-high grass. The slate shingles of the chapel they stacked at the end of the yard, and when they finished looped a heavy chain through the wrought-iron grillwork of the gate and around the supporting bar at the frame in the wall and joined ends together with a padlock bought at the hardware store in the ("stinking disgusting wasteland of a") mall. In a lane off the main road there was a tavern, a beat-down, friendly affair which Jonathan took to be a remnant of the pre-mall, predevelopment days with truck drivers and locals in bib overalls sitting along the varnished bar on tall stools, and Jonathan stood Dill a drink. They would be late for dinner.

"What kind of name is Dill?" he asked, and listened to a story of the anise seeds stolen from his mother's spice rack and sucked on like candy, handfuls of dill seed—"stimulant *and* carminative," his mother once said, exotically, from the rolling universe of her rocking chair—under shade trees, until he became sick with hiccuping and crazy as tensely strung wires in an electric storm. After a second drink Jonathan was drawn enough to Alma's fiancé's good temper that he almost broached the topic of Owen's insanity, but held back in deference to a lingering propriety—that, and a cloud called "family" which his brother Red had appreciated, had honored, as had his grandfather, and those that lay in the cemetery, but which to Jonathan seemed always thinner, wispier, insubstantial. What bothered him the most was that he began to see that this trait had come from Owen, if anyone—Owen, whom Jonathan wished to resemble less than he did any other man on earth. He caught a glimpse of himself in the mottled mirror that ran the length of the bar and listened to Dill.

Tell me about Red, was what Dill was asking. Hadn't Alma filled him in about any of them?

Red happened to be born in Virginia, Charlottesville, when his mother, Sophie, away from her young husband for the first time and for all purposes the last, had gone there to visit her father. He was premature, a seven-monther, and mother and child returned to Berkeley house in the great, round Plymouth which Owen had driven down to get them. William Hurley Manfred Theophilus Berkeley—names culled from the family tree as if against the prospect no other child would ever come to redeem and embody them. A masculation, a paying the piper in advance. Jonathan bestowed on William the nickname Red not for carrot-colored hair or an Irish complexion, neither of which he had, but for the only syllable in his hyperbolical name he could as a child pronounce.

"William Hurley Manfred Theophilus Berkeley, but even more, add to that Private 1st Class, didn't you notice back there? Born August 7th 1948 Died December 6th 1967 In Valor Pro Patria?"

"Vietnam?"

"Bien Hoa," he answered more emphatic, coming awake. "Bien Hoa Province in the south, Company A, 4th Battalion, 12th Infantry, 199th Light Infantry Brigade, they ran into a battalion-sized force and, I don't know what happened really, he was shot. Died in the field. This priest sent Alma his helmet."

That evening they deliberately got drunk, outside in the draft that stirred from the river uphill. The Milky Way shone like an erased cloud. Jonathan said he wished he could remember names of the constellations. He and Red as children had carried their father's telescope out to the edge of broom-sage fields behind their house on summer nights and picked out Orion and Canis Major with its bright dog star. Air so weighted with honeysuckle it made them dizzy, they watched for shooting stars, counted aloud in unison "one one thousand! two one thousand!" or on a particularly clear night they spotted satellites, Russian or American, as the race to space was underway, cutting slowly across the sky. How their mother approved. She didn't know about Red bringing the stolen cigarettes. Nor how britches down they would masturbate together. Once Red beat off Jonathan, who listened to his brother panting behind him, listened half in horror half disdainful, with what wits he had left to him as his brother's hand coaxed "Mr. Cucumber" and Red's own penis filled, stood insistent and awkward along the small of his back. It was everything Jonathan could manage not to pull free, pivot, slap at his brother's mouth. That business he would never let happen again; dutiful, he came in Red's tightening fingers. But the stars, the stars . . . they hacked on dried-out cigarettes and stargazed. Now it was all he could do to pick out the Dippers (which he recalled his father called "Chas' Wain") and the North Star at the end of the Little Dipper's extravagant handle.

"How easy everything's just forgotten, just like that. Alma, do you still have Red's helmet?"

"You didn't see when you were over at the gore?"

"See what?"

"The helmet, I put it there, a long time ago, it's on a ledge there. I planted flowers in it, some perennials."

"What the fuck did you do that for?"

"I didn't do anything."

"Well, it's not my fault, so don't blame me, but it was rusted through. It looked like an old chamber pot."

"What are you saying?"

"I chucked it, I thought it was garbage, so I threw it out. You couldn't even tell what it was."

"You threw it away?"

Jonathan hadn't intended to raise his voice so much; what Alma cried back at him he could have predicted was coming: "Since when do you care about it so much? You act like I did it on purpose, but you never cared about it one way or the other."

"Alma."

"Leave me alone." Alma ran inside, she stood in the foyer holding her tears back, not breathing, listening for sounds upstairs that might tell whether or not her father had heard them argue. It was silent. Out of Dill's view she composed herself by staring into the hall mirror. She went upstairs. She would change sheets. The light bulb in the bedroom was burnt out. Because she knew the room by heart she was able to strip the bed and remake it with fresh linen. The room she could dust and sweep in the morning. Pulling the case over the heavy pillow, at the smell of the fresh linen she began to weep. She walked to the window; she could hear Dill's footsteps coming up the stairs after her. Something was stirring below. It was her brother, bottle clutched at his side; he was walking down toward the field at the foot of the long terrace. He was humming to himself. He was hunched over, and seemed like a man crippled by age struggling to make his way forward with each step. Once he reached the dark field, far out of Alma's sight, he fell forward unceremoniously to his knees on the soft dry ground and rolled over onto his hip. "Whasza news up there Red-boy," he made a puttering sound, faintly, took a drink of bourbon, coughed, set the bottle at his side, burying its bottom slightly in the soil. He lay back flat and gazed at the sky of stars. They jumped, jerky; smoothly skated all with luminescent tails like a coliseum of candle-bearers turned upside down. For a moment the whole flat dome of sky was white. Jupiter burned like an irregular point pricked by a pin or by the tip of a pen in black construction paper.

Owen heard none of this. He busied himself in the offices. There was a letter which he wanted to draft. It was too late to prevent them from coming, and anyway he wanted them to come. Nevertheless he would write them about several details in the first history of It that continued to bother him, if only for his own peace of mind. For one, he had found a book in the library here which gave a much modified portrayal of the surrender of Gil González Dávila who had marched against the gentleman in question from the Olancho valley. He had checked out another book and actually read Cortés's Fifth Letter to King Charles of Spain where he found evidence of horses swimming, horses drowning, hamstrung horses—but nothing of horses being eaten. Dogs, yes. Dogs were apparently bred and fattened and eaten. Pigs, yes. But no horses.

Cortés's account of Francisco de Las Casas's escape from prison in Naco, and his capturing Olid, differed also from what Owen read in the epistle from Honduras. Seems that both Las Casas and Gil González were sitting in a room in Naco one night, arguing with Olid, when Las Casas who had been trimming his fingernails with a penknife simply seized Olid by the beard and stabbed him, crying out, "We can suffer this tyrant no longer," or something of the sort. Guards rushed about, inflicting blows, ensigns shouted, and Olid escaped amid all the confusion, only to be found a few hours later and placed under heavy guard. True to the epistle: the following morning he was sentenced to death, though a source for the events after decapitation Corless would have to provide, still.

All in all, the history of It was, it seemed, completely full of holes. Naturally, he thought to add as a postscript, any of the discrepancies these alternate histories might point up ought to have no effect on their original intentions and negotiations.

* * *

The third and final epistle reached the post office in Danlí soon after Krieger had responded to his others. Whatever might have stood behind the indiscrete sense of urgency in the timing of his communiqués (the fat man was reminded of a time when sent to an auction in New York as personal representative of His Excellency Tacho Somoza, with "buy bids" for several oils, French Impressionist, he raised his hand at the opening bid and did not lower it until the lot had been declared his own; there combined then the inebriate of power with a strange shame—abetted by silence that emanated from the small, bitter audience around him—of somehow recognizing he had poorly played the game)—whatever lay behind Berkeley's nervousness intrigued Krieger nearly as much as it delighted the fat man.

In essence, he waived caution in favor of expediency. The esteemed Corless was instructed that the photographs and what documentation he planned to send ahead for approval need not come before—or independent of—the product in question. Having given the kaleidoscope a great deal more thought than he had when he had written his second letter, Berkeley now reasoned that no body of supporting evidence could possibly be substituted by anyone interested in empirical proofs (as was he) for genuine firsthand acquaintance with the "subject/object" in question. There was no way, in other words, to go about expediting their transaction other than to import It directly into the country. While it was understood that the buyer had to be satisfied with what he had purchased, and that if there were an invoice (there wasn't) it would be marked *On Approval*, the fat man understood Berkeley's latest (and last) epistle to show every sign of weakening will.

"I realize," Owen wrote, "that this alteration in procedures may complicate matters ever so slightly. I also comprehend that for a gentleman such as yourself who must deal daily with sums and situations vastly greater and more ostensibly dire than the one at hand this might present an impediment which makes our whole business together less worthwhile for you. But, I do not mean to be (as my mother used to say) persnickety. It just seems to me that to undertake the responsibilities and debt this purchase represents to me personally, without a direct examination of the property under discussion, would be foolhardy of me, and deplete what admittedly small resources I have at hand to work with. As I take it there may be a missing piece in a puzzle I have worked out for a very long time without solving—and I think my chances at relative success are greater than those which ancient scientists bent on devising, say, a perpetual motion machine, might have had. And so it strikes me as well worthwhile to proceed apace here, showing every sign of optimism that what it is we propose to accomplish will be done to the satisfaction of all involved, not the least of whom might be the subject/object, himself . . ."

It was just this waiving of caution that Krieger'd been looking for in order to lock into place one of the final bits of his jigsaw program. Madeleine Berkeley Work was there, in invisible effigy, in his back pocket. Maddie loved her secret privacy at the crazy ranch as much as Hannah, and loved it doubly for the peace it afforded Henry. If the good Dr. Berkeley was willing to order the import of product and documentation posthaste, the esteemed Corless might easily divine the urgencies involved and take it upon himself to skip the meeting-in-Manhattan step, and suggest (impel by threat) that it would be so kind of Madeleine to take Lupi and Olid on up to Owen herself. Wouldn't that be simpler for everyone, all round? Wouldn't it, truth to tell, be one more binding reason for those at the ranch to keep their mouths forever shut? Neat idea, might be worth a little surcharge.

5.

THERE was a quixotic quality, touched by pathos and qualified by absurdity, that obtained in this man who had chosen to spend the better part of his life drifting toward deeper and deeper reclusiveness—from society, from friends, from his wife and children—so that he might devote himself to the contemplation of such obtuse and dated works of scholarship as Metchnikoff's *The Prolongation of Life* and Flourens's *De la longévité humaine et de la quantité de vie sur le globe*.

But the books were there, part of the family library—two double-shelved walls of quarter morocco with embryo-shaped marbling on their boards, old speckled cloth gold-stamped on the spines, tree calf dried into dust. They had been there for as long as Owen Berkeley could remember. Biology, entomology, geology, zoology, physics, all the natural sciences were represented; but it was longevity and its sister study, eugenics, that captured the child Owen's interest. Buffon's *Histoire naturelle générale et particulière* . . . Sir E. Ray Lankester's *Comparative Longevity in Man and the Lower Animals* . . . Weismann's *Essays upon Heredity*. An uncle Owen had never known, whose name dangled free and leafless in the genealogy of the family tree, one of the grander eccentrics in the Berkeley pantheon, had assembled the specialized library decades before this attentive disciple was born; none of Owen's ancestors had touched the library, but Owen had been familiar with it from youth. What could be gotten out of these books he took. Voraciously. By adolescence what he lived for were his theories and his mice.

The first of his mice was Rochester. He had named it after Jack Benny's butler, to whom he listened religiously on the big Zenith Sunday evenings. Benny made him double up in laughter when he drawled out the name, "Raaaw-chestr." Owen would go to his room after the program and mimic, "Now, Raaaw-chestr?" Then, conjuring the mouse's repartee, "Yahsah mihstah Benny?"

Those were the good days. Rochester was a fine specimen, adept at memorizing routes that would lead him down corridors (made up of bricks on the parquet floor) to a cube of cheddar cheese at the other end of the labyrinth, and a glorious acrobat on the treadmill and the little Ferris wheel. He seemed to respond positively to the attention his young owner lavished on him.

Rochester was never allowed to eat the cube of cheddar cheese that lay at the maze's end. Instead, he got a teaspoon of sour cream and honey which, for want of other choices, he gratefully lapped up. What Rochester (in fact) lived on was a strict diet Owen concocted out of Metchnikoff. Products of soured milk were its few staples ("milk become acidulous," the boy explained to his mother, "under the influence of lactic ferments"). He noted that Rochester developed a taste for such things as plain yoghurt and boiled bananas. His cage was kept spotless under Czerny's edict, which Owen had read in the Master's *The New Hygiene*: "means of preservation against cancer . . . rigorous cleanliness . . . and perhaps the giving up of raw food." He followed Metchnikoff's notion that the principal agents in the process of degeneration were the products of putrefaction that had their tenure in an animal's large intestine before being passed out of the body. These toxins, he understood, are absorbed into the blood and thereby carried through all the tissues of the poor creature's body, slowly but surely contaminating it. Thus, duration of an animal's life—or, by extension, that of a man—could be prolonged if measures were taken to counteract this process of autotoxification. Metchnikoff's solution was simple, by Owen's analysis. To combat or suppress the malevolent (the evil) bacteria—"our redoubtable enemies"—that thrived in the large intestine, butyric and putrefactive, one needed only introduce by gradient exposure the presence of lactic (the good) bacilli which produced bacterial flora that might happily live in the alimentary canal. Hence little Rochester's diet. His food was boiled into unrecognizability. He subsisted on whitish, gruelish mush. This spartan diet was all for his own good and Rochester's contentment and health were a consuming preoccupation of his young keeper, who could not imagine, with the exception perhaps of his own mother, a finer friend, one who would play the straight man to Jack Benny jokes, who would on the coldest wintry nights be taken into the linen sheets, bedclothes blue under the moon that peeked out from the snowy sky, the linen itself clean and warm and evocative of grandmothers and great-grandmothers who had slept in them through similar winter nights, and who would curl there against him, like his own little progeny, his great funny pal. No! he thought, he—Owen—was going to help Rochester live longer than any of the Himalayan goatherds he had read about. It was not beyond his imagination that if the mouse could live enough beyond his normal term, and be kept not only fit but through a series of exercises which might release vast amounts of blood through the cortical region to enrich and stimulate the brain, Owen might in time be able to teach Rochester rudimentary words. The squeaks, squeals and squawks he already made during the day fascinated Owen, who early on had begun jotting down their variations and the date and hour when each sound occurred. He looked for pattern and coherence in the cries that came from his sleek rodent, something that might indicate desire or pain or joy. Several Big Chief tablets full of notes had been amassed, but the boy could make no sense of his data. Still, he held out for several years the hope that someday he and Rochester could do a Benny routine, roles reversed.

His mother followed this precocity with supportive enthusiasm. Rochester would prove to be his earliest success. The normal life expectancy of a mouse, he well knew, was five or six years at the outside. So when Owen volunteered to join the army as a medic, in 1940, at the age of twenty (his colitis having kept him out for three autumns running), Rochester had already acceded to the age of six years, four months, one day. His coat was as lustrous as a healthy mouse half his age (and Owen had by that time acquired half a dozen new colonists with which he could make comparison). His eyes were sharp, hearing fine, his scent keen, his physiognomy resilient; yet when Owen came home never would he have expected Rochester to be waiting for him.

What was his grandest success might also be deemed his greatest calam-

ity, and his doting mother's worst mistake. On seeing her son back from
France, and his astonishment at finding the mouse still alive, how could she
bring herself to admit that Rochester had in fact died a week after Owen
left? how bring herself to recount the lengths to which she had gone to
locate, at a pet shop in Albany, another mouse whose coloring, shape, and
character so resembled the beloved Rochester that the loss of him might not
seem so awful?

Owen had been sent home and discharged from duty after he had stepped
on a short but razor-sharp sickle in a field in Burgundy: blade, hidden in tall
ryegrass, plunged up into the sole of his boot and pierced cleanly through
his foot, emerging between its laces. He was an ambulance driver, had just
been transferred from Germany, had labored under the three-week delu-
sion that fighting in France would be lighter than what he had seen near
Karlsruhe and Stuttgart and Heilbronn. Yet here he was, heavy emergency
kits in either hand, following two medics at a dead run, to reach a patrol
with wounded, cut off by sniper fire. The sniper, heedless of their red
crosses, fired shots as they endeavored to traverse a clearing to reach the
farmhouse where the men were sequestered. Running half-crouched the
three continued up a slight hill as the crack of the rifle reported from
somewhere within a dense stand of pines to their left. Owen had pressed
ahead half a dozen steps through the thickening rye before he noticed the
presence of the sickle, its blade like a crescent sticking up through the
boot's tongue, its wooden handle twisted underfoot. The sight of it made
him feel faint, and he sat back singing with pain as one of his buddies
withdrew it. He came to under the spirit of ammonia, foot and calf
throbbing, in the back of his own ambulance, in the company of two other
injured men. His arm and chest hurt; each was wrapped in bandages; he'd
been hit.

When his ship docked in New York harbor some weeks after, it was only
a matter of months before VE-Day came. For the rest of his life he would
walk with a slight rolling limp. The puckered scars at the back of his biceps
and at his ribs were the only emblems of his bullet wounds. Sometimes he
believed he'd been cheated, in that he was never given a medal for his
actions. They were liberally dispensed to others in his unit.

Owen never graduated from medical school. He was home-educated,
and it meant he was seen as an eccentric by professors and fellow students.
"The liver is a diplomatic organ," began one of his essays. "The liver—
that hardy, black-brown sieve, the largest gland in the body of man—is the
centerpiece of evolution. Consider the very word itself. *Liver*, or, one who

lives . . . " He dreamed of having the skill to perform liver transplants on stray dogs, and was convinced that such operations would lead him to prove that the furry patients that received the foreign liver would both live longer and accept other organs more readily. Puppy liver into an old bitch, aged liver into a young mutt, the results would be constant. The next step was easy to imagine. The genetic makeup of a dog—its maudlin behavior aside (Owen had a physical aversion to dogs)—was complex. There was nothing interpretable, genetically, in this mystery, so long as its principals were terriers and corgies. But mice and rats? right down Owen's line. The genetic makeup of a rat is simple. An albino rat is going to have a harder time accepting a liver from a black rat than from another white rat. But white into white? You would have to work as fast as a sacrificial priest, those Mayan priests who could remove your heart with their stone blades and show it to you in the open air before you died; one hundred and thirty to two hundred seconds, he estimated, to resew both artery and vein. But there were things one could count on. White rat liver into white rat liver: results, one dead liverless rat, one rat whose lifespan ought to double, tail pink, coat shiny. Take a spotted rat, graft its skin onto a white rat, and the white rat can take a transplant from another spotted rat; if spotted rat number one lives five years, spotted rat two may expect to live ten. The snow-pure genes!

His diaries filled up with designs, but the love affair with the liver was never consummated, nor were those he contemplated for other glands and organs of the body—the pancreas, the kidneys, the heart, the brain. While his grades were high, his willingness to remain in the academy wasn't strong. Couldn't all this be accomplished at home? He hated Baltimore, hated the very words Lock Raven, the avenue where he kept a room. At Easter, having come home to announce that he intended not to go back, he met Sophie. Or, met her again. And for a time, livers were the farthest thing from his mind.

A big-boned girl with flaxen hair that lay in coils across her head, Sophie had known Owen since childhood. When they were children they swam with other friends all summer long at a cove in the river known as Roan Oak Point. Sophie was the only girl Owen had ever kissed. They were married in 1947; Red was born a year later. In 1951 Sophie gave birth to Madeleine. The family did not live in poverty but neither was it well off. Sophie had been able to work occasionally before the twins, Alma and Jonathan, were born, and Owen received military benefits. Mostly they lived on family money—an exigency that depressed Owen but which he felt only fractionally compelled to change. He was not lazy, but even on the lowest of days when his studies fell into a lull he found it preferable to stare at the patterns, the bats and blossoms, in the well-worn oriental runner that lay on the floor of the offices, than to waste his time learning some trade.

Twice he had gone down to New York seeking work. This was what he told Sophie. He stayed one week each visit. His telephone calls home were distressing. "I seem to be completely unemployable," he confessed to her. In the background he could hear one of his daughters crying, and his heart would sink in guilt, since in fact he had passed the day not interviewing for jobs, but lost in the monumental and cool corridors of the Museum of Natural History and calling down books in the reading room of the Public Library. On the bus back home he acquitted himself by the admission he hadn't stamina enough to make the commute every day in any case. He would devote his life to science. It was all that mattered. There might be some sacrifices, but in the end it would measure out, it would come to be seen as worthwhile.

Sacrifices were made—all issues, active and inactive, of stocks the family possessed he sold the next morning; he put up for sale the last considerable acreage of Berkeley land that remained—all but a hundred acres, incorporating the paddock and stable which he would not have to relinquish until later. The estate was now eaten away, as he saw it, to a hermitage. His mother, whose signature he had forged in order to liquidate certain of the stocks, wasn't told about the measures he had decided to take. Sophie could only worry, but she did not argue.

"We'll put it all in savings, draw interest." Much of the money, after those first careful years, went into equipment. Packages arrived and were spirited away up into the offices, contents never to be seen by the family.

But all in all they got along well under the circumstances. He had some rats, a gerbil, some mice. The gerbil was put on a diet of chicken-embryo cocktails. He looked through the catalogues of biology supply houses, hoping to find one which offered the cells of unborn lambs. Injected, they'd revitalize aging cells of any mammal. The search was in vain. However, Segal's 1932 experiment, the protein-restricted diet affecting the brain by altering chemical balance, he was able to reenact. Results were of dubious merit. He did spend spare time developing, patenting, and selling two inventions to companies for manufacture. While they did not give him the same satisfaction or exhilaration of these other experiments, they did earn some money. One was a whimsical device: a multi-tined gadget that would debone a fish by lifting both spine and entire system of ribs free of the meat in a single upward stroke. The other was much more ambitious and more directly connected to what he fancied his true work. Here was a railway car for transporting livestock over vast stretches of land to slaughterhouses. The car, in Owen's design, would be fitted out with a complex bank of high-intensity sodium lamps so situated that each of the animals—whether hog, cow, or sheep—was fully bathed in visible and infrared light for the duration of its journey. It was Owen's contention the pineal gland in the animal's brain would under these conditions be artificially inhibited and that as a consequence its secretion of the hormone melatonin would be suppressed. By decreasing or eliminating melatonin from the animals' chemistries Owen proposed a higher-quality meat might be produced at slaughter, one from which this depressive and sedative hormone was largely purged. The company—Belle Star Farms, of Dearborn, Michigan—that bought the patent outright from him saw in the theory a prospect for marketing a line of morning sausages that could be promoted as "The Perfect Way to Start Your Day." It was something the FDA might have moved to nix had it ever been foisted on the public as a life-improvement product. No one would ever know what their reaction to Glad Patties might have been, however, as Belle Star Farms filed for bankruptcy shortly after a check made out to Owen Berkeley for three thousand dollars was sent, and cashed.

6.

YOU can't come here disrupt everything and simply pack and go back again, and leave me with him. And now Maddie. Maddie-talk. Maddie Maddie Maddie—I had a sister and her name was Maddie, they called her skinny and they called me fatty. Everybody in the world is more important to John than his own flesh and blood. You can't go yet. Maddie was always the favorite, with pa, too, always he let her come in and read with him or help out, but me never. And that once when at dinner wasn't it, there was Maddie, and she was already sneaking out with Henry, even in the middle of the night when I could hear them down in the haze that one summer, when what was it came up I don't remember, but there she was saying to everybody at table Alma's a *much* better name than

Madeleine. Can you still believe that? Alma means dawn or at least that's what she always bragged, but what does Maddie mean? Maddie means nothing, that's what they had told her at school and of course it was true, deep down I felt, yes, yes, that's right, Alma is me, and Alma means something beautiful and important and why should you who I know what you're doing with that Negro stable man, why should you expect better? It was almost then and there I blurted out what I knew was god's truth. John, can I imagine how his face would have looked then, because for all he thought right along he was the rebellious one and setting off on his own course away from pa, and William was already gone into the service then, John saying over and over as if it was something for him to be so very proud of at the time that he would never go and fight that he'd leave the country first, become expatriate, which is more or less what he has gone ahead and done, I mean, anyway, isn't it? Why didn't I say it there and then? Pa, ma, John: Maddie's getting it from Henry, yes, I know it is, it's a hard thing to say, but I heard them, yes, and saw them too—though that would have been a lie. Almost once when I was running the brindled mastiff down by where the broken bridge and the forsythia rows are, and big as life he came quick from around behind the shed, the one for the scythes, Dill and John in there yesterday, cider press, spigots, the old maple buckets, and always the yellow jackets around looking for some sugar—he came quickly from behind the shed zipping up, that nervous humble look on his face, and who came after him all glowing with smiles but Maddie? nobody but her. Well, hiya-there Almy, hi brindle-Joe, that little speckle foal got crazy and we're down here looking for it you two want to help? I mean, Jesus, Madeleine— the speckle foal got loose?—but that smile glowing on her face made it all very clear that she never expected me to believe that excuse, in fact she made it sound frivolous and false because she wanted me to know what had really happened, she wanted to outrage me. I believe that even now, don't I?—even in face of the fact that she has stayed with him, Henry Work, stuck by him all this time. Who would've ever guessed? I don't know. I don't know, maybe I don't believe it so much anymore but there had to be truth to it then—at least, I mean, that once, her hair with twigs and leaves in it and her skirt mussed.

Jonathan, no. You can't go this time. Will went, Maddie went, you went, and where did that leave me, and all the time I know that pa is Alma-this and Alma-that, but it's Maddie he misses, and even Henry Work because Henry never minded helping him in the offices all that clutter.

Will, I'm sorry about your helmet, you know I didn't mean to wreck it that I was planting flowers in it where your head had lived and it seemed to me a sentiment, a sort of sweetness. But you know that, wherever you are.

. . . As much as I love you pa I have the right to my opinion do you have any idea how embarrassing this is to me? You don't, do you. How, right along, from school on, it was forever the same terrible laughter, Alma's father? why he's squirrelly, cracked, bats, and look at what her crazy sister went and did, nearly drove poor feebleheaded Sophie Berkeley to distraction. I mean, though, not that any of their families ended up having done so much better that car crash who was it and they found out what's-his-name had been drinking killed his two best friends, and that family where the daughter got pregnant and her boyfriend busted for pushing, and some of the worst of them who just went on ahead and graduated high school, went off to college, got their job, settled right back into the same predictable routine they despised their parents for following. That much, John, I give you. You did get out of here. You went ahead and did something that at least makes some sense of what you were protesting about when you were younger. You made something of yourself, I mean you invented yourself, made yourself up, and you're still at it, so that much cannot be taken away. Aren't I doing that a little bit, too? I live mostly in New York now and that's something in itself, right? I'm finding a career for myself, not as quickly as you did, I know, but . . . so, John . . . I'm sorry, I apologize, you apologize, and there is this business of taking care of pa and so we'll do that, right? *right*.

Jonathan lit the citronella pots Alma had arranged at intervals around the porch. He liked the tang (sliced lemon) and the light (flickering orange) they cast: they were supposed to be used to drive off the mosquitoes that rose up from the stagnant inlets at the river's edge, or in busy clouds off nearby brown ponds that would be tarped in August at their shores by algae. Alma thought they'd help warm up the porch so they could sit outside and talk. The pots gave a Halloween atmosphere to the night.

"When you haven't seen somebody that long it's hard to picture them moving, it's more like assorted snapshots," as he shifted the pail of yellowish-orange wax to a low ledge. It gave off smoke. "We haven't seen her since she was sixteen. She seemed different—more special than the rest of us—but for example, I can't remember what her voice sounded like. Alma's accused me of romanticizing her."

"I have not."

"But I can see the day, but in a kind of dream, when she left. She took me into town to get my hair cut. It used to be there was a paved road, that ran back there about a quarter of a mile behind the part that went up and down the towns along the river. She took me on the bus into town. She had a knee-length green coat on, with black buttons. There was snow but it was just in patches under trees or along the shady sides of buildings. She took me to the barber's, so strange because I can smell the place as I sit here, sweaty, sweet. You know the kind of place, mirror behind the swivel chairs, the shelves of pomades and talcs, witch hazel. Lucky Tiger. Wildroot tonic. Funny-shaped bright bottles. The leather strops they used to use, for honing their razors, those old straightedges. She went out, to get something from the drugstore. Mario Schianello, Alma you remember him? He was the barber, he knew the family fairly well, knew Owen. They were friends, odd pair, played cards once in a while, before he"—and Jonathan pointed a finger up toward the second floor of the house—"got so reclusive. Mario didn't think anything was amiss until about an hour later. He was finished with me, and no sign of Maddie. He must've sent somebody out to look for her but nobody had seen her in the drugstore, or anywhere else. To cut a long story short she had run off with this black man, named Henry Work. I always liked him."

"I always hated him."

Jonathan thought, Poor Alma's the same dyed-in-the-wool bigot as her father. "I remember being so surprised I thought it was that I just hadn't understood, that I was too young to understand why everybody was so upset."

A bat swooped through the dark in the middle distance just beyond the lights cast from the porch where the three sat. It scissored the darkening atmosphere. Its thin, high peeps marked acute angles and broad curves. Dill heard it, wondered what it was doing here so late in the season, and chewed his fingernails, obliviously. His hands were sore from the little cuts that covered them, the result of working that afternoon with Jonathan.

"The barber drove me home. The house was in chaos. I remember feeling like it was all my fault."

"They put the police out after her and I was thinking to myself, What's all the commotion? She'll come walking in here any minute now laughing her head off at us. That would have been Maddie all over."

"Well, that was it, though," continued Jonathan. "She never did come back, the police never caught up with them. She did, two or three weeks later, send a letter, saying that she was all right, she was happy, don't worry about her. When it arrived, I don't think there was any mention of Henry Work in it, but Owen made up his mind immediately, and never changed it after that."

Dill, who had been sitting in the canvas chair, in his white shirt, now slipped on his sweater, buttoned it in one place, rolled back the sleeves. The lemon scent given by the hot citronella was waxy and full and had grown stronger.

"He legally disowned her."

"When that letter arrived—"

"Can't we talk about something else?"

"—he seemed calm at first. Ma had sent me to the offices to get him and when he came downstairs she handed him the letter without uttering a word. I think sometimes she was afraid of him, you know."

Jonathan looked up from the mosaic pattern of the brick porch whose cracks were tinted by moss and through which the sprigs of dead dandelions poked in clusters. He turned to Alma for affirmation and saw she'd left. The porch, situated adjacent to the kitchen on the west side of the house, was covered in a second scent. The parsley which Alma now was drying in the oven smelled of a hot confiture: grape preserves. Too, Jonathan's subconscious study of the design in the brickwork, over which his vision trailed as he spoke, produced another analogy, and then two more: a tartan's kilt; the fretwork in a molding of a Doric cornice he once saw on a trip to Greece. And the image of a herringbone jacket, stain of ice cream, butter brickle, on its sleeve. These transpired within the time it took him to inhale the twilit air, air charged with hot parsley, citronella fumes, grass, his own breath, "But so was I really."

"Maybe he's changed."

"I think my fear of him came from the guilt of being the last to see Maddie, as if there was something I could have done." Jonathan rubbed the back of his neck. "After he read her letter, I'll never forget as long as I live what he did. He read the letter. Didn't utter a word. We were all there with him in the room, Alma too, all waiting for him to say something. Well, he folded the letter back up and put it in its envelope and put it in his"—

herringbone, Jonathan realized, *herringbone with a butter brickle stain on its*

"—jacket pocket and left the room. We were all standing in that open foyer off the front door. He went upstairs. There was such deliberateness to the way he went up those stairs. We might have looked at each other, Alma and I, but we knew better than to say anything. I think by that time mother might have been crying. Upstairs, we could hear him going to it. He was in Maddie's room breaking things. Chairs, pictures. By the rhythm of it, though, it wasn't like a demolition executed in a rage, so much as it was like a kind of scientific dissection of each of the pieces and elements that went to make up the character of the room. Maybe I was hallucinating by then but I swear I could hear cloth tearing, slowly. Dresses, her sheets she slept in. One of those frilly canopies over her poster bed. It was finally a terrifying experience, to think about it now. And with ma there, crying quietly, trying to weep with a kind a stoicism. Pathetic. All of us. She kept saying, 'Don't. Don't.' But you probably know how those moments go. You never really know whether the 'don't' is addressed to one person or another. The whole thing was over in a few minutes. Here he came down the stairs again and in his hands was a beautiful porcelain bowl. It was her favorite object in the world. She used it for potpourri. Anyway, he brought it down with both hands, and walked to the front door. He tucked it under his arm, opened the door wide. Then he threw the bowl onto the porch outside. Some of the potpourri blew back in. He shut the door, didn't slam it. And he said something to the effect that as of now this family has five members—"

Three deer were grazing a hundred yards away at the edge of a clearing north of the toolshed. Dill craned his neck and squinted. Presences in the twilight, they lifted their heads, conscious of the slight change in timbre of the voice that emanated from the hill above. Behind them the sunset spread a violet murk above the line of trees.

"You've never heard from her or Work again?"

"Well," and Jonathan lay back in his chair. "They weren't that hard to trace. Ma put some man on to finding them. She had to do it behind Owen's back, but that didn't stop her. You see, Work's mother was a maid. Penny. When we were growing up she'd come here a couple of times a week to do laundry and some house cleaning. Penny Parker Work. She didn't know how to drive, so Henry would bring her out in his car and we kept some animals, some horses, a goat, laying hens. So after a while, Henry was hired to take care of the stables. He was an ex-Marine. He was a boxer, too, in the service. I gathered that once he got out of the service he lived with his father down somewhere in the South for a while, but they didn't get along, so he moved up here to be near his mother."

"And that's how he met Madeleine."

"She was always a rebellious one, and she didn't try very hard to conceal things. Work would bring his mother out in the morning and pretty soon began chauffeuring Maddie to school. They'd see each other at lunch. Half the time when she said she wanted to go out in the evening with girlfriends, Alma and I knew where it was she really was going to be. My father wouldn't tolerate it, so he fired Work's mother and told Maddie not to see him anymore. It sounds ridiculous, but I didn't even understand in the beginning that Owen's problem with Maddie's running off was because Henry was black. Didn't gibe with his politics, didn't gibe with his science."

Jonathan glanced down the hillside but it was too dark at the edge of the park to see whether the deer were still there grazing.

"Ma had them traced to Work's father's place down in the South. They were living together in a trailer house in back of his old man's. They'd gotten married. To make money, Henry had gone back to boxing, traveled some circuit doing exhibition fights, whatever was available, I gather. Ma might have sent some money to them, but it's all pretty vague after that."

"I wonder where they are now."

Jonathan sat forward forearms on his thighs. Dill saw only half his face, illuminated orange by the light of the flames; the other half was lost in shadow.

"I know that Henry Work was beaten half to death by some young fighter in a training camp down South. He only worked the circuit for a year or two and then he was hired on somewhere near Birmingham as a sparring partner for younger fighters. Well, as I understand it, he was really badly hurt, taken off to the hospital only half-conscious. He's never been able to get in a ring again. And I know, too, that an acquaintance of mine found him a job in New York somewhere. These calls that Alma's been telling me about—has there been anyone named Krieger around here?"

"I don't think so."

"What about Corless?"

"No."

A light went on upstairs. Jonathan looked up. A form left the frame of the window, a shadow. It had to have been his father up there, peering down at them.

"Maddie was his great love. I'm a bit of an outsider in this family, so it's easier for me to see it. He was never going to get anywhere with all his ridiculous gerontology-fussing upstairs, and he must have known it. The whole thing was very dumb and very privileged, if you ask me. This business of collecting sugar cane from Vilcabamba, manuscripts of neurological research in Abkhasia and the Hunzucuts, wilco seeds, aculpa, the list goes on—doda of the shamans of Ecuador, cascarilla bark, matico, all this crazy junk. It all got out of control after Maddie left."

"Alma believes that his work is important."

"I'm sorry. She's wrong."

"But he's been telling her that he's on the verge of some sort of break-through."

"What he's on the verge of is a break*down*, and anyway he hasn't been serious about any of his work for years. He collects things for the same reason most people collect things—he could never do it himself, so he surrounds himself with bits and pieces of others' accomplishments, that ship's prow in the front room, such hokum."

Dill felt as if he were being asked to choose sides in a dispute he was neither qualified nor inclined to judge. "Why'd he get so interested in longevity in the first place?"

Jonathan laughed and looked up to the window. The light was out. "That's the best question of all."

Alma was calling them to dinner. Jonathan snuffed out the flames in the citronella pots. The whitetails had drifted closer to where they sat, talking, unaware. They could smell the lemon smoke that trailed in ribbons down the rise, before their breathing dispersed these in skeins moistened and warmed by giddy lungs. They couldn't hear the man's answer to the other man's question. "It's not like he's interested in ours," was all Jonathan could come up with.

7.

OWEN opened the leaded windows. It took some effort, so long had they been kept closed. They were half fused into their casements. He looked down where Jonathan and Dill were doing something but his eye caught on a frail frame of lead and followed its course around a pane of glass. He was struck just for an instant—fully struck, even overcome—with a sense of remorse. The window leading was like a vein run dry, a capillary out at the farthest edge of the house. Who knew how much blood continued to flow through the rest, or whether its heart beat at all? He listened. No, he still could faintly hear its pulse. And the air which came tentative into the rooms assured him the thing was yet alive—the house, that is.

A voice. Alma's. She was going down to join them. What were they doing? Jonathan had a scythe out, was mowing like a symbol of death the bridle path grass. Busy with something always, Jonathan, or he wasn't happy. Not like Will. Will has more of a reflective nature. Had. He could sit still when sitting still was the thing to do. Also, he could fight, meaner than any lion, if that was what he was called to do. And who could remember Madeleine anymore?

Jonathan had been in here. Nothing was out of place but the rooms felt different. You didn't spend so many hours of your life in a place and not come to know a fourth, or fifth, dimension of it. Always busy, that boy, remember how he and his sister used to come back from their afternoons of exploration with some piece of bric-a-brac or other from who knows what generation of the family, little locked diary hidden in the south attic once, broken meerschaum pipe carved with the elephants and the dolphins. Alma, and John—who would guess them as twins now? Same busyness coming in here, all predisposed to incriminate and judge. The cages undisturbed. Horace, Virgil, Hesiod, Lucan, Valerius Flaccus, Theocritus, and all the others. The wonderful routine of their feedings. Augustus the monkey, the hamsters Martials I, II, III, Phoebus-pig, all of them hardly more than glorified pets at this stage of things, and at that hardly glorified. Solitude and prayer, and Mahler on the looped tape. Not such an awful life, not necessarily squandered given the prospect ahead.

That stagy exchange down at dinner, though. The fish, the urine, the Alma bring me my milk. It was pathetic, shouldn't have laughed. Sometimes it is better to be seen as half off. Sometimes better to be seen as all the way off, right off the edge. Which tribe is it in the Andes, the oldest amongst them generally allowed to act the craziest, carry on with their polygamy, skip the chores, and the same true of course of the females, the maids who don't marry, sleep around a little, and far outlive their married sisters and friends.

Could ask Jonathan, he'd know. The response time of youthful cortical tissue, one of the wonders of the world. Could have Alma ask Jonathan.

But he had been in here, and of course he would have known. Anyone would have known. Owen made no effort to conceal the materials which anyone who gained entrance into the room might seek—it was as if (he knew this to be true) he would welcome an end to the process. The process which, in and of itself, sought to deny ends. He himself could not stop it, although in a way he knew, just like the house, his heart was no longer sufficiently in it to push the blood, so to speak, to the ends of its body's thought anymore. Houses tire, and men and women tire, too. There was the primary struggle. They're both pulled down and down because the gravities caused by all the spinning and whirling made it so. Intervention would have to come from without. He was far beyond the threshold of responsibility. How grateful he felt toward Alma, though this too he could never show, for her having sent for her brother. The little histrionics worked—he was here, wasn't he? And Jonathan, after all, must have been the bridge by which Corless came into their lives in the first place. How else? No other way. So, as far as that goes, Jonathan was culpable.

The worst part was that he hadn't been feeling in the clear, excruciating heart of how it could function, that obsessive drive to his work anymore. Not for years. The obsession had dried up, was parched, the will had fallen. There was only the presence of inertia left to carry him forward—inertia as much as anything brought along by business, money, the transaction, the supple joy of the letter-writing and the other arrangements, getting the guest rooms ready, washing the linen, pressing the extra pairs of pajamas. It was all actually happening to him. He turned around and sat against the sill, arms folded. That *was* part of it, wasn't it? the merest great-good sense of mixing it up with the world, engaging.

What would he do once he had taken possession of this extraordinary property, who even now was probably preparing to come? Laser technologies and the promise of genetic-recombining surgery, who knew?—perhaps even at the prenatal stage, perhaps even in preconceptual matter, the very tissue of the egg under the sharp thread of light in this post-Lord era, worrying the double helix, searing it in an atomic furnace and redelivering it back through the eye of the needle into a strange new world, but girded, strengthened against itself as well as everything else, protected from its own tendencies to break down, crumble from the inside as Sophie had, perish like Will, into the unimaginable void—the one he himself faced soon enough.

He could not follow that particular road. Pioneerism was over, in a certain sense, in a pure sense. This was all musty science fiction, was it not? It felt like that, as Alma's laugh rose up the hill to the house. He stood away from the familiar window, his favorite, the one he'd passed so many years behind, looking down.

Alma down there hugging her man. No more children for this house. No more name, no more house.

And so let it come forward. Perhaps we shall become fast friends, I and It. No, absolutely, we will be friends. It will be good.

We can teach It to speak, as if a mouse.

It will be the mouse-king; that is what he shall be.

Owen drew the windows closed and rested his forehead against the cool glass.

The texture, the slow wave of skin that fell away from where his head lay on the damp pillow, until it reached a delicate, soft point, a place rather, where he could see his own hand cupped into the waist, and beyond, where her hip rose and the frame of flesh, a pear, curved down, buttocks, the straight dark indentation, her feet, the puckered soles of them, side by side, innocent and intent. Alma's head lay in the concave dish of his belly and for her it was like being carried away from all of them, her brother, the question of her father, even away from Dill himself although of course he was right here beside her on the bed. She could hear his breathing, and her head rose and fell with the pulse of blood that occupied his arteries, heart, veins. He tasted of nothing in her mouth, but she was familiar with him, with his projection, his scent, the blue threads heavy and thin that traced this arcing flesh. Sometimes her eyes were open, sometimes half closed, sometimes shut so that what image formed itself, willed itself into being and motion, was seen on the insides of her eyelids. Her eyes now were open. The engagement ring on her own finger caught a fragment of the light cast from the bathroom as ring and finger it banded rhythmically moved toward and away from her face. She moaned, in response to Dill's moan, which she could hear behind her. His hand she could feel on her waist; its fingers were splayed, then drew together. Slowly they projected, like the ribs of a fan whose paper had worn away, and moved from her waist over her hip. Gently, she was plied open by this palm, these fingers; Dill shifted his torso so that he could reach her from behind between her thighs. In his memory he was able to conjure with great precision what she looked like between her legs. It was a flower, crushed to fusiform, a carnation whose system of petals was reduced, fashioned of meat, or jelly, of flesh. Her breast hung heavily to the sheet and he knew that while he had touched other breasts, studied them, kissed them, this was the one his own child would someday feed at. His hand moved to it, cradled it, weighed it, found its nipple that projected like a brown pebble: this he pressed lightly between his fingers. He closed his eyes, concentrated on the sounds and what he touched. He opened them and looked up.

The paint on the ceiling was chipped in great triangular pieces. The house was coming down a fragment at a time, Dill thought. It didn't seem likely that either Alma or her brother, or their father, could stop the process of decay even if any of them knew where to begin, which—so out of touch was one from the others—none clearly did. He closed his eyes again, and breathed the house into himself. There was the slightest scent of her perfume from the night before.

Her hair lay over her shoulder and across his chest. He brushed it away from her face and smoothed it out over his own flesh. With the tips of his fingers (which began to quiver, as she moved her tongue, fluttered, hummed, around the head and stroked him with her hand along the saliva-wet shaft) he tucked her hair in behind her ear. She pushed her mouth and lips forward deeper into his lap, warmly took him in. She could feel him pulling her head back away from his lap. Her mouth gave him up and she allowed herself to be drawn back and as she did she could feel her feet go numb with heat.

She was in the bathroom, running water in the bathtub. Dill was still lying on the bed in the dim light that came through from the bath, his face moist and flushed. He was trying more carefully to study the cracks and peeling paint on the ceiling. He imagined an upstairs sink, above, overflowing, rust water from the old well of this house, leaking through poorly spackled tiles or chinks in the linoleum, soaking through the planks beneath, through crevices and bad joinings, dripping down the interstices between floors to pool above where it spread to form in the ceiling, once so nicely plastered and painted eggshell white, a stain the shape of a blossom first, and began to rot away. He even imagined, but just for an instant, that Owen might have made himself a peephole up there so that he could watch their mating procedures. Just a simple idea. His eyes traveled over the surface. No. His mind'd wandered. Who would blame the old duffer even if he had?

The water in the bathroom was shut off. Alma was toweling dry. In the shower she had been humming to herself. Christmas carols. O come all ye faithful. God rest ye merry, gentlemen. Now she was quiet.

Dill sat up in the bed. She came into the room. The towel was wrapped about her and she stood just inside the room for half a minute, saying nothing. He finally asked, "Why don't we go out and get ourselves a Christmas tree this morning?"

"It'd be dead by the time Christmas comes."

"We'll get another one."

"Don't be dumb."

"What's the matter?"

"Nothing."

Dill frowned, but she could not see his frown in the light. Once he understood this the frown dropped away to be replaced by a sigh; still no response, repeated, "Nothing."

"You know, Jonathan doesn't have the faintest idea how much I loved her—envied her. I mean to me she was the end-all, the object of something like total admiration. Graceful, beautiful, thin, smart, there wasn't a guy in school who paid attention to me I don't think for any other reason than finally to get a chance to meet Maddie."

"That I doubt."

"It's true, though, and I even understood maybe even sometimes I counted my blessings she was my sister, or else nobody'd have paid any attention to me at all."

"Alma."

"But it's true, I mean it. I went into her room once, everybody in the house was asleep, she had a cat named Willie Winkie, Willie was the only one who saw me, he was lying curled up next to her and I looked at her for the longest time and realized she was the most beautiful girl on the earth and it'd be best if I learned to live with that because that was the way it always would be. She was pa's favorite"—finding her bathrobe, and the damp towel was tossed on the end of the bed where Dill distractedly drew it up and began to wipe himself—"I think that's why he was so hurt when she ran away, they all were. And Maddie had no concept or else she didn't care. But I stared and stared at her that night. She was old enough she must've been involved with him, with Henry by then. But she was such perfection."

"Just like you."

"There was no way for me to measure up, doesn't make me very proud of myself but I must have been partly happy when she did it. Not that he transferred any of his affection for her to me after she left, god forbid. Just withdrew. I guess even that felt better than having to stand there and watch all his . . . adoration's the only word for what he felt."

"I think you're being very hard on yourself."

"He's all that's left of the family now, all that's left for me, and I wanted this to go, I had some ideas about his coming up that I guess weren't right. Maybe it would be the best thing if he did find Maddie, maybe he's right, what do I know?"

"Hey."

"What."
"Come over here."
"No."

Another pair of eyes studied another ceiling in wonderment though they had seen so many things of wonder before. The eyes ran with tears at the spectacle. They had seen only moments before the night where stars twinkled not just in the heavens but on the earth, too. He giggled, Who would ever believe the stars could shine in the earth, too? But they were there to see. He was witness, and Sardavaal's emissary, who stood with his arm around his shoulder, was witness, also. Some of the earth-stars were in colors, but most were white and flickered like the heaven-stars. Then they left the flat plateau of roof and went down a stairway carved at the most perfect angles the old Indian had ever seen, turned through a doorway, and came into a great, beautiful land that wasn't like home but reminded him of home, all green and with the animal noises. The big difference was that down here it was day. He stared at this bright and blue sky. Sardavaal, he thought, is bringing me to a miracle.

VI

Tercer Mundo

1.

HENRY liquefied the stuff, heating it in the bowl of a tablespoon whose handle flared as he passed it over the flame of the lighter which illuminated a number, neatly painted in white, centered on its crenellated edge. The critters gathered behind him, where he hunkered a little and suffered the rush because of the candy that seemed to have gone straight to his heart. They peered in a bunch over his right shoulder, giving off the same blue as a jay tail and Henry knew at once what it meant, this blue, even though they hadn't come around visiting for a while—meant they were about to take their leave of him again. That was quick, but it didn't make him unhappy. His face settled into repose, tiny teeth withholding his tongue, moist and heavy in the slack mouth. His eyes strayed inward; no more blue. All across the pate of his wide head fine gray coiled hairs encroached the glistening black. At the temples he'd gone white as an apple core, the hair frizzled out before two pronounced cauliflower ears. Maddie, it's because they're here again, you don't know them, but they're here and . . . he apologized, deep down inside where it was dimmer than even the Saturday night around him. Maddie answered, it seemed, that it wasn't to forgive, that she was there with him, although he knew she really wasn't. He was humming to himself a tune which freely drifted from one song to another and the words to two melodies, favorites of his father George Washington, came to his lips in a deep tenor.

> *"Rock of Ages down in the land of cotton*
> *Old times there are not forgotten,*

> *Cleft for me, cleft for me*
> *Let me hide myself in thee . . ."*

which seemed to work pretty well all gummed up and, having opened his eyes into the most brilliant, burning blue, he kept pushing,

> *"Let the water and the blood*
> *From Thy wounded side which flowed*
> *Look away,*
> *   look away,*
> *Look away,*
> *   Dixieland."*

The plastic syringe he had already removed from its acetate wrapping and a fresh-boiled needle had been attached to it. No, the critters didn't like even the crinkle of the acetate. They knew it as well as he did. Neither we, troth to tell, likes the crinkle. Not air enough, even out under the moon like this, for all of them. And the critters say, Don't sing no more baby Henry, and he remembered about their not enjoying that, so he took up another verse.

> *"O, I wish I was in Dixie*
> *Hooray, hooray*
> *Cause I'd hide myself way down in thee*
> *And I'd live and die in Dixsee . . ."*

but Henry, man-Henry not baby Henry, preoccupied with drawing off the liquid into the barrel of the syringe—it had been some years since he had done this—faltered on the melodies, and the songs trailed away.

So having aspirated the goods of the bag into the plastic cylinder, he set down the spoon, whose heat he could not feel through the heavy calluses on his fingers. He rolled back the left sleeve of his shirt and, syringe tucked like a carpenter's pencil behind one ear, commenced slapping the muscular, rubbery skin at the juncture between forearm and biceps.

"Come on," looking for the vein to rise.

After tightening the elastic tourniquet just above the elbow, he clasped the angle of his arm and screwed his clenched hand on the flesh. He looked to the surface for results. Nothing. He wagged a finger, scolding, scissored the skin between this thumb and first finger, kneaded, all concentration, regard fixed over the voice which was already beginning to leave him although it was his own, "Come on . . . you bad girl not come on up."

Presently, the vein began to articulate. It rose, pulsating, like a reluctant worm sheltered beneath the skin. He slapped it several times back and forth with the back of his fingers and the fronts, as if he were dusting the skin. The vein responded, the worm grew excited. Henry daubed it gently with tissue soaked in rubbing alcohol.

"Come on sweet, that's it you got it," he said, remembering the years when he did this to assuage the pain, recalling also how the pitter-patter of talking made it all so much easier.

After he finished, critter-blue spluttered over his shoulder and at least some of the contingent slipped and fell into the ceiling of the silo, complaining, then splashed, sloshing upside down out between the columns, sloshing into the heavens. He hid away the punch, the elastic tape, the spoon in a small niche behind a loose brick. Some great breaths, and the cold, for it was chilly, radiated into his chest. He knew he'd be missed, knew that Maddie, Hannah, Hammond, possibly even the stranger Lupi would by now be searching for him. Soon enough they would find him. He looked out from the silo to the north. There the Citibank building glowed, a stout amber chisel prepared to chip the sky, the hue of a sun-bleached and time-weathered shack. The three tiers of lights on the Empire State were ash-white, shining up at the great syringe where they used to park airships. In a week, now that Christmas neared, they would change the lights to green and red. He shook his head, chin to shoulder, and beamed at the thought of the windows at the department store, the dancing ladies in their frilly gowns twirling on the arms of their tuxedoed beaux, the wooden elves hammering together toys, children gathered by a hearth and beside it a tree covered in ornaments, ringed with tinsel, popcorn and cranberry strings.

It had been an unusual afternoon for Henry. Payday. But a day, too, in which he had located a door behind which were stairs that led him down, flight after flight in darkness illuminated only intermittently by the wan red of bare light bulbs enclosed in metal cages that put him in mind of catcher's masks. He had come into a lobby. The metal door had sprung shut behind him. He tried it, but it was locked. He slapped his trouser pocket for his keys. They bulged there. He had no idea whether or not any of them would let him back into the secret stairwell; he would find out later. First, he had to get out, get away from them all, not for long, but just an hour. Not to think necessarily—what was there to think about? The critters had clued him in. Maddie, they said, had matters to settle, and they couldn't protect her from matters no more. She didn't need their help, he answered. But they'd already rolled off to mulch themselves from green to blue in the electric hay. So, he had to get out. It was hardly his choice.

First there was a concession stand. A woman with a moustache leaned over its cluttered counter; newspapers, candy, cigarettes flanked her— framed in glossy magazines suspended by clothespins on wires. He bought not quite twenty dollars' worth of Snickers, Baby Ruths, Three Mus- keteers, Milky Ways, and paid for them with one of the bills Hannah had given him. Candies thrust into the pockets of his overalls, Henry acknowl- edged the woman's comment, "mighty hungry," by ripping the paper wrapper off the end of one and starting in. Henry knew that for him the horse and the candy went together—that was the way it had always been. The critters don't like horse, and they don't cotton to candy, neither. Why'd they come around now? now that they'd been gone so long?

One critter had told him straight to his face, Cradle's gonna fall out of the tree baby-O.

Was that why he was here?—was this what he'd come downstairs to think about?

Another critter, just as fond as his mates of communicating to Henry in nursery rhymes and children's ditties, saw that Henry had not understood the first critter, and spoke in a soft soprano voice, making sure not to let it slip into song, Four little, three little, two little Indians. One little Indian boy. Get it baby Henry?

Henry did get it. It was evident in Maddie's and Hannah's behavior. He thought, I don't need critters to tell me that, but just as he held the thought, the first critter continued it, saying simply, You're a bad boy Henry. And Henry thought about this and saw that yes he was nice to the Italian Lupi, because he liked him, because he could see that this was not a bad-hearted man—but the critter interrupted, You're spoiled spoiled spoiled boy you don't know how to say thank you. Thank the lady, Henry baby.

Henry looked up into the eyes of the woman at the counter. They were runny, behind a thick pair of glasses. "Don't cry."

The woman shrugged, another nut.

"Well, thanks," he finished, listening for more words from the critters. They didn't answer, and besides, most of them had gone ahead to the park.

Thanks—just what he'd told Hannah, what he always said on wage day. Henry was grateful to Hannah; no, he was devoted. Hannah had taken them in, sheltered them, had given Henry this job, working with the animals, doing the chores—a tidy, narrow, protected, calm life with Madeleine a farmer's wife, elegant brave Maddie. Remember that night when the first of the animals was brought in? how it seemed so huge and sleek and beautiful, how it settled down by the touch of his brush across its coat? Then some of the birds were brought in. They took to that old beat-up berlin right away—and after Henry had gone to so much trouble constructing a proper coop. The makeshift dumbwaiter used to bring down feed from the silo he rigged up, with sliding doors and heavy rope for rigging. He replastered the rooms in the loft, using sand and good unslaked lime and cattle hair to bind it. He set up the grain room, the shed, the stalls, the drainage furrows for the barnyard. 200 pounds 10-penny nails; 100 pounds 20-penny nails; 50 pounds 8-penny nails; 75 pounds 5-penny nails. He hammered together the movable plank floors for the stalls and prepared a secret chamber for the beasts to be hidden in if the ranch were ever to be penetrated. A bench, a sink, an oil stove, hoods, ventilation flues to gather, cocks in the tubs he placed high so as to allow for water being drawn into pitchers. He spread the macadam grit and shoveled soil for the garden on the roof, laid the tar roof on the bunkhouse, mended a broken cornice on the water-tank tower with Sakrete and advice called up from below from Hannah and Madeleine who he could see was happy for the first time since they ran away. She had always loathed the South, its marsh earth and bayou air, hated its hatred of her, young white woman who'd taken this decision with Henry, who had experienced in half a lifetime as much racial prejudice as most of Henry's friends and members of his family, who themselves were resistant at first; slow; leery.

As these were the best of days those were the worst—the boxing camp and the critters; primarily the terror of the critters. He'd succeeded in keeping them at bay until the accident, but then it was as if the lock on a door had been broken, the door removed, the walls, the roof taken away, and a new house, made of critters, put up in its place, with a brand-new lock and key for the door.

Henry had no clear memory of how it had happened. He was wearing his old headguard. Such a flurry of smart jabs to his face he had never been forced to ward off before, but nothing hurt. The fast little middleweight had drawn a bit of blood out of his mouth and nose—not enough to cause the trainer (a slip of a man, wisps of hair beneath his battered porkpie cap, mouth pulled far into the left cheek beneath his nose, crimpled, where a mirror of bubbles percolated under his hoarse yelling) to stop the round. The kid was getting a good workout, his rhythm was on. Work was his second sparring partner that day; everything seemed to be in order. The trainer growled, clapped hands, shouted, spat, whistled, and the sallowbrowed waterboy cheered. That flurry of punches was all: it seemed every time the kid let up and Henry relaxed back into an easy bob, block, duck, jab, on he would come again, backing this rugged flatfooter up toward the ringposts in the corner. All the commotion Henry heard like memory as they gamboled, fed-back, rang and vanished into nothing. Sometime came the backward trip and tumble, and at the base of his head there the turnbuckle flew up to hammer his skull; one clean blow was all it took.

Flash cards, Henry could remember. Flash cards, with little color pictures on them of a shoe or a doggie, and those what them dogs do hate, those kittycats. A cob of corn, for instance. An antelope, a cantaloupe, sun, moon, Plymouth Rock. Who was the first President of the United States, Columbus. Who had ever heard of Leif Erikson? Cobs of corn were easier to name than shoes. Cobs, and robin redbreasts. A gun, an apple. Apples, do they go woof, meow, boom, or? No they crunch when as you eat them. Doggie? gruhf. Gun? boom. Is Crunchy a candy? You want a Crunchy? Tell me what color it is and Maddie here will give you the Crunchy she brought with her. Brown, the brown of chocolate, and pretty Maddie who sometimes hid herself in the closet of the ward so that after visiting hours were over she could come and lie with him in the bed for a while, how happy his answer made her, and to make her more happy he said, chocolate, chocolate, pronouncing each of the sounds of the word distinctly.

In time, came back words like cat. Came back sentences like *I am Henry Work and I love my wife her name is Maddie*.

Maddie took him home. She told him that they were no longer going to be able to live down here, that she had found a new home for them, one which Henry would love, because the doctor said that he couldn't ever be hit on the head again or that would be it for him. He listened, and understood. Everything would be fine. A man had called her and seemed to know what there was to know about them (which, in fact, made her nervous, but since they couldn't go on like this she thought it was worth the risk)—there were bus tickets in the mail, an address.

On paydays often Madeleine and Henry would have supper up in the bunkhouse with Hannah. They would sit around the table out in the garden, and eat bean salad and chicken rolled in white flour and fried in bacon drippings—

What was he doing down here in the lobby of the building, then? he wondered. Everything was so odd, all these people. He thought backwards to where he'd thanked Hannah, slipped into his pocket the money she gave him, and left the bunker to go downstairs to Madeleine, who was waiting for him. But he had taken instead an innovative turn in the stairwell, descended, purchased the candy and leaned his massive frame against the glass door that delivered him blinking in wonder into the street. Here was a place of noise and multiple movements, a place of anxiety, of pushing and pulling. The smell of something poached mingled with diesel. Above all, the sweet scent of candy, its coconut, caramel, gooey and chewy there out before his nose, which followed it, the scent, as his feet placed themselves one before the other, transporting him eastward. He thought of Maddie upstairs waiting for him to knock at the door of their small apartment, waiting for him to enter the room, hand her the envelope Hannah had given him; Maddie who'd remove the money and hide it in the plastic bag she taped under the table. This was their saving-up money. Henry wasn't sure what the saving-up money was being saved up against. It seemed to him there wasn't another place on earth quite as fine as the ranch, and though he was down in the street just then, he knew he would begin to feel that old anxiousness again—those critters (he didn't know whether he called them that or they had named themselves), the nerves that came along toward the end of a boxing round, came in different forms but mostly in the shape of ice-blue crystal-like stars which waggled at the upper reaches of his field of vision, made his fingertips, toes, and the nape of his neck tingle; the old critters on their way to visit him and he would have to run back, find the door he'd opened, and escape once more into the safety of the ranch and Maddie.

But he discovered he'd walked out the front of the building, considered the critters, looked east, west, started east, walking until he reached Fifth Avenue. He proceeded downtown, eating his candy bars one by one, pausing to read the names, pronounce them aloud before making each selection, broadcasting their colorful wrappers into the gentle breeze, until he passed under the shadow cast by Stanford White's gray-streaked arch in Washington Square.

The great central fountain was dry. Henry sat down on the low concrete wall that traced its circumference. He felt tired from his walk. He wished he had bought a couple of bags of M&Ms when he'd had the opportunity. He did not seek out the kid among the lively scraps of humanity floating near him, under the spell cast by the mink-black squirrel that was now pitching itself, tiny leaps at a time, across the grass. Leaves left in the trees rustled under the winter bound sun. The squirrel stopped in a shadow on the grass, fixed its eye on this large figure seated at the fountain, hands placed flat on knees, head cocked heavily to one side to return its gaze. Was there a critter hiding inside it?

After a psychotic instant that scuttled space and time the squirrel took charge. In arcing jabs it closed the space between the two of them. Henry was bewitched by its furious sanguine eyes and its tail that brushed the air at each thrust. He wanted to get up and run but was transfixed.

The litany cut across this macabre ambush like heaven-sent absolution. "Sess-sess-sess," came the baleful hiss. It issued from a stocky short Hispanic whose face was only partly obscured along the lean line of jaw by a beard. "Sess-ss-sess."

Sin semilla, that much he knew.

Grateful to this officer of his momentary reprieve (for the squirrel retreated to continue stalking food to bury for winter, kernels of lime-green popcorn, a hickory-smoked almond, fragments of pretzel), Henry spoke up, "What?"

"Hey, man."

Henry echoed, "Hey." Nodded. Okay, man.

"What'll it be, man."

"What?"

"What'll it *be?* I mean, like what can I do you for?"

"Oh," said Henry. Unvexed, he reached down into memory and came up with a potential word, one picked up from the trainer, the only person besides Maddie to whom Henry had ever disclosed any details about the wild blue critters and the terrible pain which Maddie never knew the half of since Henry felt that to tell her would be dishonorable, in view of all the pain she had suffered through for him. He had told the trainer about the pain, though. It was a good thing he had, he thought. They started him on the morphine, light doses at first. But sometimes this other was more easily come by. At first Henry hated the needles but when he saw how the critters dispersed and the pain let up he grew accustomed to their presence in the locker room. He was warned under threat of having the—(word? the boy still was waiting for it)—taken away not to tell his wife about the medicine. And Henry could picture him there, a placid man whose soul showed in those bloodshot aggie eyes, a golden aura floating under that frail black skin. The word was there and it was just a matter of bringing it up to the lips. It seemed like an exercise, a test. Then he remembered, it was from his trainer Henry learned the word which protected him from the critters and now he pronounced it not so much to make a request as to gratify this nervous young man's need, as Henry perceived it, to communicate, saying simply, "Horse."

"Huh?"

He sat mute, his expression tabula rasa.

"Hey, whoa man," swiftly walking away, hands immobile at sides, gait angularly jaunty on the balls of his feet. He circled the fountain and came back. "So, hey."

"Hey," smiled Henry; the air smelled fresh, sun was warm. He threw his head back into it, stared into the backs of his lids—no blue crystals there.

"So uh hey, smack, man?" but even as the question dropped away to a caustic whisper the dealer took a step back, looked left-right-farther-right-left, masterfully jerking his shoulders up and down, paying homage to the forgotten television prototype on which he had crafted his own street behavior, the prototype designed from a bogus version of what he, in fact, was, here in this park, working the top of the circle.

"Horse," Henry repeated.

The kid smirked, "This ain't no rodeo, man."

Henry laughed. If only the good old trainer—he must be dead now—if only he'd heard that.

"Fuck you man, what am I spost to say to my main man?" and his voice shifted up to black, "Hey so this dude comes up to me like, no I din notice his threads, no he din have no sick threads on man, anyway so he comes up to me and like what he wants is dope?"

Henry was confused, but the monologue gained its own momentum.

"This guy's like about nine feet high you think I'm gonna say no man I ain't givin you no dope man, you tellin me you say no big man I ain't sellin you no dope, ain't nobody here gonna sell you dope man, ludes okay sure some snow right, I mean look, mescline I say sure man. But dope."

"Horse."

"You . . . no wait man, hold everything man. My ass man, I smell you a mile comin, *narc*."

Henry laughed again, genially. The world wasn't so bad. He felt sorry for the kid. The kid, he thought, could use some fathering, a good trip out to a woodshed where Henry himself could paddle his little back porch—not too hard, not too gently, just enough to force a few tears to the eyes for the soul's sake, and for the conscience some fear of the belt.

"Fuck you fuckhead," wondering how far he could go before the man turned ugly on him, but he perused his customer, measured him and was satisfied he (who regarded him with a genuinely beatific look) was not a narc. "Hey okay, fuck. Junk, dope? Lissen to me nobody carries no dope on 'em man, okay? Hang here I be right back."

Henry studied the skirt of grass against the possibility the black squirrel might return. A soccer game, trash cans set up as goalposts, was being played on the concrete before the backdrop of the World Trade Center, to Henry's left. He watched them play, guys in their twenties, some in street shoes, one barefooted and barechested, all freewheeling, aggressive, passionate players. One had his hair conked and dyed to an iridescent orange. Henry's eye took in the brief conjunction, the split instant as the orange ball lofted in the air to be head-butted by this player, then the ball bounced off at a new angle. The goalie, whose earring was dazzled in sun, caught it and without hesitation dropkicked it back into the field of play.

The light slanted down on the square, on Thompson Street and on the two towers that shined silver as Kit Kat foil at the bottom of the island. They reminded Henry, these silver skyscrapers, of two gargantuan Pez dispensers.

Pez, how had he eaten all that candy? He looked down.

Again the squirrel had approached him. It was crouched, tail a jet plume, not two yards from where his feet were crossed. He nearly fell backward into the empty fountain. And yet once again the dealer intervened. He, too, noticed the squirrel.

"Go on, get outta here," he stamped his foot. The squirrel's black tail switched several times before it left, bounding away in a direction opposite the soccer players. The kid addressed Henry, who had recovered his balance and was now standing a shoulder over him. "Okay, chief. Ten bucks a dec, thirty bucks a clean dec very good stuff very good."

"Okay, man," Henry echoed.

"You follow me, chief."

Henry was led to a corner of the park where he made his buy—two pure decs—from a handsome man, conservatively dressed, with the melting eyes Henry knew as those of a flash-card giraffe.

"How much of that does *he* get?" Henry asked, indicating the kid who stood at a discreet distance, now blowing into his hands and dancing in place, foot to foot.

"How much of what," abrupt, clipped.

Henry nodded at the jacket pocket in which the money had already been stowed.

"How much of what, I don't get it. You got your stuff, right?"

"How much does the kid get."

"Gets enough."

"How much is enough?"

"Time for you to take a walk, clown."

Having said that, the handsome man moved briskly past where the kid had taken up his position. Henry waved the kid over, not knowing what he would say if he came (he didn't).

He tucked the packet into his shoe and strolled back to the bottom of Fifth Avenue, retraced his steps home. Up stairs, past the red light in the well, and out on the roof. The door to the bunker was open and without a word Henry walked inside. No one was there. He first snatched the table-spoon out of a drawer. The syringe he took from the veterinary medical kit and the needle—boiled with a batch of others by Henry himself that morning—he selected from the dispensary drawer. The syringe and needle were among those used to inject the dog subcutaneously with vitamins, or calcium. In the dispensary there were much larger instruments, which they used for the cattle; intramuscular injections of penicillin and antihistamine. He walked out and cut across the garden, covered with winter rye, to the silo. He had not been seen; in the impertinent peace the city can offer up to one of its dwellers, Henry was able to perform his bang, keep the critters at bay, watch the trees pitching against the band of dirty salmon that hugged the outline of the hills and skyline. It looked, the sky, like blue litmus paper dipped into the acid horizon so that the damp pink rose along the chemical-treated bottom edge . . . and Henry stared hard into the wide sliver of pumpkin sun like . . . warmth rent him through like . . . his eyes like teetered merrily like then the chill shook through and then the heat like . . . cartoon nystagmus like . . . this helicopter like it . . . made a booming . . . it made a tremendous booming racket rotors pommeling the island air like . . . pushed across the big old smiling mother moon.

2.

LUPI found him—fetal heap dozing under the flashlight beam, snoring loudly, shivering—and was a little surprised at his own sense of enthusiasm at having been the one who solved the problem. If Madeleine had been correct in blaming Henry's disappearance on Lupi in the first place, Lupi who had come to ruin the delicate balance of their lives, this would go some way toward setting things back again. Crouching down to pat Henry on the shoulder, he found himself angry at Krieger.

A vigorous wind played in and around the silo. It was just after midnight and Hannah and Hammond were still out walking the streets searching for him. Hannah had gone downtown toward dusk, walking a crosstown pattern a block at a time from east to west and from west to east along the next street down. She had circled through Stuyvesant and Union to thread her way by sunset into Washington Square. Passing under the bronze regard of evergreen Giuseppe Garibaldi she made her way to a bench, sat down, footsore and nervous. Krieger had once sat here in the park with her many years ago (which bench was it from which they watched in sunlight people, birds, trees?). They'd sat there like lovers. She recalled how she'd reached over for his hand, where the fingers were spread across his knee, and how while he'd not taken hers into his own he didn't move it away—he was caught up in explaining the patriot Garibaldi who in a long life of expeditions, exiles, invasions, victories, escapes, defeats, once arrived here in Manhattan, penniless, after being pursued through central Italy by the combined armies of France, Austria, Naples, and Spain, and having successfully fled them all, set himself up first as a chandler, a supplier of goods to ships that docked in the harbor, and then as a trading skipper who piled up a small fortune with which he returned to the homeland to buy his own island, the isle of Caprera, in 1854.

A wop, Krieger said, but a man with a grade-A American mind. "Hannah," it was as if she could hear him now, that last time he had come to her. No threats in his desperation that week, no telephone messages—instead he had waited for her across the street in the Cuban-Chinese takeout, sipping cups of their tea, and when she'd come down he'd followed for a few blocks, as he later told her, building up the courage to call out her name. "Hannah, I've found him."

"Peter?" having turned to see him, gaunter and paler than ever. "You look terrrible."

"Always the compliments," but something was missing from the normal sharpness of the sarcasm. "Hannah, I found him for you."

"Found who?"

"For christsakes, Nicky of course, Nicholas. Didn't I tell you I'd find him? well, I have."

"Franz told me you were somewhere in Central America."

"Central America," distracted. "You want to see him?" Krieger leaned against the brick of a building.

"I wish you hadn't bothered," she said, a little unconvincingly. "I'm happy the way things are. I don't want to go rooting all of that up again."

Krieger pushed himself away from the brick, looked at his palms which were stained with soot, clapped them together, turned and said, "Did I get that on my suit? never mind, I'll see you."

Hannah stopped him; he looked pathetic, shoulders hunched down, arms hanging at his sides. "Where are you staying? I've got to think. Maybe I should see him. But, you're not okay, are you."

"Krieger's fine, little defeated, little homeless, little out of work, legal or peripheral, but fine."

"Can't you stay with Franz?"

"That bridge is burned."

The week which followed was calamitous insofar as it was the romance Hannah had never allowed herself to imagine with Krieger. Her femininity (womanly more than ladylike; girlish as a rough cub) was never greater than during the hours they spent in the double bed in the back, the one in which Olid now lay sipping quinine. Hannah knew she was neglecting the ranch, and intuited that Maddie was uncomfortable about this visitor lingering so close to their secret lives, but she wasn't able to get herself to bring it up either with Krieger or her friend.

About Nicholas she found herself irresolute. That Krieger had seen him seemed enough to her. She was both father and mother to this invented family, and to go back now was impossible. Why had he bothered? Krieger. He never loved anybody, certainly not Hannah, did he? That was another time Hannah asked Krieger about his own parents, his childhood, and Krieger's reply was that he simply couldn't remember ever being young, ever having a childhood, there was something about an aunt, a spinet piano which he'd taken lessons on, so far out of tune that even he who ended up having no ear for music could hear that any chord struck on it sounded off—childhood, he offered, not so horrible, he said, blank slate, maybe a few trinkets of memory ("costume jewelry covered in cobwebs") but nothing necessarily based on anything further from reach than the merely plausible. Now can we change the subject? and, anyway, you already tried that on me way back when, the first day we ever met.

"It's not such a horrible thing to have parents, a family."

"You've never given birth, all that ooze, that slime, and out comes this, this thing."

"Since when do you know about it?"

"I'll be right back," Krieger'd said, even kissed her on the side of her head, and walked toward the telephone stands in front of the library. She watched him but suppressed the impulse to follow. She'd noticed he had begun making calls again. He arrived at the stands, lifted the receiver and cradled it on his shoulder as he dialed; Hannah slumped back into the curve of the bench and gazed at the people walking by. When she looked again toward the library he was, of course, gone. That was the last time she had seen him, the last time, too, she had slept with him, or anyone.

She rubbed her hands now over her face as if to wipe Krieger away. How could she have not foreseen that contingency, and this: that Henry might someday end up on the streets—Henry who was innocent as (what? hardly a kitten?) a stable cat, but who knew too much about the workings of the ranch to make it very safe for him to leave. And poor Maddie crying; it was clear Henry could not care for himself out here alone.

She thought of the possibility he had been taken in by Krieger, and winced. If only she had been kinder to Krieger? She placed her fist, closed tight, slowly down on her thigh.

"Running a small cattle ranch in the heart of Chelsea violates," as Krieger had been careful to point out on the telephone when he had first made arrangements for Lupi and Olid to stay with her, "New York City Health Code, Title IV Environmental Sanitation, Article 161.09 Permits to Keep Certain Animals, sections (d) and (f), to wit: 'Except on premises abutting upon slaughterhouse no person shall yard horses or keep or yard cattle, swine, sheep or goats without a permit issued by the Commissioner' and 'No person shall keep a cow for the purpose of selling milk without a permit issued by the . . .' "

There was a time when Hannah could have given it up, the pasture, cattle, chickens, the roof garden, silo. She hadn't exiled herself from the Nebraska flatlands only to return from her Manhattan, defeated by this inheritance, to go back to Babylon, its tall empty sky, its tornadoes and dust, its endless yellow dirt, its memories, apparitions, the stench of the junkyard behind the barn heaped high with generations of objects that reverberated each with the dissolution of the family. There was no returning. It was as if Babylon had been an island, a penal colony where only her nightmares resided, and now was cut free of its mooring to drift away into the sun's furnace.

It was gone; Hannah's bank account was converted from several hundred to over two million. A few thousand acres outside Red Cloud became a quarter block on the West Side. All conditions of the will were satisfied, every object her uncle had owned down to spoon and suspender, flyhook and button box, chicken and cow . . . all were shipped in, each with its identification number painted, branded, carved by uncle himself to check off against the master inventory.

She saw a quarter lying dull on the pavement not ten feet from where she was sitting. Someone stepped on it, walking through the park. Franz Wrynn, she thought. She should call him, tell him what fruits had come of their champagne-dizzy day so long ago, up there in his own invented world above the waters in the reservoir and treetops of the park. She had always meant to, after all, had always wanted to pose the question: What had Krieger said? or worse yet, What had he been willing to do, that would somehow coax from Franz her new identity in the world—and where it was she had assumed it? She could almost hear his friendly yawn, the decorous optimism which would ascend through the answer as he figured out some way the situation could be finessed to the abiding happiness of all. He would say he had nothing to do with it. He would deny Krieger had spoken with him at all. More disquieting than the obfuscation, however, would be the chance that Franz would tell the truth—she adored him too much to want to hear it.

"Manhattan," Krieger had gone on, "city of hills where the Injuns came in summer, from their colonies up the Hudson, came by quaint barques, to vacation, to fish and trap and fuck, as colonies of nudists—Manhattan: verdant, often precipitous, as from Beekman's or Peck's Hill, in the neighborhood of Pearl and Ferry streets, or Nassau Street down to Maiden Lane. Water flowed between these hills. Canal Street gratified Dutch recollections of home, left behind across the Atlantic. Broad Street was a tidal inlet. Near Peck's Slip existed a river which at high tide ran up in union with the Collect (Kolck) and joined with Lispenard's swamp on the other side, to produce a waterway that ran clear across the city. The high grounds along either side of Pearl Street sometimes had to be crossed by ferry boats, farms dotted the island, proliferated, like the goddamn Injuns, just faster, as settlers pushed back the tribes. Sophistication festered, then reigned. By 1641: a cattle fair was established, held annually on the fifteenth of October; prize steers were showed by proud, competitive Dutch farmers, under the shortening sun and leaf-yellow breezes. The rich land outside the bounds of the town walls (Wall Street looming a century away) was designated public grazing grounds for cows, sheep, swine. Governor Stuyvesant himself bought the 'Bouwerie' (translates 'farm') in 1631 and procured himself, for the sum of sixty-four hundred guilders, besides the land, a dwelling house, barn, reek lands, six cows, two horses, and two young blacks. His cattle climbed around the hilly island, drank from inlets and the East River bless them, where they wandered as the windmill whirred over the broad way, the town kine, sheep, swine, and stood in the staved activity of shadows, indifferent to youths that watched by their gills of brandy or maids by their quarts of cider. Stuyvesant's descendants were made wealthy by the sale of these farmlands and there now in overcoats on the hottest day of July, shoeless on the coldest snowy day of January, is a dude doing windshields at the red light at Houston and Bowery who's gonna finish up, clean as piss, then off! boom—eat shit mo-fo."

Pin oaks, yellow locust, ash, plane, the ghosts of American elms. Under their darkening canopies the pushers, roller skaters, hotdog vendors, and students sat, stoned, listening, waiting for something to take place, anything to happen. Nothing happened. Except the break dancers twirled like lunatic windmills—paying homage to Dutch forebears—on plates of cardboard to the music belting from an enormous silver badbox . . .

> "I'm the Duke of Rap
> And I'm on fire
> Baby look at me
> I'm your heart's desire
>
> The Duke of Rap
> Your thang's desire
> I won't stop rappin
> Till I expire . . ."

(The cardboard flat, fashioned from a large carton with Hi-Dri Paper Towels printed over its smooth brown surfaces, would be appropriated later in the night by an ingenious wanderer, who used it to construct a kind of lean-to home against the side of the restrooms at the south edge of the park.)

> "The Duke of Rap says
> You My Slave,
> Ya gotta spoil me
> Till my dyin day
>
> Gotta do what I say
> Love what I do,
> You gotta spoil me
> Cause I'm royaltee

. . . If ya stick to me
You'll stick like glue
It's the natural thang
For us to do

So come on baby
Doncha hollar doncha kick
When the Duke of Rap
Pulls out his lickin stick . . ."

The soccer game disbanded after the fist fight broke out. A pair of mounted cops continued indifferently to chat as the fight drew a small crowd. At the top of the circle blue-sleeved arms reached out the window of a patrol car to frisk a man with a heavy Rastafarian helmet of hair. Hands turned their suspect around and palmed skinny torso, bottom, thighs inside and out before giving a slap on the rear to send him stumbling on his way. The crowd was dispersed of its own lack of interest, was reabsorbed into a larger throng whose legions were changing guard from the daytime to the nighttime corps.

Oak, plane, ash, and locust. Hannah got up again and strolled around the wide central fountain. Krieger's voice went on.

Washington Square had once been a field, too. The Minto farm once bordered this field along its northern edge. Certain trees dated back to the time when tobacco and corn crops were sown close by, tended by slaves, fed by springs. Through the first quarter of the last century this had been the city's potter's field and, conveniently, its hanging ground as well. This old elm had served as the gallows, plausibly. Or that plane tree, its heavy branch extended over the sidewalk. Execution day brought out hordes to gawk as the convicted was stood up on a platform, neck in noose, blind-folded, quaking, before his footing was kicked out from under and he dropped into a bob. A finch preened its wing there now.

How had it gotten so late? Out of the square, through Waverly to Sixth, she ambled back toward the ranch, still searching faces in the streets. Her feet hurt, she needed coffee. She sat alone in a short-order Greek diner several blocks shy of the loft, and drank black coffee until her vision began to redouble images that soon became parallax. The pocket of her wallet was pulled back to show her she had seventy dollars to run with.

*   *   *

When Lupi announced, rather more full of the glory of accomplishment than the situation prescribed, "I found him, up in that tower," relief passed over Hannah, the parallactic world receded, and she smiled a wide tired smile that in turn made Lupi smile reflexively, in sympathy both with her and consequently with himself.

"The silo? but we already looked up there."

"I know."

"Well, where in the, where was he all this time?"

"I think he went away down there, but he came back."

Hannah strained over her boots, which resisted coming off.

"Where's he now? can you help me with these?"

"With his woman."

"He's all right, then."

"Not very all right."

The boot came off, Hannah falling backwards. "My feet they're so swollen, I guess I'd better go down and see him—"

"I don't think there is much to do for him."

The other boot came off.

"What about Hammond?"

"Mr. Hammond's down with the animals."

"When'd he get back?"

"Hour, no two hours ago, Mr. Hammond was pretty tired, very tired. And mad, too, very mad. He came back, no luck. I thought I'd take another look up here and there he was. I found some things. These, he tried to hide them."

Hannah went outside, mounted the stairs to the landing in the silo. She easily picked her way under the twinkling, reflecting lights of the city, and in any case already knew about Henry's loose brick. When Madeleine had come up to the bunker that afternoon searching for Henry, this was the first place Hannah had come to look. Behind the loose brick Henry kept a not-so-secret menagerie of sacred possessions—mostly candy bars, gum, cookies. Hannah peered into the rectangular chink but it was too dark to see. She felt around its depths with her free hand. It was empty. She replaced the spoon and syringe and put the brick back in its place.

Downstairs, she opened the doors on the pasture. "Ham?"

She could hear the asthmatic breathing of the cattle as they slept in a group, huddled under the deep glow of the heat lamps. Hammond was snoring in his canvas director's chair, his Stetson fuchsia above his tilted head.

"Good boy," she whispered to the dog who too had been asleep but was vigilant to any unexpected intrusion in the pasture. He made a pleasant little squeal as he stretched beside Hammond's chair and meandered, tail wagging widely, over to Hannah. Hannah patted him on the head. The smell of manure pervaded the loft; no one had mucked out that afternoon. Hannah flicked a switch on the wall by the door. The low hum produced at the far end of the pasture came from industrial ceiling fans that began to draw air out of the space, thus to deposit it in an atmosphere where it was simultaneously unique and indistinguishable.

Stetson rose, was removed by a hand; a cough came from beneath.

"Stinks."

"It does. That's no good."

"What're you going to do, whole afternoon lost looking for that junkie."

"He's not a junkie."

"Still and all," Hammond said.

"Don't worry about it, it's my problem, not yours."

"You know what shape that spic found him in, though."

"Lupi's an Italian."

"Whatever he is, him and the old fart."

"All you need to think about is helping me muck. Then you go to bed, sleep lying down, okay?"

"Listen to this, now she tells me how to sleep."

Hannah folded her arms.

"I don't muck," he concluded after a moment.

Hannah ended the wrangling with a calm "Shut up, Ham."

"You didn't hire me to muck, is all I'm saying. That there's Work's thing."

"I'll muck. You hold the light. I don't want these cattle woke up if I can help it."

Hammond broadly yawned and as he did the dim red light fell across his face, exaggerating the cleft in his chin and the dimples thimble-deep and scarlike in his cheeks. His accent was Midwestern. His face was lean, angular; he had a fine, straight, large nose, furrowed brow, a handlebar moustache; roustabout's muscles, taut and supple, were strung through his legs and arms. It was the darnedest job he'd ever had, this one; but what do you do?—you're furloughed, as they called it, three weeks from your last job, wander east to see the city sights knowing that a three-week furlough generally means unemployment when you show up again, and what do you find right there in the paper but a classified ad for ranchhand. You call. You go to the address, still thinking it must be a joke. There's this fine-looking woman who offers you more than you're already making. The single requirement is silence, which is something you prefer anyway, silence, solitude, a little rum, screw the banter.

"Bacteria level's got to be way up. Did you check the moisture level in that forage?"

"Sixty-seven percent."

"What was the sugar level?"

"Didn't look, guess as it'd have to be up some."

One of the cows came awake in its bed of straw. It made a low gulping sound.

"Well, get us a wagon," Hannah said. "I'm sure we're going to rile them no matter what we do. We've got to clean this place up but fast or we're going to have a real mess on our hands."

With a grunt Hammond got out of the chair. "Hey, what time is it, anyways?"

Hey is for horses, she thought—the face on her watch was obscured in the carmine shadows.

She guessed, "Twelve, twelve-thirty."

"*Gee*-sus," Hammond declared. "What a goddamn circus."

Hannah didn't hear him. She was worrying whether the silage, manufactured of a green forage wilted to about sixty-five or seventy percent moisture which was created by makeshift humidifiers in the silo, had gone bad. The silage recipe, her own concoction with trace minerals added before they took delivery (always in the middle of the night, always with the chance of being asked by a sleepy policeman what it was they were delivering into the freight elevator—smelled like hay), had worked well over the years, but now had begun to turn rotten enough that by evening the odor, like field-rotting squash or a gulp of maize glutton or barley taken up the nose, hung strong in the air. The watering trough needed to be drained and replenished. Flops like discuses of bronze and hay shafts had to be collected and the slurry discharge of silage liquor flushed. It would take hours to bring the ranch back to normal.

"Goddamn zoo," he said, and got to work filling a bucket with disinfectant, another with detergent, got the brooms and brushes, connected the hose up. He noticed the bottle of rum—his—on the floor, half-drunk. "Whose been into my? that damn Work."

"What now?"

"Work's been into my bash."

Hannah laughed, though it made her head throb. "No, that was me, I'm sorry."

"What d'you know next?—saint Hannah drinking bashes? The world is coming to a wicked end."

"I'll replace the bottle."

"No need to replace the bottle, you only drank three-quarters of an inch." Hammond took his hat off, and his face had a gentler look to it. "You doing all right?"

"I'll survive," she said.

"I mean, I don't mean to be a pain, like."

Hannah was sympathetic, but seemed to him so solitary, in her smiling, "Of course you mean to be a pain."

Why hadn't he and she ever sparked it off? he wondered, taking the shovel, a snow shovel, out of her hands and throwing himself into the heavy work. They were very different people, he knew, when he first came. The surroundings and the labor itself were so peculiar that if it hadn't been for Hannah at the middle of it all, he knew he'd never have come to the ranch in the first place. She was good. He wasn't that bad, was he?—maybe not all that bright upstairs, but solid, right? It was Krieger who showed up once who made him understand that she and he would never go that way, down that love way. Some nights it bothered him, most nights not. "God-damn zoo," he finished, and rubbed his hands together.

3.

THE sun rose, misbegotten heap of fire, to bursts from .50-caliber machine guns. The air was awash with deaths. When they heard one of the machine guns reporting they knew it was being fired by a boy of sixteen or older. Boys and girls younger than that—twelve, thirteen, fourteen, fifteen—were given lesser weapons, the best among them AK-47 automatic rifles, worth twenty-two hundred dollars less than .50-caliber machine guns. An old cowboy herding cattle was seen to fall off his horse; the horse then fell on him. A squadron broke across a narrow clearing where his cattle had been grazing the sweet grass which had grown through the wet season, and wrestled one of the beasts away into heavy brush. The others in the herd went about, muzzles to the ground, as if nothing had happened.

It was past the border and it had gotten worse during the night. A militia of government soldiers had crossed into Honduras in hot pursuit and had gotten themselves cut off by another band of insurgents circling behind, over a long ridge of pitted boulders, to pin them throughout the darker hours before sunrise. There was a shaggy moon and many stars to fight by: a thin worthless aura of light that illuminated the heavens but not earth. The troops that happened to encounter each other at unexpectedly close range were obliged to take aim at yellow bursts of enemy fire the size of pinheads out in the sultry forest. One didn't smoke for fear of being spotted. One didn't speak. The enemy was so close one could feel its breath and sense its reciprocal fear. A canteen clanked and the immediate sky was alight with crossfire. An hour of silence and a lone pistol would go off in the dense black.

Then a mortar broke on the dawn's refulgence to detonate in a murky unmanned swamp area, pinkish in the sunrise. Way off target it boiled up only spattering mud and wet sand, birds and small reptiles, onto trees and stone. The boy who had been given the opportunity to use this wondrous instrument, after ten days of training with other boys, lived through this skirmish (which lasted far into the morning) but was later dressed down by the commander of his patrol. Having deployed three rounds of mortar at a cost of four hundred dollars, over twelve thousand córdobas, he had succeeded in burning out some cedar trees, killing small wildlife and shattering the tympanic membrane in his right ear. He was not worth the cost of his gear and subsistence.

The fat man too faced into the pink sun. The molten image of it danced on the black surface described in his coffee cup, which he soon replaced on its chipped saucer. Sounds from the deadlocked engagement did not reach this garden nor the ears of the fat man or the young girl who sat with him, although it raged—convulsive, in eruptive gusts—not seven miles away.

In the other house Krieger soaped and shaved. One of the few superstitious traits he allowed himself was the way in which he performed this particular task: without variation he began with the razor at his right sideburn, shaved down that cheek, working his way under the chin midway. After, he shaved the left in the same manner, leaving the upper lip for last. He rinsed, put on his shirt and went into the dusty house.

"Finished already?" he noticed as he stepped out onto the roof garden, ducking his head under the low-bowed lintel.

"You look terrible."

"No sleep again."

"I don't understand how it was you managed to hold down a job, in a corporation all those years," the fat man said. "Suit, tie—look at you now . . ." raising heavy eyebrows at Krieger's tiger-striped stockings collapsed in ringlets about his ankles, frail white stretch of hairless flesh above.

"Absurd accident is what, can I have some of that?—pardon me, way I managed it was I never slept. What I did, I slept on Sundays."

"Like God."

Krieger frowned: he did not like the fat man's daughter; he did not like any of the fat man's children, of which there seemed to be endless numbers. "What?"

The girl answered. "Like God, 'on the seventh day God ended his work which he had made and he rested on the seventh day from all his work.' That's the Bible. My papa makes us all read the Bible every night, don't you, papa."

"Like God then sure why not," Krieger rushed along. "But none of the resources I was securing in His Image for good old Standard Fruit ever much found its way into a Banco Capitalizador account under *my* name."

The tiny, shimmery green insect that hovered lit and was slapped at as sole response to Krieger's complaint—palm came away from forearm: nothing. "You and your money obsession, money money money. You can see how easy money is to get. It doesn't ultimately pertain to my focus in here."

"Oh no?"

"Obviously it's a necessary tool, but only a tool, like a saw or a hammer. But they're not buildings, not architecture, you can't live under a hammer."

"A profound observation," Krieger said, dryly, and watched the thick-jointed fingers of his colleague drum the table. How was it Krieger had never before noticed that diamond nestled into the fold of skin at the knuckle? its soft shine an irrelevant detail obscured under the first blanket of smoke that shrouded it. Ugly, evil hand. He looked at his own, along the edge of the cup. It was almost the opposite: slender, fine.

"Your cynicism is juvenile and insults my intelligence, this is fine with me you are undertaking this for the profit" (flickered smirk) "and my promise is always good that, after, if you still want to set up within my jurisdiction wherever it may end up being you will be protected and safe. We both know someday it may all come out, some reporter tramping through on assignment to another story altogether and stumbles on the remnants of our fund-raising efforts" (waiting for Krieger to laugh or taunt, and when he didn't continued) "and you will be happy to know some people in positions of authority who can arrange to block extradition.

Then, you will be grateful to the more serious ramifications here than money."

"Your *part* of the money."

"No need to harbor any foolishness against *me* for godsake. A war zone always has been, is now and foreverafter shall be a perfect place to make money, legitimate money, a lot of money, you'll get more than you could ever use in three lifetimes down here."

"It's too bad I despise your politics."

"You'll come around."

"When Allah dons a yarmulke."

Abruptly, a shift of wind, and churning was heard. The helicopter scattered a colorful flock of birds. It lifted away from the grass strip to the west where it had touched down for five-ten minutes, and shattered the morning atmosphere, faint as drawn-out afflatus beyond the overgrown garden. In its casement the rough-sawn door of the house very slightly rattled.

Now there'd be some casualties, Krieger thought, and looked with curiosity at the face of the fat man's daughter which displayed indifference to the racket of artillery fire. Flesh of his flesh, cold-hearted little thing— but it was, to her, routine as church bells on a Sunday morning. Even more routine.

"*Id debajo y traed los fósforos,*" he instructed his daughter and watched her as she disappeared past the door to find matches for his cigar. To Krieger, "You hear that?"

"Hear what," as the door shook softly.

"That."

"Yeah, so what? earthquake," Krieger smiled.

The fat man smacked his lips, "Earthquake no, that's either UH-1H Huey, or maybe Mi-8 transport, gunship, I don't have any idea what they've started to ship in to those bastards, earthquake no. This is all starting to wind up, I can smell it in the air."

"Wind up? wind up! it's just begun, they haven't even got underway down here. But it's not going to make any difference."

"What do you mean by that?"

"Just what I said. There is no winning this war."

"My politics which you despise so much, Krieger, if you believe what you say that things are going to get worse, knowing what a pragmatist you are how could you be stupid enough to despise my politics? You know my politics are bound by the authority of money being placed behind them to win out in the end. You want to end up on the losing side?"

Krieger's face seemed abbreviated, half there, before he said, "Money? for once you're wrong about money. You're the one who doesn't care about money."

"I don't."

"But here you are saying you think money heats the blood as hot as patriotism does? the kind you see in a young country that's just blown off a hated pharaoh. And it hardly matters how much you loved him."

"He was a friend. He's dead. I'm alive. But money? Yes, money tends to do that. It's not the way I work, but I see it in others all the time."

"You're wrong and I can see why you're wrong. Because you come from old money, musty money, the kind of tired money that's cranking this war up, retread money, *gringo* money."

"I don't care how old the money is and I don't care where it comes from—it buys what's needed to make things happen that have to happen."

"You sound like a junior State Department boy on his first company picnic. Forget it, this is a dead end."

"Why? because it's the truth?"

"The truth! Talk about dead ends! The truth's the biggest dead end ever invented. No possibility of further supposition. So, yeah, because you certainly aren't going to be talked out of thinking that is accurate and anyway I don't see where it would do a hell of a lot of good trying to convince you otherwise, so . . . dead end and, fuck it. Off to the wars."

"It's only a matter of time," the fat man finished. "If we didn't extract them, the community, they'd be disappeared by any number of others anyway. *Accidentes personales*."

The girl returned. "I can't find no matches."

"No? oh, look here, papa had some in his pocket, forgive papa?" She was too old to pat on the head, although he tried.

4.

HENRY saw Madeleine first among those regarding him. Her ruddy face, the sere blue of her irises, pools dried down to mercury. Worry that worked like the furls of a flag over her white forehead. Here was her only movement. At least at first. Her severely angled hair, so dark, marking off strict borders about the face. And behind, as if she were caught in the old painting taped to a wall in the bunkhouse, in the background grottoes, mysterious pewter crags, the wild forests, and at the center of a tiny orchard the Statue of Liberty, yes, the Statue of Liberty itself, dazzlingly bright pink!

No, the Statue proved to be an old inspection tag dangling from one of the steam pipes that ran the length of ceiling; the grottoes, crags, trees, were peeling paint, white layer, gray layer, moss green. At present Lady Liberty fluttered in the balmy, rain-rinsed morning air that entered by the open window.

Henry could smell Maddie on the pillow next to his. The breeze that wafted into the room was shot through with sea salt and diesel. His head felt clear as cold water. His limbs were flush with blood, and were supple. He could hear the city, huge mechanical beast with engines in its belly and for armor fastigiated tops of skyscrapers. It bestirred itself, hurlyburly, beyond. There was a ferocity to the city noise, but benign and in party with Henry's cheer. He half sat up on his elbows, glanced around the room for Madeleine, but he was alone. He looked at the pillow where she had slept. He put his cheek down on it, breathed in deeply. One of her hairs, soft copper ray, curled on the case.

The clock read eleven. Henry pushed away the sheets and got up. He stepped into his overalls. There was a rap at the door.

"Maddie?"

The door came open; Hammond.

"Oh, good morning," Henry faltered.

"Says you, Work."

Henry hitched the straps of his overalls. Close quarters, bad tempers. It was like this at boxing camp sometimes. He sat on the bed, with his back squared, and pulled on boots over his bare feet, began with concentration to lace them at the hooks.

"Guess you had a pretty good time of it yesterday," Hammond said. He stared at Henry's broad back, awaited some response, but as none was forthcoming simply reiterated, "Yeah, pretty good time."

Hammond had taken several more steps into the room. The door remained open behind. He had never been in this room before last night, when he and Lupi brought Henry down from the silo tower and laid him on the bed. Madeleine thanked them, asked them to leave. Now Hammond scrutinized the room with fresh eyes. Her dress was draped over the painted metal stead at the foot of the bed. Its buttons, flat false-pearl disks, he took as a taunt.

"Wish I'd had me half as good a time."

Henry finished with his laces, stood up. Even the creaking of the bedsprings remarked the transition from peace and well-being to this.

Hannah had arranged shifts so he and Hammond seldom encountered each other; their primary sense each of the other was gleaned intuitively, through observation of the work accomplished by one when the other was at rest. Henry knew Hammond was capable of honest, hard work, but that recently he had sluffed off.

"What d'you want?" Henry asked, at last.

"Well, by my watch it's eleven-fifteen. Your shift started three hours and a quarter ago."

Beneath one of the windows was a footlocker. Henry opened it and fetched from it a pair of heavy suede gloves, blackened and well broken in. "You seen my wife?"

"Your wife? Your *wife?* Hey, son. First I have to tuck you into bed, then I have to shovel your shit for you, and now you want me to dog your old lady? You're in trouble if it's got to that."

Henry turned slowly to stare at Hammond across the room.

"Best you keep your tongue in your face about your wife," Hammond concluded, returning Henry's stare levelly. Only his voice dropped away slightly at Henry's gesture.

"I do my shift now," Henry breathed. "Then I do your shift tonight. That squares us."

"That's polite, but I'll do my own work."

Henry's face tightened. "How many hours you put into my shift?"

"Who cares. Too many. One'd be one too many."

"You let me know how many hours you put in," Henry said, moving now toward the door, "and I pay you my wage for it."

Hammond preceded Henry into the hall. Henry closed the door behind.

"You ain't my boss and you don't get to go paying me for my labor."

Henry left him. The cool walls radiated chill to his warm skin; his heart seemed too full.

"Nope, no way brother," Hammond called down the corridor, but the words receded, faded in scale, and were attenuated. Henry closed the door on him even as he said, "No siree, I like it that you owe me one and can't pay."

Henry proceeded directly to the pasture. Usually he would go on up the stairs, onto the roof, and across to the bunker for breakfast. But he had no appetite this morning.

"He was a philosopher, this Diogenes, and he lived in a bathtub in the marketplace in Athens."

Henry summoned all his attention and directed it at Lupi's mouth.

"And all Diogenes owned, besides the bathtub, all he owned was a cup, this wooden cup. And then one day he noticed someone take a drink of water by putting his hands together like this."

"That's cupping," said Henry.

"And so Diogenes threw away his cup, it was something he no longer needed. And then once, Alexander the Great came to Athens, and visited Diogenes and asked him if there was anything he could do for him, and Diogenes said, Yes, you can stand out of my light."

Henry laughed.

"So Diogenes has always been a great symbol of what men can do without. But all I was saying was that I envied Diogenes for his bathtub, you see. At least he had a home."

Henry stopped smiling; putting his hands together palms upturned he switched into his role, self-assigned, as finishing teacher in the subject of English: "What's this?"

"That's cupping," Lupi said without hesitation.

5.

AN unhappy task it was that Carlos undertook—informing his brother that the boy Bautista had been murdered, had been *asesinado* (in war one cannot be *asesinado* but only *matado*, killed, butchered, but Bautista had not been—strictly speaking—at war). The task caused him trepidation not just because the fat man would be upset by the inescapable fact his boy, his son, was dead, but also that the death represented an encroachment, an untimely drawing up of the curtain upon a stage not considered set, propsmen caught unawares, the lights all wrong, actors not yet fully in their makeup.

The *bolsón* was refuge only so long as the counterrevolutionaries allowed it to remain inviolate, for it consisted of nothing tangible besides the several crude houses which abided the restraints made by incursions of forest and the disposition of hillsides' declivities—the walls and roofs offered shelter only from rain and wind. What the fat man's survival depended on more than anything else was the kind of benign indifference of those few who knew of his presence here—indifference, underscored by the sense that he was someone who so recently had been looked upon as superior; educated and while possibly not now wealthy certainly one who knew how to be wealthy (to their minds, a dark art indeed), and who seemed to promise an authority that one day, when power was retaken, God and foreign powers willing, would be of use.

All this was spoken through the appeasement of capital. Not large amounts, for he played a careful double game of having (symbol of his frightful transcendence) and not having (symbol of his common suffering), but a steady stream that here could buy such necessities as gasoline and drugs. The double game worked on both sides of the frontier, if only because what constituted the border was with each new day less clear.

Carlos told the fat man, dispatching the information in a series of laconic phrases the last of which was a request to leave the room. Outside the sky seemed heavier as he picked his way, footfalls flat, across the dirt courtyard to the other small house where he found Krieger and in his slow Spanish repeated to the world the same news.

6.

LUPI came awake even before her hand touched him lightly on the shoulder and above it his name was whispered. He might have responded—acknowledgment, assent—in order to recover from sleep, to bring himself up one more time to bear against this dark which hovered like the filth of so many human fingers that had in reverence and by routine touched the bottom of a fount, the one seen up in San Alessandro, always touched by the pilgrims and the tourists, but almost never filled with holy water, as the priest had often been too ill to bless it. It was as if the fount were there on his face, the same fount he'd seen from where he and his friends hid in the shadow-black nave watching people genuflect with their dry fingers tapping forehead, heart, left breast and right breast, muttering *Nome Padre Figlio Spirito Santo*, leaving behind film of their own dark sweat in the dry, carbon marble of the basin. He might have said something, but a palm (not a fount) was laid across his mouth and the words were smothered.

Maddie helped him find his clothes in that same dark, and had hardly to explain what it was she had decided to do.

"Does Hannah know—" he began, but her hand rose across to touch him on the mouth; he finished dressing, woke Olid, got him dressed, and followed her out.

In the cab which bounded up the nearly deserted avenue, she said, "We're just making the last train up there tonight. I take you up to him, deliver you, then I leave, I won't stay I won't see him. I deliver you and I'm gone, understand?"

He began to nod.

Grand Central was surprisingly busy for the late hour, although clearly some of those who meandered over the broad distension of stone shined to gloss by innumerable soles were not travelers looking to make night trains, but the station's denizens, people who created a constant echo shuffling about the cavern. Having bought their tickets—for herself round trip, for Lupi and the old man one-way—Madeleine led them to the gate, down-ramp, into an empty car. It was apparent her timing had been planned with some care for, as they took their seats, the doors drew flush and the train pulled away.

"Why does everything have to be so complicated?" She exhaled over her shoulder, hunched up as she'd spoken, and the shoulder fell, actually dissolved into an obtuse angle against the vertical line of her neck.

Lupi almost spoke. It was as if he intended to attempt some answer to her question, face averted to the window that reflected hers not in profile but directly on. Their eyes met on the reflective glass; unlike his, Madeleine's gaze persisted beyond the plane of the window itself and out into the train-yard rocking away under its eerie glow. The train picked up speed as it pulled clear of the city, north into the night. Madeleine's eyes refocused to catch his stare: she immediately invented meaning for her having looked through the glass and him at it: what that signified (nothing, she would conclude in a moment) was at first flatteringly plumbed. Soon it became muddled into neutrality.

Half an hour trailed away before she spoke again. What she said came from the same pattern of thought as her earlier statement, the question this time not rhetorical.

"Can you tell me why it's this money stuff, power, whatever it is drives everybody, I don't know off the brink, makes them so willing to get involved in such silliness?"

When he saw the question was as serious as the cast of her face, a candid stare now, stiff-necked, he fumbled for his response. "I, well, people get afraid—" yet she kept speaking as he found his own words, and hers plaited his.

"What are you so afraid of you'd be willing to do all this, I mean how much can they possibly be paying you?"

"I, my, why I got involved with these men, it wasn't just for, I had to. . ."

Both stopped.

"You had to? don't you think that's everybody's answer? they had no choice, just had to?"

He yielded to the dramatic degree of letting his chin drop and fingers trace the back of his head from crown to hollow down the neck. What did he look like? He wondered whether she would consider any argument and decided she wouldn't. Olid, who slumped in the seat in front of them, snored, and Lupi reached forward and patted him on the shoulder fraternally.

Maddie smirked. Her words persisted: ". . . not that I think you stood or stand to gain much in all this, as you pointed out before. I think you don't, and didn't. Not that that's a virtue."

She waited and the silence was obligingly filled by a shudder of the carriage as it ran over a rough section of track. "I've made all kinds of mistakes," Lupi said, "and I, well this certainly couldn't be the worst but what I mean is, there weren't many other ways for me to go. I had no place to live, was cut off and as they told me down there these well, things were closing in."

"And so you came to the New World to escape the powers of tyranny and oppression, and to drag a poor old man around in the middle of the night."

"You're cynical," he countered. "No; there weren't to be any violence, wasn't to be, and there hasn't been. There won't be. All I am supposed to do is I am supposed to carry this proposal up to your father, accompany this gentleman, that's all, and then I am paid enough to set up somewhere in Italy, go clean, get work, be quiet. It's all I want."

"It hasn't occurred to you they want you to fend for them because they wouldn't want to be caught with him themselves."

"Yes, sure certainly."

"There have to be easier ways for you to exist than this—not that I care really since, like I said, if it wasn't you it'd have been somebody else," pointing up (like people always pointed up) his expendability and the venal nature of his crime, he saw. The car had remained empty until the conductor came through with his ticket punch. An air of intimacy began to grow, measured by the rhythmic clacking: a primitive intimacy which submitted to her growing cruelty and his grasping away at worthiness.

"I am sorry I don't seem to fit some idea you have about how people should be." (This was an awful line of shit, he knew.)

"You should know what a terrible thing all this is, this insipid idea, four-hundred-and-sixty-year-old specimen—"

"How do you know that?"

"Hannah told me all about this. It's kidnapping you know, fraud, God knows what else."

"Not fraud, this guy really is, I—"

Madeleine laughed, a surprisingly husky laugh. "A few people get sold some fake antiques, some money passes hands, you collect yours and go back to business as usual, am I wrong?"

The train made its second or third station. A young man walked the aisle of the car and exited by its rear door. During the time it took him to do this Lupi sat in silence. He considered leaping off the train and disappearing into mysterious, night-clad America.

"Why is it I have to be put in a position where everything I count on is put into the hands of somebody who doesn't care about anything at all?"

"I didn't mean, what I—"

"You don't think I know that?"

"I mean—"

"You don't mean anything. I don't know you and I don't want to, but I can tell when a person doesn't mean anything."

"All right. Whatever you say." His voice dropped away. He lay back in his seat to stare first at the mosaic of lights on the ceiling, then at the red handle (if he shattered the glass and pulled it down, would the train skid to a clamorous halt in a storm of sparks?) and thereafter, for no reason other than to evade Madeleine, at the double doors at the front of the car. He saw it then.

It was inconceivable to him the fat man had been willing to go to such lengths to have shown his humble courier all that sham omnipotence, all that supposed omniscience, merely to work himself around to this. Posing (*presentation*, as Krieger'd said). The maneuvering had been deft, yet still more desperate than he could have fathomed until just now, when the face appeared and vanished in the half-light down within the rectangulate windows of those doors connecting theirs with the car ahead. A grand conceit, an apparently necessary one, if the face he glimpsed proved to be Krieger's.

It slipped, past Olid's head, into view and out. Had seemed quicker than it should, a rind of vellum caught in the open corridor and buffeted into sight, the dichotomous moon blinked at only long enough to recognize that deadpan face that has looked down, mute and frozen, upon a trillion deeds each night, one less admissible than the next.

Res ipsa loquitur once more, though this time (partly because Madeleine would not in any case listen to him) he would live up to his resolve to be more mendacious, a little subtler. In his peripheral vision he remained attentive to the twin dark fields beyond the empty seats of the car; were the face to reappear, he could pretend that he was looking at the billboards inside the car—the Steinberg Manhattan, the bikinied woman who emerged, a brown Venus, from pearly water onto the white beach of Jamaica (or wherever). He scratched his face: an act in keeping with the turmoil he felt within but which couldn't be allowed to show. He could excuse himself to find the toilet. Madeleine would probably not trust him to leave her with Olid unaccompanied; nor would Krieger, if accosted, be likely even to show any sign of recognition much less explain what he was doing. Lupi crossed his legs, not meaning to brush the tip of his shoe over Madeleine's calf; nonplussed, he watched her draw in, feet pressed together, arms crossed, eyes fixed on the window.

The train was already making its curve, slowing, as Madeleine stood to clutch the overhead strap, then lead them up the aisle to the car ahead.

The night was damp, outside. November rose off the river in chill fingers to come at one in snatches. Seeing the old man shiver, he turned the collar up on his coat.

Glancing behind he could not see that any other passengers got off the train. The gravel first and afterwards the hollow bell-like tone of the iron stairs under their feet sounded into the peace of the closed-up place. No one was around. Lupi was not disappointed, but a little disconcerted at Krieger's nonappearance on the platform.

Above, along the gradual hill that lifted away from the river and the station where the last car vanished, were houses hidden in the trees, from which the glow of an occasional light was apparent. As they crested the first rise and came to the road something happened to cause his suspicions to be stirred up again; the chiming resonation echoed so softly behind, one dull musical note repeated more or less—each a possible requital of all the invalid visions, the bad ideas, the mistakes he had made these several weeks. He said nothing, followed a step behind at the woman's side.

Madeleine neither heard the footfalls on the iron stairs, nor would they have evoked the monotonous bell of San Apollinaire in Classe had she. The connectivity of everything presently fired Lupi's imagination: Krieger's presence here (?) and how it had to signify (or so he thought) that he and the fat man in fact didn't know just where Owen Berkeley was (no—that couldn't be); how they'd expected Madeleine to take him up the river; how once they did know of what further use would he be to them . . .? (Where was she turning now up this narrower lane, the streetlamps shimmering along the wires that swung low between?) Like a boule player, he tried to think out the gamut of strategies. He stopped to retie a shoelace and was able to catch sight of the figure. It was Krieger's build and height, walking close by what seemed to be a privet hedge gathered in the shadows. The figure froze, blended into the aberration of light like a hint of blackness, an underexposure mark in a photograph.

Already Madeleine's doubts about being here began to crowd in. Finding her way up through the village after so many years was easier than she might've thought, even in the dark. To think of those she had known as a girl—the Schianellos, Henry's mother, friends at school, her own family— and how some of them could no longer be alive, and how the death of, say, Mr. Schianello could (did) take place in her absence. The day she ran away with Henry. Schianello must have been so upset. Her decision (made so long ago, it seemed), how it temporarily changed everyone's lives, but how time passes and all these lives—even Madeleine's—weren't forgotten as much as put aside at first and then turned under in the continuous march of things, personal histories piling up and each individual event seeming significant beyond all else in the instant of its own birth, then being buried, instant by instant by instant, under other instants devoted only to their own ascendancies. How at Mr. Schianello's funeral not a single person gave a thought to little Maddie Berkeley, wherever she was, whomever she had become after that day she dropped her brother off at the barbershop. She could picture her father, perhaps in dark glasses, seated in a front pew.

Because of her love for Henry and "plain obstinacy" (Henry's phrase, one learned from his mother) tinged by pride—the same pride that saw her through the worst years early in their marriage—she had never once considered begging her father's forgiveness. Only twice was she tempted to contact her family. When she'd miscarried, and when Henry had the boxing accident. (In the waiting room of the hospital, her skirt rumpled from the ride in the station wagon, Henry's head a weighty stone on her lap, she conjured Alma; a sister could talk to a sister no matter what. She didn't place the call.) She could wonder what became of them, Alma, William, Jonathan, and she often did, but Henry had become like a particle of her (she of him) and she'd come to believe it would be a transgression against herself to break that resolve, though Henry sometimes urged her to. The idea was fixed.

A time would come, she'd imagined. A time to return. She would not have been able to guess its admittedly unconventional form, retracing the path now along the promontory that edged the river—it sparkled countless quick ships of light under the moon—with such a stranger. Another instant so self-important but unwittingly wrapped in its own invisible winding sheet and ready for burial.

He was talking, he was saying something. She stopped and looked down through the trees that framed the Hudson. Somewhere, far off, perhaps across the river itself, a car's engine raced.

He was telling her to slow down. Why was he telling her to slow down? What was he doing now? Was he out of his mind, calling out like that up the path? His accent seemed more pronounced when his voice was raised like this, more emphatic in night silence, indeed not all that loud but more a sharp whisper made relatively strident in all the close calm. Or was it that edge, like a quaking or serration at its turns where the word broke into three, the tongue clapping the roof of his mouth. It was a dry sound. Mahdeh-lenn.

He had fallen behind. She knew the bridle path so well she had quickened the pace without noticing. As he caught up, a pale white spume of breath appeared with him.

"What are you doing?" she said, and her voice too seemed loud, as if her own voice here so near again to Berkeley house were rejected by the old air.

"I, you got ahead, and he doesn't walk that fast, and," Lupi took the *viejo*'s hand.

Madeleine saw this, no longer knew what to make of it. "You'll be there soon," she said, and continued forward.

"Listen, can I ask you a question?"

"Why are you whispering?"

"*Senti*, what am I supposed to do once we get there, four in the morning, what am I supposed to do in the middle of the night? I can't just walk in in the middle of the night."

"You can wait for morning, then."

"You'll wait too?"

"I already told you. No, I have just enough time to get back for the first train down. What you want to do once you reach the great Owen Berkeley's is your business." Lupi hadn't heard this, however; he was certain now he could hear the breathing, regular and unlabored just as it had been in Honduras, behind, the occasional pebble overturned to scuttle down after the sole and his nervousness over what Krieger might do made his blood withdraw into his heart and belly, leaving the surface of skin exposed to the dense dew at which he shivered—Krieger, who preferred everything and everyone to be tipped to the side in order that he might appear to be standing up relatively straight. Fumbling for the collar he drew it up, struggled with the top button, blew into his cupped hands breath from down inside his body. He recalled, *cupping*—

Imagine a museum turned on its side to produce a free fall down a corridor, exhibitions flying past, with no chance to pause, to loiter and admire, maybe read the wall label—which brought out in him a kind of renewed adolescent sense of things? He didn't mind. These were fresh sensations. This reemergence of a feeling of his helplessness and the newness of the world had made him susceptible to something that developed within the last days, unexpectedly, happened so naturally that he never noted it for what it was until now, cupping his hands to warm them before his face.

Henry Work; Henry. Madeleine's Henry, Hannah's, but also his own. Lupi had recounted for Henry the story of Milo's abduction, the crossroads faced below Fiesole, the Christmas theft at the house of his parents, and explained (if only to fill up the silence left by Henry's attention, which amplified his sense of guilt about the incident) that he returned to them what he had stolen, by mail.

Henry's response: "If I'd been your pa I'd found you and brought you home to where you belong."

They were down in the pasture. He had reached the point where he could no longer bear sitting up with Olid, who communicated less and less. He had told Henry his story, not knowing why. He had heard Henry's words and walked away. Henry kept talking. He had eight cousins. Five had been to jail at one time or another. Not that jail is a place of redemption. A stall to rot in. Some had since been set free, some hadn't. What he was getting at was time is a good tool, time can be put to work.

Lupi had walked away along the painted walls staring at the rural frescos, stroked out in a multitude of colors which became more abstract the closer one approached. Much of the brush work had been accomplished furiously with what seemed to be a matte-finish house paint. Henry told him Hannah had painted the walls herself. The tracklights were on timers with mechanized rheostats (an affair of winches and pulleys, thin iron rods arranged in rows with hooks at the bottoms through which wire was run laterally in series) that effected an indoor sunrise and sunset scheduled more or less to be coincident with their counterparts in the world outside. Filters which hung by cord down the row of lights could be lowered by hand one bank at a time to fall in front of the bulbs to create a rosy dawn or brilliant puce sundown glow. Henry was fond of this supplementary attachment, which was of his own devising, and generally he was the one who amused himself and troubled the roosters with its possibilities.

At that moment it was just past sunrise, filters dropped into place for a warm, humid midsummer day. Lupi came back, sat beside Henry on a low stool, knees spread wide, and considered the movie prospects of the scene just set into motion: who would ever have thought that a matinee cowboy like me, my hero, would find out his own old daddy was black as the bore of his pistol? "You'd have had a time finding me, nobody else was able to," he said, though the other voice had not altogether faded.

"I'd of found you."

"Maybe," *res ipsa loquitur*.

"I'd of found you without hardly any trouble at all."

Into the mottled silver steel pail the rhythmic streams of milk shot. Out of the corner of his eye Henry could see how intently Lupi watched him.

"Tell me, you ever done this?"

"No."

"Well then, want to give it a go?"

"I don't think so."

"Come on now, nothing to be afraid over."

"It's not that I'm afraid, I just don't think I want to."

"Here you go, give'r a whirl," said Henry, climbing from his knees, fingers glistening like rubber as he steadied himself against the flank. This was an exercise in balances and counterbalances to which the cow was accustomed. She neither flinched, withdrew, nor looked about with her noble head to train a violet eye on the man at her side.

"I, just—"

"Get in there," he said, amused and tender.

"Like this?"

Henry wiped his hands on the back of his overalls. "That's right, go on. They ain't gonna bite. Grab it, no get that one there, that's fine. That one too, take them both."

"Like this?"

"You're just fondling. Don't do that, you're liable to—"

Henry was laughing, affable, benevolent, administrative.

"Well, how then?"

"Look, like this here," extending his arms around Lupi, whose frame felt dwarfed within the half-embrace, and, as if he were knotting his first cravat or coaching him through his first attempt at tying a shoelace, grasped his hands forthwith over the cow's teats, began to squeeze and knead.

"No, easy," he urged, chin settled briefly on the other's shoulder, their ears bumping. "Relax man."

"I, just, but—"

Until the blue-white milk came forth in hard living streams, first from the left and shortly after from the right, and Henry released his grip, slowly, remained hunched over him, pantomiming the proper motions, conducting his hands, all Lupi could think was how absurd a situation this was. By what prerogative? he wondered. His chest heaved. Riddle and regret. But when the milk came and he could hear Henry's pleased chuckle and smell his fresh warm breath across his ear and cheek his heart released and he heard himself exclaiming, "*Guard' un po' che bello*."

"There you got it."

"I do I think."

"Don't stop now, keep it going, keep going."

Too full, the moment became unhinged until there was a twist, a mischief, an alteration so that within that moment all was feint, simulation. Its irrational joy flew free of nonmovie. For the time it took to quarter-fill the pail, for Henry to slap him on the back and (was it possible?) tousle the hair at the back of his head. The joy soon ended. No. This was a sad, sappy, sentimental movie, like the early one Lupi once saw that starred the child Elizabeth Taylor and her mutt-dog which she trained to be a shepherd dog, the same dog her otherwise adorable brothers mistook for a deer while they were hunting, which they shot, but of course after a dark period of tribulation and after the vet had come and said there was nothing more to be done the mutt-dog got well again, only to be run over by a truck, and again survive, what was the title of that movie? the smeary superreal colors, the puppy forever in some sort of trouble, and Elizabeth Taylor devoted to it through to the very end?

Lupi stood up smiling against what he knew was next as the dominant feeling of precariousness and moreover emptiness—that, surely—pressed in again. But he had milked a cow. Everything was possible. Henry had seen the funny crimp in the smile as Lupi got up, his cheeks reddening, overreacting to the smallest most basic gesture in the world. The smile was full, but already showed a shadow.

Movies. He had seen too many, had made too many up. This was movie also. He was catapulted onto a shiny screen. It happened, it always happened whether he resisted or not. Milo had felt like movie, or had at times. The whole thing shaken out when the children screaming and caroling turned the corner. The thing a little recovered in the burglary, when the door to the safe came open, as he loaded pockets with possessions not his. There were many movies. Black-black-haired girl, far too young for a political conscience, was it in Bologna, the bomb intended for the commuter train: she was movie. The bomb had either not been planted or it failed. He was gone. He was in Sardinia. Sardinia had succored movies. The camera left behind in Capri, the ferry missed, the connection stupendously criminal for the first time, and the night spent in under rock shelves that shot out over the white sand, the cold tide rolling up to within a few meters of where he lay. That was movie, nearly completely. And now the river here. It was dimmer, and surely its waves could not be heard. He heard them. The character at the center of the scenario correctly assumed a shiver ran through him, causing his teeth to clatter. They did so in a fit, a paroxysm, then stopped.

Madeleine was close to him. She seemed old, her face harsh, and her hair was lusterless in the starlight where everything is glazed with sheen. Her cheeks seemed meager. He felt as if he ought to kiss her on the cheek, or on her lips. Not penetrating but chaste, and he tipped one shoulder forward to do it before her words came through.

Someone was following, she said. Back on the bridle path. She was sure of it. Steps up the old station staircase. Maybe, she had told herself, it had only been the two of them trailing behind.

"I think you're probably wrong," he lied softly into her face.

The movie-feeling gave way to seeing this other deception—the tangible one—through. As the movie languished so did the desire to kiss Madeleine. It occurred to him how shocked she might have been had the performance carried him forward.

"No, I'm—"

She was studying the brush and the trees below. Lupi hesitated.

"We can wait. I can go back. You wait here, and I can go back and look."

Was it the movie again that made Lupi feel less afraid for himself than Olid, or her or by extension Henry, even Hannah?

"No," she said. "Nothing, it wouldn't matter if it were, something, this is all your business."

"No, I mean—"

"Let's just get it over with," turning.

"Whatever you think, that's what I'll do."

She turned and looked hard at him. He wanted to say something that might prevent her from insulting him, thought to repeat, "That's what I'll do," but suspected it would only benefit that audience beyond Madeleine— the greater one, the one not so substantial, since inexistent: the movie watchers. Whatever it was she had said they might collectively have heard; he hadn't. Its tone had not been contemptuous, but acknowledging, an altogether different note.

Nothing further was audible from below. Above, the house was squared as a mass within irregular shapes and textures of flora. Its chimneys, sharp-pitched gables sandwiched between constellations.

Along the parapet they approached this black confection. By contrast, the grass beneath their feet, blanched under the moon, and the soil beds— circular, a fancy octagon around the south corner—showed the house was still being cared for, at least minimally; someone had mowed in expectation of winter; the wilted flowers had been dug under. They walked the perimeters.

"Now what?"

Madeleine thought, Maybe he's dead.

The kitchen door was neither boarded over nor locked. Inside, there lingered the faint aroma of cooked meat (fish, but also an odor of gas). She felt her way forward into the room, and as her fingers found the switch, so familiar an object, cool, rim consumed by so many fingers into roundness, her thought moved toward the conviction, he was dead.

A single light came on, in the pantry. It threw easy shadows over the kitchen. A skillet sat on the stove. On the counter were tins of food and a disarray of utensils. There was a provisional, a transient feeling to the arrangement, obtrusive but unwilling to move in. Lupi, too, might have noticed this but he was taking all cues from her face (just as Olid looked to Lupi) rather than rely on any insights of his own. A difficult read, engrossed and changing as the eyes took in every surface. Enough time had passed (though it was hard to measure under the exhaustion of the journey, and the anxiety—still present—of the Krieger apparition) and Lupi spoke.

"I take you back to that, where that path comes off the road. I find my way back." (He was exhausted, the English was crumbling.)

She was already into the adjoining room.

Threads, tapers, ribbons, blotches, a variously faint light bled through the chinks in the windows, lending more a transparency to the air than illumination. Stumbling, his palm faltering onto the carved newel, an acorn, its foliation snagging his fourth finger, where the ring would have popped on the mahogany, he found himself awkwardly following the dimmest trace of her, the quick creaking and padding her foot coaxed along the hallway and ascending these stairs.

Was it another lamp flashed on behind them below where they had just come?

On the long landing Madeleine slowed down. Seemed to be light up here, too—not the yellowish hue of the bulb that gave up the stairs (the staircase Lupi saw, with its half-landing at the turn, much like that in Fiesole, though there the steps were made of marble, the cheaper material at the time), rather the thin frost-white through glass.

Yet another light came on and Madeleine went to it. The door was ajar. The face she saw was guileless, much older than she could have thought. There was a running behind them in the hallway, the thuds restrained on the thick oriental carpet.

Lupi understood something had gone wrong. He took Olid's sleeve and pulled him, in a single movement, to his side. When Krieger entered the room, a wide and reputable smile across his face, he took the envelope from Lupi without even looking at him, stretching his other hand out as his head twitched to one side—a gesture of obscene apology—and said, "Mr. Berkeley, this is all so, you know you simply haven't made this easy," and Maddie fled the house.

VII

The Reparation
of Chelsea

1.

THE various dawns' early lights. All of the little blindered suns cast their artificial radiance over the landscape of the loft. The hens that lived in the old berlin wagon began to come alive. So did the cocks that were perched in a row on its decayed hood, the cocks that crowed proudly and adjusted their feathers and stabbed beaks at the feet of others crowding their roost. Lengths of cable soon pulled taut across the ceiling. The circular tinted filters rotated into place under the bulbs and gave the atmosphere a fresh morning hue. Basking under them, these suns, their artificer stirred and the sweet, wet, friendly tongue of the dog ran across her cheek. "Oh, go away," she said. Tail wagging, the dog stepped back, barked, two sharp yaps, then two more. Hannah winced. She had a galloping hangover.

Outside, the city was clustered under its own sunrise whose air was so sharp and fixed that each building and every brick and beam and chiseled stone in it seemed to emanate its own live glow. Crisp wisps of smoke from chimneys, green billows of steam from grates and manholes along the street, curled upward into a clean blue.

Flat on her back she came toward consciousness, but through the unpleasant sensation of cold concrete. This penetrated skin and skull, as a humid wound, at one with her spine, a pain so at home it did not deign to pulsate.

She waited through the minutes that were required to wake up. The dream this pain had called her back from tarried, tattered and beat as a clock whose works were hooked up wrong so that the hands ran backwards from noon to morning to midnight. There was something about a monster, something about people, men, women, children, out along an old road, and they had their belongings with them but no homes to put them in. She wondered if they might not be refugees; she also had the nagging feeling she had been with a group of children gathered in a circle playing marbles, the only girl among the noisy boys, her hair pulled back and tucked into the collar of her shirt.

The bottle of Jamaican rum inches from her eye went some way toward explaining why her body ached. Such a scene of contentment on the bottle's label. The sugar-cane field. The honest laborer on whose shoulder were slung stalks of sugar cane, smirch of smile daubed on his swarthy face—a happy worker. The factory with its benign brown smokestack behind. The three kegs of rum neatly nestled under the yellow Caribbean sky.

"Rum?" her head toiled—it had to have come from Hammond's locker, for rum was Hammond's weakness, not Hannah's; rum and Coke, a mixture he was not proud of loving so. Myer's Jamaican came to Hammond early, through his grandmother to whom in life there were three things worth living for: her dachshunds, her bingo, and her rum. Her rum she cut with lemon juice and honey. This was a drink she called bash. The dachshunds grew grand long livers lapping bashes. Hammond, who liked his bashes as much as any dachshund, learned when he got older to hide the bottles in his locker, because other transient ranch workers agreed to a man (and Hammond had, shyly, to agree with them) that rum was *too damn exotic* a drink for one who works with his two hands.

The concrete floor was underneath Hannah's feet. The herd came forward in a loose group, her presence—standing up, at least—having implied to them: feed.

She went, staggering a little, to the haybin next to the silo chute (it felt as if she were walking with someone else's legs) and barehanded she hoisted a bale out of the bin by its wires and hauled it over to the cattle, its weight against her thighs and her back bent away to counterbalance. A pair of tin shears hung on a nail in the workshack. She dropped the bale, walked into the shack, returned with the shears, cut the binding wires and pulled them free of the bale. The hay came apart in slabs. As the cows moved forward each gentle clop of a hoof made her ears sing, and she stepped back to watch them, the long shears dangling at her side from one hooked finger.

"That's it, come on."

One looked up, shook its head, and its ears flopped.

"Don't give me that"—her voice was wearier than they were accustomed to—"I know it's late."

Another switched its tail, and also looked at Hannah.

"Eat, you silly fools," and she hung up the shears.

Their teeth gnashed together like marbles jounced in a bag. She walked, beginning to remember what it was to use her own legs, and sat down (Indian-style—Columban coinage?—Peter would know, Peter who was to blame for all this) in the midst of their ample soft female bellies where she could smell the hay, its rich, vegetable-earth odor and cattle's breath and their dung from the night, over past the concrete meadow in the corral.

Other vapors limned the inner air. They brought what actually happened back to her in a rush, and prompted a flicker of hysteria, then a calm, which came into her face. Paint. Turpentine. Her head hung down and she noticed her hands clasped in her lap. They were stained with various colors, primarily white, silver, splotches of iron-black, blues, and around her cuticles alizarin crimson, every possible color but green.

—and then she thought, No, Krieger's not to blame for all this—

Well, he is. And isn't.

Lupi and the old Indian had disappeared.

The sheets and blanket on Lupi's pallet were left in a knot, the small square of a pillow on the floor under the gray of Hannah's flashlight, the very flashlight (metal, ribbed, nice and heavy in the palm) she so long ago held to the farmhouse floor in Nebraska the night after mama Opal had died and she moved into her room, set up the rickety cot beside her bed (she would never sleep in her bed; that would be a kind of sacrilege) and made it up with linens and a comforter from her own. She had thought to keep vigil. She kept the flashlight under the covers with her, and when she found she could not sleep directed its beam along the wainscot and up the wall, papered with mazes of printed petunias, as a kind of game. Under the oval of light the petunias took on fierce faces and she shrank away. She remembered having slept head in her hands in the kitchen the night before. Soon it was all gone into a misshapenness and she awoke in the night with her flashlight in her face, pillow on the floorboards, and mama Opal's room smothered in cold. She snatched the flashlight away from her chin with a cry, pointed it down beside her.

And here all these years later, white eyelets frayed, grayed, and mended on the pillowcase, not much of a pillow anymore with its goosedown half gone, under the beam of the same old Sears Roebuck torch. Hannah kicked the pillow. She sought it out and kicked it again so that when she drew back the torch's shaft in her hands and played the beam across the dark smooth space there was a cloud of feathers fluttering all around her.

Next she searched both rooms of the bunker, paced the roof, climbed the tower stairs to the silo. Above the city she smoked one of Henry's hidden cigarettes. Damp and stale, it made her cough. She flicked it away off the roof. Someone in thirdhand mufti later would snatch it out of the gutter, with an arthritic quiver relight it and continue toward the river.

Black stirrings in the so-called dead space downstairs, those rooms on the massive floor a flight below the ranch itself: unused and each at a different stage of dilapidation. Vacuums with shabby remains of lowered ceilings (acoustical panels dangling from cheap aluminum supports, flat dry tongues panting at their silver lips) the only ornament in a featureless cubicle. One room was filled with broken, partly dismantled sewing machines, vintage units with heavy filigreed legs and wooden cabinets, awaiting a repairman who would never arrive. Fifty or sixty of them. Light, with its cat's-eye center, matriculated over this junkheap and even across the shattered bulbs strung on wires along the walls. Familiar acquaintances, but no sign of Lupi or the old man. She leaned against the doorjamb and chewed at a fingernail; her mouth was dry and she was thirsty. In the dressing mirror that was propped against a naked, headless mannequin, whose slight breasts and unarticulated genitals suggested that once it had been clothed in dresses with sashes, glass buttons, bows, the look of anxiousness she wore dimly spread and was rebuffed by a frown of surprising scorn.

She thought to talk to Hammond first, but petulant and cross and defiant is all Hammond had been ever since the arrival of the two strangers. And at the playback of the voice on the telephone-answering machine he had made no comment but Hannah knew at once Hammond recognized what he heard; he had said nothing, collected a bucket of ice to sink the poor lame calf's hind leg into, glanced from under his Stetson brim at Hannah and afterward at Lupi, and left quietly, shutting the door behind just as the message concluded. Hammond observed the unraveling from the supreme distance of his own discontent (or so Hannah took it).

He had been in the bunker by chance when the first call came through back in September, the caller so articulate, his English formal and perfect, pushed through the barrier of his thick Spanish accent, and then the voice on the line she knew well.

Krieger . . . Krieger? Jaunt to Norfolk, the rear-end collision, panicky call from Norfolk Community, a Franz, Mona, moray eel and a curious beast called a banana wrasse, the story about how Krieger spent sixty-five dollars at the tropical fish store on a certain glorious emperator angel, carefully introduced it into the tank, only to come back a few minutes after it was set loose to find its tail sticking out of the grouper's mouth, and how he tried to pull the angelfish out but it would not come, and how because it was the same size as the grouper that tail stuck out for the rest of the day as his expensive fish was digested. Then the goddamn moray eel ended up devouring everything in the tank—including the grouper—before retreating behind the plastic castle to float there listless. Krieger? *that* Krieger? and every irreducible week that intervened, grown like some hideous sponge which could accommodate the entire waters of not just Krieger's old black-light-illumined tank but the Hudson which, on the right day at the right hour, was reflected through it—only a tiny distorted image wedged between the gables and vines—upside down. Krieger, Krieger? yes, that made sense.

Once Hammond divined if not the exact character of Hannah's problem some elements of its workings, he subsided into captiousness. He went on with his chores but he went at them more lazily. Pitchforks he wouldn't touch. He wouldn't turn a clock key or pull a toilet chain. Hannah saw this and while she was upset by it knew there was nothing to say. If Hammond was not sure something was wrong with Hannah before that, he was certain of it when no comments were made about his insidious behavior. Then Matteo Lupi appeared, solitary and lost, escorting Tiresias, half blind in an ill-fitting suit and deerskin overcoat whose sleeves dangled past his fingers and seams touched the heels of his handmade tire-soled sandals. It was as if she had stepped back into her childhood, those glory afternoons up in the hayloft, making her way down roads in her head with her ancient friend Lucretius, and once there made another step, but this time across the friendly scrim into the evil (what a word, what an empty, useless word, she thought, but nevertheless:) evil world on the other side. What was most surprising was this: the evil world was no more a twilit, dark, maddening place than its counterpart. The evil side of the scrim shown just as bright. The flowers smelled the same, the shit, the same, everything was unmistakably the same. Except that this was the other side, as opposed to the other side.

She didn't even need to go down and check—Maddie'd gone ahead. That was okay. It was Maddie's life, too. She might have told her she was going but must have figured she—Hannah—was asleep.

Okay, have a sip. It all came down to this. That fucking Krieger.

* * *

Hammond's rum had been disgustingly sweet and viscous. This time she really would have to replace the bottle. No three-quarters of an inch this time. The whole darned thing. After the fifth, or the ninth, or twelfth tilt she'd cultivated both indifference to its taste and pleasure in its modifying effect. Krieger withdrew into distance, as did the cattle that right there were industriously bellowing because they had not been fed at the hour of their schedule—so painstakingly devised. Lupi and Hammond receded also. Hannah looked at the painted scenes on the long wall before her and thought, What this wants is a city.

In the janitor's closet she found cans of leftover paint and brushes. The can of battleship gray would be useful. There were cans of black, reds, other colors, and gesso, too. Most of the brushes had been ruined because they had never been cleaned: sculptural blobs—mucous gunk—of hardened paint attached like puppet heads to the bristles. With turpentine and scissors she soaked and pared the salvageable brushes, tossing the lot onto a dropcloth, dragged the materials to her wall as the herd quieted down to watch. This had been one of the lushest, most inspired meadows in the whole landscape, with a burnt-umber creek trailing S-patterns down through the verdigris grass and the figure there in straw hat, blue-jean overalls, barefooted, rod out over a pool and cork bob near the farther bank where several white rings promised a cutthroat trout, a rainbow, brownie; a grayling lay under the shadow and considered a grasshopper which flinched on the end of the hook. The figure had been the only self-portrait in the enormous composition, although Hannah had never fished, nor worn overalls or straw hat. It was first to disappear under the brash vertical strokes of opaquing gesso. The fumes were delicious. They conjured up her first months in the loft when she primed the walls with a foundation of calcimine and cartooned out the Great Plains panorama. She might have flinched a little when her brush came to the goat in the mural, the mysterious goat with the yellow eyes which Henry had always wondered at but had never had the courage to ask her about. She touched the image that had held Gerald's ghost there nicely, and painted around it for a while before taking the decision the ghost would be fine, maybe better off, resting beneath another coat of paint, another image. And so with a few strokes it was gone, too.

Buildings, bridges, people in their windows, cars and buses on their spans; an upstream barge hefted mounds of sand or garbage; there were avenues and some leafless trees worked up along their sidewalks which she dotted with passersby; a row of townhouses, a spire, a church, two churches; quays licked at by a river whose blackness came from the middle of the large sheet of glass which she used for mixing her colors, there at the center where all the hues ran together to make a sum of each, a dirty unnamable shade. And just prior to passing out, her cheek pressed to the cool drain-slough that ran from feeding area to a sump which wanted periodic flushing and stank of urine (which the cattle had already begun to lick at for the salt there) since it hadn't been cleaned, just before she fell asleep, her clothes, face and hands covered with paint, she traced out a small open boat at the edge of the water and put in it the explorer Henry Hudson and his son, set adrift by a crew of mutineers three hundred years before without compass, water, or food, and never seen nor heard from again.

Her temples no longer throbbed. She had to get up off the floor. There were so many things to do.

Her eyes sank momentarily under their thin sheets of flesh and afterwards the flesh drew back and above her were nostrils and broken teeth. The exhalation served as a reference, as did that gentle, insistent nibbling at her head. The cow wanted the shoots of hay that had gotten tangled in Hannah's hair.

2.

TEARS that welled in Lupi's eyes made driving at this high speed—down a road he had never seen before, into the depths of a country he did not know—even more difficult and dangerous than it might otherwise have been. A bead cut down his cheek and formed like a dot of mercury on his chin. The map was so uninstructive. A rise in the road and the car caught flight. But it wouldn't crash. There would be no shattered glass to shower across the gray fields, no flower of brazed metal, no wheel discovered tangled in a snow fence the next farm over. This exodus would continue until Lupi was able to carry out what he'd promised himself he would do.

"Wake up, Garibaldi," Krieger in his Corless guise had called out an hour before, with a solemnity only the morning star trapped in the gradient blues of the old leaded glass could make more manifest.

Where am I? he'd wondered, and the ride up to Berkeley house and the wholly unexpected invitation to stay the night, as guests, all returned.

Krieger was staring down at him where he lay in bed.

"The spirit is very strange it has an obligation to create, so said the great Mircea Eliade you with me kiddo?"

By distempering reality with movie Lupi had gotten through the odder developments and twists of the few days before. Yet even movie hadn't been potent enough to force Krieger's performance into focus the night before—he had moved with such apparent aplomb through every problem.

"Hey," he was saying, now walking away from the bed, "is kiddo Italian for kid?"

In the fresh-washed and ironed linen of the bed Lupi tugged his shoulders up about his ears in tandem response (though he might have feigned a snore) to Krieger's question—and Krieger himself in the pajamas that had been laid out on the other bed in the guest room, the pink room, an oriental theme room with a vellum-covered desk and the silk rug rich in its mango grove and cranes. Lupi wished he felt less ill at ease. Less sunk in dread. But it was there, in him—an overwhelming sense of shame.

"And that obligation takes on different forms I mean this is me talking now but this one is in a class by himself, Berkeley here's very classy, I don't mean classy so much as, I don't know it's not like you could say this was an upper-class setup, but it's not middle-class, that's for sure, it's not intelligentsia, which is a subsidiary of lower-class, maybe just a notch down below lower-class like a wart on the toe or something, but whatever I still haven't digested this wardrobe routine etcetera, trust him about as far as I can push this mansion up the hill. The not being available to talk business last night is the worst but what are you going to do, when in Rome, right?"

Lupi sneezed. He was coming down with a cold. How could he ramble so?—Lupi wanted to slap him, though of course he knew that he never would. Besides, he reasoned, he was weak.

"*Gesundheit*," as a handkerchief fluttered down. "You okay? I mean you realize you and I are up to our asses in alligators here, so forth, I mean we're in this together now."

When Lupi heard dialogue like *We're in this together now*, movie framework began to inform the action. Here was a movie about a man who came to realize that the choices he had other than the one where he would give himself over to the real mess he found himself in were reduced to none; his sorry "yes" was an utterance of surrender. He could almost (but not quite) hear the strains of a single violin playing background to the scene. The notes were sweet—couldn't he use what strength he had to bring them up, yes he could, there they came—watery, high, beautiful, of no recognizable composition, but so lovely that Lupi listened to the soundtrack for a few more moments and missed the segue—

> "When up to one's ass in green gators
> It's good to have waterproof waders,
> Salt, pepper and flour,
> Which fry for an hour,
> And serve with a rasher of taters."

Krieger roared with laughter, "You ever eaten gator tail, Lupi? Down in the Everglades, sure, absolutely delicious, tastes like a cross between chicken and what you find between the legs of you know what."

"No, what?"

The violin trilled, perhaps, fluttered, before it faded away under the track of laughter.

"That's my boy. What was that one, something like Youth's a blunder, manhood a struggle, old age a regret, and if we can get through this we won't regret it, agreed? right."

"I don't know."

Krieger was studying his tongue in the mirror. "Now look, it's time to check on our friend."

"Olid," Lupi muttered, as if in the midst of other confusions he had forgotten his main purpose.

Krieger scowled.

"What's an Olid?"

"Olid—"

"Memory about as long as an inchworm under a Benihana cleaver they have those over in Roma? burn your food for you right there at the table, juggle a few meat cleavers remind you who's boss, but as I was saying may I remind you our friend's to be referred to here for the sake and safety of all involved—"

"It," Lupi said.

"Correct, good boy. Hey, Lupi, did you ever hear of *The Mr. Ed Show* over there in Italy?"

"Krieger don't call me a boy."

"*Ragazzino* then, anyway, did you?"

"What."

"Hear of Mr. Ed?"

"No."

"No? but I thought you were such an aficionado of the medium, but anyhow this Mr. Ed, the talking horse you see he was a horse and he could talk, that was the bit, great camerawork the way they got his mouth to sync with the, anyhow it was a great program and its theme song went:

> *'And no one can talk with a horse of course*
> *That is of course unless the horse*
> *Is the famous mister'*—etcetera . . .

You never heard that?"

"No."

"You remember that Beatles song, 'I Am the Walrus,' you play it backwards it says Paul is dead?"

"Who cares?"

"Dante's got circles in hell for guys ignorant as you, boy, so anyhow you play the Mr. Ed theme backwards and it says something like, Your mama sucks Satan—"

"Krieger, don't ever call me boy again, I'm tired of this, I just want to finish up here and be on my way, I don't care about talking horses, I don't care about intelligentsia, I think what we're doing here is wrong."

"Yeah yeah, what am I supposed to do, applaud?—run down some sort of lick like—life's tough, life's this, life's that? Look b-o-y, it's like you can put lipstick on a hog but it don't hide the ugliness down underneath."

Surprising himself, and Krieger as well, Lupi sat up, spat to the side on the carpet, and said nothing.

Krieger's voice hardened, "Time to do your Latin thing, come on, rise and shine," and while he spoke he produced an envelope from his briefcase (briefcase? Lupi hadn't noted a briefcase the night before). "Here's your ticket, a few hundred bucks, a new passport, just in case for some reason we happen to get separated this morning."

"Why would we get separated?"

"We won't but look, better to be safe than sorry, to coin a phrase right?"

Lupi opened the ticket folder and saw the flight left New York for Miami, and thence to Managua.

"Managua? I'm not going down there again."

"How welcome do you think you'll be in Tegucigalpa? They're probably looking high and low for you."

"That's beside the point."

"There's a hotel in Managua, the Hotel Intercontinental, looks like a prefab Aztec ruin, very comfortable, booze, chicks, very historical place, great favorite of the old dictatorship. We'll meet there. And yes, I think they are looking for you in Honduras."

"I'm going back to Rome."

"You can do whatever you want, we'll talk about it in Managua, just you and me. If you want to go home, you can go from there. I know your feelings about my colleague, but you never can tell, we might be able to branch out on our own, you know. There's a lot we could do, and you've handled yourself brilliantly with this particular expedition."

"I haven't done anything."

"You've done what you were supposed to do just like any good mercenary. We'll talk about this later."

"I won't be there."

"For reasons I'm not at liberty to explain right now I would strongly urge you to do what I've said. In any case, you'd better get up, we've got to finish here."

Painfully, for his joints already ached, Lupi pushed himself out of the bed. Cristóbal had been quartered in a smaller bedroom that adjoined theirs, directly connected by a low-paneled gallery. The sun was coming up, and its winter purple suffused the room where Lupi threw on a bathrobe with a monogrammed "B" on the pocket, rubbed his sore eyes with his knuckles, then followed the other man down the gallery to the anteroom. At the entrance Krieger stood aside and let him pass.

Olid lay there in this hermetical light stiff and motionless on the bed. The instant Lupi saw the old man a strong feeling of the loathsomeness of their procedure came over him. From far away over the hills a Mahleresque passage was played by a phantom orchestra. Lupi willed the symphony away as his eyes darted the length of the slender figure wrapped in bed-clothes and it was as if his own soul suddenly went rotten, or else apperceived its inherent rot, since how could it be possible to arrive at such a juncture without the soul having already decomposed to a certain state of rottenness?—but this instant carried the bittersweet of an apple fallen to the ground where once the wasps were done with drinking at it, it browned in the breeze, was adopted by a worm, say, sank into the soil, producing a spoiled place. The sour taste of phlegm rose at the back of his throat. He coughed and swallowed.

"Say something to him, tell him it's time to wake up, tell him we're here this is his new home or something."

Lupi stared at Cristóbal's face. It was still. The narrow jaw lay slack into the pillow. Fingers of his hand curled palm up on the coverlet as if they were grasping an unseeable ball, holding tightly some invisible orb. The gesture reminded Lupi of an owl's claw.

"He's going to ask me about Sardavaal."

"So what?"

"So what am I supposed to say? All along I've been putting it off about Sardavaal by saying he would meet us here."

"Who the hell told you to say that?"

"You didn't tell me not to. I still don't understand why you sent me up here alone with him if you intended all along to follow us up the river."

"Strategy, Lupi, in any case never mind, just say, what, say Sardavaal will be coming along, he was detained, whatever, anything to get us through the transaction and the hell out of here, just make it so he doesn't bring Sardavaal up with Berkeley."

"Since he can't speak English I don't see what difference it would make."

Krieger waved his arms and cried in a low voice, "Tell him whatever you want, just wake him up he doesn't look that great."

"You shouldn't have given him so much of those drugs."

"What? the Nembutal? dosage weak enough you couldn't put a fruit fly out with it."

"That stuff wasn't necessary."

"Spare me the medical opinions, would you."

"He wouldn't have said anything, is all I am saying."

"Fine, I'll make a note of your objection to procedure now come on, hurry up. Tell him it's time we get cracking."

"I think he's dead."

"Oh for godsakes," and Krieger moved forward, raised his hands toward Lupi's shoulders and reached to pull him away from the bed. Lupi withdrew. Krieger quickly said, "How do you say rise and shine in lingua Latina?"

Lupi thought. "*Surge et . . . surge . . .*"

"*Sirgay*? fine okay, got it. I'll take care of it."

"*Surge et . . .*"

"I got it. Why don't you go take a shower, you smell more like a barn than a businessman, same stink but a matter of degrees of pungency."

Lupi took a step back, and as he did Krieger noticed in the morning light how deep an olive color his face was. He had never really looked at the surface of Lupi before, and the recognition of so tiny a particular struck him.

"What are you staring at?" Lupi said.

"What?"

"Listen, Krieger. Who is this poor little fellow?"

"Huh?" Krieger managed an incredulous frown, although he had anticipated this question for some time. He had begun to believe Lupi's participation in the project might have been a mistake.

"Well, that is, he's not any four hundred years old, you know."

"So you're the scientist now, right?"

"What about the Latin? How is it he speaks the Latin?"

"Listen honey, history's full of missionaries with hard-ons for two things: acolytes and Indians. The washed, the unwashed. It's a different kind of AC/DC. All on the same frequency. The Latin didn't have to come all the way from Europe with him, it's true. One fucking missionary with a Vulgate and the right emotional chemistry and if it's a bit of Latin they want? well, him who wants water give him water, who wants wine, wine."

"What planet are you from you come so cold?"

"Hey, champ?"

"What."

"Hit the showers."

Lupi left without saying anything. Once Krieger heard he was down the gallery hall he turned to the *viejo*; a look of intense impatience in his face, he furtively felt for some pulse at the wrist, but it was hard, cold, and Krieger noted the greeny circles beneath his eyes.

This was reprehensible, no matter what angle it was approached from: disgraceful, he thought, as a piece of ancillary business, to be sure, but also unquestionably revolting as (what?) simple human conduct . . . simple, not so simple, human, well, not so human either—but Krieger reiterated mutely for the benefit of the cobwebbed light fixture that never before had he himself perpetrated a . . . death, yes a death, and even this . . .?

Invariably Krieger had left it to others to sacrifice themselves for this unjustifiable cause or that. With a sort of mechanical abstraction he placed the wrist down, and at once began contemplating the various plausible scenarios: immediate flight; and if not that, then what stories might be concocted in order to push through the agreement?

On the floor was Cristóbal's satchel. It lay where Krieger had put it the night before after administering another dose of the drug to the old man. He had arranged the shoulder strap of the satchel over its closed mouth to make it look as if it had casually been tossed there. He memorized the position of the strap so that if during the night the satchel was tampered with he would be able to tell. Evidently no one had come into the room, and by all appearances the bag had not been searched. Krieger looked over his shoulder to see if Lupi had come back. The entryway was empty. Swiftly, silently he opened the satchel, removed the few articles Cristóbal had brought with him for the journey—a small pipe, a candle, the passport with its maroon covers—then with his pocketknife cut the stitched threads along one edge of the false bottom. Feeling with his fingers under the woven wool layer of fabric he was satisfied that the plastic envelope remained just where he had so carefully planted it back in El Paraiso; proprietarily his forefinger pressed at that hidden parcel, its layers of plastic, coffee grounds, and the white powder. He tamped the false bottom back into place and replaced Cristóbal's effects, considered for a moment where best to keep the satchel now that it was obvious his original agenda had been altered by this unfortunate death. The back of his hand brushed over the weave of the *mochila* as he pondered. Other considerations aside, it was still too early to displace the ownership of those contents from Olid (characterized by Krieger's current fantasy as not only a smuggler but a suicide) to himself. He did take the precaution of half-hiding the satchel under the bed; it would have to wait until later to be retrieved.

Hastily, Krieger dressed. The knot in his tie came out right on the first attempt which, since he always had difficulty with this little task, he took for a positive omen. Lupi was still in the shower when he left the room to go downstairs.

"Good morning," as he walked casually into the kitchen. He would approach this in as cheerful and professional a manner as possible, and thus wore on his face the countenance of any ambitious young banker possessed of formulae, blueprints, means of pushing forward through the bizarreries of commerce. Alma watched in continuous disbelief as he took a mug from the cupboard and poured himself coffee from the Pyrex pot on the stove. *Being very strange, the spirit has an obligation to create* . . . Krieger experienced the maxim once more before contriving, "Well to skip the hustings and trivia, I mean if you don't mind, that is your hospitality much appreciated and so forth but I can see your father's not down yet, what I'm wondering is whether he's had the opportunity to go over the papers as yet."

"You're in a rush," Jonathan said.

Always the dangerous-innocent around to gum up the works, he thought, looking on Jonathan with eyes of disgust. "As a matter of fact I'd hoped to get all this settled last night by the way you never did tell me how that went with Sardavaal that time."

Jonathan refused to answer.

"I was glad to be of service, always trying to help."

Krieger drank, careful to maintain such a look of dispassion locked in his features that some of the more obvious questions these two might want to ask would be at least flustered, if not altogether suppressed, by his air of tranquillity. That is, the esteemed Corless (here embodied by Mr. Krieger) should consider these circumstances prosaic in the extreme—it was just a day in the life. Too, Corless-Krieger (as the spirit invented him) worked strictly with the principals in any such deal, and should make it known that meddling could result in trouble for all. Ceremoniously Krieger drew up a chair to the refectory table where Jonathan sat, and as he did a twinkle of threat passed across his eye appreciable to Jonathan for precisely what it was, including its underlying sense of fallacy—the fallacy of the thin perfectly knotted tie on a Sunday morning, of the accommodating manner with which he had accepted the "gracious invitation" to spend the night here and trade thus an absurdity for an absurdity, and now this stylish drawing-out of the impossible situation like a vaudevillian looking for his last joke before the big hook appears from offstage to loop around his waist and drag him away. "When," Krieger smiled, and the smile felt like candy on his teeth, "can we expect Mr. Berkeley to come down?"

"I'm not sure you can expect him to come down."

"May I ask why not?"

"This is insanity," Alma inserted, as she shuffled the black-and-white photographs of Cristóbal in his former state of grace in the mountainside village. The sameness of background and foreground in the frames suggested all the shots had been taken with a telephoto lens. "I don't know why we just don't call the police."

Krieger answered quickly, and very calmly: "I can think of several reasons, but what interests me right now is why after we've come all this way at your father's insistence you're telling me I can't expect him to come down a flight of stairs to discuss our project."

"He never insisted," Jonathan guessed.

"I have it in writing, which is of course one of the reasons the police would not best be involved here. Not only that but he—Mr. Berkeley— agreed to reimburse for all expenses if he determined against custodianship." Krieger turned to Alma: "Would you mind putting those back in their envelope, dear? Can't have grease all over them, kind of ruins the prints."

"Well I determine against custodianship," Jonathan continued.

"That's fine but I have no business with you nor you with me, so if you don't mind I'll just wait here for a bit, or better yet maybe you could go up and tell him that some of us have schedules to keep and anyway *l'exactitude est la politesse des rois*."

"Let me see what you have in writing."

"I don't think that'll be necessary. If you don't mind, I'll finish my coffee here and wait for my translator to join us and then, well, if it turns out Mr. Berkeley has changed his mind we can settle up and be on our way."

To Krieger's intransigence Jonathan could make no response, yet in the silence that passed between them none heard the paltry resonation through the wide-planked floor where Lupi had caught his shoe on a footstool and fallen with the corpse, which he'd wrapped in its sheets together with the satchel he had found under the bed. He moved quickly and with a combination of tenderness and mortification lifted the body again into his arms, to start quietly once more for the door. Krieger was being abandoned to his own genius and the punishments of Mircea Eliade's dictum. Lupi had decided his own participation in this death (this *ucciso*) was inescapable, and when in the shower (the banality of the setting for this epiphany did not escape him) it all came so clear in its perversity, its horror, he began to weep not only for himself but for what he saw as the great calamity all people routinely—with such deftness and enthusiasm—bring upon themselves and others.

This was it. This was it. He owed Olid what he had owed ambassador Milo, that other casualty, so long ago in the Fiesolean winter.

It would be the first of many necessary atonements. Somewhere he would find a pleasant meadow, perhaps near a stream or spring so that once he had succeeded in digging past the hard ground along the surface where the long dead grass lay, softer soil beneath might make the task easier. Maybe there could be a grove of trees there, like the trees Cristóbal had been accustomed to seeing down in El Paraiso. That would be comforting. And if he was able to locate a rather private edge in that meadow where the roll of the earth just began to ascend, say, up toward a knoll that faced eastward, then every day could commence with an unfolding of dawn over his place, and when April and May came around the grasses and reeds would grow thicker, some white violets, snowdrops, and other early flowers would emerge. Also Lupi had thought it wisest to bury him with all his earthly possessions, what few articles he had brought along in the *mochila* for the journey; he was ignorant, he knew, of what customs or rites the villagers of Olid's tribe practiced during the burial of a man, but he speculated it would be proper to send him forth furnished with what he had been familiar with, and with what was rightfully his own. He had—he thought, feeling cleansed for once by the water, feeling clean in fact for the first time in so many years—he had it all worked out.

As light as the bundle was he had some difficulties negotiating his way down the back stairs and out into the morning. The keys were in the ignition and the engine turned over quietly. He drove down away from the house, glimpsing the baroque facades and collection of chimneys he was leaving in the rearview mirror. A willowy film of dust lifted out from under the tires and made it difficult to see whether anyone followed him out onto the flat terrace where the car had been parked. Since at the foot of the hill he could see that there were no figures on the parapet waving their arms frantic at the sight of this escape, no one running headlong down the lawn in pursuit, he knew he had cleanly gotten away.

Once he reached the short stretch of road beyond the gateposts that were hidden by a thick forest of ivy-shrouded, leafless trees he stopped the car long enough to move the body and satchel from the backseat to the trunk.

"*Poverino,*" he whispered. Poor thing.

He had forgotten to steal a shovel, but there was no going back. Fingers quaking, he counted how much money he had left. Four hundred twenty dollars. If he could find a store open on Sunday he could buy a shovel and still have enough money left for the flight back home.

Disoriented, he drove as if velocity might compensate for his lack of direction. Everything was behind him except his atonement and some still unformed conceit that once he made his way through customs at Aeroporto da Vinci he might set out on a course that would lead him back to Nini.

Nini. The steel trusses whipped by. The sun, he thought. He had come west from east and he knew where he wanted to go was therefore east from here. The fat man and Krieger with all their theories of history and how civilization for better or worse moved always like the sun from east to west. They both had missed that one simple detail—how simple things can seem at ninety-five miles an hour—that detail which surely figured into this catastrophe as well as any (and who should understand this better than an Italian?). Explorers looking for the East Indies sailed straight into what this short span of time would come to conjure as just the opposite, the west, here, this, and in the beneficent and extraordinary spirit of blunder (blunder! was *that* the word to define the whole experience?), the first tentative, dainty, stealing, killing boys set out, the first who could see their way to making up a total fiction? beginning with using the word Indian to mean a man, a woman, those who they found here in this place now so perverted that the House of Pancakes (what was that?) . . . how sad, how sorrowful, how tragic a thing it seemed to Lupi, and it was gone as quickly as it had appeared.

He was no better than the rest, was he. He was worse than most, in fact.

That's how it was. The car easily slowed to a stop. There was a young man standing beside a tractor in a lot not far from the road. Lupi ran, tripped, out into the field and asked him which way was east? The farmer pointed back down the road. Lupi thanked him, and returned to the car, whose engine was still running. He put it into gear, turned it around and accelerated quickly in the other direction. Full of confidence he drove half a mile before pulling over to the shoulder of the road once more and swung the car around again. His eyes ran over the dash, and down across a road map.

The map was not an illusion but its smear of alternatives was seductive. He saw where he was, or at least where he had passed the night. There was a red-inked circle along the printed river and beside it the words "our house." No matter how fast he'd been traveling he knew he was still in the vicinity of the red circle and the words—although in fact rather than speeding in the direction of New York, his flight to freedom was headed out toward a different freedom, to be found beyond the Catskills caught by the great sweet curve of the Susquehanna River, strung out like a basket between the towns of Binghamton and Wilkes-Barre. But before he would get there he saw the ragged blue and pink and yellow flags strung along lines across the fenced lot of a drive-in movie which tempted his attention away from the map and when he looked up he was past when he pulled hard at the steering wheel to make the curve that broke into a field where the road narrowed to a tight lane fenced along either shoulder, and as he did tears came fast again in his eyes but he laughed as the wheels of the car still made rubber bites in the road and he could see the partial reflection of his eyes in the mirror and it made him laugh the more as suddenly he felt happy here in this dislocated tangle of garden because he knew that both he and Cristóbal de Olid were going to be fine they were going to be just fine they were going to make it through.

3.

THE face brightened into a smile deficient in no measure of courtesy, even relief, as Krieger had remained mindful of the complicated mess he had manufactured upstairs in the small anteroom with its single bed and the human specimen stretched out cold in it no longer able to provide his client much to work with. The twitch he felt in the muscles at his temples, a tic that showed deeper nervousness than what he wanted to display, he converted as best he could into a wink, both eyes closed for an instant, while he took Owen Berkeley's outstretched hand into his own and shook it in a suitably clerklike manner, released it, and said, "Of course, for a minute there I started to think, well Corless it's true you came quite a distance but it's not like this is the first time you have gone a long way and sometimes things have gone up in smoke, and you'll go a long way again no doubt and, sometimes things won't go just the way you thought they might. It's just the nature of the, the beast, nature of the occupation."

"You take a philosophical approach to life," Berkeley retorted. He had not shaved, and as he spoke the light from the window sparkled in the silver grinds collected in his hollow cheek. The morning suit he wore, complete with its waistcoat and gold chain that fell in a catenary arc from watch fob to the pocket opposite, weighted with a boar's tooth and an Irish gold coin, had a sheen like ice so many times had it been worn; the edge of the collar and piping along the buttonholes showed almost through to the pale buckram lining underneath. Nevertheless, elegance pervaded, or rather, an old-worldliness.

"Yes well, but I thought, this Berkeley he seems different than some of the others, flattery aside—was thinking of some speech or other of Patrick Henry, you know well of course you must know even better than I do, but this speech?"

"Yes . . ."

"Of Henry's? I think it was before the Virginia Convention where he said and I quote, If we wish to be free, if we mean to preserve inviolate those inestimable privileges for which we have been so long contending—and I think here you and I know whereof we speak, don't we—if we mean not basely to abandon the noble struggle in which we've been so long engaged and which we've pledged ourselves never to abandon until the glorious object of our contest shall be obtained—we must fight!"

"That may well be the case, Dr. Corless," he breathed.

Despite himself, Krieger was impressed by what he viewed as absolute insolence in the nod that Berkeley made, a deep and tardy nod designed for some different era, a time whose history had no obligation to embrace the quark or the curvature mathematically deducible in the soul of a straight line. "I've been challenged by both your children here to take advantage of your absence and their what . . .? What can I call it? their superior abilities to understand the nature of your needs, the needs that is of your important work here and I must say, well, *fight* is the word."

Owen Berkeley turned to his daughter but before he could say anything she rose out of her chair and announced she was going back to New York: "I give up. I don't care what you, like what's going on here. I just don't care. I've done everything I can do."

"You'll do no such thing," her father shouted after her, but she had already left the kitchen.

For such a heavy door the sound of its slam was sharp.

Krieger's eyes shot over to Berkeley senior to see that he did not recover his composure, because he never lost it.

"Jonathan," the man said, evenly, bored even, "go talk to your sister."

"You're the one who needs to be talked to. For openers you might be interested to know that this man's name is not Corless—"

Ignoring him, Owen poured the fresh thick milk from a canister into the top pan of a double boiler, produced a match from his vest pocket and struck it on the wall. He lit the gas burner of the stove.

"I believe it's important that I know what's going on here, I've had dealings with this man in the past, maybe you'll remember, and I think I'm better equipped to judge the value of whatever it is he's trying to sell you than you are," continued Jonathan. "I also happen to know what lengths you seem to be willing to go to, to get the money together for this insanity, and since this is my house, too, I think I ought to have some say."

"Your house," were Berkeley's words.

Krieger stood politely back into the room, having sensed the expediency an almost Edwardian deference might have under the circumstances. It was so plainly *rhetorical* a gesture that Jonathan recognized it for the value it had; "Goddamn it," he said.

"Pardon me, Corless," Berkeley muttered and left as the great oak door pitched into its frame with a slow quiet dignity, meaning to Krieger that all was well, a matter of moments just to be tended with patience, almost with love, so that this little journey—like all the others—would bear its fruits. And as he waited for Jonathan to speak, he thought, What dire and unexpected slapstick, as he began then to detach himself from the proceedings. The hiccup of a laugh stuck in his throat. It felt anguished, this air stuck in the contraction of flesh, but it was best left in his body, and at the same moment he pulled his face into the purest blank stare. It worked and he was grateful when Jonathan followed his father out of the room without having done more than mutely clench his fist and raise his middle finger out of it, holding it up so close to Krieger's face he was sure he could feel the warmth of the skin radiate there at his forehead. He had not flinched, would not flinch, and the gesture had received only that blank look for all its incipient violence and passion before the door was pressed shut, this time with a crack which reverberated through the china in the cabinet, and Krieger was left alone.

Presentation, he reminded himself, presentation, presentation, and when he poured another cup of coffee he concentrated on the play of the steam, its fickle wiry tendrils, as a meditation. He seated himself at one end of the table. The coffee had a dismal thinness to it. He crossed his legs, uncrossed them, tapped his fingertips to replicate the sound of cantering hooves of a horse.

Gloomily he looked around the room. The calendar with its great empty squares for each day and the photographic scene of a comfortable and quaint town, New Hampshire or Vermont, under the winter's first dusting of snow, its white clapboard church and steeple reaching into the parrish-blue sky of morning. The utensils. The potholders, one shaped like a lamb. The reproduction of Renoir's *Le Bal à Bougival*. The drooping shelves weighted with their cookbooks—Betty Crocker's *Picture Cookbook*, revised and enlarged, the High Maples Farm book of recipes, *The United States Regional Cookbook* by Ruth Berolzheimer—on the spine of the dust jacket, the cock, the beehive, the bull, the idealized face of the Spanish girl with a red flower in her hair, the faggot of wheat, and the sober Midwestern girl above with her bonnet, brown eyes, and cherry-round lips. (They were arguing in the next room. The voices came through the wall. Somewhere in their exchange of tones Krieger descried the music of his own adolescence, although Krieger thought of himself as a man without a childhood and far removed from the possibility of such words as those he now could hear.) He got up and pulled down the Berolzheimer.

He opened it at random. Zoete Broodjes, he read. Sweet rolls. Dutch. Zoete Broodjes for company. 1 pint milk. 5 tablespoons shortening. 4 tablespoons sugar. 1 teaspoon salt. 1 cake yeast. 6 cups sifted flour. Melted butter. 1 cup brown sugar. Directions. Scald milk.

"I apologize," Berkeley said when he returned.

Krieger snapped the cookbook shut, ran his fingers over the faces of women depicted on the cover.

"Would it be better, Dr. Berkeley, if I came back another day?"

"Absolutely not, Corless. I appreciate your patience," and he picked a head of garlic from the strand that hung by a cord from a cabinet and began to separate and peel cloves on the counter as he went on. "You have children, Corless?"

"No, I don't."

"You're a wiser man than most."

"Seems like a heretical statement for a gerontologist."

"It does?"

"Of course."

"Maybe on the surface."

"Well look, no children no subjects for your study, the point goes moot, doesn't it?"

"No children, no longevity, no death, no gerontology, but if I were more interested in the personal aspects of the research I suppose I'd have managed by now to get myself into an academic setting, or some kind of lab in an applied-sciences division of a corporation, pharmaceuticals or whatnot. But I've never been able to abide committee decisions. The minor disagreement with my children just now, it's a perfect example. The process intrigues me more than the product, the pill, the poultice. You see?"

Berkeley had placed a handful of pungent aromatic cloves of garlic into a mortar and began crushing them under the porcelain pestle's head.

"But nevertheless, take my advice, whatever it is you might want with children, do it with other people's children, otherwise I think you'll discover they're a joyless enterprise, an illogical and wasteful, dreary piece of work. You raise them, try to create the semblance of a home around the idea—a borrowed idea, by the way, a received tenet, not something you could know *a priori*—and what happens inevitably is that they turn on you. You're either swept under the rug, or mollycoddled, blamed for a whole host of problems you never created. You become an instrument for their own mercenary tendencies."

"I'll bear it in mind for the future."

"Do," and Berkeley mixed the garlic juice with warm water and drank it. "Would you like something?" He held the empty glass up toward Krieger.

"No, I have my coffee."

"Alkaloid caffeine, behaves like theobromine, overstimulates the vascular system, nervous system, a rotten fuel. Balzac died of it."

"Well, we all have got to die of something."

"We seem to, but coffee's suicidal, you have a moral—almost—responsibility, liability not to consume it."

"To get back to what we were saying," as Krieger placed the saucer on top of the cup, "it wasn't that I minded your son's—what's his name again? Jonathan? yes well Jonathan, not that I minded his concern, just a touch combative is all, might have learned something if he'd asked a question or two, could have used the opportunity to orient himself about his father's discipline, but of course I wouldn't know, don't mean to sound presumptuous . . ."

"Presumptuous? No, you've been patient—I apologize for not wanting to proceed with matters last night but as you know you did go over my head, coming straight here, I thought we'd agreed to, well, no matter—"

"I'm sorry about that."

Krieger glanced at his watch; these preliminary formalities were taking too much time.

"In any case, the three of you slept well?"

"We did."

"Fine, well, I believe we have some business to conduct."

The milk had come to a soft boil; the kitchen was warm with a yeasty steam. Berkeley poured it through a sieve of cheesecloth into a bowl and brought it to the table. Fingers disquieted by his apprehension lifted the bowl uneasily to his lips and then set it down beside the thick manila envelope. He began to untie the string that was wound in a figure-eight under the two circular tabs. Krieger watched the fingers and saw how they tapered to the fine yellow nails that showed in their length many weeks' growth. "What's your real name, Corless?" he said, flatly.

Krieger hesitated, improvised, "Ingram."

"Ingram."

"Yes. Ingram, I think it means angel-raven, the first element deriving from *Ingil*, the second from French or German, *Ramn*."

"That's pretty good, Corless."

"Thank you. By the way, before we discuss the project, etcetera, I've brought you a present." Krieger lifted the small rectangular wooden box off the floor beside his chair and handed it across the table.

It was the kaleidoscope. With imperturbable skepticism, or so it was played out, his face drawn down into a docile enough frown, Berkeley removed it from the bed of dried leaves which had served as padding for the journey (and he noted how the leaves' strong scent lent the object some sense of antiquity, veritability—this Corless had seen to everything). He held it up to the light and turned the barrel. "Very lovely."

"I told you, didn't I?"

"Well." Berkeley put it back into its box. "That is to say the images are quite pretty, but it has as much value as a three-dollar bill if you still claim it was made, what, several hundred years ago."

His words went unheard. Lupi should have been down by now. Precious minutes were twisting past, each full of increasing contortion. The profound sense, here under the hollow ticking of the wall clock, that something had gone awry began to trouble his nerves. The silence startled him. Krieger looked up and said, "Whatever you say."

"I've done a bit of reading about the area you say It comes from, and I have to admit it is distinctly, well, plausible that this Spaniard through Mayan techniques which none of us in our pragmatic blindness would so much as bother to investigate might have discovered some combination of methods to prolong his life, well, if not as long as you claim, at least—who knows, and if the village is pristine . . . well . . ."

"Pristine?"

"Uninfiltrated by moderns."

"I assure you."

"Well it *was* pristine that is, was before, but we can't lose sight of the possible benefits that can be derived."

Krieger stood up. He heard voices, the voices of men, deep voices echoing from some large room nearby in the house.

"May I have a look through the photographs of the village?"

"What?"

"The photographs?"

He did not answer; his head was erect, chin pushed out forward. He noticed the unlatched window that gave out onto a fallow garden and mist of gray woods beyond. The voices were very formal in their address.

"I'll just have a look at the photographs and then we can go up and have a few words with . . . the photographs, yes here . . ."

Krieger casually took several steps in the direction of the window. "Fine," he said, forehead wrinkled.

"But these aren't Spanish-looking faces particularly, tell me, which of these in this group here . . . or . . ."

Berkeley glanced up just in time to see Krieger's hand abandon the crackling white paint of the sill, a mere jot of salmon—his hand—shredded into the pinch of chill wind that blew in by the open square and caused the pile of photographs to flutter beside the ring of milk.

4.

"HOME," Maddie read aloud in Hannah's dictionary. Hannah'd taught Maddie that when a word interested her she ought to look it up in the dictionary. They had such different levels of value, Hannah told her. If one got into your head it was good to look it up. This was the best way to find a passage for it back out again, and into the world. She seldom did, but this word in Maddie's head wouldn't leave her alone. On the train she thought the word, over and over, home home home home home, thought how she had but didn't have a home, Henry had but didn't really have a home, and Hannah who was both mother and father to the ranch that served as home to each of them, Hannah least of all had a home. That monstrosity up the river was no home now, and never had been. What was it? She had no idea. (And when Maddie had got back to New York and returned to the ranch she was so tired she could hardly focus. Henry kissed her. Hannah asked her how it went. Henry went down to work, down to feed the cattle. Hannah listened to what had happened, how Krieger had made his unexpected appearance, and then she left to walk and think. Krieger was here, nearby. Hannah knew that this wasn't over. She had to leave the loft, get out in the streets and think.) Couldn't you home in on something, too? yes, of course. This was wonderful.

Home (hōm), n. and the words under the sharp light of the lamp Maddie saw in succession, then guessed aloud at how they might have been pronounced in Norse or Lithuanian or Greek or whatever . . . *ham* and *heem* and *heimr* and *keimas* and *keitai* . . . abode and the world and a village and he lies down. Strange. All these coming up through people's mouths out of the single idea of home. It seemed impossible the richness of the word! It made her feel warm. Contented for the first time in days, the first time since Lupi arrived in the darkness of early Friday morning. She found a pencil and underlined the cross reference—See Cemetery—at the end of the etymology, flipped quickly back through the pages until she came to the word. She read through the entry; finger followed the small type across the page. What she found was that Cemetery referred her not only back to Home but also on to both City and to a word which she didn't understand, Incunabula.

"Incunabula," she said aloud.

She looked up Incunabula and there it was; it meant a cradle, a birth-place, an origin.

Strange, she thought, it was a full circle.

On the Norge the teapot whistled emphatically. Maddie turned off the gas. After pouring hot water through the strainer into a cup she put her overcoat on. She checked its pockets for loose bills, discovered a dollar crumpled into a limp ball. Leaving the door ajar she skipped down the flights of stairs and out to the doughnut shop past the corner. At the bakery the girl saw her come in and knew that she would want two glazed doughnuts and a plain cake. Sunday conversation centered on the weather. On the way back to the loft Maddie conceded to herself that this was something that stood, too, for home: all the tacit understandings between people. But routine wasn't enough, was it? She was back upstairs before the tea had finished steeping, and the routine itself began to conjure its own calm, just as she had hoped it would, the routine of the tea, its bouquet, the Norge, its solid circle of flame, the kettle, its intractable clownish whistle. She put the two glazed on a dish for Henry, arranged them just so, and everything was beyond human fouling; that recess from her paradise— hers, Hannah's, Henry's—during the night journey all but canceled now in the soft morning which omitted the vision of Berkeley house buried like a spider's nest under the low-clattering rails of the riverside train.

One's own dwelling place (she read), the house in which one lives, one's abode after death (she had never heard it used that way), abiding place of the affections, habitat, a place of refuge and rest, hence an asylum. She pulled the bulky dictionary up against her and hugged it.

The photograph on the front page of yesterday's paper, which she was about to slide into the bottom of the cat's litterbox, as the telephone rang, caught her attention for a moment as she crossed to answer. Several dozen Salvation Army Santa Clauses, their fake beards held in place on boozy, crooked faces by elastic bands, all waving mittens in the inky image, one (she noted) as fraudulent as the next, and surrounded by "At Relief Camp in Ethiopia Scenes of Horror . . . Three Koreans Killed as Soldiers Ex-change Shots in DMZ."

"Hello?" (how could children be expected to believe the nice old myths?).

"Hannah?"

"No, who is this."

"Hannah, I'm tired, it's late, it's early."

"Who is this?"

It was Krieger. "So you must be Madeleine Berkeley, just the person I wanted to talk to."

"Hannah's not here and I don't have anything to say to you."

She stared at the Santa Clauses. There was an unsteady whisper over the line, and an echo, as if he were calling from far away. In his voice there was feverishness, a kind of rattle. He had said her name once more, firmly. "Madeleine, I'm furious with you."

"What?" she said, absently reading now the article about how the elections in Honduras might have to be suspended next year so that the president could continue making great strides toward a real democracy— but, of course, she was only trying to block Krieger out. His voice grew sharper.

"You know it takes a hell of a lot to get me mad, what is this bullshit chicanery I mean you can appreciate with all the endless assholes to mix a metaphor all the endless assholes over the years I've dealt with whose brains you could measure out with cokespoons, but you my dear are a troublemaker of the first order and I don't like outsiders meddling with my business and it just may be all my goddamn good breeding but I always settle scores."

"Mr. Krieger, what are you talking about?" She pictured the face of the man who had stayed in the loft with them all those years ago, Hannah's lover—the same face she'd seen hours before in her father's house.

"All this does is make me a little angrier, Madeleine, so I advise you to cut the born-yesterday routine. I've been working on this for months, trying to bring a little happiness into the world, turn a couple dollars, etcetera etcetera, and you have to go a-cantering on your little do-gooder hobby-horse blow the whole kit and caboodle sky-high, I mean where do you get off lady?"

"What've you got Hannah involved with? why can't you leave all of us alone?"

Madeleine's pitch, almost a scream, revolted Krieger.

"Involved with? nothing very worse than the clandestine and unsanitary menagerie she's got going down there in Chelsea, as you well know, I mean of all people you, I mean I know more about you than you think—"

"So what is that supposed to mean?"

"Mean? means nothing except of course—"

"None of this is your business, I've got to go now, I'm sorry you're angry with me but in fact I have no idea what you're talking about, I've got to go."

"Except, well, naturally you recognize your Hannah there is breaking more Board of Health codes than there are hairs on a calf's ass, and all I have to do first thing tomorrow morning is give them a little jingle her whole fantasy world her little Oz-within-an-Oz comes crashing down around her ears, board the place up escort our friend to Bellevue where she'll be safe from society society'll be safe from her."

Madeleine waited.

"What I want to know is what you think you've accomplished here besides squander a lot of important people's time and energies with your goddamn meddling."

"What?"

"Right. What. What. Good word, what. Like what the fuck do *you* know about Central American politics or eugenics or business or guerrilla war or emigration laws or longevity? You're just another spoiled rich girl on a Hindoo holiday." Krieger was breathing hard, struggling to maintain the authority of his impetus. It was clear Madeleine didn't understand what he was talking about. Turning his face to the black and gold towers of the American Radiator Building, thus giving the two pedestrian policemen just then crossing Sixth Avenue a view of the back of his head (for, how far had things gone? how quickly would a bulletin dispatched out of the Hudson valley travel downstream ultimately to reach regular gumshoes like these?), he tried to figure out who'd duped him and what response to take, besides the obvious—to flee New York and environs as soon as possible. But it nagged him, so fresh the outrage of presenting his product, so close to having had payment in hand (the police passed behind, and his head accordingly revolved to face south toward the financial district), then—all hell. Not quite a quarter million dollars of pure heroin in Olid's vegetable-dyed *mochila*, planted there before they had caught the bus to Tegucigalpa, Krieger's own side venture to smuggle material into the country secreted on the person of a man who himself was secreted and entirely separate: this would, when discovered, no doubt make news. And Lupi, having bolted out of the house like a crazed jackal, stealing that car before they showed up, running off with the single piece of evidence that would hang him, thought Krieger now at the phone booth. By now he's probably treading water in the sewage waves out beyond Staten Island.

But Madeleine. Surely she hadn't hung up, because she was afraid—yet this meant nothing, her first few words assured him of that, which left only Hannah.

He caught his breath, "Maddie?"

Madeleine continued to say, "Why don't you go away just leave us alone you just go away . . ."

"Maddie stop it, listen, never mind, I believe you."

"Believe what? just go away, I wouldn't ever say anything, we wouldn't we just want to be left alone."

"Right, right. You know what? You're right. I hear you. I believe you. You may be right. I think you didn't have anything to do with this. But, look, it's kind of a mess, Madeleine, and I need to see Hannah."

"She's not here I said."

"I know, but I need, what I need is for you to let me in there at the ranch and I'll just wait around until she comes back, I won't get in anybody's way I'll have my chat with Hannah and then I'm gone, poof, but first I have to talk with her."

"I can't help you."

"Maddie?"

"Sorry, no."

"Let me just come down for a minute I'm right here not that many blocks away, where is this, I'm in Bryant Park, I'll come straight down there in a couple of minutes."

"Go away." But all she heard was a siren in the telephone. Krieger had dropped the receiver (thinking to himself, Just like Washington Square, Bryant Park, another goddamn potter's field—) and it swung by its aluminum-coiled cord in the dank, raw day. Maddie pictured the bluejays out in the trees crying *jaaeh*, then *queedle queedle*, slurring harsh first, flashing belligerent blue over the gray and crashing delicately about the branches, charlatanic and idiot, and when the siren finally passed away into all the other sounds carried over the phone she hung up and dialed Berkeley house with a memory that went back to her childhood and no real idea what Jonathan could do to help.

Her father answered and when she asked for Jonathan he mistook her for her sister.

"Alma, I'm so glad you called you know how they said they were going to come here and saw down my dead dogwood? Well, they showed up with their chainsaws and I walk up to the offices for half a minute come back and what do you think they'd gone and done but take down that big mulberry we put in there all those years back."

"Pa?"

"You got to stand me witness, Alma, and I know they'll listen to you. I'm going to sue."

"Pa?"

"People just ruin everything, don't they?"

Madeleine replaced the handset, slowly, deliberately, fingers quivering at her lips. She would go tell Henry she was taking a walk to find Hannah. She would take the service elevator in the back to avoid Krieger.

5.

WHY Washington Square struck these resonances in her and not Central Park or any other park on the island, Hannah didn't know. Full half the park was capped in unevocative pavement, the fountain rarely filled with water or its jets turned on to shoot spray above the circle, the grass was straw-yellow under the leafless trees, a pigeon on the pocked statuary head of Alexander Lyman Holley, his face in an alert stare under the deposit of a vermicular dash of green-yolked guano. It seemed anything but romantic, this place, the dingy scaling plane trees, the red brick toilets, the playground a halfway house for nocturnal derelicts. Unlike Central Park, so carefully laid out, here there were no fanciful outcroppings of granite, schist pushed to the surface; no bridle paths, evergreens, hills, hollows, gracious duckweed- and lilypad-blanketed pond, no shepherd's meadow. Nevertheless Hannah sat on a bench breathing deeply as if the air could come in and wash her blood of rum, here in steelman Holley's view in the late morning unusually abandoned except for those two of indeterminate gender and race at the chess table over in the southwest corner, gloved hands dropping the lever on the timeclock, and felt the mystery of the earth rise up from its caverns far, far down under the city's weight.

She was still mildly tipsy. Maybe it was the dead buried in their paupers' graves here, or the canals' underground susurration, the palavering trickle of ancient mineral-heavy water two, three, four hundred feet below her still ticktocking the same paleontologic language it echoed before the earliest Indian trail was cut or first divining rod was carried, witch-hazel fork jumping like a quick hare. There was a tiny quadrant nearby, fenced off and allowed to grow wild; a sign indicated the tract represented precolonial Manhattan, with sassafras, shrub evergreens, oak, maple, and thriving at their trunks a litter of bottles, plastic, paper, a dead, disintegrating pigeon: time capsule run amok.

But here—here.

They swelled, swirling through wire and rock in an upward vortex, these impossible rhythms, shifting up and up until they reached the soles of Hannah's feet and continued up through her body like a palpable fugue to make known to her that it was always the earth's intention to wrest itself back to its elemental condition; that the predisposition of all organisms and all organic matter was to come again and again to composition.

"Yes," she said.

Sunday, a good day she thought to listen to the earth as it communed with the bottoms of her feet. Then the water-voices broke their bonds and came over her with such a fury she jumped.

She stood on the green-slatted seat of the bench. Immediate silence followed. She shook her head, hands on her ears. On the back of the bench she sat, feet still safely propped on the seat. Her hands came together and thumbs twiddled quickly, and she found herself whistling, and the whistling reminded her of how, when she was a girl, back on the plains, she would whistle an aimless tune just like this when she didn't know what to think or what to do next, when she most missed mama Opal.

A chessplayer coughed: respectful dignified sound muffled in the palm of a wool glove whose fingers had been cut off. Hannah looked over to see it meant the same as toppling a king; concession, and composition. And the clicking of pawns and knights and rooks established that a new game would begin. She stepped down and set out briskly in the opposite direction, back to the arch. Behind, a body swung, ghost shimmering like Hannah's breath in the thick air, from the limb of a gallows-tree, hands tied behind, ankles bound, a strangulated grin made by the handkerchief gag tightly tied at the back of its neck.

Hannah left the park with her hands dug deep into her pockets. Looking up the avenue the whole gray heart of the city was like a photograph of ruins. A light wind stretched out from the north. The wind rushed at her face in vertiginous simplicity and clarity.

6.

THE terms of their arrangement, such as they were, had never been enforced by Hannah since they had never been challenged by Hammond. Nothing was put on paper since it was an agreement between Westerners, as each understood it and to differing degrees (Hammond more involved with his image of urban cowboy), and pride held it together. The principal item in their understanding was that the ranch be kept secret. Each felt that survival of the place depended upon a clandestine approach, Hannah less from a sense of its questionable legality than her own vision of how the city would reject them, as a body an artificial heart, were their presences at its center made known. There was something pure and fundamental about the ranch, and both Hammond and Hannah felt protective toward it, and even jealous of its anonymity.

Regarding each other, their feelings were mixed. Hannah, as they both saw it, had the alien strain of Eastener in her; both saw it and suspected it, even though it was Hannah who perpetrated this romantic subversion. And Hammond's sexual innuendos about Maddie and occasionally even Hannah herself (which she shrugged off) were inoffensive insofar as they were flippant. He was cocky by nature, Hannah concluded, and mouthing off was allowable so long as it remained an attitude, and did not progress toward an idea.

Hammond kept his keys in his hip pocket on a chain that was secured at his beltloop. They crunched as he walked, in syncopation with the stab-thud, stab-*thud* of his boots.

Hannah entrusted him with a set of keys to the green-and-silver graf-fitied metal door on the street. She never asked Hammond where he went during his off-hours—long periods of time, six, eight, ten hours at a stretch, staggered nights and days—although sometimes she wondered. There was Hammond's life at the ranch, circumscribed by the painted walls, the schedules for hosing down the floor, feeding the cattle, exercising them on the windmill walker, but out in the city what did he do to fill his time alone? The possibilities were myriad.

This morning Hammond's head was full of drowsy sweetness; he had awakened in a room that smelled of—? baby lotion? and heard his stomach issue a gentle soughing that sounded like a baby crying. His hand went down to gather it in, the palm to heat it there, for it also was full of the pain of his gastritis, but his fingers jogged up against another hand and as they did his mouth slackened and cakey eyes blinked and thoughts went sour.

He pushed himself up on one elbow and could smell the cheap (it might have been expensive, but smelled cheap) perfume. Across an enveloping cloud of mist he gazed, and framed in the window casing were the midrange floors of the Empire State Building, indifferent in deco elegance.

Naked under the sheets, he faced the bank of windows and his focus of attention moved inside to the soft cast of the bedroom. On the mauve carpet lay the party dress, effulgence of stiff lace and low satin top, blinding pink in the shadowless almost-winter light, and tissue-paper falsies, disconsolate articles, accusatory, disdainful and crinkled there beside the little Caucasian prayer rug. The smooth tanned thigh and calf thrown over his legs ruined his sense of well-being and when he drew the sheets back—flannel, with a dish-ran-away-with-the-spoon and cow-jumped-over-the-moon pattern—and saw her, thin as a boy, asleep in the bed, he sighed. It was not a pleasured sigh, but beleaguered. He blinked and looked out the window again, thinking that he had better start thinking. On her dressing table were photographs in standard-size chrome-plated frames. He saw her (what was her name again? Myra? Myrna? Mona?—that was it, yes, Mona, because he remembered in the depths of his drunk singing to her, Tell you Mona what I'm gonna do, gonna build a house next door to you) standing between what must have been her parents, father with an especially proud smile on his face under the CAT-tractor cap, the mother willowy, pretty though a bit poker-faced in her lily-print dress. The girl Mona (definitely not Myrna, for Myrna was aunt Wilma's manx cat) could not have been more than twelve or thirteen when the photograph was taken. There was a house behind them, also, off to the edge of a pond, a modest one-story with a ramshackle jetty added to the back porch and rowboat tied to a piling. A Labrador retriever leaped in front of the family, captured by the camera as a kind of benign blur, teeth predominant in the form of a triangle but making a smile. Mona's face was caught midlook, snapping out of a childish pout into a giggle at the dog's treachery.

Hammond could not smile. He knew the night cost more than it should have, and her loan to him of the two-fifty was not as kind a gesture as it might have seemed at the time since she ended up tooting the better part of it up her own nose, as his guest. "Conflicting signals"—maybe it was her way with people like Hammond (who for all his cocksureness still came across very hick)—had led him into thinking there might be some way out, a calm and equitable discussion of who owed whom what, and so he consoled himself, settled down to watch her dance through the explosions of purple strobes, her torso writhing gaily, hips revolving at such a wide and suggestive orbit they seemed detached from her body, hands flung into the smoky air of the club and fingers snapping to the steady bass of the speakers. He was lulled into having fun until the idea that she was a pro escort seized him. That, after all, had happened to him before. What was that other girl's name? . . . (hardly a *girl*, sexy Rita, who shed her wig at the critical moment to revert back into someone named Raoul). This idea passed. She was simply what she was, a bar-crawler. A nice girl, underneath the drugs, the drinks, the craze. He remembered nights, shade-drawn afternoons, mornings smelling of bacon and douche but couldn't recall a room as homey or comfortable as this. Homey and comfortable, and an unlikely reminder of the mobile home in Boulder where Hammond had grown up, his mother an elementary-school teacher, his father a day-laborer on a chicken farm. Hammond's room had been just off theirs. The long, narrow house, drafty in the winter, once had nearly toppled in the heavy wind that blew down the canyon and across the chautauqua field, but it had the same hominess as this apartment—the family portraits and combs and pillbox, the beveled mirror at the dressing table, mounds of costume jewelry on its glassy, laminated surface. There was a way out of this debt, he thought, and the new idea fell together.

One foot then both feet silently found the thick-piled carpet and Hammond was out of bed and climbing into his briefs, had his shirt on, stockings, his watch, neckerchief, turquoise ring, before pulling his blue jeans on, whose percussive jangle at the keyring woke her up, "Hey what're you think you're, oh my head . . ."

"What?" he said, belligerent yet accommodating. He did not pull up his zipper. Act of obeisance.

"What time is it? Hey, could you get me some aspirin, right in there in the bathroom."

Hammond brought her three aspirin and a glass of water.

"What'd you do last night hit me in the head with a building?"

"I," and he'd begun edging around the bed toward the door which led into her front room.

"You headed somewhere you think you're headed?" She pulled the sheets up around her neck, closed her eyes, and rubbed her temples. He was stuck, he felt, and watched her. She glanced up at him. The sun, reflecting off windows of the building across the street, was harsh on both their faces—they saw each other as older, more flawed, than imagined in the artificial light of the club where they met. Each understood it as a reflection on him-herself—not getting any younger in all these wars, or so ran the basic thought.

"Listen, I, about last night, I better go out and get you the money I owe you."

"I think I'd better come with you, just give me a minute, let this aspirin work."

He climbed over the bed, ran through the door into the small front room. "Wait a minute you sonnabitch. I knew it."

The fuzzy tabby screeched at Hammond's shoe having caught the tip of its tail. Yanking at his zipper, Hammond flung the door open and ran down the wallpapered hallway; behind him he could hear her shouting. He pushed the button with the down-arrow for the elevator but took the stairs three at a time down the emergency exit until he reached ground. Composing himself, he walked past the doorman and into the crowd along the avenue. A cab pulled hard to the curb. The driver took him the few blocks. Hammond reached down into his pocket and paid with change, then stepped out and breathed the morning air. Halfway up the fourth flight of stairs inside the building, and just as he was beginning to register the feeling of joy at having escaped his predicament, expediently, deftly, with the connoisseurship for timely action that only the superheroes in his comic books regularly displayed, he realized something was missing.

His heart sank (it felt, as if down to the basement). His face warmed and fingers involuntarily flexed up to his open mouth. He had forgotten his coat. It was back at Mona's apartment neatly hung in her front closet, his billfold in its breast pocket. As he trudged back downstairs he started inventing lavish scenarios whereby she might if not forgive him, at least take the money he would now have to ante (post facto) and let it ride for a bit of outlandishness.

Nothing very convincing had come to mind when he pulled the downstairs door open to find Mona standing there with a confident smile playing above the crimpled party dress she had worn the night before. "Hees yall jacket, Tex." The aspirin had brought back her wits and her accent, which she thickened for his benefit.

He didn't like the Tex. "Ahm, I yes," he managed, ready to go into a confession coaxed both by her smile and the way she simply handed him the tweed bundle as if nothing had happened.

"Yall have a good time last night there? yall think I's a pretty worthwhile piece of tail?"

"That's well not that's not quite the way I'd put it."

"Why'd yall go running out on me like that? If I remember right, you owe me some bread."

Hammond couldn't think. "I don't know, I mean I remembered I was late for this appointment, then I was going to go to the bank and get the money and come back to your place."

"Late for an appointment." She picked a cigarette from the pack, put it to her lips and waited for him to light it. He dug for the matches in his pocket.

"I had an appointment." He could feel the shame and silliness of the lie rise in sweat over his face; could she see?

Mona's lips puckered before the flame and the magenta flecks of yesterday's lip gloss transferred to the filter tip before she blew smoke into his face saying, "What country you think this is, Tex?"

"I don't understand what you're getting at."

"What I'm getting at is this isn't Russia you happen to be in America, pal."

"So what," he countered.

"So what this is what, land of equal opportunity, I've got the same constitutional rights as yall do, correct?"

"I don't understand what you're getting at."

"Look, amigo, can I come in for a minute? we got to talk a couple things over."

"No, I already told you I've got an important appointment."

Mona's face was a hard read, her clipped nose and chiseled features stationary as she remarked, "Listen now, you said yall had a fine time with me right? I loaned you the two-fifty and now I'd like to have it back, you see. This is how a gentleman behaves. Sad part is I kind of liked you. But obviously you're just a jerk."

"Yes, but I got to go now. Why don't we meet later? And anyway, you gave me one-fifty, not two-fifty."

"It was two-fifty, man."

"Okay, we'll talk about this a little later."

"When later?" she said, still cool, stylishly brandishing her cigarette, wearing the air of world-weariness which the party dress under daylight and the unbrushed blond hair highlighted matching pink at the temples only emphasized. She knew that he would close the door (he did) and heard the lock mechanism clack into place; that it came open again so quickly surprised her as she had not thought him to be so astute.

"All right, okay, where's my billfold?"

"It's safe," she said, "but short. Can I come in?"

Hammond stood, stolid, dumbfounded, said, "No you can't," but she inclined forward and took the step into the imperforate darkness of the foyer, the standpipe, the stairwell, and he withdrew into the prejudice of her rank perfume, the closeness of her skin and a recognition that she had displaced any authority—whether by a locked door or a fabrication—that he had held. The breach of trust here, unwritten law of Hannah and Hammond both that no one enter these precincts, opened wide, and he felt panicked she had gained entrance to the ranch itself. "Now hold your horses you can't be coming in here this is private property."

"My privates's property too, bub. You owe me. Only twenty bucks in yall's wallet there what kind of mental midget goes out has himself big old time on other people's money loans? You must be wet behind the ears, buckaroo, must have an ocean in behind there or something, I don't know about you."

"Listen. You can't come in here."

Mona had disappeared into the vault of blackness as Hammond, guided by the echo of footsteps, moved into the burgundy rendered by the exit lamp. "Vamoose on me expecting not to pay me back you ought to be ashamed, god what's that smell smells like pony shit."

Her shoeleather creaked exaggeratedly; then a palliative silence. The tip of her shoe had driven into something malleable—a pile of burlap bags, she could smell them there, seed-scent, oats, and a remembrance of her father's shanty stable, and her Shetland pony. Fermentation and excrement, a mix that summoned up a queer kind of anger, impatience in her; she kicked the mass of burlap, saying, "What in hell yall got going here, Tex?" just as Hammond jerked her by the elbow, and the orange point of ash pitched away and the air ducts augmented her high scream.

Mona retained enough self-confidence to cry, "Let go of me."

He released her, retreated several steps. Everything had fallen to redness. Her poise returned instantly. She rubbed her hollow cheek, defensive but unintimidated. "Three hundred."

Hammond laughed airlessly, "You said two-fifty."

"You ever heard of interest?"

"I'll give you a hundred and fifty dollars, that's what the amount was and that's what I owe, and besides you used up most of the stuff."

"What is this, some kind of auction? I want three hundred or I'm going to have to get some of my friends to look in on you."

"I don't have it."

"What's that stink in here anyways? Three hundred dollars. I got your wallet, I got friends, I don't like you, don't like this stink here neither," a weasel quality to her voice confounded him, angry now and his gastritis had him half doubled over in agony. Was she being heard upstairs?

"I don't have, I'll have to get it."

"So well?" and already Hammond had skipped ahead as he led her out, not noticing that she wedged, as a precaution against his running away, the empty cigarette pack between the latch and the bolt.

7.

HIS anger over the way it all had gone off center and deviated out of control did not, apparently, equal his fear of being captured. Given this, Krieger's choice to take the train back to New York might have been viewed as tempting fate were it not for the fact that those voices of provincial authority he had heard back in Berkeley's high-ceilinged foyer found nothing but three unmade beds in the guest suite. The burlier of the two officers did decide it was better at least temporarily to confiscate the parcel of unusual photographs (they seemed pornographic, all these National Geographic sort of nudes, but turned out not to be) Berkeley had spread out on the kitchen floor.

But beyond that there was little to be done except take notes toward filing a report. Even when they were called out again to investigate Jonathan's claim that a car had been stolen (he was to be vindicated some weeks later when it was discovered in West Virginia, where it had run out of gas on a stretch of rural road and been abandoned) no further credence to his first charge could as yet be provoked.

Precedents deliberately established by wise men are entitled to great weight, they are evidence of truth, but a solitary precedent which has never been reexamined cannot be conclusive . . . was a bit of intellectual trinketry, a tidbit dislodged by the quickening pace both of Krieger's progress from midtown down into Chelsea, and of his heart, which was unwontedly faint even given the pressure he suffered at finally having taken the biggest chance in his career and, for all intents and by every sign, come up with nothing. Hannah had been a waste of precious time, but what precedent did Krieger have to work with under the circumstances? Was that why the bombast of one of Henry Clay's speeches to the Senate was regurgitated at this unlikely moment? There was another fragment. It went, more or less: The arts of power and its minions are the same in all countries and in all ages; it marks its victim, denounces it and excites the public odium and the public hatred to conceal its own abuses and encroachments. That was one he had tried to teach the fat man, not only because he perversely reveled in the idea of a nineteenth-century American senator's words besmirching the tongue of a twentieth-century Nicaraguan reactionary, but also because he thought Obregón (the fat man's name, after all) might learn something having it by heart. However, inexplicably, the lush Latin sierras whisked it up in a forgetful funnel to deposit it—who knew where? anywhere—on the moon. Good old Henry Clay, pedant and bombast, what for the love of Lucy would *he* have done, Krieger contemplated, and even as he did realized none of this was taking any of the pressure of failure off him, nor was it useful in imagining what he might do next. Without question he knew he had to find Hannah, lay the blame on her for the unhappy appearance of detectives and immigration officials up at Berkeley house, and then study her reaction. Krieger knew craftiness was not one of Hannah's long suits and that no matter what she said by response to the question, Krieger would have his answer. What nagged him was his suspicion that, just like Maddie, Hannah had no part in the bust.

"All I know is," he rehearsed as he rounded the corner, "that Nembies wasn't *my* idea . . . I mean I don't take drugs I have a record so clean it's Martinized—Nembutal, hell—you know like those paper rings they put on the toilet seat in some of your finer hotels let you know nobody's gonorrheal ass . . . whose? whose what? whose idea? oh, well sir, let me tell you there are at minimum a couple of senators, ambassador or two and a latrine-full of businessmen going to be pretty fucking upset by the answer to that question . . . see, it all started with Vanderbilt ran a ferry and carriage service across Nicaragua middle of the last century, the idea being to help get people to California for the gold rush? you know, cash in? Where'd they all come from? I don't know, same dumps as always Miami, Parma, Alexandria, you name it, and then how the board of directors of Vander-bilt's company with the Senate's compliance, good old U.S. Senate the same as ever, cigars, cigars, helped this character William Walker? this soldier-of-fortune Rambo type, helped him out he came in there with American troops invaded declared himself the new president of Nicaragua, ask a simple question, right?"

The monologue ceased abruptly at those two pale pink high heels and fragile ankles. Krieger raised his eyes as the strange couple passed him, frowns giving off every indication of domestic unrest, and when they had passed, he was sufficiently struck by something that he stopped, turned, watched them recede toward the avenue, the man bowlegged and looking like he'd lost his rodeo, she propulsing, sashaying, brightest color in the immediate area, and as they abandoned Krieger to the block she tossed her head to glimpse back at him, the pale man in a khaki suit, white shirt, loosened tie, rather elegant, mumbling to himself, face angelic but crazed.

Krieger was inclined to wink but it was too late; instead he looked up the side of the building, admired the fluted cast-iron pillars in the fake balconies along its fourth story—there were no fire escapes. He had done this some years ago, when he originally found out Hannah had come into some money, found out down the (as he'd termed it) octopine grapevine, and by process of elimination rediscovered the door that led to the two floors at the top of the building. Back then, how many years ago was it?, there was a small buzzer (mammiform, like the pendulous part of Columbus's globe) and Krieger had pushed it and after several minutes Hannah had appeared before him, happier than Krieger'd remembered her to be. That was when she'd first moved in, first begun converting skills used as a billboard painter (Deutsch had since gone out of business, subsumed under the revolution of printed paper rolls and glue) to her great—if, as Krieger concluded, "dippy"—murals. Times had changed. Hannah, visionary and (again Krieger:) "animal-husbandry counterrebel," had gotten herself in far over her head. Krieger stared at the blank bit of wall hung with frayed posters, fragments of smiles, blocks of color, and shreds of words, where the buzzer had been. Only the briefest remembrance of how soft she was, her skin, he allowed, before shaking it off, moving ahead. That would never happen again.

What he saw by the door handle was more than he might have wished for, given the way his fortunes had failed over the last hours: it was ajar, held ajar by a crushed cigarette pack, and he pressed the heavy door which gave way into a cloud of musty smoke. He coughed, and fumbled at the bank of light switches, flicking them up and down but, like the buzzer, they were disconnected. Eyes smarting, he could see the stairway and next moved toward it concentratedly, and noticed that smoldering odor, foul and stubborn, now mixed with an atmosphere of—by agency of his accelerated memory—his grandmother's nannyplum tea, and then as he ascended quiet as a cat burglar landing by landing, his fingers running along the time-smoothed metal of the handrail, what came to mind was the contradictory tangle of motives that clustered to bring him inside this building, where he didn't know his way around, and put him at real risk of being caught (just when he ought to be stowing out for Lisbon or Panama City)—and why? to ask Hannah questions he'd already divined answers for? or was it just the curiosity of seeing for himself the circus he'd used for leverage, blackmail, waystationing? Lupi might be up there, also, and if he was would be worth killing, Krieger reckoned, although he had no weapon and was not by nature inclined to kill.

The smell was thicker on the top floor. Urea; oats; dung threaded with hay. Krieger moved with great caution, saw no one. The dog's bark broke a simulacrum of peace. Krieger spread himself against the nearest wall. Two more yelps, silence. He considered this for a moment, concluded it was not a watchdog as its bark was too self-pleased and soprano, then skipped quickly to the double doors behind which the sound had come and closed his fingers around the handle.

By now he had heard them, the other noises, disturbed by the dog into deep-pitched lowing like an electrical transformer shorting out, or the glissando of the lowest notes on a tuba. "Semper Fidelis" and "Stars and Stripes Forever": with the last vestiges of these barbaric melodies playing through his head, doubling, redoubling, Krieger crossed the border into another desolate, but madly colorful, country. Raucous wilderness annexed onto his own and it stretched out, its stench so pronounced his forearm came up to cover his nose as he stared across the length of the ceiling, thousands of square feet of flat clouds, still flocks of birds and the multitude of tracklights, shades varied as those down the barrel of Olid's kaleidoscope.

"Hey mister," Henry emerged from the shed at Krieger's left. Krieger hadn't noticed him.

"Well, hello there."

"You're not supposed to be in here who're you?"

"Department of Health, Animal Rights Division."

Henry said, suspiciously, thinking that he had seen this face somewhere before, although he could not place it, "I'm just a hand."

"Hand . . . fine, well now, can you tell me where I can find let me think" (tapping thumb to the bridge of his nose) "—Ms. Burden, yes a Ms. Hannah Burden?"

"She ain't with you?"

"No, no."

"Then how'd you get in here?"

"I was let in, downstairs, it's all prearranged you see, I'm scheduled to have a meeting with Ms. Burden, need to find her right away, you see, something about farming restrictions, that sort of thing, entrepreneurial-legislative, nothing of course for you to be concerned about."

"Well you might find her out in the bunkhouse."

"The bunkhouse, and where would that be?"

Both doors to the corrugated-tin-sided bunker on the roof were locked. Krieger, having left Henry in the urine-sweet loft, first knocked lightly and then, raising no response, attempted to kick them in. The broadening breeze rumpled his hair and cut erratic through his clothes; in the midst of his wild exit from Berkeley house he had been forced to abandon everything but the freshly pressed suit he had worn down to breakfast in expectation of having a relatively formal conference with his customer, who Krieger presumed would address him with the touch of Old World manners Corless had come to enjoy.

It looked and smelled as if it was going to snow. Few, few shall part where many meet, the snow shall be their winding sheet, and every turf beneath their feet shall be a soldier's sepulcher.

"Hey mister whatsername?" Krieger turned to see Henry had followed him outside, and the double-barreled shotgun upraised comfortably in Henry's arms with an aim directed imperceptibly above Krieger's head defied the cool with which Krieger said:

"Yes? and may I ask what the fucking firearm is all about, bub? I assume you have a permit because if you don't your ass's going to be in a sling."

Henry's stare did not vacillate. "It's Sunday," he said.

"So what," and Krieger was walking obliquely toward him.

"You say you're with the Board of Health what're you doing work on a Sunday for, sounds pretty fishy to me, and anyways what you kicking the door for?"

Krieger passed him, teeth clenched irate and eyes narrowed into a look of painful insult, flouting Henry's weapon and his questions. If there were more time Krieger knew that he would be tempted to accompany the man back into the cattle loft where, by alternately fulminating and reasoning with him, accenting the whole with non sequiturs and quotations, he might learn some useful information for the future. However, he knew the axis itself was turning dangerously and it was time to vanish. "These sons of bitches first they evade their taxes, I mean are you people incorporated here? and if not you have any concept what kind of unincorporated business tax must be owed, operation this size, I can't begin to guess, five-six figures, you'll be hearing . . ." as Krieger's arms flailed where he hurried for the stairwell only fractionally worried a blast might at that moment erupt to spray his back with a pool of pellets.

"Stop, you."

"You'll be hearing from me. I don't like the looks of this place."

"I said stop."

"I'll be back."

An orange flicker chewed at the air. A hot roar centered a cloud. The fire was still a tight bundle of flame surrounding the cigarette smoldering there in the burlap, lurching playfully off its surface. On the wall there was a poster. He'd never noticed it before. *L'eau qui chante et qui danse*. The water that sings and dances. A man and a woman were seated at a small round table, a bottle of mineral water between them—the poster was old, older perhaps than Krieger himself. Already the smoke from the fire had begun to darken the paper. Sing and dance, he thought; sing and dance away.

And as Krieger reached into the little bonfire at the bottom of the stairs, coughing in the heavy smoke, and began to fling the burning burlap sacks about, mindless as a child hypnotized, fascinated, delighted by the spreading fire, he could think of no appropriate quote from that massive stock so long ago memorized out of Bartlett's. When he saw that it had built into a formidable blaze as a result of his work he fell out into the street making sure that the door was securely drawn closed in its jamb.

8.

FIRE speaks jargons all its own, but it is not selfish with its tongues. Like a master linguist it converses easily with whatever or whomever it happens to encounter along the way, always speaking the dialects of territories through which it travels. Like some irrepressible gossip it is not to be snubbed or spurned, deaf and blind as it is to the subtlest condescension, to whom jibes and jeers mean nothing when weighed against the thrill of moving among the company of others. Like an epicurean aesthete it runs its fingers appreciatively over the surfaces of everything it admires. Sometimes patient, sometimes not, it becomes a part of its environment with the alacrity of a quick-change artist; wondrous pantomime it plays oak for oak, glass for glass, flesh for flesh, before insisting the game be played in reverse so that flesh, glass, and oak try to mimic flame. Prickly to the touch, and sinuous, let it be said it has its vicious side. But it is never disloyal to the elements with which it communicates: with the dense it is persistent, with sluggards slow, and with the volatile explosive.

The metaphor itself was beguiled then. Soon enough, none of the individual voices in the corridors and rooms on the lower floors could be picked out and separated for translation. Instead, what could be heard, if there had been anyone there to listen (there was no one), was the overriding accent of fire itself. This was to be so efficient a manifestation of the thoughts of the building that no matter how many different notes were struck or topics offered, the whole would not degenerate into quibbling but emerge into the declaration of a unified theme. And though, of course, all of the inanimate constituents involved in the growing document could not "know" the meaning of their labor and sacrifice, there was, as there is always in the heart of any fire, a sense in the singularity of direction, as it leapt up farther and farther from earth only in order to drag everything back down.

This is what was happening.

The burlap feedsacks which Hammond had neglected over the past few days to put out in the garbage burned hot and pure. Whiskers of flame caught along the thick paint on the walls, chawed through the molded tin ceiling to get at the buttresswork and supports. They moved vertically up the staircase and by airshafts, and horizontally through struts, doors, drywall. Upon hitting one of the gaslines on the second story, the speed and ambition of the fire were increased. The line burned out in an explosion which rumbled through the girders like a drowned vesper bell. A grand old furnace was sent into splinters and with it glass in doors throughout the central section of the structure blew. Still, because the course along which the flames fed was toward the core of the building, this salvo did not shatter the windows facing the streets. In stale offices it grew stiffer, working through file cabinets, across the tops of desks, melting a plastic pencil sharpener, blackening memos, eating a wall calendar, cracking into a closet to reduce an umbrella to ash. It brawled and broiled, mad and constant. Full of its own strength it began to breach the ceilings that stretched out between it and the sky.

Henry heard nothing and as yet neither smelled nor saw the smoke which ran like dye into vents and cracks.

But the conflagration could not keep itself a secret for many minutes more, and when a section of floor fell through under the weight of a row of linotype machines, the animals upstairs started together in a jittery run then abruptly halted, each with its head cocked sideways on a massive neck. Henry set down the shotgun, which he had busied himself cleaning to pass time after Krieger had left. When he pushed open the double doors he encountered a wall of noxious brown; the heat rose and after he closed the doors he realized his hands were scalded.

"Maddie?"

He had seen a fire once before, a barracks gutted in high wind one Texas evening. Brigade lines made up of all the young enlisted men, buckets slopping water onto the wet hollow, the sergeant's face lit up like a pomegranate under the harvest moon. Two men died trapped in there before pumpers arrived to soak the glow of cinders and metal ribs of the quarters.

"Maddie?"

The freight elevator on the west wall was either jammed or had fallen to the bottom of the shaft. Sensing which direction would lead them away from incipient danger the cattle had skittered heavily to the far side of the pasture, east, and as they did the lights went out. Under miasmal diffusion let down in shafts from the central skylight, Henry jogged, coughing with fright, the length of the loft to the service elevator. A familiar sound followed his turning the key and pressing the button—a series of clicks and the hum of cables. These noises came as such relief: not all the electricity in the building had been blown out yet. Somewhere far below, he heard the first sirens converge upon the block.

Weight capacity for the elevator was twenty-two hundred pounds, and since most of the animals weighed roughly half that amount it wasn't stress on the equipment that made Henry nervous. The cabin was square and small. "Come on, girl," Henry urged. She lunged shoulder first at the compartment then immediately reversed, panicked, bellowing loudly, and stamped her hooves on the floor of the elevator which wobbled under the strain of the weight and violence of the activity. Henry stroked her along the flat plane between her ears in an attempt to pacify her; the dog having some notion of what Henry wanted her to do helped marshal her into the cabin and Henry closed his eyes as the cage slid shut and after a repetition of the clicks the elevator started uncertainly down.

When they reached the first floor and emerged into a damp, chilly loading area, Henry began to wonder whether he had made some kind of mistake in judgment upstairs and had acted prematurely. Perhaps the fire had been confined to the loft corridor. Still, he knew, it would be better to move them down here and hope that no one would find them.

He left Leonie and went back up. The heat was intensifying and the air was thinner. Smoke rushed in thick bundles, multicolored, over the cattle's backs. The floor made a sound that was like gulping. Henry cupped his arm over his mouth and nose and walked forward toward the nearest animal, the lame calf. One by one he brought them all to safety. On the last trip, as the elevator cage clanged to and Henry pulled the lever, he witnessed a ripple roll like some soft wave presaging high tide, heard the plump enigmatic snap of superheated steel quip at the first jets of water that had begun to shower. Henry had never been in an earthquake but he imagined that the new roar which carried on its crest to this remote edge of the pasture must be something similar; it was as if he were under the wheels of a subway train, sparks cascading and railroad ties ringing, and presently the cabin seemed to break loose of its hectored cables, caught again and bobbed against the shaft's walls. Reverberations were heard throughout the length of the seemingly endless journey down, and the animal powerfully pushed forward when they reached the ground floor. Terrible tart smoke had found this corner of the building, too, and it was then Henry sensed what was inescapable—there was a paradox—inescapable fact he had no choice but to open the door onto the loading dock and let the animals make their own strange steps to safety and freedom. What would become of them, of him, there was no way to predict.

He flung the doors open and they cantered outside, moved down the inclined plane where they found themselves in an empty back lot. Around the corner from them men in bright yellow and blue waterproof suits moved across the asphalt strewn in hoses. Fourth and fifth alarms had already been sounded as the building's structure began to convolute under the diametrical influences of white heat and stone-cold water.

The cattle moved away from the growling gable and the dog loped along beside; Henry followed at a cautious distance, having no idea whether to bind his fate with theirs, wherever that might lead him, or give himself over to a meaner instinct that proposed he run as far and fast as he could in the opposite direction. As yet they had not been observed, but once they reached the end of this alley and turned left into the street this anonymity would be concluded. Tails switched, dignified gleaming bodies gently touched one another, and behind this family that clopped like a benevolent race come back out of time to visit the island that once was theirs, Henry lingered for another moment before marching out to the sidewalk, arms swinging at his sides, to join them where they were, there on the cobble-patched gutter, less frightened than he, and indifferent to the devastation left behind. That mask of confidence he set on his face meant in its own manner to preclude anyone's approaching him with a question like, Look here now, what is this supposed to mean? However, the attention of the crowd that had gathered deep into the adjacent streets focused high on the swordlike plumes of water that showered across the structure at two tons per minute from each bright nozzle held forth into the green-and-black air.

Krieger watched the fire with all the others, from a comfortable distance of a half a block. As with many phenomena he knew how this worked, what he witnessed here with his fellow spectators; there was still something—a dust-filmed pane on his retinas—that prevented him from feeling the impact of what he saw. It was a powerful deprivation, this distance that grew out, an empty form, between one Krieger in the body and the other Krieger out there slogging away, kicking and punching through life. He looked at the faces of the men and women in the crowd that began to gather and recognized in their profiles the horror and fascination, too, and he gazed up again at the palatial cloud that rolled away into the sky, opulent as blackberry jam, and he wanted to step out before all of them to make his rightful claim that what they were experiencing together was of his own making, something he had been obligated to create.

At nine hundred degrees a flame remains red, he could tell them. Twice this and fire burns to peach orange and pale yellow. Twenty-five hundred degrees and everything blanks out to white, not bone but the radiant white of a glass of milk held up in the sun. He took several steps forward, pulling at the sleeves of a few people in the crowd, to edge a little closer. He tried hard to believe he'd never been so alive as at that instant, though he couldn't take it into himself like a physical thing and couldn't feel it for the great flood of sensory excitement he knew it must somehow be down in the tissues of his own body. He rubbed his chest with his hand in a circular movement. He pulled on his slender nose, and chewed at his knuckle. Across his face was extended a tight smile and his eyes were dancing. Nevertheless, the Krieger up there of black smoke and fire, and the Krieger of plumes of water which misted and shot in funnels from the cherry-pickers, the Krieger of continuous sirens and distorted cries through megaphones, so prominent and effective, could not be reached by the Krieger who stood below, feeling himself a neglected element, not even a significant point of reference in the equation.

What was it, this empathy that swirled about him just out of reach? He could imagine the steel beams expanding, exposed girders faltering and twisting as their critical load strengths were passed, some buckling now where the walls still held, others pushing the walls away from the floors, the floors collapsing and marble stairs spawling like crystal under the torrents of water falling and flooding down toward the basement, swamped in a tide of ash and metal tines of coal and roar of steam. The cornice that had gotten red before coming loose to plummet seven stories all in a piece to the street presaged the belltower sinking into the roof just above that painted image of a woman's finger, that fragment of some long-lost advertisement, its polished nail still bright. With this—the cornice may or may not have caught someone down below, it was impossible to see over all the shoulders and heads—the collective mood delicately shifted from awe to fear, and the crowd drifted back on itself away from the growing sphere of fire.

Krieger was itching to talk, yet as he studied those around him his mood sank more. The girl standing next to him, holding forth against the retreat, skateboard under her arm, would have to do—they were all morons, anyway, he ascertained even while his own sense of power abruptly faded. "I started this, you know."

She stepped away from him, held the board against her chest.

"The fire," Krieger explained. "I started it."

She looked away, said nothing.

Perhaps she hadn't heard him. After all, it was noisy out here. He repeated what he'd said, and continued, rather louder, "No, I did in fact, really. There was a little fire already going in there about twenty, twenty-five minutes ago and I, there were these burlap sacks on fire and so I spread them around, gave them a chance to prove themselves."

Still no riposte.

"You know what else? See up there along the top couple of stories? There was a cattle ranch operating up there, half a dozen head."

Bullshit, Krieger said to himself, on her behalf.

"I mean it," aloud in his own voice.

Like you mean a regular cow ranch like?—inventing the voice of the young girl in his head.

"Right," as Krieger.

You mean with like those mechanical kind of bulls that chick in the Travolta picture, what one was it, where the chick like in the tight jeans rides like she's getting screwed on the mechanical bull, that brown-haired chick—

"No, no you ever seen *Bonanza*?"

Huh?

"Sure, Little Joe, Big Joe, Hoss, all that crap? Just like that, painted prairie, seasonal crop, silo, the whole shmear."

"What?" the girl said for herself, dazed by the strange performance. Krieger was startled she'd spoken. "Why not?"

The imagined girl: Yeah well, why not, okay. But why'd you want to go burn it down for?

"Hey, honey, why not? right?"

The girl coughed at the rubber smell and looked up at the thick columns of smoke plummeting upward, forming a vast curtain over the streets. The street lights radiated down through the smoke, and produced heavy cones, pink as if it were nightfall. Aside from sirens in the distance, it was very quiet here. The traffic must have been diverted away from the area for blocks around. Cherrypickers carried men in twos up into the curtain, and a tearing sound was made by the water as it hit the stone and bricks. She could also hear, she was sure, the sound of water boiling.

Krieger breathed in. The air was perceptibly warmer. "It's beautiful though isn't it?" and his eyes moved up the building which now had begun to collapse in stages under the weight of the water upon the failing architecture. "You kids everybody's gotten used to thinking fire's just destructive, but the old cultures thought it had all kinds of different powers, put it to use, forest management, hell they were smart, fire was the souls of their ancestors, I mean they thought fire lived in wood and other things, your boyfriend's underpants for example, and that it could be sprung to life by friction see? like making the beast with two backs, you've done that before haven't you?"

"What beast?"

"Shakespeare."

"I better go."

"Making the goddamn beast with two goddamn backs! Use your head, I mean fucking, fucking and you know what fucking is? all fucking is is friction, you ever heard of the French philosopher Diderot defined love as an emotion caused by the rubbing together of two epidermises, but as I was saying these Herero, South African tribe, these Herero believed both they and their cattle came from fire, dig this at Mostar in Herzogovina? the bride sits her little black maiden pud down on a bag of fruit and here she is and she starts to stoke at the fire in the hearth, one two three times, and this is the only way she'll conceive, same with the Hindus they pray to fire-gods, same with your Aryans, your Slavs, here you have the bride all hot and bothered ready to get down to it and so she pokes the fire with a stick and as many sparks that fly up so many cattle and male offspring'll come, it's true all over so this is like a creative process here, a beautiful act, like fucking it's like I fucked this building and the fire there it's like an orgasm."

Krieger didn't like what he saw then in the retreating, wide-open eyes that searched his face. He was gazing, he thought, into the eyes of some new species that had dragged itself up out of the murk and shaken off its tail, left it there on the sandy shore and evolved without pause into its civilized stage as apocalyptic pioneer. He found this neither pitiable nor as comical as his temperament usually dictated it to be.

"You're all a bunch of fucking morons," he said, simply enough, and turned his back on the vision of the fire and the girl.

He kept a rigid steady pace through the crowd, looking back only once to see the girl talking to a policeman, pointing in his direction. At this Krieger's heart approvingly lit up.

9.

IT was a procession or a parade, Hannah thought, but here Sunday had come and she had been so entrapped by the necessities—for this is how she would view these days: how the devil else?—necessities of survival, that the holiday being celebrated had slipped her mind. There was Thursday, of course; Thanksgiving. She felt a little remorse at how that festivity had gone uncelebrated this year—Thanksgiving which, despite all, had always been Hannah's favorite day of the year what with its cranberry sauce, its goose and its rice pudding, the mincemeat and squash pies mama Opal laid out and which, when Hannah could stand chin high to the burners of the stove, she taught her daughter to prepare with the same special, secret enthusiasm she herself had. Hannah shook her head at the overcast sky. Neither she nor mama Opal ever had much to be thankful for. All the mirth with which those pies were made had come unquestioned, as if it were entrusted to the calendar's logic, like a rationale wryly held there in the date itself lavished every year in praise and sauces. And how accustomed it had become to Hannah's homage each November, Hannah who, even after mama Opal had disappeared, carried on as its shy new celebrant. The evening of Thanksgiving 1956 had been the only time when uncle LeRoy had lit a fire of old pine logs in the dining-room hearth and helped Hannah wash dishes after supper, even tucked her in bed, awkward and tender and as confused as a sparrow which accidentally had flown in through an open window. That was a night their edges seemed to overlap. Such a moment seldom came again.

Then, what was this? she thought. It couldn't really have been much of a parade, for there were only a few people that lined the fence at the corner of Fifth Avenue and 11th Street. The church behind was massive and dignified.

Hannah stood up on tiptoes to see what the laughter could be about. No, this couldn't have anything to do with Thanksgiving—that was days ago, although she had to admit it seemed like so much longer, the pleasing vision of Henry, happy, across the table reading from one of LeRoy's books. What can you say of macaroni, of spaghetti? what are "raised biscuits" and what are "beaten biscuits"? what should be done with bread when it is taken from the oven? what injurious gases are developed in foods by bad cooking? why is New Zealand preferable to the common spinach ("because it is so far away," said Maddie)—and as he read she laughed, as did Hammond who grabbed away the book and read, "What are the bottoms and the choke of the globe artichoke" (which sounded metaphysical)—and then came Hannah's own turn at it; she turned at random to a page to read aloud, "In rural regions, both in the United States and in Europe, farmers sometimes cooperate in the maintenance of slaughterhouses and storehouses, thus making it easier to obtain fresh meat in hot weather. In a 'meat club' in this country, which was said to be successful, the members took turns in providing animals (lambs or heifers) for the slaughtering which was done in a special shed on three Saturdays of each month."

"Hannah, stop," Maddie said.

But she hadn't heard, and continued, "The meat was distributed among the members according to a system previously agreed on, the different cuts going to the different members in rotation. A fixed price per pound was agreed—"

"Hannah."

"—on at the beginning of the season and at the end of the season accounts were balanced according to the weight of the animals provided by and of the cuts—"

"Hannah, please."

"—no, cuts supplied to each member. Such a plan seems capable of extension to meet (meat!) a variety of conditions, particu—"

Someone whistled. Someone else pushed his way through the group of people which had gathered, shaking his head. Someone—it was a boy in a Sunday suit, but Hannah could only see him from his elbows up—made whoops of pleasure and bobbed up and down weightless and excited. Uptown there were the sounds of sirens and when Hannah looked up at the stately Gothic central tower of the First Presbyterian at 11th Street she saw a cloud that rose not so many blocks behind it, lifting quantities of blackness up into the sky to form a swirling pool almost precisely the shape of a child's spinning top. It was very beautiful, in fact, she thought.

More immediate to Hannah's eye were her cattle here in the grassy courtyard of the church, grazing indifferently at the long grass beside the crab apple trees and the brownstone walls embellished with tracery of quatrefoils. Henry sat on the steps of the church, behind the cast-iron fence. Madeleine could be seen standing in the doorway talking to a gentleman who seemed thoroughly confused by whatever it was she was telling him. The cattle seemed so small in their new surroundings and their delicate fawn coats and faces. The boy in the Sunday suit whose legs spread around the ribs of one of the cattle tired quickly of his game but, unwilling to climb down, lay his head against the back of the animal's silky neck. Mounted police entered the scene from the square below.

Parts of the building that hadn't trailed up into the air, or been carried by the overflow of water down into the flooded gutters and thence between the grates of corner drains, were taken away by the city, for the structure—a grand old pile the records showed to have been designed by De Lemos & Cordes so long ago—was, while not completely consumed, adequately weakened as to be condemned on site by the first inspectors who arrived the next afternoon to begin picking through the char. It hissed well into the night, well after many of the auxiliary crews pulled out. Because of the peculiar nature of the fire, which had progressed so extensively within the stories of the warehouse before burning its way outward quite literally in search of air, there was little chance of salvaging the building itself. Hardly a chaotic fire, it seemed to those who had fought it, and to those who began the work of sorting out how it might have started, remarkably systematic, almost—tidy. For one, as a result of the heart of the structure having burned out first, creating a white-hot empty center, almost like a vacuum, once the flames reached the outer walls and roof, the constituent facing, the cast-bronze fluted Cabaret pillars, brickwork, molding, cornices, and all the rest obligingly collapsed, gable by gable, inward on itself and not out into the streets. What was left, then, was a rectangular mass over which stood individual upright supports and shafts, stationed like columns of giant soldiers ordered to stand stationary guard over the devastation.

Guards were not needed. There was no looting because nothing worth stealing survived. Within days they were relieved of their dubious duty as a wrecking crew moved in to topple the walls and bulldoze the debris into heaps stacked high in dumpsters so they could then be taken away. The rubble of uncle LeRoy's possessions would eventually end up half in a landfill on Fountain Avenue in Brooklyn and half on the deck of a garbage barge to be taken some miles out to sea ahead of a churning, burly tugboat, and dumped into the water to mingle with the remains of Henry Hudson and his son, John.

For twenty-four hours it was a *cause célèbre*, although the sudden appearance of half a dozen head of Guernseys grazing the lawn of a church at the bottom of Fifth Avenue and the destruction by fire of a huge warehouse in Chelsea could in no responsible way be connected. As if they had materialized under the crab apple trees of the lawn the animals appeared to have no owner, and no one stepped forward to take possession of them aside from the man who seemed somewhat befuddled at all the questions that were asked of him, the man in overalls and boots who according to the police report was first to notice them and with the help of his wife pastored them safely off the street and into the fenced parvis.

Insofar as the owner or owners of the said building were not immediately identified (as some surmised, because the city was unable to trace ownership beyond a rural route box in, of all places, Nebraska—unable, that is, within the first day or two in which these events were purported to be news) no one, likewise, came forward to talk about the (as one paper put it) "fiery conflagration."

After the cinders flamed out into the rotation of what was considered news and what history, a curious situation arose in which some authorities began to construe a connection between the fire and the orphaned animals. At any rate, the woman who had initially offered to take care of them also turned out to be the owner of the building. Her interest in the matter seemed puzzlingly intense. She visited them daily where they were temporarily stalled in the police stables on the Lower West Side. She taped sprigs of mullein foxglove on the walls, claiming it was necessary to prevent evil spirits from entering the compound. She brought flowers which had been woven into daisy chains that could be hung around their necks.

Jonathan recognized neither his sister nor Hannah in the photo in the newspaper, but Henry was unmistakable. He studied the image for many minutes, alone in the library. Madeleine's back was turned to the camera, to the left of the group, her hair blown from behind to obscure her profile. As he looked at the outline a remembrance of that day in the barbershop emerged, and Madeleine herself emerged, and Jonathan knew immediately what to do. It was easy to trace them down to where they were staying in two small rooms in a run-down hotel near the Port Authority.

The next morning he went up into the offices, calmly entered from the sewing room through the pink door, pulled back all the curtains, and opened up the cages one by one, freeing the mice to make their own way, circumspect and virginal, into the recesses of a less discrete world than the one they were used to. He would explain later his action to Owen. He announced downstairs that he was taking the first train down to New York. As he was leaving, Owen asked him why he was going to New York.

"To bring Maddie home."

His father had merely hummed, distracted.

"And Henry too," Jonathan added.

"I see."

The desk clerk at the hotel said they were at the police stables. He made his statement with a wry smile and a cat's cradle of wrinkles working at the corners of his eyes and along his white cheeks. Jonathan decided not to wait for them to return. He took a subway downtown.

"Them they left here about half an hour ago," he was told at the precinct station. He took a cab back up Sixth. There was one more place to look.

The circular lamppost plaques which reproduced the coats of arms of the republics of Nicaragua and Honduras swayed gently, buffeted by the wind that had swirled at the very top of the avenue around the bronze body of José Martí's statuary steed, before picking its way along the glass walls of the buildings on the journey here. Having located a fine spot where it could play with delicate, filmy leaves of ash and bits of blackened debris in this large lot where only yesterday it had encountered solid rock, the breeze lingered for a time at the site of the fire, and caused the woman who was there in the middle of it, picking among the rubble, looking in vain for the familiar binding of her Lucretius, to turn up the collar of her coat. Jonathan stepped out into the mist which had tapered down from the sky and was reflected there in the oil-stained pools of water which stood far out from the gutters into the street. Henry and Madeleine were nowhere to be seen, but he approached the woman whose name he knew was Hannah.

"This is—what happened here is terrible," he said, scoffing at himself at the fumbled words.

She knew, of course, that even if she found it—which she wouldn't, not in this mess—it would be ruined. And if she discovered it, miraculously saved, what would that mean? Maybe it, too, was better left to pass.

"They're saying this was tied up somehow with those people who found the cows at that church, but I don't see how they're making any connection the one with the other, do you?"

She began to walk away.

"Hannah?" and he ran up beside her.

"How do you know my name."

"You are Hannah, aren't you?"

She continued walking. "What do you want?"

"Hannah, I'm Madeleine's brother."

"Your name is Jonathan?"

"That's right."

Still, she walked, and he followed her, resolute; Madeleine would come home now, and Henry, and this Hannah, too. He would see them soon, for Hannah was leading them west toward the Hudson, back toward where the hotel was, and this was what he knew he could say once he reached them, and could speak. Sure of this, he quickened his pace until he was walking beside her. She looked at him, and he smiled. His smile was not returned, but Hannah brushed her hair away from her face, and said, "That land back there, that's mine, that land."

"You mean where the fire was?"

"That's my land. I own it."

"I'm sorry."

"There's nothing to be sorry about," she said.

"Madeleine and Henry are all right?"

"It's my land, and you know what I'm going to do with it?"

"What."

"Nothing."

"What do you mean?"

"Once all the rubble's cleared I'm going to leave it alone, throw some seeds in, let it do whatever it wants to do."

"It won't do much," said Jonathan.

"Fine."

"What?"

"Henry and Madeleine, they're fine," she said, while a flock of pigeons started from the street which had been worn down to its cobble, circled round, rose, came directly over them, wings clapping like little dry sticks, and threw an imperceptible shadow which retreated in an instant before the whiteness of overcast returned.

Wrynn told the doorman to send her up. He looked at himself in the hall mirror. The gilt frame on the mirror was flaking. He'd have to get it refinished. After some hesitation he saw his face. Not that awful, really. He had kept himself up. He swam every day, fifty laps, used his rowing machine. Hannah would not be shocked. In the guest bath, quickly, he daubed some powder over the forehead, and beneath the sideburns. The chime rang and he went to the door composing on his face a look of nonchalance—nonchalance impossible to maintain. He folded her fondly into his arms. They were friends.

"Sweet Hannah," he said and realized he'd only embraced her once before—and wasn't altogether certain why he was holding her now, though it seemed like family.

Hannah was talking and Franz didn't know what she was talking about, had heard nothing about a fire in Chelsea, but when he began to ask questions—had she seen Peter? there was no Peter? had she ever found Nicky? why didn't Nicky take it on himself to find her?—she stopped him. "You remember that once we talked about doing the James Riding journey?"

"The who?"

"Baja, the trip down to Baja."

"Oh, sure," but it was obvious he couldn't recall.

"Hey, Franzy, have you got a boyfriend right now?"

"You're talking too fast."

"Well, do you?"

"Sure."

"What's his name?"

Franz told her his name.

"Has he ever been to Baja?"

Franz doubted it.

"Well, why don't the three of us go?"

Why didn't they go? all right, they would go. Then what.

"Where's Baja?"

Franz, Baja—Hannah looked him in the eyes. Kansas. Why did she think Kansas? she meant Nebraska. Franz had asked once, What is Nebraska, What is Kansas, or where, hadn't he? Franzy, eyes young surrounded by the skin and the powder he used to cover it, the lotion; the head framed in part by the watercolor of wrens on the wall behind. She couldn't remember what kind of wrens, rock wren, winter wren, house wren—

Hey—had he ever taken the day-trip boat up the Hudson, the milky brown dirty clean old Hudson?—not so very beautiful this time of year, all the leaves fallen and the almanac promised snow coming but she knew some people up there she wanted him to meet, what harm could there be in them trying that?

"No harm," he said.

"And then we'll buy some seeds, some little saplings, but strong ones, some oaks, they're strong, chestnut, gingkos, lots of saplings, and plant them down where the building was, and then this spring maybe we will find him."

"Find?"

Whoever else, the patron saint of pawnbrokers.

10.

TWO places on earth that are safe, two inviolate havens, thought Krieger. Churches and bars. He felt at home in neither, but the bar-priest was generally the more discreet individual, stools were more comfortable than tight-angled pews, the whole architecture of taverns scaled more to human endeavor than any cathedral's. Besides, neon burned its welcome colors day and night, but the rose window? Forget it.

Scotch, sacramental and chilled by ice, arrived on the paper coaster although Krieger did not want scotch (where was the goddamn haggis, then?)—it was a key to further presentation here, as he saw it, where the other men gathered to view the girl crouched on the small stage (for this bar provided services beyond meditation and simple communion), her pasties trailing mirrored surfaces (was this legal on a Sunday?) and the black beads visible between her thighs where the spangled string jumped between buttocks. He may have watched the show with the others but it was as if it were played out—late disco (very post-Hustle), flesh pounding itself—in the exceedingly distant mouth of a tunnel. It was not like a dream, since he knew he could walk along the cave walls and emerge from the tunnel, come back out as it were into the sun. Plato's cave; which happened also to be the name of the place.

Instead, he closed himself inside the telephone booth at the end of the bar and placed one call which got him aboard the flight he decided he would have to take, and a second call which afforded him only the briefest instant of immeasurable pleasure—of a kind so close to torment it had to exist on some wretched border in between—when he heard the voice of Franz Wrynn repeatedly asking, "Who is this? who is this?" before he was disconnected.

Later, while the jet taxied through the crisscross system of runways at Kennedy to reach the end of a line awaiting clearance, he breathed into his sleeve and saw a group of herring gulls out beyond the tarmac huddled in active disarray about the remains of—something; vile, no doubt, thought Kreiger, as he looked at the rosy round insignias on their beaks, marked as Cain, but who knew why? And as they bounded in and out, flashing, beaks pecking at the thing fallen which he not only could not see but would not allow any symbolic meaning to be attached to—and his breathing into the sleeve, this was against his allergy to the fumes— . . . none of this had the least actual significance (he almost said it aloud) as the plane came around and began its movement down the runway and lifted off over the water.

The last of Krieger's quotes risen like flotsam from the chaos of his retentive mind was out of Camus's essay "The Minotaur, or the Stop in Oran": "It is impossible to know what stone is without coming to Oran. In that dustiest of cities, the pebble is king." Yet here substitute an unrecorded Mayanesque perched village for the tenth-century Moorish port in Algeria. Substitute, further, the obese and appalling figure of Krieger's former colleague, Obregón, for the pebble in Camus's construct, since there he stood in the flawless sun-warmed afternoon on the short balcony of the crude *palacio*, dressed up in the regalia of a shaman, headdress elaborately fashioned from the long iridescent tails of sacred quetzals, coarse woolen robes so tightly woven that a spear could not penetrate nor a poison-tipped arrow find its way through to his heart, his face painted with a white pigment. Krieger adjusted the focus of the binoculars in a seizure of disbelief.

As he steadied his hands and the glasses they held, blew breath from his lungs like a marksman, blinked and squinted once more through the binoculars at the sight he had beheld from this perch in the perfumy shedding cedar tree, the fat man was still there pantomiming some magical rite, some invocation of powers from who knew what kind of pantheon, what manner of pantheon, and all for the benefit of this muster of Indians that stood or crouched in a semicircle in the cool green thrown by the shade tree at the plaza's center.

The fat man now become a noble savage? a hermit crab that had scuttled sideways somehow into the shell of virgin village to present himself as successor to their own elder (and who knew, finally, just how old?) and metamorphosed out of a sense of self-preservation into a fake prince come to govern this tiniest world, a world so detached from the one that engulfed it that it might be called a fourth world, a fifth world, like a subterranean society or a colony out in space?

Behind him, hard-eyed and in need of a shave, stood his brother Carlos. Fatigues and beret. High-laced combat boots scuffed into a pearl-shell finish. No attempt to etherealize this, the nature of *his* presence there in the quiet yard. His shiny FAL automatic rifle he held confidently, barrel down. The placidity about him was only remarkable within the framework of incipient, or at least preparatory, violence, and such colorful shamming. Having scanned the rest of the village that was to be seen from this perch, Krieger concluded the fat man had moved in here with a relatively sizable entourage of family and supporters. The Indians seemed delighted at his histrionics. He went about his dance in spasms, tremors, and thrusts. He was as confident as he was grotesque. One adorned with such natural girth and fantastical bangles must surely be the emissary of a god if not a god himself; so Krieger reasoned on behalf of the charmed villagers.

With brilliant dignity the fat man took the African gray parrot—the very one which had repeated with such authentic, if unknowing, zeal Olid's quaint Latin—from a pouch in which he had held it concealed. Calmly he broke its neck before the silent audience. He shook it like a rattle. He put it back into the pouch, then washed his hands in the stone fountain. The dying god now dead. Carlos brought him a cup and he dipped it into the tainted water and drank. He passed the cup into the hands of the elderly Indian that sat on his heels beside the fountain and the Indian, seeing his role, drew water from it and also drank; shortly, all the villagers had participated in the ceremonious ingestion of the ancient. The power had now flowed into the person of Obregón.

Just how this fake shaman had betrayed Krieger was not clear. Krieger understood, as he watched the bizarre performance which continued below his point of vantage, what motives the other would have had to see him at least temporarily removed from the scene by the authorities—for one, this occupation was legitimately an act of war, far outside the bounds of law to be sure, but not much farther beyond those bounds than what anyone else was doing down here. This had become the fat man's private real estate development program, and as he lacked the means to piece together an army he was forced to create another framework for the passage of power. Dominion in his new sanctuary, what would it mean? Would he recall all of his family here to this desolate spot? And the villagers, whose contact had been confined to those visits from Sardavaal, how easily would they suffer their conversion into serfdom or slavery? That's what was bound to happen here, was it not? A question there was no need to answer was what Obregón had figured Krieger's importance might be to his project. Their relationship had always been loosely bound by the necessities of commerce, but while it was true the fat man had noted more than once that the two of them, historically, were opponents, Krieger took it all rather glibly.

"I'm a businessman," he had said once, "and as such I understand that, well, to be sure, until there's only one left standing, holding the whole damn wad in his hand—and I don't mean one corporation, one partnership or committee, or anything like that—I mean one man and nobody left to merge with or take over, that would be it, the whole history of it wrapped up, but until we've reached that point I know we're all opponents."

"You're very wise for someone out of the middle classes," the fat man chided and he had started for a door as he thought he ought better.

Krieger's smirk faded. "You're pretty smart for a . . ." *spic* was the word on his tongue at the time, but he had swallowed it, rather self-conscious of his own cowardice. He now regretted both the bilious, sharp taste of the word and the laughter that followed the broken phrase. The insult, Krieger considered, like any insult, might have provoked a response which he could have interpreted, and which might have in turn given him a clue that what lay ahead was not a continued partnership, but a private coup. It was not like him to miss such opportunity but, as he reasoned even here, brothers and other family members standing about with machetes and carbines can influence the dialectic of any debate. Might is right, and forever shall be—some of the old adages were inviolate.

Whatever the fat man had said next must have been conciliatory since Krieger could not remember it. That had been the beginning and, by all evidence, the end of their argument, such as it was. Thereafter, business was conducted as usual and if anything this curious colleague—Krieger's supply-side partner, as he liked to put it—maintained a friendly and circumspect attitude toward the Northerner. The only other time he had said something truly combative was when he'd interrupted Krieger who was monologuizing about the potential profits they were to make: "Tentative," Krieger said, rather breathless, "but nevertheless positive and probable customers in what, not even six months, that's a conceivable half million to post in receipts from starting up, two million per annum at no growth, which would mean with expenses of I don't know, a hundred thousand tops, say just an expansion of ten percent after costs, that would leave one point nine no eight million, about a hundred and twenty million córdobas on the white market in the first year. Figuring conservatively—"

"You people have no culture, quantum theories for manufacturing money, all the rewards for being able to have made so much, a bright people, but no culture."

Whenever the fat man pulled out a pipe or cigar, or even on the rare occasion a cigarette, Krieger knew that he proposed to lecture. They were, he had long since decided, meant to prop up the relative authority of what ideas were launched on the wings of their smoke.

"You're going to patronize *me*?" Krieger countered.

"No culture."

Krieger interpreted the cigar (he remembered it was a cigar, not of the best tobacco, and not fresh, for he could remember its foul scent) and rebutted. "Culture? There's a word I don't trust, always comes weighted down with fartloads more promise of something great and grand than it ever comes through with. I say stick a pin in it."

"What?"

"Like a voodoo doll, stick a pin in it. I'll bet you don't even know what it means, not that it matters, not that you'd know the difference, but comes from something to do with plowing a crop. Cultivation, the same thing.

Plowing, tilling, you people ought to know a little bit about that particular exercise. Wetbacks, backs in the sun, backs browned, butts browned, tilling, culture, doesn't that all connect?"

The fat man raised his hands, and dropped them to his sides. "No sense of culture."

"Who the fuck needs it."

"No sense of history or culture—"

"You're starting to sound like me at about age ten."

"No sense of the meaning and beauty of dirt."

"The beauty of dirt?" Krieger scoffed and then paused before saying slowly in a deep, low voice, "Stick a fucking pin in it."

"You're no better than an animal in the yard but you don't even have that much common decency for—"

"Listen, patriarch."

"No sense of dirt. Mud, rock, the land."

"Go make me a taco, make yourself useful." (It wasn't going the way it might have.)

"To you, everything is only to understand if it is made over in numbers, I'm convinced it has something to do with the polar icecaps. All your philosophers like to frown on the peoples of the equator—the darkies, the spics" (*spic*—he can use it) "the ragheads, you call them, you call us—we have no culture you say because our heads are cooked in the sun too long. But meantime you people are frozen."

"He who's got shall give, who's not shall lose, right?"

"You yourself, you don't understand anything unless it's abstracted into numbers."

"So the Bible says and it still ain't news—but what you're not getting at here is that you were born with the numbers, man, with the numbers on your side, hombre, and so the numbers like you, the numbers will always come back to you—you know it for a fact. Shame on you for turning the basic tables on me in a simple discussion, when you know all the facts just for what they are."

Krieger was actually wagging his finger. The fat man saw this and sneered. "Numbers, it's all you know. When you die—"

"Me?"

"When you die the dirt won't take you, you'll end up like a cipher written in a cloud."

"Very poetic and if any of it were true you think I'd be sitting here talking to the likes of you?"

—was, more or less, Krieger's rebuttal. He was not satisfied with it at the time and, considering of it again, he could still think of many things he might have said—most prominently, in reference to his colleague's status as mere beneficiary to the same civilization he so freely condemned: his rhetoric was almost revolutionary, but no matter what it was Krieger understood it as accurate if worthless sermonizing . . .

It was a neat trick but would have been neater had the fat man's tip to the authorities of a very sad and twisted transaction about to take place in a big, strange house on the river that flows down past New York come a few minutes sooner. The whole matter could have been deemed allegorical had the timing clicked.

But there was Krieger, still, up in a tree, viewing the fat man's new mistake, as at first he persuaded himself to think of it, through the magnifying lenses of the pair of binocs.

He watched until the light began to go and he could no longer see what was happening. The masque, or ceremony—whatever it was—went forward without pause throughout the hours of the afternoon. For a time, they ceased. Everyone dispersed. Yet as if they were automatons or individual elements in the works of a clock, the villagers convened once more as the afternoon shade spread longer across the stone concourse. The fat man appeared again, now in fresh, if more recognizable, raiment—battle fatigues, high black laced boots, folderol of medals encrusted like some nutty carapace upon his expansive chest. The helmet, Krieger muttered to himself, was straight from central casting, but so elaborately accurate, so completely anachronistic and at the same time out of sync with the rest of the fat man's fairly normal battle garb, that its effect (it was a conquistador's helmet, half-moon steel brim cocked up away at either end into the sharp points of a banana-split boat) was as terrible as anything Krieger had ever witnessed. This time he carried with him a shallow basket filled with water lily leaves. Power play, thought Krieger, laying the sacred water lilies on these Indians. Where'd he get water lilies? Were they plastic?

Someone was led off. Krieger adjusted the binoculars and saw that it was an elder. A machete fell even before hands rose away into the plaza and the liquid green of the surrounding leaves broke in on Krieger's periphery as he dropped the glasses to avert his gaze. He caught himself, looked again, understood that the longer he studied the scene below, the less certain he felt about its significance. Weary, increasingly agitated, and shivering a bit from the chill that had set in as the rain-forest fog lowered itself into its slate-blue mountains, Krieger gave up his vigil, climbed down out of the tree, and began to descend the hill in the opposite direction from the village. What the fat man had accomplished set his head reeling. A bravura performance all around. How long would he be able to keep the village, how long maintain his shamanship without going crazy, without giving in to deeper tribal dictates like having himself tattooed with the geometrical shapes of the Paya, ornamentally scarred on the face and teeth chipped like the Sumo men? How long would he have before the war, its shrapnel, its flames, its almost biological imperative to grow, rage, would sweep across him here, overwhelm him in the fiery wave of its advance? Among the Sumo and Mosquito a man who has been wronged must avenge himself or be considered a coward. Poisoning is the honorable method for murdering an enemy. How long would he have before he was given, perhaps in some repast so lovingly prepared by a concubine, the secretions from a frog, the *dendrobates tinctorius*, the juice of *Hippomane mancinella* which is swift and very lethal? Not that long, not that long. Hath swallowed down riches and shall vomit them up again. Weights and balances. Only good in it was the reversion to primitivity. An absolute reversion to primitivity. Admirable ploy. Not even a ploy, a decision made in the marrow. Cristóbal de Olid came to mind. Which of them had chosen that name out of the encyclopedia?—not that its aptness hadn't brought laughter even that first evening when Krieger happened to be traveling north from Matagalpa not so long ago and came—and this was hilarious too at the time—posing as a Maryknoll priest, into a particular village, quiet, comparatively, clean and well supplied, comparatively, overseen by a local strongman, Carlos.

That night, safely distant from the village, sheltered in a narrow crevasse that backed up to the ridge where he first had shown Lupi what brave and basic sights the jungle could produce, he sat with a blade of grass pulled taut between the balls and tips of his thumbs, which were pressed together. He blew hard into the opening, trying to produce a tune. The coals of his small fire gave off a friendly light. He hadn't tried to play the grass harp in years. It might be a good way to relax, to calm himself, but try as he might he found he'd forgotten how to make more than three notes, and those could not be kept much in one order or another. With a stick he prodded at the coals, making orange flickers of spark. He spat in the fire and saw the plume and heard it hiss as the heat consumed his saliva in a quick boil.

A spasm of anger passed through him, thinking again of Lupi and how he had never showed up at the hotel in Managua that morning, as he was instructed. It had been suicidal of Krieger to rent that car in the capital and drive straight north on the road past Estelí into the war zone. He had never done anything like that before, but had enough experience down here to know that the safest way to avoid ambush on the open roads north of Jinotega was to drive as fast as possible, and stop for nothing or no one. He had crossed the border without incident, left the car in Danlí, set out on horseback for this unknown place. It was curious how, back in Nueva Segovia, he kept thinking he saw Sardavaal's face, over and over, a shoulder above those groups of refugees walking in families along the road, their movable possessions tied high and wide in panniers of colorful cloth on the backs of mules and oxen. Whenever he would slow the car down to look closer, the face proved to be that of someone else, a missionary, or one of the members of a volunteer brigade come from the States to help in the fields. Sardavaal, he thought, and shook his head. All Sardavaal's work, the lives he may have saved with his inoculations, the villages improved through program after program, the foundations of the earliest cultures in the hemisphere dug up in fragments of fabric and bone, bits of pottery—all of it was going to come to nothing.

He chuckled. The howler monkey that was perched atop a broken formation of volcanic stone just below where he had made his temporary camp for the night glanced up with its perfect round eyes across whose surfaces were reversed images of the flames of the fire. The monkey flinched at the several bursts of sound that came from the man up the ridge, echoed from the stone blind. It bared its teeth, and its delicate fingers clasped the pulpy branches of the limb in which it crouched.

Krieger didn't notice his audience. If he had he might have lobbed a rock down the side of the hill into the tree for sport. He wouldn't have tried to kill the howler, for he wasn't fond of monkey meat. Years ago, working for one of the corporations, on one of his business junkets to visit some bauxite mine or other, his hosts had served it proudly as an example of rural cuisine. The plates were from China, the servants who brought it to table come—way back in their families—in the holds of slave boats so heavily loaded with men and women the waves played over the decks on the calmest days. Rural cuisine, he thought, you cannibals. Dutifully, he had eaten his portion. Strings of gristle caught in his teeth for days after the meal, and the whole experience caused considerable discomfort and even a nightmare.

Monkey meat was not for him. The monkey meant nothing. The monkey too was a nightmare. His whole concentration was on this one thing that had brought him around from his attempts at making music into the coughing smile that spread over his sweat-clouded face and the sudden understanding that what he would have to do, and as quickly as possible, was get to a telephone. He had had an intriguing idea. Yes, he thought. Yes, well, that might work.

ABOUT THE AUTHOR

Bradford Morrow has lived and worked in Honduras, Italy, France, and America, as a medical assistant, jazz musician, and bookseller. He is editor of the highly respected literary magazine *Conjunctions*. *Come Sunday* is his first novel.

COLLIER FICTION

Ballard, J. G. *The Day of Creation.* ISBN 0-02-041514-1

Beattie, Ann. *Where You'll Find Me.* ISBN 0-02-016560-9

Cantor, Jay. *Krazy Kat.* ISBN 0-02-042081-1

Carrère, Emmanuel. *The Mustache.* ISBN 0-02-018870-6

Coover, Robert. *A Night at the Movies.* ISBN 0-02-019120-0

Coover, Robert. *Whatever Happened to Gloomy Gus of the Chicago Bears?* ISBN 0-02-042781-6

Dickinson, Charles. *With or Without.* ISBN 0-02-019560-5

Handke, Peter. *Across.* ISBN 0-02-051540-5

Handke, Peter. *Repetition.* ISBN 0-02-020762-X

Handke, Peter. *Slow Homecoming.* ISBN 0-02-051530-8

Handke, Peter. *3 X Handke.* ISBN 0-02-020761-1

Havazelet, Ehud. *What Is It Then Between Us?* ISBN 0-02-051750-5

Hawkes, John. *Whistlejacket.* ISBN 0-02-043591-6

Hemingway, Ernest. *The Garden of Eden.* ISBN 0-684-18871-6

Mathews, Harry. *Cigarettes.* ISBN 0-02-013971-3

Miller, John (Ed.). *Hot Type.* ISBN 0-02-044701-9

Morrow, Bradford. *Come Sunday.* ISBN 0-02-023001-X

Olson, Toby. *The Woman Who Escaped from Shame.* ISBN 0-02-023231-4

Olson, Toby. *Utah.* ISBN 0-02-098410-3

Pelletier, Cathie. *The Funeral Makers.* ISBN 0-02-023610-7

Phillips, Caryl. *A State of Independence.* ISBN 0-02-015080-6

Pritchard, Melissa. *Spirit Seizures.* ISBN 0-02-036070-3

Rush, Norman. *Whites.* ISBN 0-02-023841-X

Tallent, Elizabeth. *Time with Children.* ISBN 0-02-045540-2

Theroux, Alexander. *An Adultery.* ISBN 0-02-008821-3

Vargas Llosa, Mario. *Who Killed Palomino Molero?* ISBN 0-02-022570-9

West, Paul. *Rat Man of Paris.* ISBN 0-02-026250-7

Available from your local bookstore, or from Macmillan Publishing Company, 100K Brown Street, Riverside, New Jersey 08370